HALAKHIC SOURCES, RELIGIOUS AUTHORITY, AND MILITARY SERVICE IN ISRAEL'S WAR OF INDEPENDENCE

MILHEMET MITZVAH

Volume I

Editors:
AVIAD HACOHEN,
YITZCHAK AVI RONESS,
AND MENACHEM BUTLER

The Institute for
Jewish Research and Publications

Cambridge, MA • 2025

Milhemet Mitzvah: Volume 1

Halakhic Foundations, Religious Authority, and Military Service in Israel's War of Independence

Editors: Aviad Hacohen, Yitzchak Avi Roness, and Menachem Butler

© 2025, All Rights Reserved

ISBN: 978-1-962609-15-9

Published by The Institute for Jewish Research and Publications

Cambridge, MA

www.IJRPub.org

info@IJRPub.org

Twitter @TheIJRPub

Table of Contents

Milhemet Mitzvah: Volume 1
Halakhic Foundations, Religious Authority, and Military Service in Israel's War of Independence

Foreword: Why, How and When Do We Recite
The Prayer for the Soldiers of Israel i
    Haskel Lookstein

Preface: Confronting the Halakhic and Ideological Debate on
Military Service in Israel vii
    Menachem Butler

Introduction: 'The Army of Holiness for Israel':
Religious Ecstasy and Its Profound Significance
in the 'Swords of Iron' War 1
    Aviad Hacohen

Section I:
Rabbi Yitzhak Isaac Halevi Herzog and Recruitment of Yeshiva Students

The Recruitment of Yeshiva Students on the Eve of the War of
Independence 45
    Yitzhak Isaac Halevi Herzog
    ed. Itamar Warhaftig

Correspondence between Rabbi Yitzhak Isaac Halevi Herzog and
David Ben-Gurion on the Question of Inducting Yeshiva Students
to the IDF in Israel's First Decade 110
    Mirit Bat-Horin

The Halakhic Definition of the Wars of the State of Israel in the
Teachings of Rabbi Yitzhak Isaac Halevi Herzog ... 124
    Neria Guttel

Milhemet Mitzvah Without a King:
Rabbi Yitzhak Isaac Halevi Herzog's Halakhic and Ideological
Perspectives on the 1948 War of Independence ... 148
    Yitzchak Avi Roness

Section II:
The Religious Soldier During the Independence War

Service in the Israel Defense Forces in the Thought of Rabbi Yehuda
Amital zt"l ... 201
    Aaron Ahrend

The Path of the Religious Soldier during the Independence War ... 216
    Yehuda Amital

The Activities of Rabbi Abraham Isaac Hacohen Kook in Matters of
Security of the Yishuv ... 228
    Moshe Ehrenwald

The Draft and Yeshiva Students ... 247
    Moshe Ehrenwald

The Recruitment of Haredim ... 315
    Moshe Ehrenwald

The Involvement of Jerusalem's Rabbis in Security Matters During the
War of Independence ... 369
    Moshe Ehrenwald

Patrons of The Ginzei Nistarot Society provide support to
The Institute for Jewish Research and Publications,
*directly contributing to the growth of Jewish scholarship and fostering
a deeper understanding of Judaism and its contributions to the world.*

**To join or to find out more information,
please contact info@ijrpub.org**

אלה יעמדו על הברכה

Ginzei Nistarot Society Patrons

Anonymous

Arielle and Donny Rosenberg

Jennifer and Michael Kaplan

Hilda and Yitz Applbaum

Nancy and Dov Friedberg

Caron and Steve Gelles

Joyce and Jeremy Wertheimer

Joan and Jack Mann

This volume, along with the entire Milhemet Mitzvah series, is dedicated in honor of

RABBI HASKEL LOOKSTEIN,

whose lifelong commitment to Jewish education, halakhic inquiry, Religious Zionism, communal unity, and the moral responsibilities of religious leadership has shaped generations. Rabbi Lookstein's steadfast advocacy for Israel's defenders - through both principled leadership and tangible support - affirms the deep interconnection between Torah study, national responsibility, and the security of Medinat Yisrael. Rabbi Lookstein has long championed the moral imperative of being our brothers' keepers, ensuring that silence is never an option in moments of challenge. In that spirit, we honor the students, alumni, and families of Congregation Kehilath Jeshurun and the Ramaz School who have served - and continue to serve - in the Israel Defense Forces, upholding a tradition of duty that reflects both halakhic obligation and historical necessity.

Anonymous
Rita and Prof. Albert Baumgarten
Lizzy and Daniel Bonner
Laura and Menachem Butler
Sarah and Rabbi Noah Cheses
Prof. Dvora and Rabbi Menachem Hacohen
Dr. Jennifer and Michael Kaplan
Harriet and Joshua Muss
Dr. Jessica and Rabbi Ariel Rackovsky
Pamela and George Rohr
Lisa and Rabbi Chaim Steinmetz
Joyce and Jeremy Wertheimer
Rabbi David Wolpe

Foreword

Why, How and When Do We Recite מי שברך לחיילי צה"ל The Prayer for the Soldiers of Israel

Haskel Lookstein

I

We began to say this prayer at Congregation Kehilath Jeshurun after the Six Day War, a war which demonstrated the extraordinary bravery, skill and power of the Israel Defense Forces. Following that war, the bumper stickers in Israel featured the words

כל הכבוד לצה"ל, "Glory to the IDF."

Six years later, after the terrifying failures of Israel's leadership in the Yom Kippur War, and the glorious victory which overcame the failures, the bumper stickers in Israel read:

"ישראל בטח בה' "O' Israel Trust in God."

The *Misheberach* for *Tzahal* had a different meaning to us, post Yom Kippur War, from its meaning post the Six Day War. We all understood that, ultimately, ה' איש מלחמה "God is the True Warrior." It was His Providence which enabled the IDF to triumph in both 1967 and in 1973. It will be His Providence which will lead Israel to victory after the terrifying pogrom of October 7th.

And, so, we must fervently pray to God to give the IDF כח לעשות חיל the strength, the power, the skill and the courage to defeat Hamas and the enemies of the State of Israel and the Jewish people.

II

We used to say the *Misheberach* at KJ every time we read the *Torah*: on *Shabbat*; on *Yom Tov*; and during the week, on Mondays and Thursdays and *Rosh Chodesh*, and on *Chanukah* and *Purim*. The Rabbi recited it immediately after the *kaddish* following *Torah* reading. We followed this practice until COVID. Regrettably, COVID adversely affected many things in *shul* life, including *davening*, even after we came back to *shul* in person. People expected the service to be shorter. Many meaningful prayers and practices were dropped and, among others, the recitation of the מי שברך לחיילי צה"ל was discontinued during the week.

It is unfortunate that an accelerated service brought about the partial elimination of this prayer. Let us analyze why this *Misheberach* is so important for us.

III

We recite the Prayer for the Israel Defense Forces for two reasons:

First, we recite it because Israel cannot survive without the power of the IDF and the fear that it instills in the enemies of the Jewish State.

Israel lives in a very dangerous neighborhood of hateful murderers and beastly butchers. We always knew that, but, for some time, we didn't pay enough attention to it. After the pogrom of October 7th, we understand clearly that the only thing that stands between a secure and blessedly peaceful Israel and the Kishinev-like pogrom of October 7th, is the fear of a powerful IDF on the part of our enemies. We have to pray, fervently and tearfully, that *Tzahal* wins this war. We must pray at every possible opportunity, for the success and the safety of the soldiers of *Tzahal* and for God's support of the first line of defense for Israel and for us. The life of the Jewish State and our people depend upon it.

But, there is a second reason for reciting this prayer regularly, particularly for us as Diaspora Jews. Most of us have been reciting *Avinu Malkeinu* since October 7th on both weekdays and Shabbat. Rav Hershel Schachter made an Halakhic decision, right after October 7, that we should recite *Avinu Malkeinu* even on *Shabbat*. His basis was that when Yom Kippur falls on a *Shabbat*, we do not say *Avinu Malkeinu* because we do not petition God on a *Shabbat*. The exception, however, is at the closing prayer, *Ne'ila*, when the Gates of Repentance are closing and the Jewish people is in danger (Sakana). At *Ne'ila*, we pull out our entire liturgical arsenal and we recite and sing *Avinu Malkeinu* with heartfelt feelings, before we say *Shema Yisrael*.

This was an unprecedented *psak* by Rav Schachter. It was inspired by his clear understanding that we are in a שעת סכנה - a period of ultimate danger to our lives. At such a time, we have to pray to our Father and our King with utmost fervor.

At KJ, we began reciting *Avinu Malkeinu* at every *Shacharit* and *Mincha*, on weekdays, and on Shabbat, starting the prayer with אבינו מלכנו שמע קולינו חוס ורחם עלינו, "Our Father, our King, hear our voices, pity us and have mercy upon us." The rabbi chants the verses and the congregation responds until the end of the *Avinu Malkeinu* passages when we all sing the last *Avinu Malkeinu* with a fervor that I have only heard at the closing of *Ne'ila*.

I understand that, in Israel, most do not add this prayer. But, even if that is so, we in the Diaspora should continue to say it. Israelis need no reminders that they are in an existential struggle. We do. They live, for the first time in a long time, in great vulnerability. They live it night and day, in many ways. We do not. They all have close relatives and friends who are risking their lives on the front lines. We do not. They experience rockets and missiles exploding around them. We do not. Their own lives are at stake in this war. Ours are not. They can add or subtract prayers as they wish, but we must change our liturgical routine in order to keep this struggle at the forefront of our minds for as long as the crisis lasts, until Israel destroys Hamas and wins this war. If our davening is elongated thereby by three minutes, so be it. Our prayers and our constant thoughts about Israel and its citizens make that necessary. This is our struggle too.

IV

Finally, how to recite the מי שברך לחיילי צה"ל. I have heard this prayer recited in any number of shuls. It is usually recited by someone – sometimes the rabbi – hastily and with very little feeling – like a routine prayer. We have never recited it that way at KJ. We recite it with utmost gravitas and *kavanna*, with an entire congregation standing in silence, at attention. We realize that we are praying for the lives of the soldiers of the IDF; we are praying for the survival of Israel which depends on the IDF. If we ever needed to be reminded about that, we surely understand it now. This prayer should be recited regularly and with the greatest possible feeling.

To paraphrase Rabbi Akiba's statement about *Shir HaShirim* – "If all the Books of Tanach are holy, *Shir HaShirim* is the holy of holies" – if all of the prayers in our *Siddur* are holy, מי שברך לחיילי צה"ל (the Prayer for the Soldiers of *Tzahal*) is קודש קדשים - the holiest of holies.

May God hear our prayers and bring victory to our soldiers and peace to our Land.

Haskel Lookstein

Rabbi Haskel Lookstein has been a Rabbi of Congregation Kehilath Jeshurun since 1958 and served as Principal of the Ramaz School from 1966 until 2016 when he became Principal Emeritus.

This chapter was first published in Haskel Lookstein, "Why, How and When We Recite The Prayer for the Soldiers of Israel," in Aviad Hacohen and Menachem Butler, eds., *Praying for the Defenders of Our Destiny: The Mi Sheberach for IDF Soldiers* (Cambridge, MA: The Institute for Jewish Research and Publications, 2023), 156-164.

Preface to the Milhemet Mitzvah Series
Confronting the Halakhic and Ideological Debate on Military Service in Israel

Menachem Butler

F OR OVER SEVENTY-FIVE YEARS, MILITARY service in the State of Israel has remained one of the most unresolved tensions at the intersection of halakhah, ideology, and national identity. This debate is not merely political or strategic—it strikes at the core of Jewish sovereignty and the principles defining the modern Jewish state. At its heart lies a fundamental dilemma: the necessity of national defense versus the spiritual imperative of Torah study. One side argues that Israel's survival depends on a strong and capable military, while the other maintains that the ultimate safeguard of the Jewish people lies in the sanctity of Torah study. These competing visions have shaped public discourse, rabbinic rulings, and political battles since the state's inception.

Confronting the Halakhic and Ideological Debate on Military Service in Israel

This tension is not new. Throughout Jewish history, communities have struggled to reconcile the demands of physical defense with spiritual devotion. From the Maccabean revolt, where religious zeal fueled military resistance, to medieval rabbinic debates over armed self-defense, the balance between faith and force has remained a pressing dilemma. In modern Israel, this debate has gained urgency, influencing coalition politics, legal battles, and deep societal divisions. The exemption of yeshiva students, the integration of religious soldiers into the IDF, and the broader question of Israel as both a Jewish and democratic state have only intensified in recent years. But this is more than a political or legal dispute—it is a question of national identity and survival. What does it mean for Jews to live as a sovereign nation? Is Jewish survival secured through military strength, or does it rest on an unwavering commitment to Torah? And in an era of persistent external threats and internal divisions, how should Israel navigate the balance between faith and force? These questions do not merely shape Israeli society—they may define the future of the Jewish people. Within Religious Zionist communities, where sons and daughters have long served courageously—most recently in the ongoing Swords of Iron war, enduring profound losses—the debate over Milhemet Mitzvah and the obligation of all Israelis, including Haredim, to share in the national burden has never been more urgent. This reckoning has reignited the demand for serious halakhic and historical engagement with military service.

As Israel confronts the aftermath of the October 7th attacks and the ongoing Swords of Iron War—along with the profound security and societal challenges they have unleashed—the questions explored in the Milhemet Mitzvah series are not just timely; they are existential. At this critical juncture, it is imperative that the IDF achieve success in its campaign against Hamas in Gaza. Moreover, Israel must persist in its relentless efforts to secure the release of all hostages still held by Hamas, including Hadar Goldin, whose body has been held hostage since 2014—long before the horrific events of October 7th, 2023.

These urgent issues demand immediate and resolute action, highlighting the fundamental moral and legal imperatives at the heart of this volume. The tension between Torah study and military service, between religious obligation and civic duty, is not a theoretical debate but a defining moral and halakhic challenge of our era. This moment demands more than policy decisions or political maneuvering; it requires a reckoning with Jewish sovereignty, national responsibility, and the balance between spiritual and material imperatives in securing Israel's future.

At a time when national unity is imperative, and the burden of military sacrifice is shared across Israeli society, the continued exemption of an entire community from this responsibility is not merely a policy debate—it is a test of Israel's moral, halakhic, and national integrity. Can a sovereign Jewish state endure when one sector insists Torah study alone ensures victory, while others shed their blood to defend it? Does halakhah mandate passivity in the face of existential threats, or does it demand full participation in the defense of Jewish life? These are not abstract questions; they strike at the very core of Jewish sovereignty, collective responsibility, and the ethical foundations of the State of Israel.

Yet, despite the gravity of this moment, Haredi leadership's justifications for exemption remain detached from historical precedent—particularly from how their own ideological predecessors in 1948 and beyond grappled with Milhemet Mitzvah's halakhic and hashkafic implications. Unlike earlier generations, who engaged with the realities of statehood and national defense through halakhic analysis, contemporary Haredi leadership has increasingly prioritized political expediency over rigorous halakhic deliberation. This shift has not only distanced contemporary discourse from its historical foundations but also reinforced a theological stance that is both innovative and, within Jewish tradition, a minority view. Recent statements from Israeli Haredi leadership continue to assert that Torah study alone provides essential protection for the Jewish people, rendering military service unnecessary for yeshiva students. Though framed as halakhic principle, this assertion disregards the well-established category of Milhemet Mitzvah—an obligatory war in which, as the Mishnah (Sotah 8:7) states, "everyone goes out to fight, even a groom from his room and a bride from her canopy." If modern Israeli wars meet this criterion—as Chief Rabbi Yitzhak Isaac Halevi Herzog and subsequent halakhists have affirmed based on Maimonides' Mishneh Torah—then yeshiva student exemptions are not a given but a matter requiring serious halakhic scrutiny.

As Israel faces both internal and external crises, no issue carries greater weight for the state's future than Giyus Haredim—Haredi conscription into the IDF. While judicial reform battles and the government's handling of the war following Hamas' October 7th attacks have tested the nation's political fabric, they pale in comparison to the existential challenge posed by military service exemptions. Indeed, daily reports suggest this could be the breaking point for the current coalition government. More than a policy dispute, conscription has become a defining fault line, threatening to fracture the delicate balance between religious and secular communities. It raises fundamental questions about the core obligations of a Jewish state: Is Torah study an exemption from the burdens of sovereignty, or is it integral to sovereignty's very responsibilities? Can a state built on Jewish values endure when one sector claims spiritual guardianship while another bears the physical sacrifices of war?

At this critical juncture, it is imperative to examine these questions with both intellectual honesty and yirat shamayim—a deep reverence for Torah, the Divine, and Jewish sovereignty. Only through rigorous halakhic and historical analysis, coupled with an unwavering commitment to truth, can we engage meaningfully with the responsibilities that statehood demands. To this end, The Institute for Jewish Research and Publications has launched the Milhemet Mitzvah series, a multi-volume project that examines these issues with academic and halakhic rigor. Edited by Aviad Hacohen, Yitzchak Avi Roness, and myself, the series explores the halakhic, historical, legal, and ideological dimensions of military service in the State of Israel. This book is not intended solely for those deeply embedded in Religious Zionism. Just as the State of Israel is a home for all Jews—alongside its non-Jewish citizens and residents—so too must the discourse on national responsibility be accessible to all who seek to understand it. The interplay between Jewish law, military service, and sovereignty extends beyond the beit midrash; it carries profound implications for anyone invested in the moral and ideological foundations of the modern Jewish state.

By presenting these issues through an uncompromising halakhic lens and an unflinching historical framework—even when addressing difficult or uncomfortable episodes—the Milhemet Mitzvah series offers a perspective often absent from discussions on national defense, civic duty, and the ethical imperatives of statehood. Rather than conforming to prevailing narratives, these volumes engage with the complexities of Jewish sovereignty on their own terms, ensuring that the halakhic and ideological dimensions of military service are neither ignored nor oversimplified. To that end, the Milhemet Mitzvah series rejects ad hominem attacks and ideological rhetoric. While engaging in rigorous halakhic debate, it remains firmly anchored in historical documentation, verifiable data, and meticulous halakhic and hashkafic analysis. Through a comprehensive examination of foundational halakhic sources, historical precedents, and contemporary realities, these volumes provide an evidence-based approach to a debate too often clouded by rhetoric. By cutting through polemics and historical amnesia, these volumes offer clarity where ideological narratives have obscured the facts. They feature pivotal primary texts from the period surrounding Israel's establishment, many appearing in English for the first time. These documents provide critical insight into how religious leaders navigated the unprecedented challenges of statehood and national defense. More than historical records, they offer essential context for contemporary debates, making them invaluable to scholars, policymakers, and anyone engaged in the intersection of Torah, military service, and national responsibility.

The Institute for Jewish Research and Publications named this project the Milhemet Mitzvah series in recognition of Rabbi Yitzhak Isaac Halevi Herzog, the first Ashkenazic Chief Rabbi of the State of Israel, and his pivotal role in shaping halakhic discourse on military service. As Rabbi Prof. Neria Guttel notes in this volume:

"From then until today, the understanding that the wars of Israel in the modern era should be defined as 'commanded wars,' with all their halakhic implications, has long become a foundational principle. Rabbi Herzog's teachings on this matter have become so widely accepted that they are now regarded as basic consensus. It is worthy to bring this recognition to the world and to restore to Rabbi Herzog his rightful honor. All should know that this perception was, at the time, a matter of intense debate among the great sages of Israel, and it is Rabbi Herzog who holds the 'intellectual copyright' over this crucial halakhic innovation."

Published by The Institute for Jewish Research and Publications, the Milhemet Mitzvah series explores the intersection of halakhah and national responsibility in the context of Israel's wars. Rather than limiting the discussion to political and military leadership, these volumes examine the religious and legal foundations that have shaped Jewish perspectives on national defense. By bringing to the forefront the often-overlooked perspectives of Jewish religious leadership during Israel's formative years, these volumes reframe the discourse, moving beyond narratives that focus solely on political and military figures. Instead, they emphasize the halakhic, spiritual, and communal dimensions that have shaped Jewish engagement with national defense, offering a more comprehensive and historically grounded perspective.

These first two volumes in the Milhemet Mitzvah series feature contributions from more than a dozen leading scholars, prominent rabbis, and communal leaders—primarily from the Religious Zionist communities, but spanning a broad spectrum of perspectives. Together, they provide a rigorous engagement with one of the most pressing issues in Israeli society today. By refining and presenting halakhic and ideological discussions with scholarly rigor, these volumes serve as indispensable resources for those seeking clarity on the obligations and responsibilities of military service in Israel. To further this understanding, they include pivotal primary texts from the period surrounding the establishment of the State of Israel, many appearing in English for the first time. These documents offer critical insight into the halakhic and ideological perspectives of religious leaders as they grappled with the unprecedented challenges of statehood and national defense—perspectives that remain essential for anyone engaged in this ongoing debate.

Milhemet Mitzvah, vol. 1: Halakhic Foundations, Religious Authority, and Military Service in Israel's War of Independence examines the foundational period of Israel's War of Independence and the role of religious leadership in shaping halakhic discourse on military service. A central focus is Rabbi Yitzhak Isaac Halevi Herzog's halakhic framing of the war as milhemet mitzvah and his correspondence with Prime Minister David Ben-Gurion regarding yeshiva student conscription. (Subsequent volumes in the Milhemet Mitzvah series will explore additional aspects of Ben-Gurion's communications with esteemed Torah sages during Israel's early years.) In addition to scholarly analyses of the ideological and halakhic frameworks that emerged in 1948, the volume includes newly translated halakhic documents from leading Religious Zionist figures, offering direct insight into their perspectives on military service and national defense. It also provides a detailed, well-documented examination of the role Haredim and yeshiva students played in Israel's national defense, shedding light on a lesser-known yet pivotal chapter of Israeli history.

As debates over military service continue to shape Israeli society, the next volume in the series—*Milhemet Mitzvah, vol. 2: Religious Leadership and Halakhic Responsibility in the Military Service Debate*—examines the evolving role of rabbinic authority, Torah study, and military obligation in the modern Jewish state. It explores David Ben-Gurion's policies on religion and conscription, particularly his attempts to balance religious autonomy with national security, as well as pre-state debates on yeshiva recruitment during World War II, which laid the groundwork for later exemptions and deepened ideological divisions over military service. A central focus of this volume is the Religious Zionist soldier's identity, for whom military service is not merely compatible with religious commitment but an expression of duty to both Torah and nation.

Through historical and halakhic analysis, this volume examines how Religious Zionist ideology has shaped self-perception, framing military service as both a halakhic imperative and a fulfillment of Jewish national destiny. This exploration highlights the complex interplay between faith, statehood, and national defense, addressing how spiritual conviction, halakhic responsibility, and civic duty converge in Israeli military service.

While these historical and ideological debates shaped Israel's military policies, they also sparked halakhic disputes that remain central to contemporary discussions on military service. The intersection of Torah study, national defense, and religious obligation remains a defining issue, with competing perspectives on exemption and enlistment reflecting deeper tensions over halakhah's role in a sovereign Jewish state. To further unpack these debates, this volume analyzes halakhic justifications for military service and exemption, exploring Torato Umanuto, the redemptive role of military duty, and key rulings from Rabbi Zvi Yehudah Kook and Rabbi Shelomo Yosef Zevin, and also features an in-depth study by Professor Hannah Kehat on the status of Torah in the Thought of the Hazon Ish, which examines the ideological and halakhic foundations of exemption claims. (Subsequent volumes in the Milhemet Mitzvah series will further explore the Hazon Ish's stance, tracing its evolving interpretations and continued influence.) The volume culminates with a halakhic treatise by Rav Yitzhak Sheilat, Rosh Yeshiva of Yeshivat Birkat Moshe in Ma'ale Adumim, titled "Halakhic Perspectives on Milhemet Mitzvah and Military Service in the Modern State of Israel," offering a systematic analysis of military service through the lens of Jewish law.

Following Rav Sheilat's framework, the volume concludes with Professor David Henshke's essay, a deeply personal and urgent response to the post-October 7th claims that seek to exempt yeshiva students from military service. Engaging directly with misinterpretations of Maimonides' rulings, Henshke systematically dismantles arguments that invoke the tribe of Levi as a precedent for exemption. Building on the volume's broader discourse, particularly the contributions of Rabbi Prof. Neria Guttel, which explore the halakhic and ideological tensions surrounding military service in Religious Zionist thought, Henshke expands this discussion to confront the contemporary implications of these debates. He forcefully argues that Torah law obligates all capable individuals to participate in a milhemet mitzvah and warns against the grave consequences of misapplying halakhic exemptions, emphasizing that theological justifications for non-participation not only distort Jewish law but also endanger national security and communal responsibility.

Building on the foundations of these two volumes, future volumes in the Milhemet Mitzvah series will continue to explore the halakhic, ideological, and legal dimensions of military service in Israel, addressing key developments that have shaped the discourse over the past seventy-five years. The series will examine the pivotal role of Chief Rabbi Shlomo Goren and his disciples in shaping halakhic responses to military service and in providing religious leadership within the Israel Defense Forces. It will also explore the military and national service of religious women, analyzing the halakhic debates and the evolving communal attitudes toward their participation. Additionally, the series will offer an in-depth examination of the Israeli Supreme Court's rulings on the conscription of Haredi yeshiva students, assessing how legal and societal perspectives on this issue have evolved over time. Another critical area of focus will be the Hesder movement and the religious and secular preparatory military academies which originated within the Religious Zionist community but have since expanded across the ideological spectrum. Furthermore, the series will address the role of conscientious objectors—both from the ideological right, who refuse service on religious or nationalist grounds, and from the ideological left, who object based on political or ethical opposition to Israeli military policies—examining how halakhic and legal discourse has grappled with these refusals in a sovereign Jewish state. Through these and other critical topics, the Milhemet Mitzvah series aims to provide a rigorous and comprehensive exploration of the evolving interplay between Jewish law, military service, and national responsibility in the State of Israel.

This volume follows my previous work, *Praying for the Defenders of Our Destiny: The Mi Sheberach for IDF Soldiers*, co-edited with my dear mentor and friend, Professor Aviad Hacohen, and published under the auspices of The Institute for Jewish Research and Publications. Conceived, compiled, and published within seven weeks of the October 7th attacks, that anthology explored the theological, ideological, and historical dimensions of the Mi Sheberach for IDF soldiers. It analyzed the prayer's evolution as both a liturgical expression of faith and a statement of unwavering support for Israel's defenders. Bringing together over seventy contributions from scholars, rabbis, and thinkers, it examined the complex interplay between military strength and spiritual faith in securing Israel's future. If that work illuminated how Jewish communities invoke divine protection for their soldiers, this book addresses an even more fundamental question: Who is halakhically obligated to serve? At a time when Israel's security challenges are intensifying and debates over military service dominate national discourse, the need for a rigorous halakhic and ideological analysis of Milhemet Mitzvah—and the duty of all Jews, including the Haredim, to share the national burden—has never been more pressing. This volume seeks to provide that clarity, confronting both historical precedent and contemporary realities with the depth and seriousness they demand.

But this debate is not confined to yeshiva halls or political negotiations in Jerusalem and Bnei Brak. Across the Jewish world, and particularly on university campuses in North America, the question of Israel's religious significance—and the role of the IDF in securing its future—has become increasingly urgent. Yet, in these spaces, ideological clarity is often replaced by silence or hesitation. For many students seeking a religious framework that affirms both the State of Israel and military service, the absence of serious engagement has left them navigating these issues on their own. In the more than 500 days since the October 7th attacks, *Praying for the Defenders of Our Destiny: The Mi Sheberach for IDF Soldiers* has become a foundational text, reaching thousands of readers worldwide. Copies have been distributed not only to members of the Israeli military and government but also to Jewish students on American college campuses, where there is an increasing demand for ideological content that affirms the religious significance of the State of Israel.

Yet, for a variety of significant reasons (beyond the scope of this preface), this perspective remains largely absent from campus discourse. The dominant Jewish voices—particularly within Hillel and Chabad—vary in their approach but generally refrain from offering a clear religious affirmation of the State of Israel and, by extension, the IDF. This reluctance ignores a fundamental truth: the religious significance of the State is inseparable from the IDF's role in ensuring its survival and the continuity of Jewish life. A genuine religious commitment to the State cannot be separated from the responsibility of defending it—a connection too often overlooked in mainstream campus discourse. As a result, students are often left without serious guidance from their educators, forced to navigate these complex discussions on their own. It has been a privilege to help fill this void by providing students, their families, and educators with *Praying for the Defenders of Our Destiny: The Mi Sheberach for IDF Soldiers*—a book that offers both ideological clarity and religious affirmation in a time when they are needed most.

The contributors to the Milhemet Mitzvah series were selected for their diverse perspectives and independently shared their insights, each unaware of the participation of others. While the opinions expressed in each essay belong solely to the respective author and may not align with those of other contributors, this approach ensures an impartial collection of essays while reinforcing the unity that this project seeks to convey. This volume does not claim to resolve these dilemmas with a single answer, nor does it impose a uniform ideological stance. Instead, it offers a framework for rigorous halakhic and philosophical engagement—one that rejects slogans and historical amnesia and instead demands intellectual honesty and moral clarity.

I am deeply grateful to my co-editors, Professor Aviad Hacohen and Rabbi Dr. Yitzchak Avi Roness, whose scholarship, insights, and invaluable discussions over many years have been instrumental in shaping this volume. I also extend my appreciation to all the contributing authors, who worked closely with our team at The Institute for Jewish

Research and Publications to refine their articles and prepare them for English translation.

My heartfelt thanks also go to the editors, translators, and academic advisors at the Institute, whose meticulous efforts ensured the accuracy, clarity, and presentation of these volumes, and to the patrons of the Ginzei Nistarot Society, whose generous annual support made this volume possible.

As noted at the start of each volume in the Milhemet Mitzvah series:

> "This volume, along with the entire Milhemet Mitzvah series, is dedicated in honor of Rabbi Haskel Lookstein, whose lifelong commitment to Jewish education, halakhic inquiry, Religious Zionism, communal unity, and the moral responsibilities of religious leadership has shaped generations. Rabbi Lookstein's steadfast advocacy for Israel's defenders—through both principled leadership and tangible support—affirms the deep interconnection between Torah study, national responsibility, and the security of Medinat Yisrael. Rabbi Lookstein has long championed the moral imperative of being our brothers' keepers, ensuring that silence is never an option in moments of challenge. In that spirit, we honor the students, alumni, and families of Congregation Kehilath Jeshurun and the Ramaz School who have served—and continue to serve—in the Israel Defense Forces, upholding a tradition of duty that reflects both halakhic obligation and historical necessity."

We are profoundly grateful to the patrons who have generously supported the Milhemet Mitzvah series in honor of Rabbi Haskel Lookstein, whose names are listed on the dedication page. The Institute for Jewish Research and Publications deeply values Rabbi Lookstein's unwavering support, insightful guidance, and steadfast commitment to this project. His leadership and encouragement have been instrumental in bringing this vision to fruition.

Menachem Butler

Rabbi Lookstein's impact as an educator, mentor, and communal leader extends far beyond the institutions he has led, shaping how Jewish values and national responsibility are taught to future generations. In this spirit, the Milhemet Mitzvah series was conceived not only as a scholarly contribution but as a foundation for meaningful learning and discussion in Jewish communities worldwide. Beyond the books themselves, Milhemet Mitzvah serves as an educational resource. Under the auspices of The Institute for Jewish Research and Publications, articles from these volumes will be adapted into curriculum materials for yeshivot, schools, and synagogues. These materials will be made available at no cost to educators and institutions, ensuring that this critical discourse reaches the next generation of students, scholars, and community leaders. As debates over military service continue to shape Israeli society and Jewish communities worldwide, the need for serious, halakhic, and historically grounded engagement has never been greater. (Opportunities to support these efforts remain available, and all contributions are tax-deductible. For more information, please be in touch.)

May the Milhemet Mitzvah series be more than a scholarly resource—may it serve as a catalyst for long-overdue conversations, embracing difficult questions with the depth and seriousness they demand. May it help shape an Israel not only defended by the sacrifices of the few but sustained by the shared commitment of the many.

May the study of these volumes drive deep and unflinching engagement with the enduring questions of Jewish sovereignty, halakhic responsibility, and the moral obligations of nationhood. May they challenge readers to wrestle with the delicate balance between spiritual devotion and national defense, between the eternal mandate of Torah study and the immediate demands of securing Jewish life.

At a time when Jewish power and self-determination are tested on the battlefield and in the halls of halakhic discourse, may these volumes ground the debate in its historical and legal foundations and inspire a renewed commitment to both faith and action.

May all hostages be returned home immediately, and may their families—and all those affected by the tragedy of October 7th and beyond—find comfort and strength. Above all, may the soldiers of the Israel Defense Forces—entrusted with the defense of Am Yisrael, Eretz Yisrael, Medinat Yisrael, and its democratically elected government of the State of Israel—stand firm against every threat, protected from harm, unwavering in purpose, and resolute in spirit.

Lastly, may the rabbinic and halakhic advisors who offer guidance to the soldiers of the Israel Defense Forces continue to provide wisdom and clarity, ensuring that devotion to Torah and commitment to national defense remain inseparable pillars of Israel's destiny. May the soldiers' dedication be reinforced with strength, their sacrifices honored with the highest reverence, and their mission fulfilled with clarity and success. As they defend the security and sovereignty of the Jewish state, may their efforts not only guarantee its survival but also uphold its strength, justice, and moral integrity for generations to come.

Menachem Butler, the Program Fellow for Jewish Legal Studies in the Julis-Rabinowitz Program on Jewish and Israeli Law at Harvard Law School, serves as the President of the Institute for Jewish Research and Publications, and is a co-editor of this volume.

Introduction

'The Army of Holiness for Israel': Religious Ecstasy and Its Profound Significance in the 'Swords of Iron' War

Aviad Hacohen

To some contemporary believers and adherents of religious faith, war is regarded as sacred.

While modern secular liberal Western thought frames war as a civic act—a calculated instrument to achieve political, diplomatic, or military objectives such as territorial expansion or national defense—religious thought often imbues war with a sacred dimension, manifesting in a variety of expressions.

Thus, for example, already in the Bible, the "anointed priest" or the "priest anointed for war"—a prominent figure of spiritual, not military, leadership—would go out before the people to war; similarly, the Ark of the Covenant would accompany Israel into battle,[1] and this pattern persisted in later periods. It is therefore unsurprising that even in the earliest sources of Islam,[2] and Christianity,[3] there is widespread discourse on the concept of a "holy war," victory and defeat in war were attributed to the raising of the hands of the *spiritual, not military*, leader (Moses) or their lowering.[4]

I extend my gratitude to my colleagues: author Prof. Haim Beer, Amichai Chasson, Judge and Major-General (Res.) Prof. Menachem Finkelstein, and Dr. Udi Wolf, for their insightful comments on an earlier version of this article, which significantly contributed to its refinement. I am also deeply grateful to Mr. Menachem Butler, who edited this article; his extensive knowledge and wisdom provided me with many valuable insights. Needless to say, the responsibility for the content rests solely with me. All emphases are mine unless otherwise noted.

1 Deuteronomy 20:2-7; Numbers 10:35; and Moshe David Herr, "On the High Priest Anointed for War in the Biblical Period," *Mahanayim*, no. 69 (May 1962): 36-39 (Hebrew).

2 See David Cook, *Understanding Jihad* (Berkeley: University of California Press, 2005); and earlier in Emmanuel Sivan, "Jihad: Text, Myth, Historical Realities," in Évelyne Patlagean and Alain Le Boulluec, eds., *Les retours aux Écritures. Fondamentalismes présents et passés* (Louvain: Peeters, 1993), 83-99.

3 See Joshua Prawer, *The Crusaders' Kingdom: European Colonialism in the Middle Ages* (London: Phoenix Press, 1972); Jean Richard, *The Crusades, c. 1071 – c. 1291* (Cambridge: Cambridge University Press, 1999); and Ariel Koch, "The New Crusaders: Contemporary Extreme Right Symbolism and Rhetoric," *Perspectives on Terrorism*, vol. 11, no. 5 (October 2017): 13-24.

4 Mishnah, Rosh Hashanah 3:8.

Other religious traditions frame war as a "religious commandment" rather than solely a civic action. In Islam, for example, *jihad*, one of the five pillars of faith, is regarded as a sacred duty. Similarly, Jewish sources employ the term *milhemet mitzvah* (obligatory war) to describe conflicts that carry a distinctly religious purpose and significance, transcending purely secular or civic motivations.

Similarly, various thinkers, such as Rabbi Zvi Yehuda Hacohen Kook, one of Israel's most prominent religious leaders in the second half of the twentieth century, ascribed the status of "absolute sanctity"[5] to the Israel Defense Forces, as well as to the tank and the rifle. They spoke of the "Army of God" rather than merely the army of the state. This perspective found expression in diverse and multifaceted ways, such as the assertion that "The Army of Israel possesses a genuinely divine value, a value of sanctity," or references to the "divine militarism" associated with the Master of the Universe. In this framework, war—with all its sacrifices, both physical and emotional—is perceived as a critical stage in the process of redemption.[6]

---

5   Rabbi Zvi Yehuda Hacohen Kook, "The Kingdom of Israel," *ha-Tsofeh* (20 April 1953): 3 (Hebrew), quoted in Hagai Shtemler, *Eye to Eye: The Thought of Rav Zvi Yehuda Kook* (Eli: Binyan ha-Torah, 2016), 168 (Hebrew).

6   In this article, we did not expand on the ideological and literary aspects of clothing the military and war in the mantle of "sanctity" and their role as an integral part of the process of redemption. This trend received significant development—in various styles—in the thought of Rabbi Abraham Isaac Hacohen Kook (1865–1935). In his famous chapter on war in *Orot*, he depicted it in an idealistic manner, viewing it as part of "the service of God." This worldview was further developed extensively in the writings of his son, Rabbi Zvi Yehuda Hacohen Kook (1891–1982).

For a comprehensive discussion, see Hagai Shtemler, *Eye to Eye: The Thought of Rav Zvi Yehuda Kook* (Eli: Binyan ha-Torah, 2016), 41-59, 161-175 (Hebrew), and the sources cited therein; as well as the subsequent studies by Hanoch Ben-Pazi, "The Theology of War: War and Militarism as Viewed by the Ideological Circle of Rabbi Zvi Yehuda Kook," *Moreshet Yisrael*, vol. 14 (2007): 227-255 (Hebrew); Hanoch Ben-Pazi, "R. Abraham Isaac Kook and the Opening Passage of 'The War,'" *Journal of Jewish Thought*

Religious Ecstasy and Its Profound Significance in the 'Swords of Iron' War

The ongoing "Iron Swords" war following Hamas' attack on Israel on the October 7th attacks has brought to light remarkable instances of religious fervor, even extending to extraordinary expressions of religious ecstasy.[7] To draw a stark distinction, similar phenomena have also been observed among the enemy, particularly within Hamas and Islamic Jihad—distinctly religious movements—that have encouraged their

---

and Philosophy, vol. 25, no. 2 (2017): 256-278; and Bezalel Naor, "'Master of Wars, Sower of Righteousness': The Impact of the Great War upon Rav Kook," in Aviad Hacohen and Menachem Butler, eds., *Praying for the Defenders of Our Destiny: The Mi Sheberach for IDF Soldiers* (Cambridge, MA: The Institute for Jewish Research and Publications, 2023), 457-465. For a recent translation by Rabbi Bezalel Naor of this tract, see Rabbi Abraham Isaac Hacohen Kook, "Orot ha-Milhamah," in Bezalel Naor, ed., *Orot: The Original 1920 Version* (Jerusalem: Orot & Maggid Books, 2022), 130-144, 462-467.

It is essential to recognize that Rabbi Abraham Isaac Hacohen Kook's writings were deeply rooted in the historical and ideological context of the pre-World War II period. These compositions, shaped by the challenges and realities of their time, might not have been articulated in the same manner—if at all—had they been written after the war. For further discussion, see Neria Guttel, "'Freedom for our Yeshiva Students' or the Mitzvah of Their Recruitment: Rav Kook's Letter and the Debate on Its Interpretation," in Moshe Rachimi, ed., *The Kipa and the Helmet* [=*Amadot*, vol. 1] (Elkana: Mikhlelet Orot, 2009), 25-39 (Hebrew), translated into English in this volume.

7   The phenomenon referred to as "religionization" (hadatah) in the IDF has been the subject of extensive research over the past decade. See, for example, Reuven Gal and Tamir Libel, eds., *Between the Yarmulke and the Beret: Religion, Politics and the Military in Israel* (Tel-Aviv: Modan, 2012; Hebrew); Yagil Levy, *The Divine Commander: The Theocratization of the Israeli Military* (Tel Aviv: Am-Oved, 2015; Hebrew); and more recently, with a more critical perspective, see Daniel Statman, *'Mamlachtiut', Religionization and Religious Soldiers in the IDF* (Jerusalem: The Israel Democracy Institute, 2019; Hebrew).

followers to engage in a "holy war"[8] or "the war for the Temple Mount,"[9] with the aim of defending and liberating the Temple Mount from Zionist Jewish rule.

The roots of this phenomenon in the Israel Defense Forces, the army of "the only democracy in the Middle East," can already be traced to earlier wars. One of the most prominent and well-known cases in this context is associated with the figure of Major General Rabbi Shlomo Goren, the IDF's founding chief rabbi, who founded and served as the first head of the Military Rabbinate of the Israel Defense Forces (IDF) in 1948, a position he held until 1968.[10]

Rabbi Goren was a towering Torah scholar of unparalleled genius, a profoundly original thinker, and a figure of extraordinary courage. Harnessing these remarkable qualities, Rabbi Goren built the Military Rabbinate in the IDF from the ground up, masterfully resolved intricate halakhic dilemmas, and, in his roles as Chief Rabbi of the IDF and later

---

8   See Reuven Firestone, *Jihād: The Origin of Holy War in Islam* (New York: Oxford University Press, 1999); and Reuven Firestone, *Holy War in Judaism: The Fall and Rise of a Controversial Idea* (New York: Oxford University Press, 2012).

9   Hamas's designation of its October 7, 2023, attack as the "al-Aqsa Flood" echoes the PLO's "al-Aqsa Intifada" (2000-2004), coined by PLO Chairman Yasser Arafat to bolster support against Hamas. This invocation of al-Aqsa can be traced back to Haj Amin al-Husseini, who weaponized the narrative in the 1920s and 1930s to incite violence against Jews at the Western Wall.

10 He then served as the Chief Rabbi of Tel Aviv–Jaffa from 1968 until his election, in 1972, as the fourth Ashkenazic Chief Rabbi of Israel in 1972. See Yaron Silverstein, *The State of Israel and Its Institutions in the Halakhic Thought of Rabbi Shlomo Goren* (Jerusalem: Magnes, 2021), esp. 217-353 (Hebrew); Shifra Mescheloff, "In the Eye of the Storm: The Public Image and Creative Torah Work of Rabbi Shlomo Goren, 1948-1994," (PhD Dissertation, Bar-Ilan University, 2010; Hebrew); and Aviad Hollander, "The Halakhic Profile of Rabbi Shlomo Goren: Studies in the Considerations and Foundations of His Halakhic Rulings," (PhD Dissertation, Bar-Ilan University, 2011; Hebrew).

as Chief Rabbi of Israel, delivered countless victims of oppression from the grasp of their tormentors.

At the same time, from the very beginning of his service in the IDF, he saw himself as a "Priest Anointed for War," leading the armies of Israel with a Torah scroll in hand. Not infrequently, his writings—initially published in *Mahanayim*,[11] the journal of the IDF Military Rabbinate, and later compiled in his books[12]—reflected a spirit of assertiveness alongside a strong messianic and redemptive undertone.

---

11   Another example of the integration of spiritual vision and physical strength in Rabbi Goren's leadership was his desire to name the IDF Military Rabbinate's journal *Kol Hashem Bakoach* ("The Voice of the Lord in Strength," see Psalms 29:4), a name reflecting his assertive approach to combining Torah values with the military ethos. Rabbi Goren's choice of name emphasized the centrality of divine power and strength in shaping the religious identity of the IDF. However, the editor, my father Rabbi Menachem Hacohen, objected, preferring a title that conveyed spiritual depth without an overt emphasis on force. Sharing his disagreement with Rabbi Goren at home, my father consulted his father, Rabbi Mordechai Hacohen, who proposed the name *Mahanayim*—a Biblical term evoking duality and harmony, as well as its connection to "camps." My grandfather explained, "The IDF's weekly publication is called *Bamahane*; yours will be *Bamahane* —but doubled." While Rabbi Menachem Hacohen embraced this suggestion, Rabbi Goren resisted, insisting on his original choice of *Kol Hashem Bakoach*. Despite pressure from the Chief Military Rabbi, my father held firm, ultimately securing the adoption of *Mahanayim* as the publication's name. See Menachem Hacohen, *For the Sake of My Brothers and Friends* (Ben Shemen: Modan, 2025), 53 (Hebrew).

12   See his subsequently published volumes of responsa on "Matters of the Military, War, and Security" in Shlomo Goren, *Meshiv Milhama*, vol. 1 (Jerusalem: Ha-Idrah Rabbah, 1983; Hebrew); Shlomo Goren, *Meshiv Milhama*, vol. 2 (Jerusalem: Ha-Idrah Rabbah, 1984; Hebrew); Shlomo Goren, *Meshiv Milhama*, vol. 3 (Jerusalem: Ha-Idrah Rabbah, 1986; Hebrew); and Shlomo Goren, *Meshiv Milhama*, vol. 4 (Jerusalem: Ha-Idrah Rabbah, 1992; Hebrew).

From the very beginning of his service in the IDF, he regarded himself as a "priest anointed for war,"[13] leading the armies of Israel with a Torah scroll in hand. Through a deliberate and calculated effort over many years, including scholarly Torah articles, he positioned himself—despite the lack of a continuous two-thousand-year tradition—as the successor of the land's conquerors during the time of Joshua bin Nun,[14] as well as the heir of the Hasmoneans, the Maccabees, who waged a grueling campaign to purify the Temple and restore the sacred service.[15] He also saw himself as a successor to Bar Kokhba.[16] His mission, as articulated through religious writings to bridge a two-thousand-year gap in Jewish tradition was to purify the Temple and restore its sacred service, framing his military endeavors within the context of a divine and historical mandate.[17]

---

13 Aharon (Roni) Kampinsky, "The IDF Military Rabbi: Between a 'Kohen Anointed for War' and a 'Religious Services Provider,'" *Religions*, vol. 11, no. 4 (2020): 1-14.

14 [Shlomo Goren], "Abu-Ageila Has Been Sanctified with the Sanctity of the Land of Israel," *ha-Tsofeh* (2 November 1956): 8 (Hebrew).

15 Shlomo Goren, "Army and War in the Light of the Halakhah," *Mahanayim*, no. 121 (February 1969): 7-19 (Hebrew).

16 See Shlomo Goren, "The Reign of Bar Kokhba in Light of Recent Discoveries in the Judean Desert," *Mahanayim*, no. 59 (July 1961): 6-15 (Hebrew); and on this topic, see also Haim Weiss, "'Suddenly, a Bridge Was Built Across Two Thousand Years': From Secular Archaeology to Religious Archaeology – The Case of Bar Kokhba, Yigael Yadin, and Shlomo Goren," *Theory and Criticism*, no. 46 (2016): 143-167 (Hebrew).

17 See above, footnote 7; and Aviad Hacohen, "Not by Might, Nor by Power: Conflicts Involving Religion and State in the Israeli Army," in Aviad Hacohen and Tsvi Tal, eds., *Safra ve-Saifa, The Book and the Sword: Rabbi Mordechai Piron Jubilee Volume* (Jerusalem: Mahanayim, 2013), 233-365 (Hebrew).

Ariel Sharon, Rabbi Shlomo Goren, and Rehavam Ze'evi recite chapters of Psalms together during "Operation Inferno" and the Battle of Karameh, 1968. [IDF and Ministry of Defense Archives Collection, Photograph No. 6505/0034/B1, Bamahane Photographers.]

The culmination of Rabbi Goren's vision materialized during the Six-Day War, when he joined the frontline combat troops, holding a Torah scroll and a shofar in his hands, as if embodying the biblical kohen *mashuah milhama* (priest anointed for war). Unlike his fellow soldiers, who adhered to safety regulations, wore steel helmets, and advanced cautiously toward the Lion's Gate and the Old City while staying close to the wall, Rabbi Goren ran down the middle of the road with the Torah scroll in hand, wearing nothing more than a simple fabric cap on his head. His now-iconic photograph—depicting him adorned with tefillin, holding the Torah scroll, and blowing the shofar—transcended the battlefield to become a powerful symbol of the war. This image was commemorated not only in military literature but also reproduced on postcards, philatelic materials, and in works of visual art, solidifying its place in the collective memory of the conflict.[18]

18 Shalom Sabar, "'The Year of the Liberation of Our Holy Sites': The Six-Day War in the Mirror of Israeli Folk Art," *Jerusalem Studies in Jewish Folklore,*

It is noteworthy that in these photos, Rabbi Goren is seen wearing only the tefillin for the head and not the tefillin for the arm, as required by halakha.[19] The explanation for this anomaly, as I learned from my father, Rabbi Menachem Hacohen—who served as Rabbi Goren's close aide for many years, accompanied him throughout the war, and stood beside him in the famous photograph—is quite simple: Rabbi Goren did not have his own tefillin with him. Upon arriving at the Western Wall, he "borrowed" the head tefillin from a nearby soldier (visible in the photograph), but the soldier refused to part with his arm tefillin.

Rabbi Goren, holding a shofar and wearing only the head tefillin, stands alongside a soldier wearing the arm tefillin, from whom he had "confiscated" the head tefillin. Two people over is my father, Rabbi Menachem Hacohen, leaning in and appearing to be the closest to the shofar, making him the one who most directly heard its call (Photo: Bamahane, courtesy of the IDF Archive, Ministry of Defense).

On that occasion, Rabbi Goren instructed my father to "confiscate" all the shofars held by soldiers and civilians who had arrived at the site, so

vol. 35 (2023): 37-86 (Hebrew).

19   Based on verse in Deuteronomy 6:8.

that he would be the sole shofar-blower to be commemorated in history with the liberation of the Western Wall.[20] In another photograph, my father is seen holding two additional shofars that had been "confiscated" from other soldiers, ensuring that Rabbi Goren could blow the shofar in a "solo" performance—he and no one else.

The brief proclamation dictated by Rabbi Goren to my father at the Western Wall, written on four small slips of paper, began with a blessing:

> *"Dear soldiers, heroes of the nation! The fateful, decisive, and most historic moment for the people of Israel has arrived. You stand before the gates of Jerusalem and the gates of the Temple. You have been granted the greatest privilege of redeeming and liberating the nation's Holy of Holies—Har HaBayit, the Western Wall, and the city of God, Zion, and Jerusalem. You are the emissaries of Divine Providence to fulfill the messianic vision of the Jewish people. For this moment, we have prayed for thousands of years."*

Rabbi Goren then referred to well-known prayer verses, including "And rebuild Jerusalem, the holy city, speedily in our days; may our eyes witness Your return to Zion with mercy." Immediately thereafter, however, he added, "Now this messianic mission has been placed upon you." He concluded with an impassioned call to the soldiers:

> *"Open the gates of Jerusalem for the masses of the house of Israel, with strength and spirit, in sanctity and courage! Step by step, inch by inch, let us sanctify anew, with joy and jubilation, with supreme self-sacrifice, the courtyards of the Temple!"*

---

20   Menachem Hacohen, *For the Sake of My Brothers and Friends* (Ben Shemen: Modan, 2025), 129 (Hebrew). On the prayer of IDF soldiers held on the Temple Mount on Yom Kippur after the Six-Day War, see ibid., 134-136 (Hebrew).

The repeated references to redemption, sanctity, the Temple, the "messianic vision" and the "messianic mission" in such a succinct document were far from incidental. Rabbi Goren, with his deeply ingrained historical consciousness, was convinced that the Messiah was "aharei kotleinu"[21]—right behind the Western Wall—and would soon appear, if not within minutes, then within hours or days.[22]

Rabbi Goren's self-perception as a kind of savior and redeemer, a successor to the Hasmoneans and Bar Kokhba, along with his prominent

---

21 This verse from Song of Songs 2:9 is expounded as referring to the Messiah, who stands literally "behind the wall," with his arrival imminent. Among the circles of Yeshivat Mercaz HaRav, it is customary to sing this verse in dance on Yom HaAtzmaut and Yom Yerushalayim as an expression of the redemption that is drawing near.

22 Haim Weiss, "'The Mountain that Encompasses All the Hopes and Visions of Israel': Shlomo Goren and the Six-Day War," *Jerusalem Studies in Jewish Folklore*, vol. 35 (2023): 107-128 (Hebrew). On Rabbi Goren's motivations in his military activities in general, and during the Six-Day War in particular, see Arye Edrei, "Divine Spirit and Physical Power: Rabbi Shlomo Goren and the Military Ethic of the Israel Defense Forces," *Theoretical Inquiries in Law*, vol. 7, no. 1 (January 2006): 257-300; Arye Edrei, "War, Halakhah, and Redemption: Army and War in the Halakhic Thought of Rabbi Shlomo Goren," *Cathedra*, no. 125 (2008): 119-148 (Hebrew); Arye Edrei, "From Qibya to Beirut: The Renewal of the Jewish Laws of War in the State of Israel," in Yossi Goldstein, ed., *Yosef Da'at: Studies in Modern Jewish History in Honor of Yosef Salmon* (Beer Sheva: Ben-Gurion University Press, 2010), 95-127 (Hebrew); Shifra Mescheloff, "In the Eye of the Storm: The Public Image and Creative Torah Work of Rabbi Shlomo Goren, 1948-1994," (PhD Dissertation, Bar-Ilan University, 2010; Hebrew); Shifra Meschloff, "Establishing the Independence of the Military Rabbinate: From Rabbi Goren to Rabbi Piron," in Aviad Hacohen and Tsvi Tal, eds., *Safra ve-Saifa, The Book and the Sword: Rabbi Mordechai Piron Jubilee Volume* (Jerusalem: Mahanayim, 2013), 366-389 (Hebrew); Shifra Meschloff, "The Temple Mount in the Teachings of Rabbi Shlomo Goren," *Israel Studies Review*, vol. 32, no. 1 (January 2017): 88-103; and see also Nadav Shragai, *The Temple Mount Conflict: Jews and Muslims, Religion and Politics since 1967* (Jerusalem: Keter, 1995; Hebrew).

influence on the lives of religious youth in the 1960s, found extensive literary expression as well—occasionally ironic and incisive. Examples include Haim Be'er's *Et Ha-Zamir*[23] and Adam Baruch's *Lustig*.[24]

However, it is crucial to note that alongside these grand discourses on "the Temple" and the "messianic mission," Rabbi Goren also emphasized, in the same brief document, the imperative of preserving the sanctity of all holy sites, regardless of religious affiliation. This aspect of his message underscores the broader nature of his perspective, articulating the need to safeguard the sanctity of sites sacred to all religions, not just those central to Jewish identity.[25]

It is worth noting that Rabbi Goren had articulated similar views years earlier. On August 15, 1962—five years before the Six-Day War—

---

23   Haim Be'er, *Et Ha-Zamir* (Tel Aviv: Am Oved, 2004; Hebrew). See also Orel Sharp, "Between the Gravedigger and the Anointed Priest of War – A Conversation with Haim Be'er," *De'ot*, no. 57 (2012): 36-41 (Hebrew).

24   *Lustig* (Tel Aviv: Monitin, 1985), Chapter 34 (Hebrew): "He, God preserve us, Goren, perhaps already imagines himself as a sort of savior for the multitudes of Israel, silently exulting in his heart, 'I have saved, I am saving, I will save,' while the sheen of his face glows ever so slightly with pride. This, even as he—alongside his entire army, his rabbis, his religious officers, his supervisors, his rank, his study hall, and the honor bestowed upon him by the householders whose sons serve in the military, the honor granted by Holocaust survivors, the reverence of the grasses, shrubs, and wild animals—all these, and he himself, stumble along, rattling like a bubbling kettle trailing after Ben-Gurion."

25   See Yaron Silverstein, "Sanctification and 'Sacred Sites' in a Jewish Democratic State: A Study of Rabbi Shlomo Goren's Halakhic Rulings," *Jewish Political Studies Review*, vol. 31, no. 3-4 (2021): 98-134; Aviad Hacohen, "'The State of Israel, This Is An Holy Place!' – The Formation of Jewish Public Sphere in the State of Israel," in Mordechai Bar-On and Zvi Zameret, eds., *On Both Sides of the Bridge: Religion and State in the Early Years of Israel* (Jerusalem: Ben-Zvi Institute, 2002), 144-172 (Hebrew); and Aviad Hacohen, "'How Awesome Is This Place': Holy Places in Jewish Law," in Marshall Breger, ed., *Sacred Space in Israel and Palestine: Religion and Politics* (London: Routledge, 2012), 25-48.

"Rabbi Goren at the Oral Torah Conclave," *Davar* (15 August 1962): 4 (Hebrew).

Religious Ecstasy and Its Profound Significance in the 'Swords of Iron' War

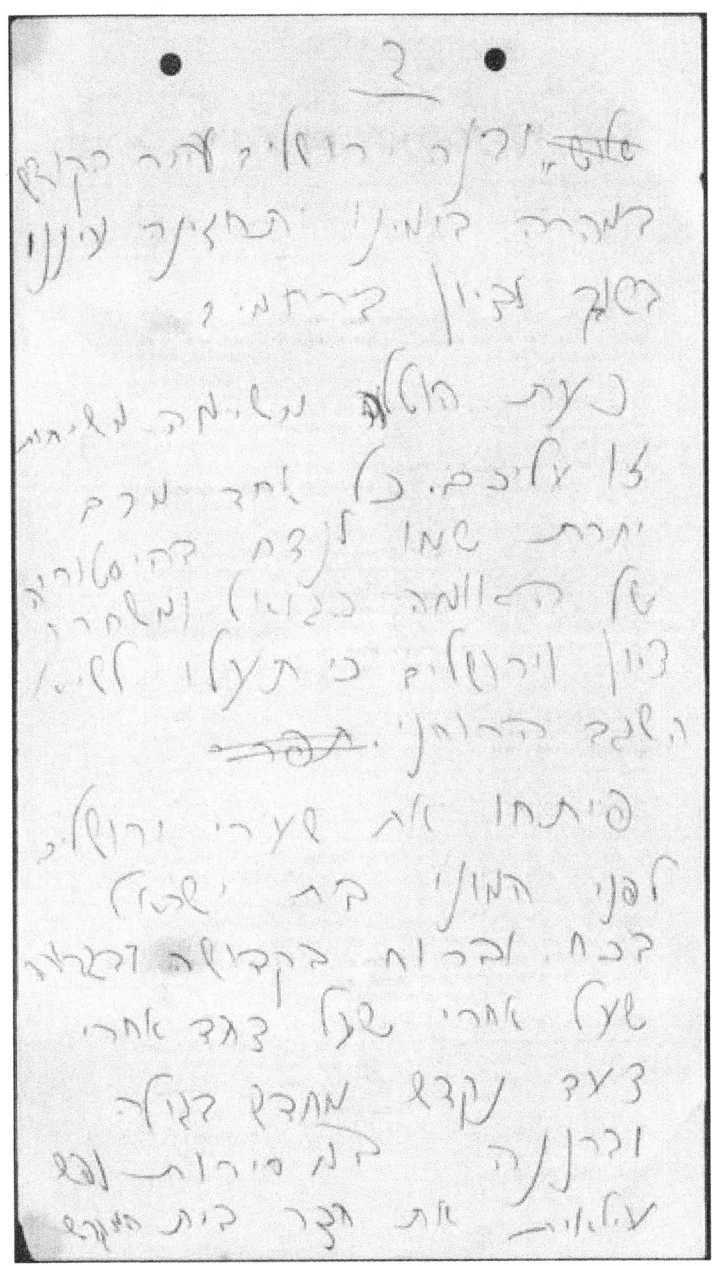

The Proclamation Issued by Rabbi Goren Upon the Liberation of the Western Wall, as Dictated in Real-Time to My Father, Rabbi Menachem Hacohen, Immediately Following the Liberation of the Wall (Courtesy of the Israel State Archives).

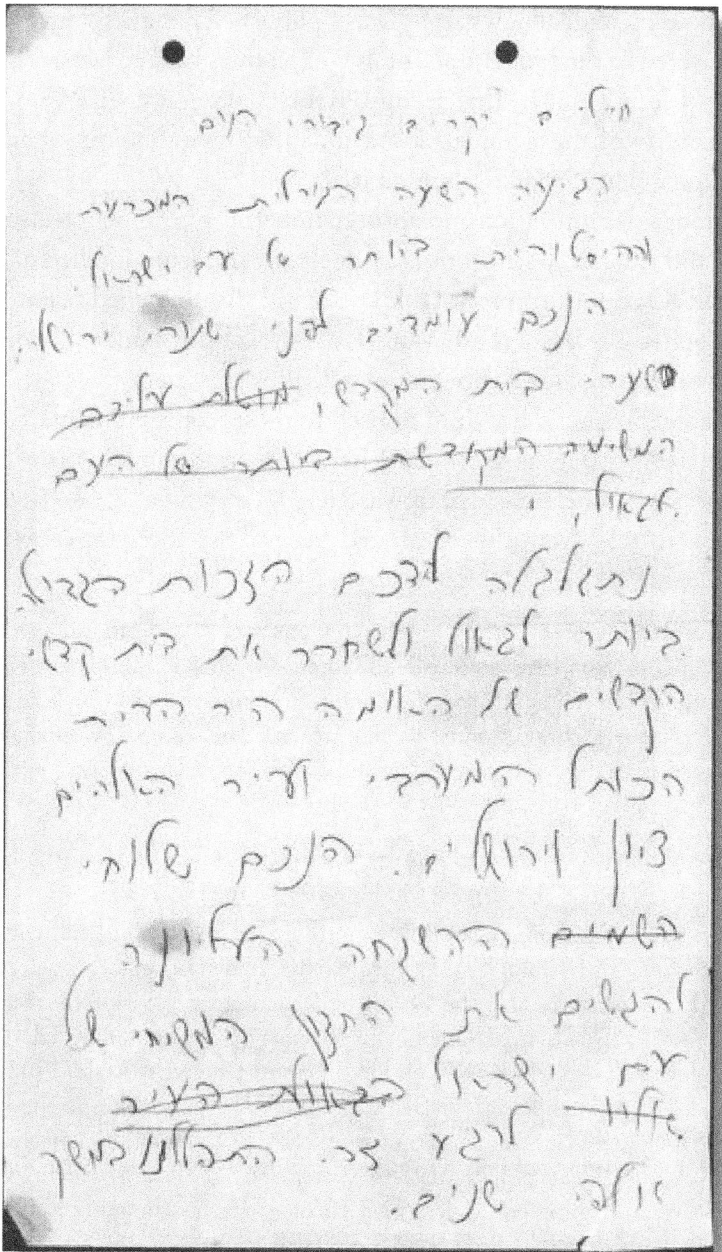
חיילים יקרים גיבורי חיל

הגיעה השעה הגדולה המצפה

וההיסטורית ביותר של עם ישראל.

הננו עומדים לפני שערי ירושלים.

שערי בית המקדש, ~~עליכם~~

~~המשאלה המקודשת ביותר של העם~~

~~ישראל.~~

נתגלגלה לידכם הזכות הגדולה

ביותר לבוא ולשחרר את בית קדשי

הקדשים של האומה הר הבית

הכותל המערבי ועיר האלוהים

ציון וירושלים. הננו שלוחי

~~השמים~~ ההשגחה העליונה

להגשים את החזון המשיחי של

עם ישראל ~~הגאולה הצפויה~~

~~אלפי~~ לרגע זה. המצפה במשך

דורות שנים.

the official Histadrut newspaper *Davar* published remarks from a lecture he delivered at the Fifth Oral Torah Conference, held at Mosad HaRav Kook in Jerusalem. In that lecture, Rabbi Goren stated: "Were we to seize control of the Temple Mount today, we would be duty-bound to rebuild the Beit HaMikdash upon it."[26]

Alongside admiration and appreciation, this phenomenon also drew scorn and ridicule, both from Haredi circles and from intellectuals and thinkers. One of the most notable critics was the renowned scientist and philosopher Professor Yeshayahu Leibowitz, who famously coined a derisive nickname for Rabbi Goren following this event.[27]

Rabbi Goren did not limit himself to these iconic moments. Shortly after the 1956 war, he ascended Jebel Musa (traditionally identified as Mount Sinai, where the Torah was given), carrying a Torah scroll and a shofar to read from the Torah and "renew" the covenant ceremony.[28]

---

26 See "Rabbi Goren at the Oral Torah Conclave," *Davar* (15 August 1962): 4 (Hebrew); and see later Shlomo Goren, "On the Contemporary Mitzvah to Build the Beit HaMikdash," *Panim El Panim*, no. 424 (30 June 1967): 12-13, 16 (Hebrew); and Shlomo Goren, "The Temple Mount and the Location of the Sanctuary in Jewish Law," in *Sefer Har Habayit* (Jerusalem: Ha-Idrah Rabbah, 2004), 47-53 (Hebrew).

27 See Yeshayahu Leibowitz, "Idolatry, or: The Clown Blowing the Shofar," *Haaretz Literary Supplement* (30 June 1967): 26 (Hebrew).

On Leibowitz's "anti-redemptive" approach, see Yeshayahu Leibowitz, "The Religious and Moral Significance of the Redemption of Israel (1977)" and "Redemption and the Dawn of Redemption (1971)," in Yeshayahu Leibowitz, *Judaism, Human Values, and the Jewish State*, ed. Eliezer Goldman (Cambridge and London: Harvard University Press, 1992), 106-122, 123-127; and see Dov Schwartz, "Leibowitz's Position in the Face of the Religious Zionism Theology," in Avi Sagi, ed., *Yeshayahu Leibowitz: His World and Philosophy* (Jerusalem: Keter, 1995), 212-214 (Hebrew); and Haim O. Rechnitzer, "Redemptive Theology in the Thought of Yeshayahu Leibowitz," *Israel Studies*, vol. 13, no. 3 (Fall 2008): 137-159.

28 It also led to a sharp Haredi remark about Rabbi Goren, suggesting that his ascent of Mount Sinai was not to symbolize the giving of the Torah or to renew the covenant, but rather to "return the Torah."

Rabbi Goren is seen at the summit of Mount Sinai, draped in a tallit, holding a Torah scroll and a shofar. To his left stands Yaron London, one of Israel's most prominent media figures, who at the time served as a military correspondent.

After the War: Ascending Mount Sinai (Photo: Alex Igor, *Bamahane*, courtesy of the IDF Archive, Ministry of Defense)

Religious Ecstasy and Its Profound Significance in the 'Swords of Iron' War

Rabbi Goren, adorned with a tallit, holding a Torah scroll and a shofar, atop Mount Sinai. To his left stands Yaron London, one of Israel's most prominent media figures, who at the time served as a military correspondent. (Photo: Bamahane, courtesy of the IDF Archive, Ministry of Defense)

(Photo: Alex Agor, Bamahane, courtesy of the IDF Archive, Ministry of Defense))

It should be noted that this was not the only time Rabbi Goren ascended Mount Sinai. In my father's memoirs, recently published in his book *For the Sake of My Brothers and Friends*, he recounts another ascent by Rabbi Goren, accompanied by "the poet of redemption," Uri Zvi Greenberg.[29]

29 See the evocative account of Uri Zvi Greenberg's journey to Mount Sinai, as described by Menachem Hacohen, *For the Sake of My Brothers and Friends* (Ben Shemen: Modan, 2025), pp. 138–140 (Hebrew).

According to my father's testimony: Uri Zvi Greenberg traveled to the Sinai Peninsula aboard a small aircraft departing from Sde Dov Airport in Tel-Aviv. The plane, apart from its pilot, carried only three passengers: Rabbi Shlomo Goren, Rabbi Menachem Hacohen, and an accompanying soldier. As the aircraft flew over Gaza, my father gestured toward the city, remarking, "That is Gaza." Greenberg turned to look and immediately erupted into a torrent of invective—not directed at Gaza itself or its inhabitants, but at Nathan of Gaza, the confidant and secretary of Shabbetai Tzvi, the seventeenth-century false messiah. Greenberg's relentless imprecations against Nathan of Gaza continued unabated. Rabbi Goren, unable to contain himself, burst into laughter. Greenberg took no offense and persisted in his outpouring until the aircraft exited Gaza's airspace and entered the Sinai Peninsula. After some time, the aircraft landed at Ras Sedr, a site along the Red Sea where Israel operated a substantial oil field. We entered the modest military camp at the location, where we had a brief meal and some refreshment. Uri Zvi then walked to the shoreline, where he stood and proclaimed with fervent urgency, "The Egyptians will invade from here! Look, they will cross here! They will march through this very place!" Six years later, the Egyptians indeed invaded Sinai, though not at this precise location but farther to the north, along the Suez Canal. Nonetheless, the mere notion of an Egyptian invasion of the Sinai Peninsula seemed inconceivable in the months immediately following the Six-Day War. Such a prospect was deemed utterly detached from reality. Yet Uri Zvi Greenberg alone stood apart, embodying the prophetic intensity of the ancient seers of Israel.

That evening, the group rested near the site of Saint Catherine's Monastery at the foot of Jebel Musa, the mountain traditionally identified with Mount Sinai. Early the next morning, they prepared for their ascent to the summit, riding camels along narrow mountain paths that precariously skirted deep ravines. Greenberg, however, refused to mount a camel, insisting instead

In any case, following the Six-Day War, and shortly thereafter, Yoram Taharlev (1938–2022), one of Israel's most renowned songwriters, composed a satirical and rhyming song about the character of "Our Rabbi, Rabbi Goren."[30] The song, laced with irony and humor, reads as follows:

> on ascending by foot. "You won't have the strength to climb," my father cautioned him, but Greenberg remained resolute: "I will climb." Reluctantly, the others left him to ascend the mountain alone while they continued on their way, accompanied by two soldiers and riding the camels toward the summit, towering at an elevation of 2,285 meters. The climb proved arduous, particularly for Greenberg, who was already 71 years old. As the sun rose higher, the heat intensified. At one point, the group entered a shaded crevice to rest before resuming their ascent. Suddenly, Greenberg broke into wrenching, uncontrollable sobs. He wept inconsolably, his emotions overwhelming him. Abruptly, he emerged from the crevice, stood upright, and, with tears streaming down his face, began to recite the Kaddish prayer. "Uri Zvi," my father asked gently after Greenberg finished his prayer, "what has happened?" Greenberg replied:
>
> "The last time I saw my parents was during my visit to Poland, just before the outbreak of the Second World War. All these years since our parting, I have not known their fate—whether they perished in the Holocaust, and if so, when or how. I have never recited Kaddish for them. Yet here, on Mount Sinai, it was revealed to me with absolute clarity: they are no longer alive. Here, too, I understood when and how they were murdered. Therefore, it is here, for the first time in my life, that I have recited Kaddish for my parents, who died as martyrs, together with millions of other Jews. May God and the people of Israel avenge their blood."
>
> After some time, Greenberg regained his composure. He declined to continue the ascent and, accompanied by the two soldiers, made his way back down to the base of the mountain. Reflecting on the experience, Rabbi Menachem Hacohen concluded: "I did not regard this as a failure. Uri Zvi Greenberg had come to terms, at long last, with the death of his parents and recited Kaddish for them. If the entire purpose of this journey had been to bring even a fleeting moment of tranquility to his tormented soul, then it was worth every effort."

30 Yoram Taharlev, *No Way Back: Songs and Stories of an Alternate Israel* (Tel-Aviv: Ministry of Defense, 2007), 81 (Hebrew).

When the people were called to action,

Our Rabbi, Rabbi Goren,

Wore his steel helmet with pride.

With a shofar and a kapote,

He rushed to the Dakota,

Fighting both in Sinai and Judea.

On Monday, he prayed by the Temple at the Wall,

On Tuesday, he was summoned to the plains.

Before he finished in Gaza,

His car was already on its way,

To purify the Cave of the Patriarchs.[31]

From there, he hastened, our Rabbi,

To the resting place of Rachel our Matriarch—

May her memory protect us forever.

He didn't stop to say "Shalom Aleichem,"

For they already called him to Bethlehem,

Since there's only one Rabbi Goren.

At midnight, he was to reach Jericho,

To bring down its walls with his shofar.

But from Saint Catherine's,

A telegram arrived in haste: "Please save us!"

So he flew by helicopter to the desert.

---

31 On the "conquest" of Hebron and the Cave of Machpelah during the Six-Day War by Rabbi Goren; my father and the driver had already arrived at the site even before IDF forces reached the location. See Menachem Hacohen, *For the Sake of My Brothers and Friends* (Ben Shemen: Modan, 2025), 130–131 (Hebrew).

And behind him came a cinematographer,

Chasing him on a motorcycle,

Racing through fire and trenches.

Some say that the IDF

Didn't advance another inch,

Because Rabbi Goren simply collapsed from exhaustion.

Indeed, it must be stated truthfully: since the Six-Day War, and especially after 1973, this phenomenon has markedly declined. The profound trauma of the Yom Kippur War significantly tempered messianic fervor, and there were even those who began to question whether we are indeed in an advanced stage of the "beginning of redemption" (*Atchalta De-Geulah*).[32]

Why, then, have such phenomena resurfaced with particular intensity in the past decade? Several factors might be considered in this context.

---

32 See, for example, Norman Lamm, "The War: First Thoughts," *Sh'ma: A Journal of Jewish Responsibility* 4/61 (November 16, 1973): 4, where he writes, "Al Chet — for the sin of premature Messianism. This presumptuousness is common to two disparate groups — those whose Messianism is primarily nationalistic, and those to whom it is completely internationalist. In 1967, a large number of Israelis, and some Americans, were convinced that the Six-Day War proved we were in a definite pre-redemptive Messianic era, and some even said so in the prayers we recite for Israel — *Atchalta De-Geulah* ('the beginning of redemption')." See, in response, Shubert Spero, "Lo Chatanu – We Have Not Sinned," *Sh'ma: A Journal of Jewish Responsibility* 4/73 (May 3, 1974): 98–100; and the rejoinder by Norman Lamm, "Aval Ashemim Anachnu – But We Are Guilty," *Sh'ma: A Journal of Jewish Responsibility* 4/73 (May 3, 1974): 100–101. See also Jacob J. Schacter, "In Memory of Rabbi Dr. Norman Lamm: Some Personal Reflections," *The Lehrhaus* (June 1, 2020), available here (https://thelehrhaus.com/commentary/in-memory-of-rabbi-dr-norman-lamm-some-personal-reflections). I thank Rabbi Dr. Yaakov Jaffe and Mr. Menachem Butler for these sources, cited in their forthcoming essay, "An Ambitious American Orthodox Initiative: Crafting a 'Unity Compromise' Prayer for the State of Israel."

The enlistment of graduates from pre-military academies—foremost among them the "Bnei David" Academy in Eli—into elite units of the Israel Defense Forces (IDF), followed by their subsequent advancement through the ranks of command, has increasingly infused the IDF's ethos with messianic-redemptive overtones.[33] One notable example occurred during Operation "Protective Edge" in the summer of 2014. Colonel Ofer Winter, commander of the Givati Brigade, was a student of Rabbi Haim Drukman (1932–2022), a leading figure among the followers of Rabbi Zvi Yehuda Hacohen Kook and Yeshivat Merkaz Harav, and one of the first graduates of the "Bnei David" Academy in Eli. He issued a "Daily Commander's Order" to his soldiers, the content of which left no doubt about its ideological underpinnings: "**History has chosen us** to stand at the forefront of the battle against the terrorist enemy in Gaza, which reviles, curses, **and defames the God of Israel's armies.**"[34]

---

33 Udi Lebel, "Settling the Military: The Pre-Military Academies Revolution and the Creation of a New Security Epistemic Community – The Militarization of Judea and Samaria," *Israel Studies*, vol. 21, no. 3 (2015): 361-390; and Udi Lebel, "The 'Immunized Integration' of Religious-Zionists within Israeli Society: The Pre-Military Academy as an Institutional Model," *Social Identities*, vol. 22, no. 6 (2016): 642-666; and Udi Lebel, "Pre-Military Academies as the 'Making' of Religious- Zionist Leadership Capital," in Rein Brouwer, ed., *The Future of (Lived) Religious Leadership* (Amsterdam: VU University Press, 2018), 186-207.

34 "Givati Brigade Commander to Officers: 'The Lord, God of Israel, We Fight Against an Enemy Who Blasphemes Your Name,'" *Haaretz* (11 July 2014; Hebrew).
In this context, there is limited room to delve into the phrasing of daily orders that incorporate scriptural verses or the changes these have undergone from the establishment of the State to the present day. Nevertheless, it is worth highlighting a well-established tradition that has emerged during IDF recruit oath ceremonies: the recitation of verses from the Book of Joshua 1:6-10, which are marked by a distinctly religious tone: "Be strong and of good courage; for you shall cause this people to inherit the land which I swore to their fathers to give them. Only be strong and exceedingly courageous, to observe to do according to all the Torah which Moses My

The final phrase is drawn, not coincidentally, from the words of King David as he stood before Goliath the Philistine (I Samuel 17:45): *"David said to the Philistine, 'You come to me with sword, spear, and javelin, but I come to you in the name of the Lord of Hosts, the God of the armies of Israel, whom you have taunted.'"*

The enlistment of graduates from pre-military academies, foremost among them the "Bnei David" Academy in Eli, into elite units of the Israel Defense Forces and their subsequent advancement through the ranks of command have resulted in an increasing infusion of messianic-redemptive overtones into the IDF's ethos.[35]

During the "Iron Swords" war, there was a growing prevalence of phenomena such as blowing the shofar before heading into battle[36] and during combat,[37] immersion in a ritual mikveh (!) prior to engagement, the wearing of an unofficial "unit badge" alongside the official military

---

servant commanded you; do not turn from it to the right hand or to the left, that you may have success wherever you go. This book of the Torah shall not depart out of your mouth, but you shall meditate on it day and night, that you may observe to do according to all that is written therein; for then you shall make your way prosperous, and then you shall have good success. Have I not commanded you? Be strong and courageous; do not be afraid, nor be dismayed; for the Lord your God is with you wherever you go."

35 Udi Lebel, "Settling the Military: The Pre-Military Academies Revolution and the Creation of a New Security Epistemic Community – The Militarization of Judea and Samaria," *Israel Studies*, vol. 21, no. 3 (2015): 361-390; and Udi Lebel, "The 'Immunized Integration' of Religious-Zionists within Israeli Society: The Pre-Military Academy as an Institutional Model," *Social Identities*, vol. 22, no. 6 (2016): 642-666; and Udi Lebel, "Pre-Military Academies as the 'Making' of Religious- Zionist Leadership Capital," in Rein Brouwer, ed., *The Future of (Lived) Religious Leadership* (Amsterdam: VU University Press, 2018), 186-207.

36 Based on the ruling of Maimonides, Mishneh Torah, Hilkhot Taanit 1:1-4.

37 Rogel Alpher, "An IDF Division Convening Before Battle for a Ceremony to Hasten the Coming of the Messiah? Precisely So," *Haaretz* (6 November 2024; Hebrew).

patches bearing the word "Messiah,"[38] and the carrying of Psalms, various types of amulets, and ethical texts (such as the Mesillat Yesharim

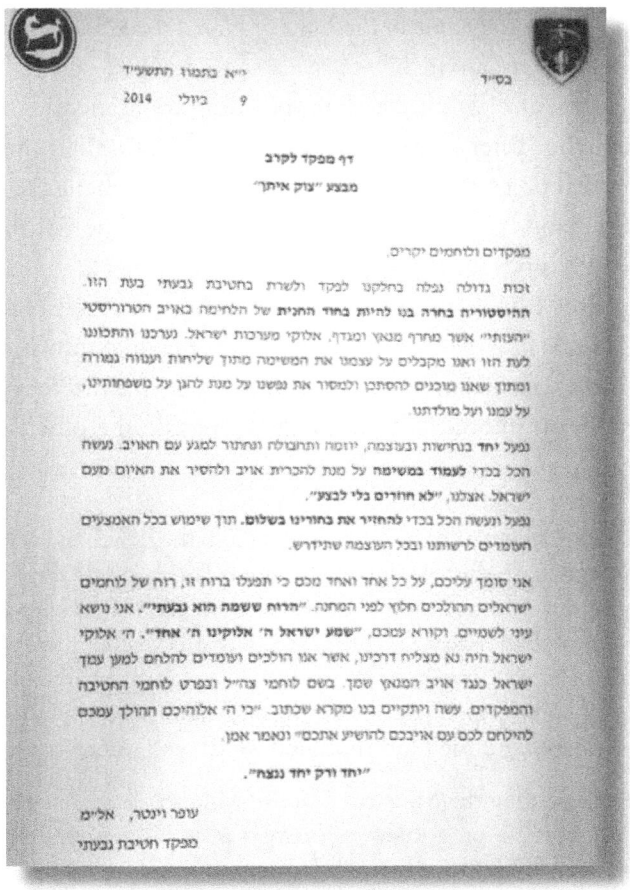

[38] "Messiah" patches, tied to Chabad's messianic faction, reflect beliefs in Rabbi Schneerson as the Messiah and often feature symbols like crowns or "770." See image from here (https://www.ebay.com/itm/166940166669).

In at least one instance, IDF Chief of Staff Lieutenant General Herzi Halevi, upon encountering a Golani soldier wearing a "Messiah patch," ordered its immediate removal. See Avi Ashkenazi, "Chief of Staff Removes 'Messiah' Patch: 'Only Military Patches on the Uniform,'" *Maariv* (22 October 2024; Hebrew). Following this event, Channel 14, a right-wing Israeli TV network, aired a mocking animated clip targeting IDF Chief of by Rabbi Moshe Chaim Luzzatto,[39] in a pocket-sized edition designed

> Staff Lt. Gen. Herzi Halevi. The clip exaggerated an incident where Halevi reprimanded a soldier for displaying a "Messiah" badge. Subsequently, the IDF condemned the content as inflammatory and defamatory, asserting it undermines the military during wartime. The incident also sparked a heated debate on social media, where comparisons were drawn between the "Messiah" patch and LGBTQ community symbols, reigniting ongoing tensions over the display of personal and ideological patches within the military. See "Fierce Debate Over the Difference Between the 'Messiah' Patch and the LGBTQ Flag," *Tel Aviv Online* (23 October 2024; Hebrew).
>
> A related controversy erupted on social media following an out-of-context quote attributed to IDF Chief of Staff Eyal Zamir regarding the IDF's policy on patches. The initial headline, widely shared online, quoted Zamir as saying, "I will not tear off anyone's patch, that's not my role." This led to criticism, particularly from left-wing commentators. However, his full remarks, delivered to senior IDF leadership, clarified that enforcement of the policy was the responsibility of commanding officers: "I do not intend to tear a patch off any soldier; that is your role. I do not plan to deal with this, and you do not want me to deal with this—it is a matter for the chain of command." Despite this clarification, some critics, including former deputy head of Israel's National Security Council Eran Etzion, accused Zamir of undermining IDF professionalism, while others, such as journalist Avishai Grinzaig, defended him against what they described as a politically motivated misrepresentation. See "Storm on the Web: Attack on the Chief of Staff – Following a Quote Taken Out of Context," *Arutz 7* (10 March 2025; Hebrew).

39 Nehemia Stern, "Like a Sacrifice Ascending from the Flames: Hadar Goldin's Mesilat Yesharim in Israeli Religious Nationalist Thought," *Prooftexts*, vol. 40, no. 2 (2023): 38-70, who examined the publication of Hadar Goldin's edition of Mesilat Yesharim, based on notes he took from Rabbi Eliezer Kashtiel's lectures on *Mesilat Yesharim* at the Bnei David pre-military academy in Eli. For the published work, see Hadar Goldin, *How to Build a Life: Studying Mesillat Yesharim with Hadar Goldin*, ed. Simha Goldin (Jerusalem: Maggid, 2018; in Hebrew); and see also Simha Goldin, "Bringing Hadar to Eretz Tzvi," in Aviad Hacohen and Menachem Butler, eds., *Praying for the Defenders of Our Destiny: The Mi Sheberach*

to fit into a soldier's pouch).[40]

In this context, it is essential to distinguish between the blowing of the shofar during combat zones as part of the morning prayers in the month of Elul or on Rosh Hashanah—an established element of Jewish prayer practice for generations—and the blowing of the shofar outside of prayer, intended for an entirely different purpose. The latter seeks to

continue the ancient tradition mentioned in the Bible of blowing the shofar before going to war.[41] For example, during the "Iron Swords" war, Captain (Res.) Yoel Kaplan, the rabbi of Brigade 162 (and in civilian

> *for IDF Soldiers* (Cambridge, MA: The Institute for Jewish Research and Publications, 2023), 232-238.

40 See the editions produced by Rabbi Eliezer Kashtiel, *Lectures on Mesillat Yesharim, 'Man's Duty in His World'* (Eli: Bnei David Publishing, 2016; Hebrew); Rabbi Eliezer Kashtiel, *Lectures on Mesillat Yesharim, 'The Trait of Watchfulness and the Trait of Zeal'* (Eli: Bnei David Publishing, 2017; Hebrew); Rabbi Eliezer Kashtiel, *Lectures on Mesillat Yesharim, 'The Trait of Cleanliness'* (Eli: Bnei David Publishing, 2017; Hebrew); Rabbi Eliezer Kashtiel, *Lectures on Mesillat Yesharim, 'The Trait of Piety'* (Eli: Bnei David Publishing, 2020; Hebrew).

41 See Numbers 10:9, though in that context specifically referring to trumpets.

life, a Chabad emissary in Albania), would gather the soldiers before embarking on a mission and sound what he called "the shofar of the Messiah, the shofar of salvation that we all anticipate and long for."

_{Rabbi Yoel Kaplan, a Chabad emissary in Albania and the divisional rabbi of Brigade 162, as reported by Channel 14, a right-wing Israeli television channel.}

In early October 2023, Captain Harel Ettinger, an officer and team commander in the Egoz Unit, fell in battle in southern Lebanon. At his funeral, his commanders and subordinates delivered eulogies, and, as is customary, concluded with the singing of "Hatikvah." Following this, spontaneously, the crowd began singing "Ani Ma'amin Be'emunah Shleimah Beviat Hamashiach" ("I believe with perfect faith in the coming of the Messiah"). The singing of "Ani Ma'amin" at the conclusion of induction ceremonies for recruits has also become a widespread phenomenon.⁴²

Unlike "the Goren phenomenon," in which Rabbi Shlomo Goren, as Chief Rabbi of the IDF, officially oversaw the management of religious life in the army, the current war has seen these phenomena become increasingly widespread among "ordinary" soldiers.

This trend has not been limited to soldiers who identify as religious or observant, but has also appeared among those who generally consider themselves secular or even outright atheists.

As mentioned before, the roots of this phenomenon began to take hold about a decade ago, coinciding with the growing integration of graduates from religious pre-military academies—chiefly the *Bnei David* Academy in Eli, whose alumni have risen through the IDF ranks to occupy prominent leadership positions—as well as from *hesder yeshivot* and Zionist-religious higher yeshivot. Many students of these institutions, often encouraged by their rabbis and heads of institutions, choose to serve in elite combat units and pursue officer training.

As a result, this phenomenon has grown significantly in scale. According to various reports, approximately 40% of IDF officer training graduates are alumni of these institutions,⁴³ despite the fact that the religious Zionist sector constitutes no more than 15% of Israel's population (and not all of its members affiliate with these institutions).

---

42   See, for example, the induction ceremony for Armored Corps recruits: once again, the singing of "Ani Ma'amin" at induction ceremonies sparks controversy. Similarly, at the swearing-in ceremony for soldiers of the Kfir Brigade near the Western Wall: "Ani Ma'amin Beviat Hamashiach"—the swearing-in ceremony of the Kfir Brigade, online here (https://www.youtube.com/watch?v=lrvSWpY30_M). See also Yaakov Kastel, "I Swear, I Believe: Religion in IDF Swearing-In Ceremonies," on the Kan Website (https://www.kan.org.il/content/kan-news/defense/282344).

43   See Ariel Finkelstein, *The National-Religious Society in Data* (Jerusalem: Ne'emanei Torah Va'Avodah, 2021; Hebrew), quoted in Yagil Levy, "A Nationalist Religious Group Has Swelled the Ranks of Israel's Military," *The Forward* (17 October 2024).

This trend, described by its critics as "religionization" (*hadatah*) of the military, has also assumed visible external forms. Increasingly, soldiers are seen with long beards and *payot* (side curls), wearing their *tzitzit* (fringes) outside their uniforms, or donning large wool hats in the style of Breslov Hasidim or the *Old Yishuv* of Jerusalem. This stands in contrast to the short, cropped hairstyles traditionally mandated in the IDF by long-standing regulations.

As noted above, this phenomenon is unsurprising. War exposes soldiers, particularly those on the frontlines, to mortal danger. It is well-documented that when faced with life-threatening situations, individuals—like those gravely ill—often experience religious or quasi-religious impulses, leading them to engage in acts of a spiritual nature that they might not otherwise consider. The religious element is also evident in the language of modern warfare, which borrows terms from religious sources. For example, the phrases "purify the area" ("*letaheir* et ha-shetach") or "purify a house" ("*letaheir* ha-bayit") are used to describe clearing a building in enemy territory of militants, explosives, or weapons. The verb "*to purify*" (*letaheir*) is directly derived from the laws of ritual purity and impurity, which are closely associated with the Temple and sacrificial worship.

Beyond the sociological aspect, these various actions—sometimes culminating in religious ecstasy or intensely spiritual experiences—carry theological implications. Chief among them is the perception of war not merely as a civic operation but as a formative step toward the ultimate redemption (*geulah*) and a crucial phase on the path to the arrival of the Messiah.

This outlook has been echoed in numerous statements during and after the war. The most extreme voices have described the horrific events of October 7 as a "heavenly act," framing them as part of the stages of redemption, which necessarily involve trials and self-sacrifice. These voices emphasize an idea, shared to some extent by both Hamas theology and certain IDF fighters, that the "October 7 War" is not merely a military-political campaign but a central part of the "battle for the Temple Mount" or the "Temple War."

The phenomena observed in the field and the discourse that follows often intertwine in ways that blur the lines between reality and narrative. A striking example from "Operation Iron Swords" is the widely circulated photograph of Lieutenant Colonel Itamar Eitam—son of former minister and Brigadier-General (Res.) Effi Eitam[44]—blowing a shofar in the heart of Gaza, his face framed by a prominent beard.[45] Itamar Eitam, who was wounded by sniper fire during a battle and subsequently evacuated to the hospital, candidly discussed, in an extensive interview with *Makor Rishon*,[46] the religious—and messianic—spirit that he felt accompanied him throughout the war.[47]

---

44 Brigadier General Effi Eitam (b. 1952) is a former Knesset member who served as a cabinet minister in the Sharon government and later became a leader of the National Religious Party. In a *Haaretz* interview with Ari Shavit, he made statements laden with messianic overtones, suggesting that, like Rabbi Goren, he sees himself as a "redeemer of Israel," in the tradition of Judah Maccabee and Bar Kokhba. See Ari Shavit, "A Leader Waiting for the Sign," *Haaretz Magazine* (22 March 2002): 14-16, 18, 20 (Hebrew); and also Ari Shavit, "Waiting for the Sign," *Haaretz Magazine* (22 March 2002): 8-11 (English).

45 Far from being a simple, spontaneous moment, this image raises questions about its authenticity: was it truly an unplanned event, or a meticulously designed, carefully staged, and orchestrated tableau intended to resonate as an "iconic picture" and shape public perception?

46 Hodaya Krish Hazoni, "'If You Will It, It Is No Dream': Itamar Eitam's Mission to Revive the Spirit of the IDF," *Makor Rishon, Sabbath Supplement*, no. 1423: *Parashat Chayei Sarah* (16 November 2024; Hebrew).

47 In contrast to the messianic militarism expressed by figures like Lieutenant Colonel Itamar Eitam, Elhanan Nir emphasizes a shift in national consciousness from external responses to a deeper, introspective understanding. Nir advocates for a transition from the "doctrine of Abel" to the "doctrine of Cain," urging a move from passivity to strength, but with an inward, reflective focus rather than through militaristic action. This contrast underscores different responses to crisis: one framed as a spiritual and intellectual challenge, the other as a divinely sanctioned, active confrontation.

Religious Ecstasy and Its Profound Significance in the 'Swords of Iron' War

Summary

As noted earlier, the phenomenon of "religious ecstasy" within the IDF, Israeli Army, is not a recent development. Different scholars have already explored various aspects of it in the past.[48]

However, a significant difference emerges between the religious fervor observed in the context of Rabbi Goren and the phenomenon witnessed in recent years, particularly during the Iron Swords war.

This distinction is evident both in the individuals involved and in the nature and scope of the phenomenon itself. In terms of scope and key figures, Rabbi Goren was, to a large extent, an isolated figure within the IDF. Throughout his decades of service, and even during the two decades following his military retirement—when he served as the Ashkenazi

48 Yonah Hadari-Remag, *The Messiah Rides a Tank: Public Thought in Israel Between the Sinai Campaign and the Yom Kippur War, 1955–1975* (Tel Aviv, 2002; Hebrew); and Elie Holzer, *A Double-Edged Sword: Military Activism in Religious Zionism* (Jerusalem: Keter, 2009; Hebrew). See also Dror Greenblum, *From the Bravery of the Spirit to the Sanctification of Power: Power and Bravery in Religious Zionism, 1948-1967* (Ra'anana: Open University, 2016; Hebrew), and see the bibliography therein.

Chief Rabbi of Israel—he remained the only soldier consistently seen carrying a shofar and Torah scroll into battle.

In contrast, a closer examination of the contemporary phenomenon reveals a much broader involvement, with hundreds—if not thousands—of soldiers now incorporating religious symbols into their personal gear. These symbols include not only standard military items like water bottles, personal bandages, and grenades, but also amulets and army unit patches embroidered with the word "Messiah." Moreover, Rabbi Goren held a senior rank, retiring as a Major General (*Aluf*), whereas many of the soldiers carrying these makeshift religious symbols today are, in military terms, *hapashim*—ordinary rank-and-file soldiers.[49]

Like any complex phenomenon, this one presents both positive and negative dimensions. On the positive side, as history has shown, religious zeal and a messianic vision can serve as powerful motivators in times of war. The invocation of messianic themes and the adoption of overt religious symbols can elevate the battlefield from a mere physical confrontation to a struggle imbued with profound moral and spiritual significance. This transformation can enhance soldiers' resilience, fortify their morale, and heighten their sense of purpose, helping them navigate the challenges and dangers of warfare.

Conversely, the negative aspects of this phenomenon should not be overlooked. The incorporation of religious symbols—such as Messiah unit patches, long payot, and tzitzit worn visibly outside of uniforms—can disrupt the cohesion of the army. These distinctive external markers challenge the military's reliance on uniformity and standardized appearance, which are essential for maintaining discipline and order. Moreover, the increasing dependence on amulets and external spiritual

---

49   This sentiment became so pronounced that some humorously proposed renaming the IDF's main induction base in Ramat Gan from Tel HaShomer to Tel HaShomer Shabbat, a playful jab highlighting the growing influence of religious practices within the military.

authorities—ranging from "miracle workers" to rabbis and Admorim[50]—poses a significant risk to military discipline. In these instances, soldiers may prioritize their personal sources of authority over the established chain of command, thereby undermining the hierarchical structure that is critical to maintaining order, unity, and operational effectiveness within the military.

Since we are still in the midst of the ongoing conflict—in the north, the south, and the east—it remains premature to assess whether the trend of religious fervor will persist and manifest in additional phenomena, or whether it will fade over time, as is often the case with various trends that rise and fall on the stage of history.[51]

On a theological level, this phenomenon sharpens the tension between the reliance on military preparedness and the conviction that ultimate outcomes rest in divine providence. It challenges the traditional rejection of the principle "my strength and the might of my hand have achieved this victory," prompting a deeper examination of how faith-based perspectives reconcile human agency and divine oversight within the framework of military endeavors.[52]

---

50   See Levi Cooper, "Hasidim Praying for Soldiers," in Aviad Hacohen and Menachem Butler, eds., *Praying for the Defenders of Our Destiny: The Mi Sheberach for IDF Soldiers* (Cambridge, MA: The Institute for Jewish Research and Publications, 2023), 173-197, which has since been greatly expanded into Levi Cooper, "Hasidim Praying for IDF Soldiers After October 7 2023," *Contemporary Jewry*, vol. 44, no. 4 (December 2024): 847-883.

51   This article does not address the potential impact of the increased integration of Haredi soldiers into the IDF, as well as that of religious women, some of whom serve in uniform while wearing a sheitel—a prominent and conspicuous head covering within the existing military landscape.

52   I have addressed this tension in Aviad Hacohen, "Neither Seen nor Found: Why is the 'Mi Sheberach' Prayer for IDF Soldiers Absent in the Lithuanian Haredi Community?" in Aviad Hacohen and Menachem Butler, eds., *Praying for the Defenders of Our Destiny: The Mi Sheberach for IDF Soldiers*

On a moral and philosophical level, this phenomenon presents a significant and complex dilemma. In the Torah's worldview, peace is an ideal and intrinsic value,[53] while war is regarded only as a necessary and regrettable means to an end. It is no coincidence that the commandment of war is not included among the 613 mitzvot, aside from the specific cases of the conquest of the land during the days of Joshua and the eradication of Amalek.[54] Even these were bound to their historical context, and notably, the Torah refrains from using the term *milḥama* (war) in these instances. Instead, it employs terms such as *meḥiyah* (eradication)[55] or *cherem* (utter destruction)[56] underscoring the exceptional nature of these commands and their distinction from the broader concept of war.

In this context, it is crucial to underscore that the dominant currents of Jewish law and philosophy[57] firmly reject an extreme pacifist stance.

(Cambridge, MA: The Institute for Jewish Research and Publications, 2023), 265-318.

53 See Aviezer Ravitzky, "Peace," in Arthur A. Cohen and Paul Mendes-Flohr, eds., *Contemporary Jewish Religious Thought* (New York: Charles Scribner, 1986), 685-702; and Daniel Sperber, *Great Is Peace: Perek ha-Shalom from the Talmudic Tractate Derekh Eretz Zuta*, second edition (Jerusalem: Massada Press, 2003).

54 See Elliott Horowitz, "Amalek: The Memory of Violence and the Violence of Memory," in *Reckless Rites: Purim and the Legacy of Jewish Violence* (Princeton: Princeton University Press, 2006), and earlier in Daniel Sperber, "The Erasure of Amalek, Haman, and the Roman Damnatio Memoriae," in *Minhagei Yisrael*, vol. 6 (Jerusalem: Mosad ha-Rav Kook, 1998), 252-256 (Hebrew); and Diana Lipton, "Remembering Amalek: A Positive Biblical Model for Dealing with Negative Scriptural Types," in David F. Ford and Graham Stanton, eds., *Reading Texts, Seeking Wisdom: Scripture and Theology* (London: SCM, 2003), 139-153.

55 Deuteronomy 25:19.

56 Deuteronomy 20:16–17.

57 For unconventional views advocating for absolute or extreme pacifism, see, for example, Aharon Shmuel Tamares, "Freedom: A Sermon for

The Jewish tradition categorically opposes the Christian ideal of "turning the other cheek"[58] and instead recognizes the legitimacy of a milhemet mitzvah as a divinely obligatory war.[59] However, such recognition is reserved strictly for situations of necessity—an ultimate measure of survival and self-defense[60] embodied in the Talmudic principle, "If someone rises to kill you, rise early to kill him first."[61] This framework firmly distinguishes milhemet mitzvah as an act of last resort rather than elevating war itself to the status of a mitzvah, reflecting a profound commitment to the sanctity of life and the pursuit of peace wherever possible.[62]

> Passover," in *The Morality of the Torah and Judaism* (Vilna 1912), 43-44 (Hebrew); Aharon Shmuel Tamares, *Pacifism in Light of the Torah*, ed. Ehud Luz (Jerusalem: Dinur Center Publications, 1992), 141 (Hebrew); and Isaac Slater, "Aharon Shmuel Tamares and the Dark Side of Religious Humanism," *Jewish Thought*, vol. 5 (2024): 177-207 (Hebrew). See also Joseph Klausner, "In the Struggle Over a Worldview," *HaTekufah*, vol. 26-27 (1930): 435-446 (Hebrew), which was written 11-21 October 1929.

58 The Christian principle of "turning the other cheek," derived from Matthew 5:39 in the Christian New Testament, emphasizes the moral imperative of non-retaliation and extreme forbearance. In contrast, Jewish law, while also valuing peace and reconciliation, incorporates principles of self-defense and the pursuit of justice. See Aviad Hacohen, "'And You Shall Not Place Blood in Your House': The Right to Bear Arms for Occupational and Self-Defense Purposes and Its Limitations," *Parashat ha-Shavua (The Weekly Portion), Ministry of Justice*, no. 425: Parashat Parashat Ki Teitzei (17 August 2013): 1-4 (Hebrew).

59 See the essays in this volume.

60 Haim Shapira, "The Law of the Pursuer (Rodef) and the Source of Self-Defense: An Analysis of the Talmudic Sources," *Jewish Law Association Studies*, vol. 16 (2007): 250-269.

61 Sanhedrin 72a.

62 Aharon Lichtenstein, "Seek Peace and Pursue It: The Pursuit of Peace as Today's Religious Imperative" (ed. Aviad Hacohen), *Alon Shvut le-Bogrei Yeshivat Har Etzion*, no. 14 (April 2001): 189-203 (Hebrew); and

Aviad Hacohen

On the halakhic level, this phenomenon generates peculiar mutations unimaginable to our ancestors. For example, in one image from the

also Daniel Roth, "The Pursuit of Peace in Medieval Judaism," in Yvonne Friedman, ed., *Religion and Peace: Historical Aspects* (London: Routledge, 2018), 146-158.

battlefields of the "Iron Swords" war, a group of soldiers is seen listening to a Torah reading, where the Torah reader uses a steel commando knife as a substitute for a *yad* (the pointer traditionally used by the reader). This image starkly contrasts with the prohibition, rooted in the Bible, against bringing iron or weapons—tools designed to "shorten human life," associated with death and killing—into the sacred domains of the Temple or contemporary synagogue.[63] This prohibition, grounded in the principle of *kedushat ha'adam* (the sanctity of human life), or perhaps supplanting it, elevated the value of *kedushat hadam* (the sanctity of blood) and the rejection of weapons intended to spill it.

It should be noted that this blending of religious and military symbolism is not entirely new. Already in the early days of the State, military rabbis, led by Rabbi Goren, conducted wedding ceremonies where the bride and groom walked to the chuppah under bayoneted rifles, or where rifles were employed for this purpose instead of the standard chuppah poles.[64] In later years, wedding ceremonies of soldiers were even held atop tanks, and no one objected to the blending of weapons of destruction—intended to sow devastation and ruin (even for justified purposes)—with the establishment of a new home in Israel.

Similar to the concept of "holy war" in Islam, this transformation reconceptualizes war as a *mitzvah*, imbuing it with profound ethical and ideological significance and introducing far-reaching implications for the interplay between religion, morality, and military conduct.

This trajectory appears far from complete, with its final outcomes yet to be realized and its ultimate chapters unwritten. One can only hope that the transformation of the aspirational vision of peace — "Nation shall not lift up sword against nation, neither shall they learn

---

63 See Zvi Ryzman, "Weapons in Shul," in *Exploring Halachic Dilemmas of War and Terror: Discussions of Issues In Our Perilous Times* (Rahway, New Jersey: ArtScroll/Mesorah, 2024), 129-146.

64 See, for example, the footage titled "Wedding Ceremony in a Military Base" (1960), provided by the Jerusalem Cinematheque – The Israel Film Archive, available online here (https://jfc.org.il/news_journal/59790-2/91861-2/).

war anymore"[65] — into the grim reality of perpetual conflict will not become our undoing, reversing the promise of blessing into the burden of an enduring curse.

To complete the picture, we shall add that, as in every war, religious phenomena emerged beyond the battlefield and IDF encampments during the "Iron Swords" war as well. However, this article does not seek to expand upon them in detail. Alongside routine religious expressions—such as the recitation of Psalms and prayers for the safety of soldiers—distinctive phenomena also surfaced in the course of the recent war.

One notable instance is that of Agam Berger, one of the reconnaissance soldiers who had been abducted to Gaza. She refused to be released at the same time as her fellow captives as part of the negotiated hostage deal, as her release would have entailed the desecration of the Sabbath. Instead, she returned to Israel only several days later, after enduring 482 days in Hamas captivity. As she made her way back to Israel, accompanied by her parents aboard the military helicopter transporting her home, she raised before the cameras a handwritten sign that read: "I have chosen the path of faith, and by the path of faith I have returned." In interviews following her release, she recounted that what sustained her during her captivity was a prayer book she had found in one of the tunnels, from which she prayed each day. She also noted that even in captivity, she remained steadfast in observing the fast days.

Similarly, Sheli, the mother of Omer Shem Tov—who had been held hostage in Gaza for 505 days—remarked upon his release that from the time of his abduction onward, she began to observe the Sabbath. She even opened the press conference held in honor of his release with the blessing of Shehecheyanu.

Dani Yaron, the father of Omri Miran, who was abducted to Gaza over 500 days ago and has yet to return to Israel, stood in Hostage Square and offered a prayer for his son's well-being and for the safe return of all the remaining captives.

Another striking moment occurred when the singer Idan Amedi returned to the music stage after a year-long hiatus, having suffered severe injuries during his participation in combat in Gaza. At the start

---

65 Isaiah 2:4.

of his first performance upon his return, in front of an audience of 8,000 spectators who had come to see him and cheer him on, Amedi paused the music, took a deep breath, and, with tears in his eyes, recited the Shehecheyanu blessing: "Blessed are You, Lord our God, King of the Universe, who has granted us life, sustained us, and enabled us to reach this time."

In all these cases, as in numerous others, those who expressed these "religious" sentiments had not previously identified as "religious" or "observant" (at most, some of them had considered themselves "traditional"). These manifestations of religious identity surfaced only during the war and as a consequence of it. As stated, this phenomenon extends beyond the scope of this article, and there remains much to be explored regarding its full contours, its roots, and its implications.

Agam Berger, a reconnaissance soldier who was held captive by Hamas for 482 days, is seen with her parents aboard the military helicopter transporting her back to Israel following the hostage exchange deal. The handwritten sign she held read: "I have chosen the path of faith, and by the path of faith I have returned."

Aviad Hacohen serves as the President of Sha'arei Mishpat Academic College and previously held the position of Dean at its Law School. Professor Hacohen's extensive academic research encompasses Mishpat Ivri, human rights, criminal law, civil law, and their intersections with Jewish law.

Section I: Rabbi Yitzhak Isaac Herzog and Recruitment of Yeshiva Students

The Recruitment of Yeshiva Students on the Eve of the War of Independence

Yitzhak Isaac Halevi Herzog
ed. Itamar Warhaftig

[This chapter, titled "The Recruitment of Yeshiva Students on the Eve of the War of Independence," was authored by Chief Rabbi Yitzhak Isaac Halevi Herzog on January 27, 1948, during rabbinic debates concerning the partial drafting of yeshiva students. It presents a halakhic analysis of the security and political circumstances preceding the establishment of the State of Israel on May 14, 1948, and the subsequent War of Independence. The original document is preserved in the Herzog Archive at Heikhal Shlomo and the Central Zionist Archives. Rabbi Dr. Zorach Warhaftig reviewed and summarized this work in his book *Constitution for Israel: Religion and State* (Jerusalem: Yad ha-Rav Herzog, 1988), p. 236 (Hebrew). After remaining unpublished for nearly sixty years, the full article was released in *Ma'asuah le-Yitzhak*, vol. 1 (Jerusalem: Yad ha-Rav Herzog, 2008), pp. 237–276 (Hebrew), with minor corrections and scholarly annotations by Rabbi Professor Itamar Warhaftig, the author's son. This translation, prepared by Mr. Menachem Butler and Rabbi Dr.

Yitzchak Avi Roness, faithfully reflects the original content by Chief Rabbi Yitzhak Isaac Halevi Herzog, and for the comprehensive annotations by Rabbi Professor Itamar Warhaftig, please see the full version in *Ma'asuah le-Yitzhak*, vol. 1, pp. 237–276 (Hebrew).]

I. Should We Learn from the Nations of the World?
II. Torah Scholars Do Not Require Protection
    1. Torah Protects and Saves
    2. The Disgrace of Torah Scholars
III. The Poll Tax on Torah Scholars
IV. Everyone Goes Out, Even a Groom from His Chamber
V. Asa Was Punished for Conscripting Torah Scholars into Service
    1. "None Are Exempt"—Including Torah Scholars
    2. Why Was It Not Explicitly Stated That Torah Scholars Are Exempt?
    3. Why Was Asa Punished?
IV. Abraham Was Punished for Conscripting Torah Scholars into Service
V. The Curse of Meroz
VI. The Wars of the Hasmoneans
VII. The Postponement of the War by Amasa
VIII. The Wars of Joshua
IX. Partial Draft and "Its Annulment Is Its Safeguarding"
X. The Tribe of Levi in the Thought of Maimonides
XI. Kohanim
    1. The Permission for a Beautiful Captive for a Kohen
    2. The Permission for a Beautiful Captive for a Volunteer Soldier
    3. Volunteering of Those Exempt from War
    4. Draft Age
V. The Departure of the Tribe of Levi to War

- 1. Counting the Sons of Levi
- 2. The War with Midian
- III. The Anointed Kohen for War
- IV. The Return of a Kohen Who Committed a Sin Among the War Returnees
- V. A Kohen Who Killed a Person
- VI. The Cancellation of the Daily Offering During War
- VII. No Evidence from Amasa for Exempting Torah Scholars from the Draft
- VIII. The War of Independence: A Mandatory War
  - 1. Even Though It Was Not Declared by the King and Beit Din
  - 2. Saving Israel and Judaism
- III. Warfare Even Over Matters as Trivial as Straw and Chaff
- IV. The Laws of War as Listed in the Tur
- V. Saving Others at the Risk of One's Own Life
- VI. It Is Forbidden to Surrender to the Enemy
- VII. Fear of Desecrating God's Name
- VIII. The Three Oaths
- IX. The Need for Military Rabbis
- X. Hezekiah's Trust Compared to the Opinion of the Sages
- XI. One Engaged in a Commandment Is Exempt from Other Commandments
  - 1. Individual Commandment and Communal Commandment
  - 2. Conquering Territories Outside the Land of Israel
  - 3. The Difference Between One Drafted and One Standing in Battle
  - 4. Amasa Who Found Scholars in Their Study
- V. Our War Is a Obligatory War (Milhemet Mitzvah)
- VI. Torah Study Is Greater Than Saving Lives

VII. Conclusion and Summary
   1. Partial Draft
   2. Fear of Opposition and Criticism
   3. Prayer and Hope

• • • • •

I. Should We Learn from the Nations of the World?

Some argue that they [yeshiva students] are entirely exempt because the civilized nations of the world exempt their seminarians.

In my opinion, this is not a valid argument. Are we obligated to learn from them?! Although I do not suggest that it falls under the category of "how did these nations serve their gods" (Deuteronomy 12:30) or imitation of gentile customs, we must not rule on any matter of halakha, or even on the ethics of virtues based on their precedents or practices. Indeed, our teacher, Rabbeinu Asher became exceedingly angry with a certain sage who sought to resolve a difficult legal question, for which he no source in the Talmud or the Geonim, by referring to a precedent from foreign law. He shouted: "Praise God, as long as I live, I will not permit any ruling in matters of Torah law to be decided by the scholars of the nations but only from the Talmud of Ravina and Rav Ashi – 'the locale which has everything', etc." And even though in Sanhedrin 39b it is stated: "One verse says, 'You have not done according to the ordinances of the nations,' and another verse says, 'you have not done according to the correct ones among them, but you have done according to the corrupted ones among them,'" Rashi, our teacher who has enlightened the eyes of Israel, already explained it: "You have not done as Eglon, king of Moab, and Naaman." That is, you have not even done the good things that the best among the nations do, but these are not things you should have learned from the nations, for they are intrinsic to your holy Torah.

Even if some of our sages praised the customs of the Medes and Persians in matters of etiquette, this does not mean that we should resolve halakhic uncertainties based on their practices. It is almost unnecessary to discuss this at all.

There might be a slight basis in halakhah to consider this from a different angle: if this exemption of seminarians among the nations stems from a special respect for religious individuals due to the honor given to religion itself, then if we do not act similarly, it could result in a desecration of God's name. This is similar to the explanation of the Magen Avraham (Orah Hayyim 306:11), who writes that if the gentiles do not allow public building on their holidays, and we allow [non-Jewish] builders to build our synagogue on our Sabbath, it would be a Hillul Hashem. This could potentially serve as a basis for opposing the conscription of yeshiva students because if we conscript them while other nations exempt their seminarians, they might say that we do not value our sacred Torah studies as much as they value their own theological studies.

However, this applies to full military conscription in ordinary times. But in times of danger, to impose the duty of city defense on yeshiva students, it seems that this is not subject to the same argument, as the gentiles would understand the situation. I recall that in times of danger, when there was fear of a German invasion of England, they conscripted theological students into home guard units.

Furthermore, the circumstances are different, as anyone with common sense can understand. We are facing an immediate threat of siege and must recruit every available person. Who will fill the positions of those going out into actual combat if not those exempt from full conscription? In such a situation, any nation would conscript even fifteen-year-olds. This is besides the matter of Obligatory War, and immediate danger and saving lives, as surrendering to such adversaries has known consequences that need not be elaborated on.

II. TORAH SCHOLARS DO NOT REQUIRE PROTECTION

1. Torah Protects and Saves

Seemingly, there is evidence from Bava Batra 8a: "Everyone goes out to reinforce the gates of the city," referring to building the walls, and setting up their doors, etc. "But scholars do not need protection." Even though Rabbi Judah the Prince did not act in this manner, and required of the scholars to take part in building the wall, there was sharp dissent from Resh Lakish and Rabbi Yohanan. And when Rav Hisda imposed a levy on the sages, Rav Nahman bar Yitzhak protested, claiming it violated both the Torah as well as the words of the prophets and the writings. See there in Bava Batra 8a. While there was less outcry against the Nassi who imposed a tax to cover the price of the city walls, his decision was still disputed based on the verses in Psalms.

However, this argument pertains only to regular security measures. This is not valid proof for such terrible times, when our Arab enemies, secretly aided by the current British government; symbolizing Esau, the hypocrite who extends his hooves and claims purity, as derived from Talmudic interpretations, stand against us. Their inner impurity, represented by their not chewing their cud, is not clearly apparent, and thus they can deceive the world. They wrap themselves in a tallit, as if seeking justice and righteousness, presenting themselves as allies of the righteous of the world. And they position themselves on the stage of justice, as if they are meting out justice. But this is all lies and deceit, like the Roman Empire, as explained in our sages' teachings equating Esau and Rome.

In these times of immense danger, we need great mercy and the Torah protects and safeguards. Nevertheless, we cannot rely solely on miracles; we must defend ourselves and persevere until God has mercy on us. That the enemy not succeed with their plan to annihilate the Jewish community in the Land of israel, and thereby extinguish the last embers of hope amongst Israel – upon which all Judaism depends.

2. *The Disgrace of Torah Scholars*

Additionally, it is not appropriate to connect this with the claim that Torah scholars "should not join the populace" because it degrades them. For it is clear that carrying and using weapons in a time of defense of the nation should be seen as an honor, not a disgrace. Furthermore, the halakhah does not follow Rabbi Eliezer, who said that they [weapons] are only for disgrace, as the plain meaning of "Gird your sword upon your thigh, O mighty one, for it your splendor and majesty" (Shabbat 63a) suggests otherwise. Could any Jew be disgraced by an act that saves (the Nation of) Israel and the Land of Israel, and to a great extent safeguards Judaism itself?

This can be derived via a Kal V'chomer from the actions of Rav Nahman, the senior judge of Israel in Babylon, who allowed himself to do menial labor in front of three witnesses (Kiddushin 70a). And our sages have already stated that "these (lifesaving) actions etc, should be done by the great men of Israel and their sages" (per Maimonides' wording).

It is obvious that all such activities should be limited in scope and time—a few hours a week—so that the sound of Torah is never silenced, even for a single day.

III. THE POLL TAX ON TORAH SCHOLARS

And seemingly, there is proof from Bava Batra 8a regarding the karga [poll tax] that Rav Hisda imposed on the scholars, which caused Rav Nahman bar Yitzhak to fiercely object. He said that Rav Hisda had transgressed the Torah, the Prophets, and the Writings. However, from the content of the interpretation of the words of the Torah, it is evident that the intent is that even at a time when the Holy One, blessed be He, so to speak, shows favor to the nations—meaning, He brightens His face to them and grants them dominion over His children (see Rashi, Deuteronomy 33:3)—it is forbidden to impose the karga on Torah scholars, because "all His holy ones are in His hand" to protect them.

However, this pertains to regular times, and the tax was for supporting guards and watchmen in the cities and neighborhoods of Israel to protect against sudden attacks by gentile robbers and bandits. But this does not apply to a mandatory war, and in the Land of Israel, and during a time like this, which is a critical moment and a time for redemption, which could be lost due to a lack of self-sacrifice, as it is said, "If you falter in the day of distress, your strength is small" (Proverbs 24:10). There have been several moments of divine visitation for Israel, hinted at from the heavens, which were not heeded, and this brief remark should suffice.

Moreover, considering the immense catastrophe, the likes of which we have never witnessed in our national history, of the destruction of a third of our nation, which was truly the major part of the community in terms of religion, Torah, and the connection to the Land of Israel, may their blood be avenged. While the holy spirit has ceased from Israel, it has ceased from individuals, but regarding the nation as a whole, Hillel the Elder already said: "If they are not prophets, they are the sons of prophets" (Pesahim 66a). We witness a tremendous and miraculous awakening following the decision of the nations, that resonates in the hearts of Jews in Israel and throughout the Diaspora (except for a minority—from one side, overzealous radicals; and from the other, extreme assimilationists who, God forbid, wish for the complete assimilation of Israel among the nations).

IV. Everyone Goes Out, Even a Groom from His Chamber

Considering the nature of this war, when our enemies—those who besiege us—aim to extinguish the light of Israel, destroy our young men, and ultimately expel us from our holy land, there is no doubt in my mind that this is the kind of war described in the Mishnah, Sotah, at the end of Chapter 8, where it is said that even a bridegroom from his chamber and a bride from her canopy go out [to fight].

Nevertheless, one could argue that while they go out, Torah scholars do not, because even a mamzer who is a Torah scholar takes precedence over a Kohein Gadol who is ignorant. From this, one could infer that just as a Kohein Gadol does not go to war, as it says, "From the sanctuary, he shall not go out" (Leviticus 21:12). And although we have learned that a Kohein Gadol who marries a widow does not return from the ranks of the war, and from this, one might infer that he is obligated in war, there is no proof from there—because as long as he has not divorced his wife whom he married in violation of the law, he is not fit to serve in the Temple, and in this respect, he is like any other person in Israel, and we compel him to go out to war. See further below regarding kohanim in general. So too, a Torah scholar, who takes precedence over an ignorant Kohein Gadol, does not go out to war at all, for the crown of Torah is greater than the crown of priesthood and kingship, and the study of Torah is greater than saving lives, etc.

But can we really establish halakhah based on such inferences? Furthermore, the aforementioned statements do not refer to students but to complete Torah scholars, at least practicing rabbis or exceptionally great figures. And if you say that in the current state of Judaism in Israel and the Diaspora, yeshiva students have an even greater value than practicing rabbis, still, the aforementioned statements cannot serve as sources for halakhic rulings. Concerning the Kohein Gadol, it is said, "From the sanctuary, he shall not go out," and this is an actual prohibition (see Rambam, Hilkhot Klei HaMikdash 5:7), meaning he does not leave Jerusalem. And yet, we find that Shimon the Righteous went out to meet Alexander far from Jerusalem for the sake of the public good. And thus this cannot serve to exempt Torah scholars from the obligation to join the community in a place of such danger for all of Israel and for Judaism as a whole.

As for the statement "The study of Torah is greater than saving lives," it has already been explained by the Taz (Yoreh De'ah 251) that this does not apply when there is an immediate need to save lives in front of you.

V. Asa Was Punished for Conscripting Torah Scholars into Service

1. "None Are Exempt"—Torah Scholars Included

Moreover, it is not reasonable to suggest that Torah scholars would be given precedence regarding the exemption from war over bridegrooms and brides, since the survival of the nation depends on this matter. If, God forbid, there is no Israel, there would be no Torah scholars and no Torah. This is explicitly stated in the Talmud, Sotah 10a: "Rava taught: Why was Asa punished? Because he conscripted Torah scholars for forced labor, as it is said: 'And King Asa imposed a levy on all of Judah; none was exempt'. What does 'none was exempt' mean? Rav Yehuda said in the name of Rav: Even a bridegroom from his chamber and a bride from her canopy." And it is noted in the margins in the name of the Arukh: "This means, 'all the more so, Torah scholars'—for it is understandable that we can infer that he conscripted a bridegroom and bride from the words 'none was exempt', and it is written in the Torah, 'He shall be free at home for one year, etc.' [i.e. In both of these two verses the torah uses the same word 'Naki'], But conscription of Torah scholars is not explicitly mentioned here. Therefore, we must conclude that Rava derived this by a fortiori argument: if he conscripted a bridegroom and bride, whose exemption is explicitly stated in the Torah of Moses, then Torah scholars, how much more so. From this you learn that in a situation where a bridegroom and bride are obligated, Torah scholars are certainly obligated. And since it is explicitly stated in the Mishnah that a bridegroom and bride are obligated, all the more so are Torah scholars obligated." And is this not stated explicitly in the Arukh: "Even a bridegroom from his chamber, etc., and all the more so Torah scholars," showing that in this matter, bridegrooms and brides take precedence over Torah scholars.

However, we must carefully consider the matter itself: How did Rava know that Asa was punished for conscripting Torah scholars for forced labor? Isn't it more reasonable to say that he was punished for violating the explicit command in the Torah, "He shall be free, etc." as mentioned earlier, and not for conscripting Torah scholars? For the prohibition against drafting Torah scholars is less severe than the prohibition against drafting a bridegroom and bride in a discretionary war (Milhemet Reshut). There is what to explain and elaborate on this, but according to the straightforward interpretation, it is difficult: If you say, "dismiss the lesser prohibition before the more severe one," meaning that the sin of drafting Torah scholars is more severe than the sin of drafting a bridegroom and bride, and thus he wishes to say that Asa was punished for the more severe offense; if that is what you are saying, then how do you know that he actually conscripted Torah scholars? It is possible that he committed the lesser sin and not the more severe one. After all, the verse only says "none was exempt," which hints at a bridegroom and bride, as there is a verbal analogy Naki-Naki with "none shall go out" — "he shall be free at home," etc. And if you say that a verse never loses its plain meaning, and yet the homiletic interpretation should also be expounded, in other words, the plain meaning of the verse is that no person was exempt — "none was exempt"—and this includes Torah scholars. But from the fact that the text used this specific phrasing (Naki) instead of saying "none shall go out" or something similar, Hazal derived that even a bridegroom and bride were conscripted. Does this not already prove that the matter of a bridegroom and bride is more severe than that of Torah scholars, and we return to the earlier point. And it is still difficult to understand why Rava did not say that Asa was punished for drafting a bridegroom and bride. Understand this well.

I find a way to reconcile this based on the Jerusalem Talmud, Sotah, at the end of Chapter 8, where there is an explicit disagreement regarding the interpretation of the verse concerning Asa, between Rabbi Simon and Rabanan. Rabbi Simon interprets "none was exempt" as indicating that Asa did not exempt from forced labor even those of whom it is said, "He shall be free at home for one year." Rabanan, on the other hand, says that even "the great among the scholars" was not exempt from that conscription, and they do not interpret "none was exempt" in the same way as Rabbi Simon. The explanation for their view is, that it was difficult for Rabanan to attribute such a sin to the righteous Asa, implying that he transgressed explicit commandments in the Torah. Therefore, they interpreted "none was exempt" to mean that even "the great among the Scholars" were not exempt, even though the phrasing more naturally suggests it applies to a bridegroom and bride. Clearly, according to their interpretation, even the greatest rabbis are considered secondary to a bridegroom and bride regarding conscription for a discretionary war (Milhemet Reshut), and that the sin of conscripting a bridegroom and bride is more severe. And they did not want to ascribe such a sin to our righteous king. However, Rabbi Simon interpreted "none was exempt" as referring only to a bridegroom and bride, based on the gezerah shavah of "Naki-Naki," and therefore Asa was punished. And if you wish to say: it is already established that he conscripted Torah scholars—and even though this sin is less severe—why didn't the verse also mention Torah scholars? According to the simple interpretation, there is no difficulty, as not every sin is punished from Heaven in this world, especially with afflictions to one's feet with a terrible disease, especially for a king who remained faithful to God and His Torah, and upon whom all Israel depended. Moreover, it is reasonable to assume that Asa repented and prayed to God, like Hezekiah in his time, and his sin regarding the Torah scholars was atoned for. But this sin of conscripting a bridegroom and bride was more severe, and it was not atoned for except through suffering.

And if you wish to clarify the words of the sages in this Aggadah a bit, see Eruvin 100b regarding the verse "And he who hastens with his feet sins," and Rashi there. Also, in Sotah 8b: "With the measure a person uses, so it is measured for them," and it will become clear to you. The point is that Rabanan in the aforementioned Jerusalem Talmud truly believed that Asa did not transgress the explicit commandment in the Torah; he did not conscript a bridegroom and bride but rather only Torah scholars. And if you wish to further understand the depth of the sages' words and their precision on this point of "measure for measure," as Asa became ill in his feet, see Bava Batra 8a: "Rav Yosef taught: These are Torah scholars who wear out their feet traveling from city to city and from country to country to learn Torah," and this is easy to understand.

And now everything becomes clear and understandable. The Gemara states: "Rava expounded: Why was Asa punished? Because he conscripted Torah scholars for forced labor, as it says: 'None was exempt'. What does 'none was exempt' mean? Rav Yehuda said in the name of Rav, etc." At first glance, there is room to read more precisely: If, as is commonly understood, Rava derived his teaching based on Rav's interpretation of "none was exempt," which includes even a bridegroom and bride, then the language should have been: "For Rav said, what does 'none was exempt' mean? Even a bridegroom from his chamber and a bride from her canopy." Therefore, one must say that Rava's interpretation is linked to Rabanan's interpretation in the Jerusalem Talmud, as this is the Torah of the Land of Israel. Rava's intent is that "none was exempt" does not mean he conscripted a bridegroom and bride and learned a gezerah shavah of "exempt-exempt," as mentioned earlier, because one must judge this righteous man favorably, that he did not transgress the explicit commandments of the Torah. Rather, according to the straightforward meaning, "none was exempt" means he conscripted everyone, a general inclusion, since it already says, "He summoned all of Judah," meaning apart from a bridegroom and bride, who are forbidden by the Torah. Therefore, the addition of 'none was exempt' concerns Torah scholars, even the greatest rabbis, who are not explicitly mentioned in the Torah. And what is stated immediately after, "What does 'none was exempt' mean, etc.," are not Rava's words but rather Rav's words in their own right, and a period should be placed there. These are the words of Rav, which align perfectly with Rabbi Simon's teaching through the gezerah shavah of "Naki-Naki," indicating that Asa conscripted even a bridegroom and bride, and certainly Torah scholars. According to Rav, Asa was indeed punished for both, but primarily he was punished for conscripting a bridegroom and bride.

And now, although these things seem very reasonable to me, my heart does not allow me to introduce a new interpretation in the Talmud that is not found in the early commentaries, especially against the explicit words of Rabbeinu Yehiel of Rome, of blessed memory, the author of the Arukh, who interprets that "even a bridegroom, etc., and all the more so Torah scholars." Whereas according to my interpretation of Rava's words, there is no place for "all the more so," since Rava is speaking only about Torah scholars, and a bridegroom and bride were not conscripted. However, whether according to the interpretation of the Arukh or according to my interpretation, I, the insignificant one, the conclusion arises that a bridegroom and bride are prioritized over Torah scholars. According to the Arukh's interpretation, this is explicit. And according to my interpretation, Rava in the Babylonian Talmud did not wish to state that Asa conscripted a bridegroom and bride, just as Rabanan in the Jerusalem Talmud did not wish to explain that he forced a bridegroom and bride into service, since this is explicitly stated in the Torah. Rather, Asa conscripted Torah scholars, which is not explicitly mentioned but only hinted at in the verse, "Indeed, He loves the peoples, etc.," and even this was interpreted by the sages only in regard to taxes for regular protection, as mentioned earlier.

And since it is explicit in the Mishnah that in an obligatory war (Milhemet Mitzvah), even a bridegroom and bride go out to fight, we should all the more so say that Torah scholars are obligated to go out as well.

And now, as I am printing this pamphlet, which has been hidden with me since last Tevet, I have been made aware of the words of the author Hasdei David, in Ein Yaakov (Metzudat David), where he claims that Torah scholars are considered more important than a bridegroom and bride. Therefore, it is said that Asa was only punished for conscripting Torah scholars – look at his words there. Yet, it is still difficult to understand why it was not said that he was punished for both, since in any case, the prohibition against conscripting a bridegroom and bride is explicit in the Torah of Moses, whereas the prohibition against conscripting Torah scholars is, at most, only derived from a homiletic interpretation. And it does not make sense to say that "since it is derived from an interpretation, it is more cherished to him" (Yevamot 5). Therefore, the one who interprets "none was exempt" to refer to a bridegroom and bride holds that Asa was not punished for conscripting Torah scholars, as he did not interpret the drasha to include Torah scholars, as we find in Bava Batra 8, that Rabbi Yehudah the Prince and Rav Hisda also did not interpret it this way. But the conscription of a bridegroom and bride is explicit in the Torah, and for this, Asa was punished, as this was not an obligatory war (Milhemet Mitzvah), as will be explained further. And the one who interprets "none was exempt" to include even the great rabbis holds that a bridegroom and bride were indeed not conscripted, but Asa conscripted all sages, even the greatest rabbis.

And if you ask, from where do we know that Asa conscripted even the greatest rabbis? It can be explained that the rabbis inferred this based on Rabanan's interpretation in the Jerusalem Talmud. For according to the view that Asa conscripted a bridegroom and bride, and the verse says "none was Naki (-exempt)" to connect it with the Torah verse, "he shall be free at home, etc." (it is understood), But if indeed Asa did not conscript them at all, but instead conscripted Torah scholars, then the verse should not have said "none was exempt," because since it says "all the men of Judah," they are already included, as they are not explicitly mentioned in the Torah as being exempt. At most, the verse should have said "none were exempt" or "without exemption." Why did it say "none was Naki (exempt)"? From here, the sages derived that Asa conscripted even the greatest rabbis for the task of demolishing the mounds.

Additionally, it could be said that Asa would not have been punished for conscripting regular scholars, as their Torah study was not their sole occupation in ancient times. As is known, most of them also engaged in work, but they treated their work as secondary and their Torah study as primary. However, for the greatest rabbis, most of them had Torah study as their sole occupation, and in their case, their townsman was indeed commanded to work for them (see the fifteenth chapter of Tractate Shabbat).

Additionally, it could be said that if we do not understand that the interpretation of the verse exempts regular scholars from such work, yet regarding the greatest of the rabbis, the reasoning is straightforward and does not require a scriptural source. For they are the pillars of Torah, and at all times the mighty cedars of Lebanon, the giants of Torah, produce new insights and solve problems. And causing them to stop their learning would cause a great loss, and therefore, it was not appropriate to involve them in such tasks.

In any case, the author of Hasdei David does not say that this was an obligatory war (Milhemet Chovah). And although his words imply that Torah scholars are given precedence even over a bridegroom and bride, it is possible that this applies only specifically to the greatest of rabbis. In any event, his words do not provide proof for a complete exemption from a war to help Israel against an enemy that comes upon them, under all circumstances, and to exempt regular scholars.

2. Why Was It Not Explicitly Stated That Torah Scholars Are Exempt?

And I hereby continue to investigate: Is it conceivable that our great master of blessed memory [=Maimonides], the admiral of all the armies of sages and their students, would not explicitly write in the laws of Kings that Torah scholars are exempt from discretionary wars? And also, why is this not explicitly mentioned in the Talmud? Therefore, it seems they are not absolutely exempt even from discretionary wars. For the meaning of "discretionary" is not that it is only a voluntary conscription; rather, "discretionary" refers only to the decision by the Great Sanhedrin and the king, who are not under an absolute obligation to declare a discretionary war. But once they declare it, it becomes obligatory for every person, except for those explicitly mentioned in the Torah as being exempt (see Sotah, end of the chapter "The Anointed for War," and later here). And since Torah scholars are not explicitly mentioned in the Torah as being exempt, it would seem, at first glance, that they are obligated.

3. Why Was Asa Punished?

You might say, if so, why was Asa punished according to Rava in the Babylonian Talmud, and Rabbi Simon in the Jerusalem Talmud? I would answer:

a. This was not even a discretionary war (Milhemet Reshut), as Asa had already acted by bribing the King of Aram to make Baasha withdraw from him. The destruction of Ramah was not urgent, as there was no war at all here. This is akin to "digging a well" (Bava Batra ad loc). This then was the sin of the righteous King Asa, for which he received his punishment in this world, to cleanse him for the next. In the end, this is why Maimonides did not write that Torah scholars are exempt from a discretionary war in Hilkhot Melakhim, because the incident with Asa was a different matter. And to state that they are obligated in an obligatory war (Milhemet Mitzvah) he thought deemed to be unnecessary, since he had already written that even a bridegroom leaves his chamber, and a bride her canopy. And even if you say that this task of dismantling Ramah was a war-related task, it was still not an obligatory war.

b. This was not a matter of a war against enemies of Israel but rather a civil war between Israel and Judah. Even if you say that since Baasha was an idol worshiper and most of the people with him were as well, it might have been considered a matter of a war between idolaters and Israel (which is a far-fetched and strained argument), nonetheless, Baasha had already withdrawn from Jerusalem, as it is stated, "And he dwelt in Tirzah" (1 Kings 15:21). The clarification of the matter is that, initially, Baasha considered establishing his kingdom in Jerusalem, but afterward, he despaired and went back to establishing his capital in Tirzah. Thus, there was only a mere concern that his intentions might change and circumstances might shift. And an obligatory war (Milhemet Mitzvah) – aside from the wars of Joshua or similar cases, and the eradication of Amalek – is only a battle fought for the purpose of helping Israel against an enemy that comes upon them or an enemy preparing to attack them. Thus, at most, this was a matter of a discretionary war (Milhemet Reshut).

It is still worth examining why Maimonides did not explicitly state in Hilkhot Melakhim that Torah scholars are exempt from a Milhemet Reshut.

Furthermore, it is worth mentioning, to justify the righteous Asa, that the only lasting sin attributed to him in the biblical text is that he did not abolish the high places (bamot). This implies that he erred in judgment, thinking that this was also considered an obligatory war (Milhemet Mitzvah), and his sin was in not consulting with the Torah scholars. It appears that he later repented for the sin of going against what is explicitly stated in the Torah by conscripting a bridegroom and bride. However, he did not repent for conscripting Torah scholars, because a bridegroom and bride are considered more significant than Torah scholars. Therefore, he was only punished for this sin. Regarding his conscription of Torah scholars, this we truly did not learn from an a fortiori argument, but it was a tradition held by our sages. There was also a tradition among them that he did not repent or regret this sin. Therefore, he was specifically punished in his legs, as he should have learned from the interpretation of "beneath your feet" (Bava Batra 8b) that this was indeed not the case.

VI. Abraham Was Punished for Conscripting Torah Scholars into Service

Seemingly, there is evidence to the contrary—that Torah scholars are exempt from an obligatory war (Milhemet Mitzvah). This is found in Nedarim 32a, where it states that Abraham our forefather was punished for conscripting Torah scholars. The war in question was an obligatory war (Milhemet Mitzvah), to rescue Lot, his nephew, and so on. So why was he punished?

Indeed, this is not truly a real proof, since only the rescue of Israel qualifies as an obligatory war (Milhemet Mitzvah), whereas Lot did not fall under this category; on the contrary, he is referred to as wicked. [This is the opinion of Rav, and it is also found in the words of the sages (Midrash and Pesikta).] On the other hand, Abraham converted men, and Sarah converted women, and those who they converted had the status of Israelites, and among them were Torah scholars.

It is possible that this was not even considered a discretionary war (Milhemet Reshut), since, in principle, neither the Great Sanhedrin nor the King of Israel would initiate a war unless it was deemed, in their judgment, to be of significant importance to the entirety of Israel. It is no small matter that they are given the authority to requisition not only the property of Israel but also their very bodies for their wars. Even a discretionary war, when declared by the Great Sanhedrin and the king, is still a commandment. The very term "discretionary war" only means that if the Great Sanhedrin does not decree it, the king can only declare a voluntary draft. And this, too, is significant, that the Torah permits a Jew to risk his life (see Ha'amek Davar on Parashat Noah). Therefore, we must conclude that even a discretionary war is not a trivial matter at all; it is an important issue for the entire nation, for the holy land, and, consequently, for the sacred Torah.

And if you ask, despite this, why was Abraham punished? After all, as is brought in the interpretations of our sages, Abraham foresaw with divine inspiration that the kingdom of the House of David was destined to come from Lot. One could answer that there was no imminent danger of death threatening Lot and his family. Furthermore, Abraham should have trusted in the Holy One, blessed be He, that He would not deliver them to the King of Sodom for execution, since the kingdom of the House of David was destined to come from Lot. Additionally, the sages believed that it was possible for Abraham to conscript others with payment, and thus Rabbi Elazar says he was punished. In any case, you cannot derive a ruling from this, as it is not found in the writings of Hazal in halakhah or in the Rambam that Torah scholars are exempt from an obligatory war (Milhemet Mitzvah), contrary to the implication of the discussion in [Bava Batra 9] and so on.

VII. The Curse of Meroz

There seems to be evidence that even a great person in Israel is not exempt from an obligatory war (Milhemet Mitzvah), and this is found in Moed Katan 16a: "Curse Meroz', etc. Some say Meroz was a great man, etc." This indicates that a great man, presumably one who was great in Torah, was cursed for not joining an obligatory war. All the more so are we to infer that ordinary Torah scholars are indeed obligated. However, this is not a definitive proof, as it is possible that he was liable to be cursed because he actively, or by inaction, caused the people of his city, who were ordinary folk, not to come to the aid of God with their mighty. For the curse was not pronounced on him alone, as it is written, "Curse Meroz, curse its inhabitants" (Judges 5:23), meaning the inhabitants of his city. This is how the early commentators, of blessed memory, interpreted it, and it is in the commentary on Moed Katan attributed to Rabbeinu Yehiel of Paris, as published from the writings of the Harry Fischel Institute for Talmudic Research, vol. 1 (1937). And these are his words: "Some say that Meroz was a great man whom Barak cursed. He was a prominent and respected person in Israel who did not wish to come at Barak's summons. And when it says "its inhabitants," it refers to the city in which he lived, for they all followed his example, and since he did not come, the others did not come either."

This is a different matter and does not prove that Torah scholars are obligated to fight in wars. The reason Barak summoned him to come to battle was that if he did not come, the people of the entire city would not come, and this would have a significant impact on the campaign. Therefore, Barak required him to come, and, consequently, the city's inhabitants would come with him. Due to such circumstances, even if we say that Torah scholars are exempt, he would have been obligated to come. It is possible that Barak summoned him not to actually fight in the battle; it is possible that were he to have come Barak would not have required of him to enter battle, but to be there in a capacity similar to the anointed for war, the spiritual leader who accompanies troops. He would not have been so close to danger or directly engaged in the fighting, but his presence was crucial for the war effort because he would lead the entire city to follow him.

VIII. THE WARS OF THE HASMONEANS

From the words of Maimonides in Hilkhot Melakhim we do not have a source to resolve our question, as he does not list Torah scholars among those who are exempt from a discretionary war (Milhemet Reshut) nor among those obligated in an obligatory war (Milhemet Mitzvah). However, we do know from the Hasmonean wars that the warriors were also Torah scholars. There is much to investigate in the Books of the Maccabees, where, as I recall, the anointed for war and the great commander, Judah Maccabee, proclaimed the exemptions as stated in the section of the Torah portion of Shoftim. This is puzzling, for it is impossible to conceive of a war more obligatory than that one, which was about saving all of Judaism, and in an obligatory war, as mentioned, those who are normally exempt would be obligated to take part. However, this book is not currently in my possession, and I do not have the time to search for it.

And it is a simple matter to conclude that the torah scholars were obligated to take part in that war, they were required to show an example to the people, for this was a war conducted in order to save Judaism, and if the scholars would not show an example to the people, the multitudes would not endanger themselves.

In the Hanukkah prayer, we say, "the wicked were delivered into the hands of those who engage in Your Torah," indicating the participation of Torah scholars. This should be examined further in the context of the Books of the Maccabees.

IX. THE POSTPONEMENT OF THE WAR BY AMASA

From Sanhedrin 49a, there seems to be evidence that Torah scholars are exempt from an obligatory war (Milhemet Mitzvah). It is explicitly stated there that Amasa was not considered a rebel against the monarchy, even though David had commanded him to gather all the men of Judah within three days. Amasa delayed because "he found them studying a tractate and expounding the words 'akhin' (only) and 'rakin' (but)." He said, "Could this apply even to words of Torah and adornment?" See there. This was, after all, an obligatory war to uphold the Kingdom of the House of David. This implies that Torah scholars are exempt, and it is forbidden to interrupt their Torah study.

However, this proof can also be refuted: Maimonides did not list as an obligatory war (Milhemet Mitzvah) any war except Joshua's war (and similar cases) and the war against Amalek, or helping Israel against an enemy who attacks them. And this was not a case of helping Israel against an enemy, for Israel had thrown off the yoke of the House of David, and only Judah remained loyal to him. David could have remained king over Judah alone, as he was at the beginning of his reign. It turns out that this was essentially a war of Judah against Israel to expand and extend the Kingdom of David. This falls under the category of a discretionary war (Milhemet Reshut), as explicitly stated in Hilkhot Melakhim, that expanding and enlarging his kingdom is a discretionary war. See Parashat Derakhim by the Gaon Mishneh LaMelekh, of blessed memory, Derush 12, on the issue of whether David, when fleeing from Absalom, was considered a king at all. And David himself believed he had only the status of a private citizen, as he was honored with a young goat because the hearts of all Israel inclined toward Absalom, and thus his royal status was removed from him. Consequently, when he was reinstated by only Judah, he had the status of a king of one tribe. When he commanded Amasa to muster all the men of Judah, the intention was to fight against the other tribes and restore his kingship over all Israel. This was an expansion of his kingdom and not an obligatory war in the sense of helping Israel against an immediate enemy.

Furthermore, this was not a war of gentiles against Israel but rather a civil war, where all involved were [righteous]. Even though restoring the Kingdom of the House of David was certainly a mitzvah, it was not an obligatory war (Milhemet Mitzvah) that would justify interrupting Torah scholars from their studies. Additionally, this could have been accomplished without involving Torah scholars. In any case, if there is any evidence here, it is only that Torah scholars are exempt from a war that does not fall under the category of helping Israel against an immediate enemy, which is not the case in the above discussion.

X. The Wars of Joshua

You should know that during the conquest of Joshua, which was certainly an obligatory war (Milhemet Mitzvah), Torah scholars were not exempt from it. At that time, the Israelites were learning Torah from Moses our teacher in the wilderness, as it is explicitly stated (Eruvin 54b): "When the elders passed away, all the people entered, and Moses taught them their section." And it is said in the Mekhilta: "The Torah was given only to those who ate manna." And although the manna ceased when they entered the land, all of Israel continued to study Torah, as explicitly mentioned there, in Eruvin 63b. How then, could they be required to wage war? seeing as they were all studying the teachings of God? And we do not find that this was a temporary directive, for whenever the sages speak of an obligatory war, they begin with this war. On the contrary, we find there that Joshua was punished for interrupting them from Torah study, and Rashi explains there: Because they were engaged in warfare during the day, they did not have time to engage in Torah study except at night. See there. But during the day, they were obligated to participate in the war.

Yet, you might say that there is still room for one to disagree, suggesting that, in what circumstances are we speaking of? When all of Israel were engaged in Torah study and continued the tradition from the wilderness, as there was no concern that the Torah would be forgotten from Israel. For even if some would fall in battle, it would only be a minority. This is proven from its own context because, according to Rabbi Shimon bar Yohai, when Israel does the will of the Omnipresent, they do not need to plow, etc., as others will do their work for them. If an enemy were to come upon them, how are they to exist? Therefore, you must conclude that at such a time, Torah scholars were not exempt, for if they were, everyone would be exempt, and their war effort would not be carried out. However, this can be refuted, as at such a time, Israel is assured that no enemy or adversary would come upon them. In any case, the situation back then was different, and the fear of the cessation of Torah from Israel, God forbid, did not exist. Moreover, since they were all Torah scholars, we cannot draw conclusions from a situation where there was no other possibility.

However, what are we talking about? If we wanted to prove from there that Torah scholars are obligated in an obligatory war (Milhemet Mitzvah), we could refute this — as explained earlier. But a definitive proof — no. And my intention is merely to preempt the question, if indeed Torah scholars are obligated in an obligatory war, why was Joshua punished? The question has already been resolved, as they were indeed obligated in the war, but at night they were free to study Torah, and therefore he was punished. According to our understanding, we have indeed learned that even on the battlefield, when they are free from battle, Torah scholars are prohibited from neglecting Torah study.

XI. Partial Draft and "Its Annulment Is Its Safeguarding"

Indeed, all this discussion pertains to full conscription. However, partial conscription—for a few hours a week, as a guard in internal positions—is a different matter. Although this, too, constitutes some level of neglect of Torah study, we nevertheless find that Torah study — even of the entire community — is temporarily suspended for certain activities, such as accompanying the dead to burial etc., under specific conditions (Megillah 3 and Yoreh De'ah 401, see there), and a war like this should not be considered less significant than fulfilling those commandments.

Furthermore, the sages have already said (Menahot 99b): "Sometimes the neglect of Torah study is its very foundation," as it is stated, "It is time to act for the Lord; they have nullified Your Torah" (Psalms 119:126). It is clear to us, that when the Holy City of Jerusalem is in this state, and the one hundred thousand of its Jewish inhabitants, may God bless them and safeguard them, Clearly, in this situation, where there is a complete lack of participation from the yeshivas, God forbid, not only will this lead to a degradation of the honor of those who study Torah in the eyes of the people but, God forbid, to a hatred of the Torah itself. And how severe this matter is!

You might say that we could explain that the merit of Torah study would protect us more than participation in the war effort, but the people will not accept this and will not listen. They will argue that, in any case, most yeshiva students cannot be trusted to study without interruption.

And there is no demand, God forbid, by the military command to close the yeshivas. Moreover, in a situation where there is a real danger to themselves, the people know that the yeshiva students will not rely on a miracle and will do whatever is necessary to save themselves from danger, whether from shells, bombs, or the like. It is also not possible to abstain from all involvement when our soldiers, our young men, risk their lives to provide our sustenance, and if not for them we would, God forbid, die of starvation. And after all the command does not require full conscription, but rather some form of participation.

XII. The Tribe of Levi in the Thought of Maimonides

There is still a question to consider based on Maimonides at the end of Hilkhot Shemittah ve'Yovel: "Why did the tribe of Levi not receive a portion in the inheritance of the Land of Israel or its spoils along with their brothers? Because they were set apart to serve the Lord etc., to minister to Him, and to teach His just ways and righteous judgments to the masses, as it is stated, 'They shall teach Your judgments to Jacob and Your Torah to Israel.' Therefore, they were set apart from the ways of the world—they do not go out to war like the rest of Israel, nor do they inherit land, nor do they acquire wealth by their own efforts, etc." See there. And after all, what is Maimonides referring to here? He is discussing the war of conquering the Land of Israel, which was an obligatory war (Milhemet Mitzvah), yet the Levites did not go to war, etc. Therefore, it might be suggested that any Torah scholar whose Torah is his occupation, like the tribe of Levi, is exempt even from an obligatory war.

However, there are some points to note as follows:

i. Our great master, of blessed memory, sought to provide a reason why the tribe of Levi did not receive a portion in the inheritance of the Land of Israel or its spoils. His answer is that they did not receive it because every tribe fought and earned their portion through their physical efforts, but the Levites did not fight, and therefore they did not earn a portion. If you argue that they should have fought and earned, the response is that it would not be fitting for a sanctified tribe to inherit land through physical means. This reasoning only fits a war to conquer the land, however regarding a war of necessity to help Israel and prevent destruction and exile from the Land of Israel – it is not right that they should be exempted for this reason.

ii. Maimonides, of blessed memory, is precise in his language and does not say that they do not go to war at all, but rather "do not go to war like the rest of Israel." It is possible that his intention is to exclude wars to help Israel, meaning they do not go to war like the rest of Israel in a war of conquest. Or, it could be that his intention is to exclude actual combat on the battlefield with weapons, while they might still participate in war activities to a certain extent, such as guarding positions for a number of hours or providing water and food, similar to those who return from battle, so that they do not neglect in a significant manner their sacred duty of studying Torah and teaching it to Israel.

The practical difference in our case would depend on whether we interpret this according to the first explanation or the second.

i. Maimonides is only discussing the specific tribe of Levi, and this is by royal decree. From this, we cannot derive a general rule for Torah scholars. Although Torah scholars fulfill a similar role to that of the tribe of Levi in ancient times, there is a significant difference: since the Levites did not inherit land, the fighting tribes would not lose morale due to the non-participation of the tribe of Levi. However, Torah scholars, who are integrated among all the tribes and are eligible to inherit land like their brethren, it is not right that they should allow others to say of them; "shall your brothers go out to war, and you will remain sitting here" – i.e. in the study hall. Therefore, they would be obligated even in a war of conquest of the land, and all the more so in a war to assist Israel against an immediate enemy.

ii. The tribe of Levi was rightfully entitled to receive tithes and offerings in exchange for their lack of land inheritance, which is not the case for Torah scholars, who rely on donations. Even though they are assured that God will provide for them through the generosity of the people, as Maimonides states, since they depend on donations, it is not appropriate that at a time when Israel, who act as Zebulun to their Issahar, are in great danger in their holy land, they should not participate in the war effort at all. This would lead to complaints against them, potentially worsening their actions and they would cease providing for their livelihood. Note that in the adjacent halakhah 13, Maimonides does not mention war even by implication concerning Torah scholars, rather he simply states that anyone whose spirit moves him to dedicate himself wholly etc. becomes sanctified as holy of holies, and God grants him sufficient means in the world to come, see there.

iii. We know that ultimately, the students in the yeshivas, whose primary occupation is Torah study, will go out into the public sphere to receive appointments as rabbis, judges, and similar roles, and they will have to receive a salary from the community in exchange for their work. And they will not be accepted by the majority of the community if they now stand apart and do not participate at all. Thus, the very strengthening of Torah's existence itself demands some level of participation.

iv. Maimonides says that the tribe of Levi is called the "army of God," meaning they are a special holy army. But where does he derive this from? If it is from the verse that states, "And of Levi, he said… bless O' God his strength", does not the end of the verse say, "smite the loins of those who rise against him and his enemies so that they rise not again" [Deuteronomy 33:11], and a verse never departs from its plain meaning. The verse speaks about real war. Indeed, our sages emphasized this and interpreted that Moses prophesied about the war of the Hasmoneans. It is thus hinted in the text that the tribe of Levi will be destined to fight with great self-sacrifice to help Israel against an enemy. This indicates that such a war is indeed their duty.

You might object and say that that was a war to save the religion; here is your answer at hand: Despite the extreme zealots, this, too, is a war to save the Jewish faith. I know and can testify that when I was traveling through the camps in Europe, I was told that many Jews from the Carpathian Hasidim—simple Jews raised in the ways of Hasidism—fell into such despair that they stopped even putting on tefillin. I spoke with them amongst their fellow Jews and succeeded in instilling in them new hope that they would eventually come to the Land of Israel, that we are on the verge of the beginning of redemption, and they returned to righteousness. The same applies to the majority of the Jewish masses: If God forbid the ember of hope shall be extinguished, had our enemies, including that known powerful nation, succeeded in their schemes, tens of thousands would have despaired completely, and our holy religion would have begun to decline down a slippery slope, etc. etc. Enough said.

In any case, there is no proof here for a complete exemption. Moreover, there is no reason to establish a law based on the implication of the language of our master, of blessed memory, in matters that are essentially part of Aggadah in Hilkhot Shemitta ve-Yovel—where war is mentioned only incidentally. Whereas, in Hilkhot Melakhim, which is the main source, our master did not explicitly exempt Torah scholars even from a discretionary war (Milhemet Reshut), let alone from an obligatory war (Milhemet Mitzvah). And to assume that he relied on what is not even explicitly stated but at most hinted at here —and that is even of we assume that there is such a hint—it is not the practice of distinguished legal authorities (to base rulings on such inferences). In any event, even if we find an apparent contradiction within Maimonides' book, the later statement surely should be granted primacy.

XIII. Kohanim

1. *The Permission for a Beautiful Captive for a Kohen*

Regarding the kohanim, and certainly the Levites, there is truly no clear ruling that they are exempt from conscription. This matter was already addressed by one of the early authorities, the Mordekhai, in Gittin (no. 432), states that the kohanim did not go to war. He provides evidence from Kiddushin 20b: "What is the law regarding a Kohein and a beautiful captive woman?"—which implies that kohanim would go to war. However, he dismisses this by suggesting that perhaps the Kohein would return home and not actually participate in the front lines of the battle. So too the anointed Kohein for war would return home after fulfilling his role.

However, this matter requires further examination, for the Torah only permitted taking a beautiful captive woman (yefat toar) in the presence of the evil inclination, meaning during a time of war when the evil inclination grows strong amongst those engaged in battle. But it does not imply that this permission extends even before the battle has begun. Moreover, it is stated, "and you see among the captives" (Deuteronomy 21:11), etc. And look at Maimonides in Hilkhot Melakhim, where it is clear that the allowance for a yefat toar only applies after they have defeated the enemy, and entered the enemy's territory, and caused them to flee, and have taken captives. See there carefully. And the Gaon Rabbi Meir Simcha HaKohen [of Dvinsk], of blessed memory, in Meshekh Hokhmah on Parashat Ki Tetzei, concludes that a condition for the permissibility of taking a yefat toar is that it is only after the enemy has been definitively delivered into the hands of Israel, as it is written, "And the Lord your God delivers them into your hands, and you take them captive" (Deuteronomy 21:10). In a manner that taking her captive would not cause the enemy to withhold a prominent Jew in exchange for her. But as in the typical conduct of wars, when both sides capture individuals, and the way peace is made – or during the course of the war, they exchange captives who are no longer fit for battle—under such circumstances, the law of the yefat toar does not apply, as explained there. Again, I question this, for it is clearly stated in the verse, "And the Lord your God delivers them into your hands, and you take them captive, and you see among the captives a beautiful woman" (Deuteronomy 21:10–11), etc. How then could it be permitted, even for an Israelite, when they have not yet entered into the battle or begun the combat? In conclusion, the Mordekhai's position requires further clarification.

Indeed, regarding what he said about the anointed Kohein for war, suggesting that he might withdraw afterward, the straightforward understanding of the Gemara in Kiddushin implies that a Kohein… [apparently the text is missing here] … in the Sifre, the entire allowance for taking a beautiful captive woman applies only in a discretionary war (Milhemet Reshut), and not in an obligatory war (Milhemet Mitzvah). However, it is possible that from here, the Rambam, of blessed memory, derived his ruling differently from the Sifre. He holds that a Kohein does not go out to a discretionary war, implying that the Gemara discusses an obligatory war, proving that this allowance also applies in an obligatory war. Therefore, he does not distinguish between an obligatory war and a discretionary war regarding the matter of a yefat toar. This still requires further study.

2. *The Permission for a Beautiful Captive for a Volunteer Soldier*

However, it could seemingly be said that there is a difference between coercion and volunteering: a Kohein cannot be forced to go to war, but if he volunteers, he is permitted to go even to a discretionary war (Milhemet Reshut). And if you ask why a yefat toar would be permitted to him, after all, he has put himself in a situation where the evil inclination might overcome him, and he was exempt from the whole matter. This is not necessarily so, for since he put himself into this situation, the allowance applies to him as well. This is akin to being compelled, as he is already in the battlefield and under the pressure of the evil inclination. However, God forbid that one should learn from this case to another situation, for there is no coercion in a forbidden sexual relationship, since physical arousal does not occur without intent. They do not say that the person was led to sin by their evil inclination in the context of one forced to have coitus (Sanhedrin 74b, "And Esther"), and they do not apply the principle of "initially it was by coercion etc." except in the case of a woman, and this is not the place to discuss it further. But in this case, the holy Torah considered the compulsion of the evil inclination, and we are bound only by what the Torah has stated.

However, it could be suggested that for this reason, a Kohein, or anyone exempt from war, should be prohibited to volunteer, lest their evil inclination overpower them regarding a yefat toar. This aligns with the opinion of [the Radbaz], of blessed memory, who holds that even in cases of a mitzva, it is forbidden to place oneself into a situation where they would be compelled, even of pikuah nefesh, — his contrary to the view of the Rabbi Zerahiah Halevi. For someone who is exempt from conscription is not fulfilling a mitzva, and even in an obligatory war (Milhemet Mitzvah), if one is exempt, they should not involve themselves, lest they come to face the temptation of a yefat toar.

However, it is possible to distinguish that in an obligatory war (Milhemet Mitzvah), according to the opinion of Rabbi Zerahiah Halevi, it might be permissible for a person to place themselves in a situation of this type of trial. If this is so, then it is possible that the Gemara is referring to an obligatory war and a volunteering Kohein, and there is no proof from there that Kohanim are obligated to be conscripted even in an obligatory war.

But if we do not accept this distinction, then it would not necessarily follow that, in any case, he is obligated in an obligatory war (Milhemet Mitzvah). This would be true only if we assume that one who places themselves in a situation of temptation is not permitted by the Torah to take a beautiful captive woman. It would then be necessary to conclude that, at least in an obligatory war, a Kohein is obligated, which aligns with the opinion of Maimonides. However, if we follow the view of the Sifrei, it would be necessary to conclude that he is also obligated in a discretionary war (Milhemet Reshut). Yet, as is written in the Jerusalem Talmud (Yerushalmi, Maaserot, 5:4), "it is turned, and overturned again; we do not hear anything from here," – so too we have no clear inference from this source.

Incidentally, the Minhat Hinnukh (mitzvah 526) investigates the case of the three categories of individuals who are exempt from military service, whether this is not an exemption of choice—meaning that if they wish to stand in the battle, they may—or whether it is an obligation for them to return home. However, it is clear that this investigation does not apply to a bridegroom and bride, as he is forbidden to go to war, even if she relents. Even if both of them desire to go to battle, it is still forbidden (as noted in Meshekh Hokhmah, Parashat Ki Teitzei, regarding the verse "and he shall make his wife happy," and see also Sefer HaHinnukh). But regarding a Kohein, I still have no decisive ruling, and ostensibly, why should it be forbidden for him to volunteer? If it is because it is nearly impossible in war not to come into contact with corpses, whether those of Israel or even those of gentiles, with whom a Kohein is also forbidden to come into contact, this seems problematic. For there is no greater mitzvah in all of the Torah than that of preserving life. If it is permitted for an Israelite to volunteer and risk his life, then similarly, impurity would be permitted for a kohen. There is no greater sin than the desecration of the Sabbath, and yet, it is permitted even in a discretionary war (Milhemet Reshut). Therefore, impurity should also be permitted. You must therefore innovate that these matters were only permitted for one who is obligated in conscription, but for one who is exempt, they are not permitted, and therefore he is forbidden to enlist.

However, the Gaon HaNetziv of Volozhin writes in his commentary Ha'amek Davar on Deuteronomy 20:8 that there is no prohibition for a person to put themselves in battle and risk their life, but they must not be faint-hearted, etc. From him, may his memory be a blessing, we learn two things: that one is permitted to volunteer for war, and that one who is fearful and faint-hearted is forbidden to stand in battle. According to this, if it is permitted to put oneself in a situation of life-threatening danger, which is a serious prohibition, it seems that it would also be permitted for a Kohein to do so, even though it is almost inevitable that he will come into contact with a corpse.

However, with some difficulty, it could be argued that this is still not more than a positive commandment that one must guard their lives, and the severity of the prohibition of committing suicide only would apply when it is certain that one will be killed, and this not the case for the prohibition of impurity for a kohen. However, from his words, you learn that it is permissible to volunteer for war. Therefore, in a discretionary war (Milhemet Reshut) of Israel, even though a person might be exempt—such as when they are under twenty, over forty, or over sixty years old—they are still permitted to volunteer, even though in a discretionary war one engages in battle on the Sabbath. And if this is permitted, all the more so would it be permitted for a kohen, and he does not need to be concerned about contact with a corpse.

3. *Volunteering of Those Exempt from War*

And now I am perplexed by the Gaon in Minhat Hinnukh, that he investigated this matter at all, for I recall that it is explicitly stated in the Sifrei: "Lest he die in battle, etc. — if he does not heed [the warning] of the Kohein – at the end he will die in the war." According to the commentary of the Malbim, of blessed memory, he dies because of that sin. Thus, he is obligated to return. However, this applies to those explicitly mentioned in the passage, but the Torah does not explicitly write that Kohanim or Levites return from the battlefield. And even if they are exempt, it does not necessarily mean that they are forbidden to volunteer.

And it is possible that the same applies to those with physical defects who are exempt, as explicitly stated in the Sifrei. It goes without saying for someone missing eyes or legs, as it is apparently forbidden for them to stand in battle since they are likely to hinder the combat efforts. But for someone missing teeth, which appears to be merely a scriptural decree, it might be permissible for them to volunteer, and it is just that the Torah provides them with an exemption. However, perhaps this is not so, for one missing teeth may fall ill from the difficulty of chewing food, and especially in battle, as is self-explanatory, and in the end he will become a burden on his comrades.

4. Draft Age

Regarding those under twenty, or over forty or sixty, perhaps they are allowed to volunteer. However, this is not entirely clear, as the Torah states, "From twenty years old and upward, all who are able to go out to war in Israel," and our sages (Rashi to Numbers 1:3) explain: "This teaches that one does not go out to war until he is twenty." And we find that the sages decreed that one cannot sell his father's property until he is twenty, indicating that one's mind is not fully settled before twenty, and therefore he should not be brought into battle where he might bring about a failure. And if you argue that an eighteen-year-old can serve as a judge in Israel, this is for someone who has reached such a level of wisdom and maturity, having been appointed as a judge, and he is surely proved himself removed from the general rule, and it is manifest that his mind is fully developed. Judges are appointed only if they have proven themselves capable and experienced in legal matters, and they have been found to analyze the facts fittingly. This might also apply to those over forty, or at least over sixty, whose physical strength is not complete and has already declined, making them less suitable for direct combat. However, they might still be suitable for leadership roles whereby they would coordinate the armies activities, for after all this is a separate matter, and to the contrary, it is even more appropriate for one who has reached the age of wisdom. I do not presently have sources on this point from our rabbis, and it deserves further examination.

Incidentally, it is surprising that Maimonides omits the ruling regarding age limits. The military commanders today also do not follow this practice properly, as they conscript those younger than twenty for full service. However, one may try to justify their practice by claiming that this rule applies only to discretionary wars, or that the current situation is more than just a war, it is a case of danger to Israel. However, if we follow the rationale of the commandment, we must fear that they are unfit for war, and if so it should apply even to a obligatory war (Milhemet Mitzvah).

XIV. THE DEPARTURE OF THE TRIBE OF LEVI TO WAR

1. Counting the Sons of Levi

Once again regarding the Kohanim and Levites, the Torah explicitly states: "Only the tribe of Levi you shall not number" (Numbers 1:49), and Maimonides explains that they did not go to war. Thus it is explicit that the Tribe of Levi does not participate in war. This might be the source for Maimonides' above ruling, but it is not definitive proof that they are exempt even from a war to defend Israel from an immediate threat. For the context here was preparing Israel for the conquest of the land, as explicit in Nahmanides' comments, and as explained above the Levites did not participate in the battles of conquest.

Moreover, there is no clear consensus, as Rashi does not interpret it this way. Instead, he quotes the sages: "It is fitting for the king's legion to be kept separate." However, the plain meaning of the verse, as explained by Rashbam in Numbers 1:47, states: "The Levites according to their fathers' tribes were not numbered among them… for they did not take part in the military service; because their duty was to guard the Tabernacle. However, it seems that in regards to a mandatory war, which is not about conquering the land, there is no clear proof that the Levites are exempt.

On the surface, this seems to imply that Torah scholars are not exempt from a mandatory war. For it lies before you that while the Levites and Kohanim were exempted, Torah scholars were not explicitly exempted. You might argue that at that time, all of Israel were Torah scholars, and thus it was not feasible to exempt them all as there would be no one left to conquer the land. However, not everyone – even in that august generation — was equally learned. And proportionally, the greatest among them in comparison to the general population, were like the difference between yeshiva students today compared to the multitude of young men, and yet the Torah did not exempt them. Furthermore, the tribe of Issachar, who were fully dedicated to Torah study, and who had greater sages amongst them even then the Tribe of Levi, – as indicated by the Targum Jonathan and Rashi's commentary on Genesis 49:15: "Issahar bends his shoulder to bear the burden of Torah." The Sages (Yoma 26a) state: "You will not find a scholar who does not come from Levi or Issahar." Yet, Issahar is counted among those who went out to war in Numbers 1:28.

One could argue, however, that the sons of Issahar dedicated themselves to Torah study only after they had settled in the land, as the verse implies "He saw that rest was good" (Genesis 49:15), and rest was not present in the wilderness (see Zevahim 119a). Additional proof could be found in Eruvin 100b that Moses could not find "wise men" amongst the tens of thousands of the Tribe of Issahar, and we must conclude therefore that their full dedication to Torah study, like that of the Levites, and even more so, only occurred after they settled the land.

2. The War with Midian

If we consider the matter further, the question of the Tribe of Levi's participation in war is disputed between two great authorities, Rashi and the Vilna Gaon. In Numbers 31:4, Rashi writes (based on the Sifri) that the phrase "A thousand from each tribe" regarding the war against the Midianites includes the Tribe of Levi, while the Vilna Gaon (on the Sifri) interprets it to exclude the Tribe of Levi. Clearly, neither Rashi nor the Vilna Gaon would alter the text without justification, rather we must assume that there were two competing versions of the text. Rashi's opinion was that the correct version was the one claiming that the Tribe of Levi were included, while the Vilna Gaon's opinion led him to favor the opposing version excluding them.

Perhaps this was the source of their disagreement: Rashi was of the opinion that there was no need to exclude the Levites explicitly, as this was already clear from their exemption from the conquest of the land. Thus, the verse must be interpreted as coming to teach us that they were included in this war, for it was a war to save Israel, to prevent the Midianites from continuing to lead Israel to sin. Although in general the pre-emptive battle to diminish the idolaters so that they do not attack us (Sotah 44b) is not considered to be a obligatory war, this war was different. As it was clear and apparent in God's eyes that if they were left alone, they would continue to pose a spiritual threat, as Midianite women seduced Israel into immorality. Therefore, for such a war, the Tribe of Levi was included. The Vilna Gaon, on the other hand, might argue that the conquest of the land was a different matter, since the Levites would not inherit the land and therefore were exempt from taking part in the battle. Yet, I would have thought that in regard to wars like that against Midian, as well as other wars involving a direct threat to Israel's survival, that they were to be included. Therefore, the Sifri teaches us that they were excluded from this battle as well. Even so, the Levites exemption from certain wars, it is not conclusive proof that they are exempt from all mandatory wars, especially those for the immediate defense of Israel. For here God told them that they [Midian] were planning to harm them further, and yet they had still not come. We might say that in wars where there is a direct threat to annihilate Israel, all are obligated to participate. However, this remains subject to debate and further clarification.

XV. The Anointed Kohen for War

We have already touched on the matter of Kiddushin 20b. However, regarding the writings of the Mordekhai, of blessed memory, who stated that the anointed Kohen for war would return immediately [before the actual battle began], it does not appear that this was the case in the War against Midian. Rabbi Shimon ben Yohai proves (Yevamot 60b) that a convert younger than three years and one day is eligible for marriage to a Kohen from the fact that Pinchas was with them. Our sages found no other way to interpret this other than explaining that "keep them alive for yourselves" means to leave them alive as servants and maidservants. Now, if the anointed Kohen returned immediately from the battlefield, there would be no proof for Rabbi Shimon ben Yohai, and why did the sages not simply reject his view saying that Pinchas had already returned? Therefore, it is clear the anointed kohen did not return immediately.

Furthermore, the Torah explicitly states that the sacred vessels and trumpets for sounding the alarm were in his hands, indicating that the trumpets were to be sounded during battle, meaning he had to remain on the battlefield. If the commandment to blow the trumpets during battle, which as explained by the Netziv z"l in Ha'amek Davar and Harhev Davar, suggests that this was done in the presence of the Ark, which was taken out to war as described in the Jerusalem Talmud, Shekalim. Then this would indicate that the Kohanim and the anointed Kohen were indeed present during the battles. But perhaps they blew the trumpets before the battle commenced, and this needs further clarification.

However from Yevamot 60b, which we brought above, it is evident that the anointed Kohen remained in the battle, contrary to the Mordekhai's view. It might be that his intention was that Kiddushin 20b cannot be adduced as proof. For the Kohen with the trumpets was indeed present during the battle. However, this only applies when the Ark is present, but when the Ark is not present, the trumpets are not sounded, (since the requirement is to blow "before the Lord your God"). See the comments of the Harhev Davar. Likewise, the Yerushalmi states that during certain conquests, the trumpets were not blown, and this would refer to times when the Ark was absent. Thus, Kiddushin 20b proves that Kohanim do go to war, and the reference could be to the anointed Kohen for war, and this would prove he goes out to war. And when the Ark is not present, he returns before the battle begins, as explained above.

However, I have already argued above from what is said, that the permission to take a beautiful captive applies even before the battle begins, as previously discussed.

And yet it is a little difficult to understand, why did Rabbi Shimon ben Yochai not simply say, "Pinchas was with them," after all there were Kohanim with trumpets, and additional Ark carrier kohanim were also there. Why then did he not say "there were kohanim with them"?

However, it is possible that since they were all secondary in importance to Pinchas, therefore only Pinchas was mentioned.

Regarding the exemption of the Levites, it is noted that the Levites were not counted for war (Numbers 1:49). What about the kohanim? For this there is no hint. – other than Pinchas himself, and the other few necessary to blow the trumpets and carry the ark. This implies that the kohanim were entirely exempt, but this does not necessarily apply to later generations, for at the time there were not so many kohanim, and they could not be conscripted without halting the service in the tabernacle. As opposed to the Levites who were thousands strong and could be partially conscripted for war. And according to one version, "including the Tribe of Levi" – the Tribe of Levi indeed participated in the War against Midian.

XVI. The Return of a Kohen Who Committed a Sin Among the War Returnees

Returning to the proof adduced from a Kohen Gadol who married a widow, or a regular kohen who married a divorcee etc. regarding whom the Talmud in Sotah 44a writes that they do not return from the battlefield. This proves that Kohanim participated in discretionary wars, for they certainly participated in mandatory wars, where even a groom would go out from his chamber. And the Torah did not need to state that a Kohen Gadol who betrothed a widow does not return from the battlefield, for could one imagine that the sinner be awarded?!

And yet one could argue that the Kohein Gadol is truly exempt, as it says, "and from the sanctuary he shall not go forth," requiring him to always remain in Jerusalem as Maimonides explains. Even if regular Kohanim are obligated, the Kohein Gadol is exempt. However, if a Kohein Gadol betrothed a widow, he is forbidden to serve, and the prohibition "and from the sanctuary he shall not go forth" would not apply to him. Nevertheless, this does not completely settle the issue, as we do not know if marrying a widow disqualifies him from service according to Torah law. If it does not, would the prohibition "and from the sanctuary he shall not go forth" be nullified? Thus we may conclude that even a discretionary war would obviate this prohibition, as we stated above. However, the simple reading of Maimonides' words (chapter 6, Biat Mikdash) indicates that the prohibition is a Torah commandment, (for he felt the need to clarify, that if he nonetheless served – it would not be desecrated. And If this prohibition was only a rabbinic disqualification he would not have felt the need to clarify this point.

On the other hand, from what is stated about the immediate resumption of duties after a vow of abstention from her, it seems the disqualification is not a Torah prohibition but only a rabbinic fine. For if it were a Torah prohibition, how could he resume duties while he was still connected to her? Thus, is it hard to reach a clear decision either way.

Ultimately, if the disqualification is only rabbinic, then there is proof that he must be conscripted. For if it is only a rabbinic disqualification, he is included in the commandment not to leave the temple., and we must say that this prohibition is lifted even in a discretionary war. However, if the disqualification is from the Torah, this does not prove the above. For he is always exempt from conscription as a result of "and from the sanctuary he shall not go forth", and when he is disqualified from service, he must be conscripted, as he no longer must remain in the temple, for he no longer has what to do there.

XVII. A Kohen Who Killed a Person

I was also prompted by what I saw in the commentary of the Da'at Zekenim, authored by the Tosafists (I do not have the book currently at hand), which states that when Pinchas was granted a covenant of peace, it was because he killed Zimri, and a Kohen who kills cannot raise his hands (to bless the congregation). He was therefore concerned that he might be disqualified from raising his hands. This would suggest a reason to exempt Kohanim from war.

However, this might only apply to civil wars among Israel, such as those during the First Temple period, or the war against the Tribe of Benjamin. But in wars against non-Jews, it might be different. And

Pinchas is a unique case because he killed an Israelite. This, however, is not a convincing argument. Pinchas was permitted to do what he did. Indeed his act of killing was a great mitzva. Nonetheless, since he had taken a soul, he should have been disqualified. Similarly, although killing a non-Jewish idolater during wartime is permitted, it might still disqualify a Kohen from raising his hands. Even if killing an idolater outside of war is not punishable by human courts, it is still a sin and he "owes his life" to the heavens. Thus, this too should be seen as an act of shedding blood, even when permitted, and might still disqualify one from certain religious duties.

However, even if we assume that a Kohen who kills is disqualified from raising his hands, this does not necessarily mean that as a result he would be exempt from participating in a discretionary war. The concept of discretionary war pertains only to the king and the Sanhedrin, meaning that they may decide whether to go to war. Once decided, however, everyone is obligated to serve, except those explicitly exempt by the Torah. If there is no explicit exemption in the Torah, one cannot derive such an exemption since he would be henceforth disqualification from raising his hands. Similarly, the Talmud (Kiddushin 21b) does not derive the ruling that a servant who is a kohen cannot have his ear pierced, simply as a result of the claim that this would mean he would become disqualified from serving in the temple. This shows that when there is a requirement of piercing, it cannot be waived merely from this concern.

In Makkot 13a, we learn that a person who returns from a city of refuge upon the Kohein Gadol's death returns to their family's status, including the priestly service (according to Rabbi Meir). This implies that the sin is atoned for relatively easily. Yet, Pinchas needed a divine promise to reassure him despite having performed a mitzvah. This suggests that even someone who kills accidentally does not lose their priestly status completely.

If a Kohen who kills in war is disqualified from raising his hands, how much more so would he be disqualified from sacred service? However, according to Rabbi Meir, even one who killed returns to full priestly service upon the Kohein Gadol's death. This challenges the view of the Tosafists.

However, the Tosafists' claim is truly hard to fathom: It is hard to accept that a kohein who participated in war would be disqualified from his priestly duties. How could his actions be compared to the verse "your hands are full of blood"? How can we take the verse and interpret it so far from its simple meaning? Maybe they too intended to say, that the verse in regard to Pinchas simply teaches us that all permitted actions of killing, all the more so when the killing is a mitzva, would not disqualify a kohen from his priestly duties.

XVIII. THE CANCELLATION OF THE DAILY OFFERING DURING WAR

In Eruvin 63b, the angel rebukes the Israelites for neglecting the evening offering due to being occupied with war. This raises the question: if the Kohanim were exempt from war, how did this neglect occur? This implies that during war, the Kohanim were also obligated to fight, hence their absence resulted in the neglect of the offering. This is doubly challenging: If all the Levites were entirely exempt from military service during the conquest of the land, as Maimonides writes, why was the sacrifice not brought. And if they were obligated to fight, in opposition to Maimonides, why did they not leave behind a small portion who could have fulfilled the temple service.

We may suggest that while the Levites were indeed exempt from war, sacrifices in a public Bama (high space) would only be offered when the Ark was present. As a rule, they would take the Ark to battle in the morning, first offering the morning sacrifice, and then return it to its place by evening for the evening sacrifice. However, one night the Ark was not returned in time, leading to the neglect of the evening offering. This implies a significant principle: obligatory sacrifices are only offered in a public Bama when the Ark is in place.

We may also suggest that there is no proof from the above that the Kohanim were exempt from conscription, rather the members of the

Ma'amad were preoccupied with the war, and therefore the sacrifice was not brought in time. This would prove that the sacrifice cannot be brought without the members of the Ma'amad, and this deserves further investigation.

XIX. No Evidence from Amasa for Exempting Torah Scholars from the Draft

Regarding the matter raised earlier (chapter 9) about Amasa delaying the call to arms in Sanhedrin 49a, it should be noted further, that the language of the Talmud, "he found them beginning to study a tractate," suggests they were engaged in specific study sessions. Perhaps they were not exclusively Torah scholars, but rather people who would gather together for a designated period of study, and then return to their homes and fields. Similar to the "months of assembly" in the Talmud and Geonic periods. Amasa did not wish to interrupt them until they had completed their studies and were ready to return home, after which he conscripted them. Indeed, I tend to this interpretation.

However, this does not prove that Torah scholars are exempt from mandatory war, as this was not a war to defend Israel from an external threat but to expand the kingdom of David. Even though the kingship over Israel was promised to David, perhaps the other tribes did not deny the Davidic dynasty, but rather objected to David himself as a result of the sin with Batsheva. This was therefore not a war in which even a groom would be required to leave from his chamber and the bride from her canopy, nor would the scholars be required to conscript. David, in his piety, acknowledged this by not treating Amasa as a rebel towards his kingdom.

This can be seen in the fact that in Asa's case, he mobilized all of Judah, and it was stated, "there was none free." Here, it was not stated that "there was none free," implying that David himself did not consider it a mandatory war requiring even Torah scholars to participate. Therefore, it cannot be used as a proof that Torah scholars are exempt from mandatory war.

XX. The War of Independence: A Mandatory War

1. Even Though It Was Not Declared by the King and Beit Din

I have heard arguments that this does not qualify as a mandatory war because such a war requires a declaration by a king and a Sanhedrin, which we lack today. However, my predecessor, the great sage of blessed memory, expressed his opinion in Shu"t Mishpat Kohen (no. 144), stating that in the absence of a king in Israel, the public takes the place of the king. This is logical since the power of the king is derived from the nation, and the community precedes the king (see Horayot 13a).

In other words, the community, representing all of Israel, holds precedence over an individual king. And who is the public which bears the status of K'lal Yisrael? The public of Eretz Israel holds this status. Just as halakhic decisions follow the residents of Eretz Israel, as mentioned in Maimonides' commentary on Mishnah Bekhorot, chapter 4. The Jewish community in Eretz Israel is considered the collective body of Israel, while the Diaspora communities, even if they are millions strong, are like individual members.

Thus, this war was declared by local authorities, representing the public authority of each collective organization, including the religious organizations like Mizrachi, HaPoel HaMizrachi, Agudat Israel, and Poalei Agudat Israel, along with the Chief Rabbinate of Eretz Israel and the Chief Rabbis from major centers. They acted with the knowledge that this was the consensus of the majority of rabbis everywhere, with the backing and active encouragement of most Jews worldwide. Who can claim that all this collective authority together is not equivalent to the authority of a king in Israel?!

2. Saving Israel and Judaism

Regarding the war itself, its purpose is evident. The state of the nation is dire. Our terrible enemy, (may their name be erased, and together with them may all Israel's enemies be erased), destroyed a majority of "the building" of our people – six million Jews who can be likened in their value to many tens of millions. Hundreds of thousands remain in camps, their lives hanging by a thread, without a hope, other than refuge in Mount Zion. Without this, God forbid – suicide. Hatred against Jews is escalating terribly globally, putting Judaism at immense risk, even in countries where Jews are still tolerated. Our only remaining hope was the establishment of a Jewish state, recognized by the United Nations, as a sanctuary in our ancestral land.

This hope has materialized, thank God. However, immediately after, the Arabs, incited from outside, from known sources, began to kill and destroy, aiming to extinguish the last ember of our hope. Our response is clear: surrender would mean abandoning our brethren in distress, leading to the massacre of thousands by savages and the forced exile, God forbid, of the majority of our population from our holy land. It was impossible for tens of thousands of our youth to not rise-up in defense, and our ultimate fate would be annihilation as in Europe. No other ending could be possible. What rational person can deny the reality that this is a mandatory war, the defense of Israel against an existential threat, in the fullest meaning of these words?!

According to Nahmanides, even if this were merely a battle focused on conquering the land, it would still be a mandatory war, akin to the days of Joshua. I can prove that Maimonides does not disagree, and he did not enumerate this as a separate mitzvah due to a specific reason. Further explanations can be found in the appendix.

Additionally, beyond these reasons, this is also about saving Judaism, the soul of Israel. In the diaspora, Judaism is in decline, while here, despite the various degree of secularism amongst many, this is the only place where Torah study and Shabbat observance can be perpetuated until the arrival of the Messiah.

From an even broader perspective, it is evident to all who have spiritual eyes, that the extinguishing of this last ember would lead to the overall demise, if we do not merit divine revelation in the near future, of the "candle" of Judaism among the majority of Jews. The exile has lasted so long, divine providence seems hidden, and the last holocaust has overburdened everything. On the other hand, atheism, or at least skepticism, has ballooned globally. Without the hidden miracle of Eretz

Israel, the vast majority of Jews would fall into despair and from there quickly reach spiritual decay, with many joining the Reform movement or similar trends, the majority of them then being pushed into the abyss of assimilation and loss of identity.

I should elaborate more but time does not permit. Nonetheless, I must express my deep sorrow that some great Torah scholars do not recognize the gravity of the situation, and they do not understand that the opportunity given to us to establish a Jewish state, is indeed a divine salvation and eventually the beginning of redemption. While I will not deny that my heart has fear, such as do many others, from the concerns about secular elements, but thank God we have enough power – if we all unite — to shape the state so that it should at the very least not stand in opposition to our holy Torah. Ensuring no civil marriage or divorce contrary to Torah law, and securing public observance of Shabbat and kashrut, as well as a legal system based on Torah principles. Together we can ensure the continued existence and thriving of the religious education system, and strengthen and fortify the holy Yeshivot.

In conclusion, this is in my opinion undoubtedly a mandatory and obligatory war.

XXI. Warfare Even Over Matters as Trivial as Straw and Chaff

We will now discuss the matter from a pikuah nefesh perspective. The murderous actions of our enemies, both overt and covert, immediately following the UN decision, especially in Jerusalem, which according to the U.N resolution will not be passed over to Jewish rule, clearly demonstrate their intent. Our clear duty is to defend our lives. Without our defensive actions, we would already be victims, with a hundred thousand Jews in Jerusalem, both the old and new sections, may the multiply, falling prey to them. Now where do we find a law stating that Torah scholars are exempt from actually saving Jewish lives! The words of our great master Maimonides are as clear as midday: all Jews are obligated in the sacred work of saving Jewish lives. "In any place, if they come for lives or wage war, or lay siege, we go out against them with weapons and desecrate the Shabbat. And all of Israel are commanded to come and help their besieged brethren, and deliver them from the idolaters on Shabbat etc." (Hilkhot Shabbat 2:23). Maimonides does not merely permit Shabbat desecration but rather writes that "all of Israel are commanded etc."

Rashi in Eruvin 45a explains that in towns close to the border, even if the enemies have come only with the intention of taking straw and chaff, we go out against them with weapons because "from there the land is easily conquered before them." We do not assume that since they initially came only for straw, so too even if they eventually conquer the land they will not kill us, but rather they will be solsly focused on monetary matters. For it is forbidden to trust the gentiles, and we must not allow them to conquer any Jewish settlement. These principles apply to Jewish settlements world-over, not only when there is an independent Jewish kingdom or in the Land of Israel.

These halakhot are codified in the Tur and Shulhan Arukh, who only bring laws which are applicable in the current era, and thus they are clearly relevant to our time as well.

XXII. The Laws of War as Listed in the Tur

Moreover, the Tur brings in Orah Hayyim, section 249, the Baraita that states, "One does not besiege the cities of gentiles less than three days before Shabbat." This law pertains to discretionary war, but in a mandatory war, one besieges even on Shabbat. A discretionary war can only be declared by a king with the Sanhedrin of seventy-one. What relevance does this law have in our time?! If it is assumed for the purposes of this Halakha that the Messiah has arrived, and there is a king from the house of David and a Great Sanhedrin of seventy-one, then this is a law relegated to the future, which should not have been included within the framework of the Rabbeinu Yaakov, author of the Turim, Halakhic compilation. But if it relates to an era when there is no king or Sanhedrin, what could be the practical application of the laws of discretionary war?

One must conclude, that there is indeed a reality, similar to the one which we currently experience, where we have gathered more than half a million Jews in our holy land, and we have been granted the permission of the governments to establish an independent Jewish state. And it is proven that the organized community in Israel carries the status of a king and a Great Sanhedrin, even in the absence of both. It is known that Rabbeinu Yaakov, of blessed memory, had Ruah Hakodesh, the holy spirit, and with his holy spirit he foresaw, and indicated, that this authority exists — not only to declare a mandatory war but also a discretionary one, for in regards to an obligatory war, it is universally accepted that you lay siege to gentile cities even on the Shabbat.

XXIII. Saving Others at the Risk of One's Own Life

Let us return to the examination of this issue from the perspective of the laws of pikuah nefesh. I have heard some relying on the responsa of the Radbaz (vol. 3, no. 627; vol. 5, no. 218), which states that one is not obligated to place oneself even in possible danger to save another, even from certain danger. This is indeed a disagreement among the Rishonim. From the Jerusalem Talmud, it is clear that one must endanger oneself. In Maimonides, we do not find an explicit ruling. Maimonides states, "Even if an individual is pursued by gentiles, it is a mitzvah to save him… on Shabbat, even if it involves repairing weapons" (Shabbat 2:23). It is hard to interpret this as applying only to a case where there is no danger to the rescuers, since in an armed confrontation with armed gentile attackers, who can guarantee no danger to the rescuers? It seems clear to me that Maimonides rules like the Jerusalem Talmud.

If one would stubbornly insist that while it is permissible to rescue on Shabbat, it is a matter of piety to avoid danger, as concluded by the Netziv in his responsa (Meshiv Davar, no. 147). However, it is simply impossible to attribute such a view to Maimonides! But what can be done, there is no end to the claims of the stubborn – anyone with a brain in his temple will surely understand this.

What would they answer to the earlier law requiring one to wage war on the border towns, and after all warfare entails danger? They must admit that the Halakha at least when many are endangered is different, and when a town is endangered the law is different than when an individual is under attack.

Regarding the essence of the law, the Radbaz's words have not been correctly understood. Rabbi Hayyim Heller, may his candle shine bright, in his notes on the Sefer HaMitzvot (page 474) tried to probe Radbaz's intention: He quoted Radbaz who wrote elsewhere (Leshonot Harambam, 218), that there is indeed an obligation to endanger oneself to save another, as stated in the Jerusalem Talmud. However, he adds, that in a case of certain danger, or even in situations where the danger to oneself is the more probable outcome than saving the friend, there is no obligation to endanger oneself.

It is a general rule not to present a decisor as contradicting himself. Therefore I do not agree with R. Heller who is of the opinion that the Radbaz in his responsa changed his mind. I believe he never meant to rule against the Jerusalem Talmud, and that this is what he meant in the words he wrote in his responsa as well.

Standing guard for a few hours in an internal neighborhood position, does not constitute certain, or even anything close to a probability of fifty percent danger. It is merely a possible risk, and there can be no claim to shirk one's obligation based on the Radbaz's rulings, even if we pushed aside entirely any and all considerations pertaining to Israel's war.

We have never heard that Torah scholars, even great ones, are exempt from such an obligation to save lives. On the contrary, Maimonides states that is to be conducted "Only through the actions of the great sages of Israel" (Hilkhot Shabbat 2:3).

In truth, the whole issue is irrelevant to the situation at hand. The dispute pertains to a a situation where Reuven faces no danger whatsoever, while Shimon is endangered. Here there are different opinions to what extent he must place himself in danger to save his friend. However, if both are equally endangered, and both are commanded to do all they can to save themselves, and not be butchered like sheep at the hands of evil murderers. How could anyone say that Shimon should fight to save both himself and Reuven, while Reuven sits by passively – at Shimon's expense – since Shimon is a Yeshiva student?!

XXIV. It Is Forbidden to Surrender to the Enemy

Here we might detect the influence of a handful of extremists advocating surrender, not realizing that in our current state, surrender would mean slaughter and exile. This aside of the halakhic rationale detailed above, which these extremists fail to see since their fanaticism has caused them to lose their mind. Regardless, ninety-nine percent of the population would consider anyone advocating surrender as a traitor. The Jerusalem community, along with the rest of Israel, will continue to stand firm, and the started efforts would continue. Is it not indeed a mitzvah to help in the defense, and to do everything in one's power to help rescue the community, even if one's personal view is that the majority is wrong? In life-threatening situations, practical reality and communal safety take precedence.

Would someone watching another run and jump into the river intent on drowning himself, not be obligated to save them, even if it involves Shabbat desecration?! And according to our conclusion above, the Radbaz himself would agree if the risk to oneself is less than certain, that one is obligated to help out even at their own peril. All the more so in our situation, where, praise God, we have more chances of prevailing, and the signs of divine providence indicate that these are the labor pains of redemption, at least the beginning of it.

XXV. Fear of Desecrating God's Name

If a full draft of yeshiva students were demanded, it might pose a spiritual danger, potentially extinguishing the light of Torah among the remnants of the people. Even temporarily, God forbid. However, what is demanded is only partial participation, avoiding any such danger. And I ask of you: Is this not a desecration of God's name?! Why should the people say: Our young men, including religious God fearing ones, are endangering their lives to bring food and sustenance, with some being killed on the way, and they sit without moving a finger to take part at all in the joint defense and rescue efforts?!

Moreover, military leaders are willing to completely exempt exceptionally outstanding students who are expected to become leading Torah figures, and even more leniencies can be obtained.

XXVI. The Three Oaths

I have also heard the argument that all this effort constitutes a violation of the oath imposed upon us by God not to ascend in force and not to rebel against the nations. I assert that this argument is null.

Firstly, there is no rebellion here. Rebellion is only against a governing power that holds authority over us. Since when have the Arabs in the land of Israel and the surrounding regions had authority over us? The British mandate has ended, having accepted the authority of the United Nations, which decided with a large majority to grant us a state in the land of Israel. The Arabs have had no rule over the land of Israel for hundreds of years, neither within nor without. So, against whom are we rebelling? On the contrary, they are the rebels. What relevance does the oath not to ascend as a wall have here? Since we have been granted permission to establish the state, we have the right to bring our brothers who languish in detention camps in the diaspora.

On the matter itself, the early sages have already ruled that the law of "Dina d'Malkhuta Dina" which applies to foreign rulers, does not apply in the land of Israel, and it is reasonable to assume that the three oaths do not apply here either. Note that when Rabbi Yehoshua ben Hannaniah entered a public assembly where people had gathered to discuss rebellion against Roman rule, he tried to influence and dissuade them without even hinting that such rebellion was forbidden due to the oaths.

Moreover, the whole matter seems mistaken to me. Our great teacher, the master of Torah armies, Maimonides, never even hints to these oaths. It is a riddle! But the explanation is simple: just as God imposed an oath on Israel, He also imposed an oath on the nations not to enslave Israel excessively. Already in the time of Maimonides, the nations had repeatedly violated their oath, thus freeing us from ours.

Additionally, as is known, it is found in the writings of the students of the Ar"i may his memory be blessed, that the force of the oaths expired at the end of the fifth millennium. We have also found in the Midrash, published by Rabbi Eliezer Halevi Grinhut, from the Cairo Genizah, that: "I have adjured you not to awaken love — until the kingdoms willingly place the sword in your hands." This condition has been fulfilled, as the United Nations, which according to international agreements has the say about these parts, has "placed the sword in our hands," granting us, praise God, the authority to establish our state in the land of our fathers. And soon they will recognize the validity of their decision as the Mandate will shortly end. Thus we see the fruition, of that which Nahmanides already foresaw with his Ruah Hakodesh, regarding the process of redemption. That first the nations will grant us permission to found a state etc., as is well known.

XXVII. The Need for Military Rabbis

I do not understand all the uproar. It is clearly stated in Sotah 43a regarding the war against Midian that not only Pinchas, the anointed Kohein for war, went, but also the Sanhedrin accompanied him, meaning the Great Sanhedrin of seventy-one. While it is not necessary to assume they participated directly in battle actions, they were among the ranks to influence them with their spirit and their Torah. It would be nice and proper for some appropriate yeshiva students to serve as military rabbis to influence the soldiers with Torah and pure fear of Heaven, at least in places where there is no immediate danger. After all, in an obligatory war the Great Sanhedrin went to the war.

If one were to argue that there the text says "no man was missing" and that the situation was different, Rabbi Shimon ben Yohai explains, "no one was missing – no one sinned" (Yevamot 61a). And even according to the sages, who disagreed, did they have a promise from God in advance that no one would be missing at the end!?

In any case, it would be very worthwhile for the yeshivot to provide a quota of rabbis to serve as military chaplains, away from places of immediate danger, under a prominent rabbinic figure, serving as a model akin to Pinchas and the Sanhedrin.

XXVIII. Hezekiah's Trust Compared to the Opinion of the Sages

And I have heard claims that we should learn from Hezekiah, King of Judah, who placed a sword at the entrance of the study hall and declared, "Whoever does not engage in Torah study shall be stabbed with the sword." They examined from Dan to Be'er Sheva and found not a single man or woman, boy or girl, who was not well-versed in the laws of purity. "And the yoke will be destroyed because of the anointing oil"—Sennaherib's yoke was broken due to the merit of Hezekiah's oil (Sanhedrin 94b). This testimony from our Sages is indeed of great significance, blessed be He who chose them and their teachings. However, if these claimants believe that Hezekiah did not organize an army or prepare weapons, they are mistaken and have forgotten explicit verses. The verse in the Book of Kings clearly states that Sennaherib ascended upon the fortified cities of Judah and captured them. It is evident, then, that Hezekiah fortified cities, and it is certainly logical that he stationed soldiers in them. Even more explicitly, in Chronicles II (32:5), it says that "He strengthened himself and rebuilt the broken-down wall, raised towers upon it, built another wall outside, fortified the Millo in the city of David, and made weapons and shields in abundance. He appointed military officers over the people and gathered them … and spoke to their hearts" (II Chronicles 32:5-6). This shows that Hezekiah engaged in a large-scale recruitment and made numerous military preparations.

And what our Sages said regarding this should primarily be understood in relation to the period prior to the war, during which Hezekiah established a massive movement to spread Torah throughout

Israel. His intention was twofold: that the people should be learned in the teachings of God and, at the same time, to create a mighty spiritual force to purify the people from the spiritual impurity into which they had sunk during the days of Ahaz and to return them to the holy source. However, it is clear to any reasonable person that Hezekiah did not abolish agriculture and industry and turn all of Israel into one giant yeshiva, for "many attempted to do as Rabbi Shimon bar Yohai did and were unsuccessful," and the halakhah follows Rabbi Yishmael. Rather, everyone was required to attend Torah lessons in their local study halls.

Similarly, it is not to be understood literally that the Sages intended to say that Hezekiah was prepared to kill with the sword anyone who did not engage in Torah study, for we have not learned anywhere that someone who does not study Torah is subject to execution by the sword at the hand of the king or anyone else. Rather, the sword was symbolic, meaning that the future sword, the Assyrian sword of war, would come upon those who neglected Torah study. The merit of Torah study would protect those who engaged in it when they stood in the heat of battle. But anyone who did not set fixed times for Torah study would eventually fall by Sennaherib's sword.

I have a feeling, that the widespread Torah study instituted by Hezekiah was also a foreshadowing of what was to come. Why is it mentioned that the people were specifically well-versed in the laws of taharah (purity)? Why taharah in particular? After all, the laws of purity were as relevant to their day-to-day lives then as the laws of meat and milk are today—so what is the novelty here? But in light of the circumstances, this becomes clear. Hezekiah foresaw that a great war would come upon Judah, but he trusted in God and in the merit of Torah study, which he had spread throughout Israel. When the land would be filled with battles and, inevitably, with casualties, it was particularly important for the people to be well-versed in the laws of purity and impurity. And it is easy for an insightful person to understand that even in the midst of the war, Hezekiah continued to maintain the "Lamp of Torah" in Israel as much as possible. Not the entire population was fit for recruitment, and not all the recruits were occupied with war day and night. The verse "The yoke shall be destroyed because of the oil"—the yoke of Sennaherib was destroyed because of the oil of Hezekiah, which continued to burn in the synagogues and study halls—refers not only to the yoke that was threatening to come upon them, but also to the yoke once it had already been placed upon them.

It also seems that most of the people's Torah study took place at night, for during the day they were occupied with their work, businesses, and preparations for war. At night, they studied in rotating shifts throughout the night. This is the "oil of Hezekiah" that continued to burn in the synagogues and study halls.

However, the assumption that Hezekiah and his people did not take the necessary measures to prepare for war and only occupied themselves with Torah study is entirely unreasonable and contradicts what is explicitly stated in the Book of Kings and especially in Chronicles. And as the Sages said, "No verse can be entirely removed from its plain meaning." Indeed, we do not find even the slightest suggestion that the Sages disapproved of Hezekiah's extensive preparations for war, as is clearly described in the verses, including the appointment of military officers. And it is self-evident that there can be no army without soldiers and commanders, and that Hezekiah fortified the cities of Judah, which was done in accordance with the will of the Torah and the will of the Sages. Only in regard to his decision to hole up the upper waters of the Gihon spring was there any dissent (Mishnah, Pesahim 9:4).

And if you ask, why did the Sages not agree with him, since his intention was to prevent the kings of Assyria from finding water to drink? Your answer is found in the clear words of our guiding light, Rashi, who explains (Pesahim 56a, s.v. v'lo hodu), that Hezekiah should have trusted in God, who said, "I will protect this city and save it." This is particularly relevant concerning the defense of Jerusalem. On the other hand, heaven forbid to suggest that this righteous man, may his merit protect us, Jerusalem, and all of Israel, was somehow lacking in bitahon [trust] in God. Rather, it was the fear that sin might cause a reversal of fortune, similar to what our forefather Jacob feared, despite having received a divine promise. See Berakhot 4a and Rashi's commentary there. The Sages of that generation disagreed with Hezekiah only because they differentiated between a general promise and a specific promise regarding a particular situation. Jacob had received a general promise, "I will protect you," and likewise, David was generally assured that God rewards the righteous in the World to Come. Nevertheless, he feared that perhaps he might fall from his spiritual level due to sin. Similarly, in the days of Ezra, there was a general promise regarding the Second Temple: "Until this nation You have acquired passes over." But in the case of Jerusalem, there was a specific, unique promise: "I will defend this city and save it" (Isaiah 37:35). The Sages believed that such a specific promise from God should be seen as immutable—"No good ever issued from the mouth of the Holy One, Blessed be He, and was later retracted to become bad" (Jerusalem Talmud, Berakhot 9:2). However, Hezekiah did not hold this view, but rather believed that sin could always cause a change in the divine decree, heaven forbid. Even though Hezekiah was undoubtedly one of the greatest of his generation, the Sages nevertheless believed that he should have consulted with them and accepted their perspective, as they represented the majority opinion.

Thus, my inclination is to justify the actions of this righteous man. May it be the will of God that his merit protect us and that the promise "I will defend this city and save it" (Isaiah 37:35) be fulfilled for us. And not only for this city, but also for all of the Land of Israel, to save it, for the sake of God, for the sake of Hezekiah, and for the sake of David, His servants. Amen and Amen. Indeed, regarding the military preparations, there was no disagreement with him whatsoever.

XXIX. One Engaged in a Commandment Is Exempt from Other Commandments

1. Individual Commandment and Communal Commandment

We still need to examine Sotah 45b, regarding the dispute between Rabbi Yehuda and the Rabbis as to the status of a battle intended to diminish the idolaters so that they do not attack us. Rabbi Yehuda considers this a mitzvah, exempting one from other mitzvot, whereas the Rabbis see it as optional, not exempting one from other mitzvot.

One wonders why they did not explain the dispute differently: if engaging in one mitzvah exempts one from other mitzvot, then according to Rabbi Yehuda, such a war is a mitzvah and takes precedence. The king and his advisors might decide to launch a preemptive attack, finding the timing suitable, thereby making this an obligatory mitzvah. In such a scenario, anyone involved in another mitzvah must abandon it to join the war effort, ensuring they do not miss the opportune moment. Whereas according to the other sages there is no such requirement.

Similarly they might have suggested the following distinction: There is a significant difference between individual and collective obligations. War, if considered a mitzvah, is a collective obligation. Therefore, someone engaged in a personal mitzvah is not exempt from it. But if the mitzvah in question is collective, like the communal study of Torah, one engaged in it is exempt from participating in war.

This distinction was not put forth since the following coclusion is indisputable: Engaging in a personal mitzvah does not exempt one from collective obligations like war, whereas when one is involved in waging a war, all other collective mitzvot, do not demand his attention, as war is a communal mitzva.

2. Conquering Territories Outside the Land of Israel

In the Jerusalem Talmud, however, at the end of the chapter on the anointed Kohein for war, there is a discussion possibly implying that "coming upon us" refers to our conquest of territories outside Israel. Once these territories are conquered according to the proper procedure— after first conquering all of Israel—they become like the land of Israel. If enemies then come to expel us from these territories and wish to return them to their previous status, without any thought of conquering Israel itself, safeguarding these lands is considered an obligatory war only for Rabbi Yehuda. However, if enemies come upon us in our own land, it is an obligatory war for everyone.

Yet, this explanation raises a difficulty: what is Rabbi Yehuda's definition of an optional war? And why is it not mentioned? The issue is further complicated because if enemies come upon us in Israel, it becomes a matter of life-saving, and it is hard to argue that even a bridegroom and bride would be exempt from this mitzvah. According to our understanding, though, it is easier to apprehend this: One might theoretically be allowed to flee back to our ancestral land. Nonetheless, it would be a disgrace to do so. Thus, we are to declare war and fight, though in such a case we would not compel the bridegroom and bride to join in.

Regardless of how we interpret the Jerusalem Talmud, the practical ruling follows our great master, who states that when enemies come upon us, it is an obligatory war, and everyone, including bridegrooms and brides, must join.

Sotah 45b in the Babylonian Talmud, allows us to further refine the interpretation. The Tanna speaks of a certain type of war as one of conquest, such as Joshua's wars, which are obligatory. Certainly, this does not refer only to Joshua's wars themselves but rather to all other similar wars, implying that the conquest of the land of Israel always carries the status of an obligatory war.

This leaves us questioning why Rava omitted the Jerusalem Talmud's explanation of wars against enemies coming upon us. It suggests that such wars are so clearly obligatory that no explicit mention is needed. Thus, not to create unnecessary disputes between the Talmuds, we must say the Jerusalem Talmud concurs with wars against invading enemies being obligatory, and the discussion there implying otherwise, refers to a defensive war upon foreign lands which we have already conquered.

3. The Difference Between One Drafted and One Standing in Battle

Regarding the principle that one engaged in a mitzvah is exempt from other mitzvot, we must further clarify. This principle applies before a person joins the battle. Once they have joined, it is unreasonable to suggest they can abandon the battle to perform another mitzvah. The opposite is true: They are to remove all other thoughts from their mind, even thoughts regarding their wives and families. When one is already engaged in war, their duty is to focus entirely on the battle, even if it means ignoring other mitzvot. This applies even in optional wars.

Thus, the principle is not applicable during active combat. However, if one is conscripted even though he is momentarily not in active battle, he is continuously considered to be engaged in a mitzvah. However during actual battle, no one ever countenanced the thought that they would lay down their weapons and stop fighting in order to commit another mitzva.

4. Amasa Who Found Scholars in Their Study

By and by we might now add regarding Amasa who found scholars engaged in a study session, that if he had not found them already engaged in active study, they would not have been exempt from the war merely for being scholars. Since they were actively engaged in a communal and joint mitzvah, they were exempt as long as they remained so. Their temporary exemption did not stem from their status as scholars, but rather as a result of their active involvement in a communal mitzva. Once they finished the session, they immediately became obligated to join the war effort, before they would even have the chance of beginning to study a different tractate. And this point still merits further investigation.

XXX. OUR WAR IS A OBLIGATORY WAR (MILHEMET MITZVAH)

Furthermore, in the Jerusalem Talmud, there is room for further scrutiny, as the Mishnah states that the sages say: "In what case are these words said? In a discretionary war (Milhemet Reshut), but in a obligatory war (Milhemet Mitzvah)…" And according to the Talmud, in Rav Hisda's explanation, Milhemet Mitzvah refers to the wars of King David, and the obligatory war (Milhemet Chovah) refers to the war of Joshua. Where then does the discretionary war (Milhemet Reshut) fit in? Therefore, we must accept the version of the Penei Moshe, "The discretionary war is the war of David, and the obligatory war is the war of Joshua." See also Rashi's commentary on the Mishnah: "such as the conquest of the Land of Israel in the days of Joshua." Our master's wording: "such as," must mean to suggest that any additional war for the conquest of the land falls under this category, since "what was – was," see also Yoma 5.

And I ask: Where are we to classify a war in which the nations come against us? Could it be imagined that a war involving actual danger to multitudes, the prevention of exile from our ancestral land and captivity, would not be regarded as an obligatory war (Milhemet Chovah)?! This cannot be. And it must be considered to be included as part of the war of Joshua, meaning that we cannot allow the nations to dispossess us from our inherited land.

And again, I ask regarding the words of Rabbi Yehudah: "Rabbi Yehudah would refer to a obligatory war (Milhemet Mitzvah) as one in which we go out against them, and an obligatory war (Milhemet Chovah) as one in which they come against us" And I am puzzled: Where then does the war of Joshua fit in? Could it be that Rabbi Yehudah would not consider the war of Joshua to have been an obligatory war?! Surely, it was the ultimate goal of all our wanderings in the desert, and it was already intrinsically tied to the very redemption from Egypt, as it says, "And I will bring you [into the land]" (Exodus 6:8), and they were explicitly commanded regarding it, as detailed by Divine command. Therefore, surely all must agree on this point, and there was no need to repeat it. Rather, Rabbi Yehudah's intention was that this is already included in the war of Joshua, as mentioned above.

And if you challenge this, and say: If so, should Rabbi Yehudah not have said that a obligatory war (Milhemet Mitzvah) refers to the war of David, and an obligatory war (Milhemet Chovah) refers to the war of Joshua? I would answer that this is because his words were said in response to the sages' view. Since they had made the statement that the war of David is discretionary (Milhemet Reshut), Rabbi Yehudah wished to stress that at times, the war of David is not only a obligatory war (Milhemet Mitzvah) but also an obligatory war (Milhemet Chovah), such as when they [the enemies] come against us. Thus, according to all, the conquest of the Land of Israel and a defensive war against an enemy attacking us are both considered obligatory. The dispute is only regarding David's wars for territorial expansion—Rabbi Yehudah considers them to be instances of a obligatory war, while according to the sages, they are discretionary.

Now, the Penei Moshe explains that in a obligatory war (Milhemet Mitzvah) the exemptions explicitly mentioned in the Mishnah do not return from the battlefield, and the practical difference pertains only to those who are actively engaged in fulfilling another mitzva. However, this explanation is difficult, for if that was the case, a critical element is missing from the words of the Jerusalem Talmud. It occurs to me that the practical difference might relate to the laws of the beautiful captive woman (Yefat Toar), which, according to the Sifrei, does not apply in a obligatory war. Similarly, there may be a difference regarding the prohibition of laying siege to non-Jew towns less than three days before the Sabbath — in the context of a obligatory war, one may lay siege even on Shabbat itself.

Another idea occurs to me, which is that even "when we go out to attack the akum (idolaters)," there is also a distinction: if the invasion is into territories adjacent to the Land of Israel, where they have already attempted to invade our land and we have repelled them, or when they are likely to conquer at any moment, this is considered, even according to the sages, a obligatory war. However, if we are invading distant lands that have not invaded us and are not likely to invade, this is a discretionary war according to the sages, while for Rabbi Yehudah, it is always considered a obligatory war. Additionally, one might suggest, that the sages hold that a discretionary war pertains to a personal conquest—David's conquests for his own needs, as Rashi explains in Gittin 8b and 47a—but a collective conquest, meaning after all of the Land of Israel has already been captured, is considered a obligatory war even according to the sages. And "the war of David" refers only to the first type, namely, a personal conquest, while Rabbi Yehudah holds this too to be classified as a obligatory war. And an obligatory war (Milhemet Chovah) would include only cases where the non-Jews have attacked us. And the conquest of the Land of Israel, such as the war of Joshua, is considered an obligatory war according to all opinions, and similarly, a defensive war when the non-Jews attack us in the Land of Israel is also considered an obligatory war by all.

Another distinction occurs to me, which is the difference between one discretionary war (Milhemet Reshut) and another discretionary war. A war that is launched based on the ruling of the Great Sanhedrin, with the forced conscription of all of Israel, except for those who return, or who are exempt from the outset, this would be considered a obligatory war to which Rabbi Yehudah refers to as the war of David — where the king declares war with the approval of the Great Sanhedrin. However, a war in which the king organizes volunteers or hires mercenaries, such as in a raid on an enemy troop, even though it is permitted, the Great Sanhedrin does not formally declare it. And any war that is not declared by the Great Sanhedrin is referred to as a private war, and even according to Rabbi Yehudah, it is merely a discretionary war (Milhemet Reshut).

Based on this, Rashi's words in Berakhot 3b can be understood: "Immediately they seek counsel with Ahitophel and consult with the Sanhedrin," in reference to David's statement, "Go and extend your hand against the troops." Rashi explains: "To receive permission from them so that they may pray for them." And what does it mean to "so they may pray"? Surely, their permission is needed since without it the king cannot lead a discretionary war (Milhemet Reshut). – One must therefore conclude, that since the king is not compelling anyone, but rather relying on volunteers and hired soldiers, there is no need for formal permission from the Sanhedrin. Rather, he seeks their permission, meaning their consent, so that they will pray for the troops. For it is possible that the Sanhedrin opposes this war, and if so they might not pray for them, but rather advise them to stop this war, or at the very least, they might not pray with full sincerity. Thus, the king seeks their permission, meaning that he ensures there is no opposition from them. However, from a legal standpoint, he is not required to obtain their permission, since he is not compelling anyone to fight. And there is yet room for further investigation of Rashi's words.

And all of this is for the sake of "magnifying and glorifying the Torah."

For on a practical level according to the Babylonian Talmud, and the ruling of our great master of blessed memory, there are only two different categories of wars: obligatory wars which are obligatory, such as those of Joshua, the war against Amalek, and defensive wars delivering Israel from its enemies. And discretional wars aimed at expanding territorial boundaries, increasing the king's domain, and enhancing his power and glory. And I believe that the Jerusalem Talmud would concur that a war to conquer the Land of Israel, as well as a war to safeguard ourselves from an enemy attack, are both obligatory wars which are obligatory.

Regarding the conclusion of the aforementioned words of the Jerusalem Talmud, regarding King Asa, we have already discussed this earlier, section 5.

XXXII. Conclusion and Summary

1. Partial Conscription

We have extensively discussed all the above, for the sake of expanding and glorifying Torah, on the level of practical halakha, however, things are clear: Halakha is as our great master ruled: Aiding Israel against an enemy is a obligatory war which is obligatory, and there is no basis to exempt Torah scholars entirely from it. However, it is crucial to ensure that the study of Torah is not disrupted, even temporarily, especially considering our current situation where the centers of Torah in the diaspora have been destroyed, and all that remains is the torah studied in the Land of Yisrael, the holy yeshivot, may God preserve and bless them.

The military leadership understands this and wishes to avoid actions that would lead to the closure of yeshivot, even temporarily. Therefore, I believe that yeshiva heads should reach an agreement with the military for partial conscription under specific conditions, including complete exemption for exceptional students, who are like young, budding, "great sages." Additionally, efforts should be made to exempt younger students up to a more mature age, as they are more susceptible to external influences, and even a temporary break for guard duty could diminish their dedication to study.

Regarding active rabbis, teachers, and elementary school instructors, I have not addressed them, since, as far as I know, there is no intention from the military to conscript them at all.

2. Fear of Opposition and Criticism

Aside from all the aforementioned considerations, I believe that a certain level of participation is beneficial for the yeshivot themselves, as total non-participation could provoke opposition. Until now, even secular circles in Israel have respected Torah institutions. It has been reported that yeshiva emissaries are received respectfully even in secular kibbutzim of Hashomer Hatzair, and receive donations from them. Compare the respect for Torah institutions by the secular in Israel to the secular in the diaspora! However, complete refusal regarding conscription, especially for defense and rescue in Jerusalem, could lead to severe backlash.

The verse "Guard your heart with all diligence, for out of it are the issues of life" (Proverbs 4:23) reminds us of our duty to protect the yeshivot, the heart of the nation, from any harm. The yeshivot, where young Torah scholars devote the best of their energy and years to the preservation of Torah, are akin to the altar in the national sanctuary, which is the Land of Israel, with Jerusalem the holy city at its center. Our sages took great care to avoid any reproach from the masses concerning the altar (see Gittin 55b).

Well-intentioned criticisms of the yeshivot in previous years, stemming from great and good individuals, have claimed that the Yeshivot are disconnected from the general populace, and are uninvolved in the nation's revival and rebuilding. In regular times, I have rejected this criticism, explaining that while yeshiva students and their rabbis may seem isolated, this is due to their intense devotion to Torah study, which leaves no time for other matters.

However, in these times of emergency, such justification cannot withstand scrutiny. Indeed, it is true that many young Torah scholars have volunteered and served, but the official, and complete, refusal from the yeshivot could overshadow these efforts and lead to renewed criticism, not only from great individuals, but also the general populace will develop a real animosity.

In concluding this discourse, I emphasize that I wrote this amidst many distractions, in great haste, and there may be points that cannot withstand scrutiny. However, in general, I believe my conclusion is well-founded, thank God, as I wrote it with concentrated thought despite the haste.

3. Prayer and Hope

I conclude with a prayer: May it be the will of the One who makes peace in His heights to bring peace upon the rabbis and their students, and may all factions of Israel unite under one name, one counsel, and one reverence, trusting in the Rock of Israel, our Savior and Redeemer. Together with this, let us each fulfill our duties, each their own, in order to ensure the success of this great and vital endeavor, which I believe marks the end of exile and the beginning of redemption. With the unification and cooperation of all those loyal to the Torah and our sacred tradition in spirit and action, we will succeed, with God's help, to influence the shaping of the Jewish state, and guide it according to the principles of the Torah. Amen and Amen.

Correspondence between Rabbi Yitzhak Isaac Halevi Herzog and David Ben-Gurion on the Question of Inducting Yeshiva Students to the IDF in Israel's First Decade

Mirit Bat-Horin

Background

One of the burning issues on the Israeli public agenda in 2012 was the question of drafting Haredi yeshiva students into the Israel Defense Forces (IDF). This issue has deep roots in the history of the State of Israel and has been a part of the public discourse, particularly in the context of the tension between religion and state, since the early days of the state.[1]

In fact, the discussion on this matter began even before the declaration of the state, during the War of Independence. At that time, Rabbi Yitzchak Meir Levin, who would later become the Minister of Welfare and leader of Agudat Israel, approached Ben-Gurion with a request to exempt 400 yeshiva students from military service so they could devote all their time to Torah study, in the spirit of "Toratam Omanutam" (Torah as their profession).[2] Ben-Gurion decided to grant this request.[3]

1   It is worth noting that the exemption granted to Haredi yeshiva students is only part of the broader issue of Israeli youth evading IDF service under various pretexts. Shahar Ilan addresses the comparison between the exemption given to Haredim and the non-service of other draft evaders: "There are quite a few secular individuals who evade service, and there are also many 'jobniks' who spend their service time in headquarters. The reason why the criticism is mainly directed towards the Haredim is that for them, it is not a matter of a few outliers but a decision by an entire community not to serve in the army. There is deception in the very claim that it is an exemption from military service for yeshiva students. In reality, it is an exemption for the entire Haredi community. The fact that it is granted only to those whose Torah is their profession simply forces every Haredi young man to be registered in a yeshiva." Shahar Ilan, *Haredim Ltd.: Budgets, Evasion, and Law Violations* (Jerusalem: Keter, 2000), 127 (Hebrew). For more on the "short history of the exemption," see Asher Cohen, *From Accommodation to Escalation: The Religious-Secular Rift at the Dawn of the 21st Century* (Jerusalem: Schocken, 2003), 25-40 (Hebrew).

2   Rabbi Yitzchak Meir Levin (1885-1971) — one of the founders and leaders of Agudat Israel in Poland, son-in-law of the Rebbe of Gur, editor of "Eretz Yisrael," the global Agudat Israel newspaper published in Poland, and after its closure, editor of "Darkenu" — immigrated to Israel in 1940. See Yosef Fund, *A Movement in Ruins: The Leadership of Agudat Israel in the Face of the Holocaust* (Jerusalem: Rubin Mass, 2008), 5n13 (Hebrew).

3   Regarding matters of religion and state, Ben-Gurion made a clear distinction between his personal, extremely anti-religious views and the public and national sphere. He himself completely rejected any religious practice,

According to Daphne Barak-Erez,

> "This compromise was likely motivated by the desire to preserve the yeshiva world following the destruction of European communities during the Holocaust. At that time, it was perceived as a sort of 'rescue anchor' for a vanishing world that held cultural and historical value for Jewish society."[4]

The students were seen as "brands plucked from the fire" and received the coveted exemption on an individual basis, without formal legislative procedures or a government decision.[5]

---

avoiding even the most basic ones such as holiday meals, building a sukkah, or registering marriages with the rabbinate. However, he understood the need to maintain a Jewish public space that would ensure the broadest possible national consensus. Therefore, he was careful not to impose his views on the religious and traditional public. See Zvi Zameret, "Yes to a Jewish State, No to a Clerical State: The Mapai Leadership and Its Attitude to Religion and Religious Laws," in Mordechai Bar-On and Zvi Zameret, eds., *On Both Sides of the Bridge: Religion and State in the Early Years of Israel* (Jerusalem: Yad Ben-Zvi, 2002), 175-245 (Hebrew).

4   Daphne Barak-Erez, "Drafting Yeshiva Students: Between the Citizenship Dilemma and the Judicial Dilemma," Mehkarei Mishpat, vol. 22 (2006), p. 15. Barak-Erez bases her statements on Zerach Warhaftig, *A Constitution for Israel: Religion and State* (Jerusalem: Mesilot, 1988), 232 (Hebrew). See also Shahar Ilan, *Haredim Ltd.*, 126.

5   Barak-Erez, pp. 13-14. The documentation before us indicates that David Ben-Gurion later regretted this decision. For example, in a letter to Levi Eshkol dated September 12, 1963, after Eshkol replaced Ben-Gurion as Prime Minister: "The fanaticism has gone beyond all bounds, and I feel somewhat responsible for this [...] I exempted yeshiva students from military service. I did this when their number was small, but they are growing and multiplying" (Ben-Gurion Archives). And in another letter, dated February 1, 1967, to citizen Moshe Shterman: "Immediately after the establishment of the state, Agudat Israel approached me and said: In the Diaspora, all Torah centers were destroyed, and only in the land are there a few young people who want to study in yeshivas — and they requested to

Ben-Gurion's decision allowed many young men to avoid military service under the pretext that they were dedicating their time to Torah study, although many of them actually went to work for a living while most of their peers enlisted in the army.[6]

The following letters[7] from November 1958 reveal a fascinating correspondence between then-Chief Rabbi Yitzhak Isaac Halevi Herzog and Prime Minister David Ben-Gurion. This correspondence occurred following a proposal by the Ministry of Defense officials to the heads of the yeshivas, suggesting that their students undergo several months of basic military training and then return to their Torah studies.[8] A few days before this correspondence began, the Haaretz newspaper reported:

    exempt them from the army. I granted their request. Meanwhile, it became clear to me that there are many yeshivas abroad — in France, Switzerland, the United States, and more, and in the land, they are increasing, and there is no basis for exempting them from the army" (Ben-Gurion Archives).

6   This is evident, for example, from a letter by Member of Knesset Yosef Burg (of HaPoel HaMizrachi) to Rabbi Herzog dated 22 Iyar 5710, May 9, 1950: 'And so I have heard that in recent months, boys have entered yeshivas who did not consider Torah study their vocation, but upon reaching the draft age, registered as students in the yeshivas. Such a phenomenon could lead to a desecration of God's name (Heaven forbid), as it will increase the attacks on the yeshivas and those who genuinely study there, because of those who evade military service by disguising themselves as yeshiva students.' State Archives, Division 72.102, File 4251/7.

7   The documents are taken from the personal collection of Rabbi Yitzhak Isaac HaLevi Herzog (1888-1959), which was transferred to the State Archives from Heichal Shlomo with the assistance of Member of Knesset Isaac Herzog, the Rabbi's grandson. Our thanks are extended to the State Archives for permitting us to use these documents.

8   Rabbi Yitzhak Isaac HaLevi Herzog was the first Ashkenazi Chief Rabbi of the State of Israel. For more on his life and the various issues he dealt with and influenced, see *Ma'asuah le-Yitzhak: Rav Yitzhak Isaac ha-Levi Herzog Memorial Volume*, vol. 1 (Jerusalem: Yad ha-Rav Herzog, 2008; Hebrew).

"A short-term enlistment, staggered by age, will likely be proposed to yeshiva students in their meeting today with the Director-General of the Ministry of Defense, Mr. Shimon Peres, at the Prime Minister's Office in Jerusalem. The delegation will be led by Rabbi Z. Porush, the Israeli chairman of the Council of Torah Sages, the supreme spiritual authority of Agudat Israel. Knowledgeable circles noted that in Mr. Ben-Gurion's consultations on this matter with the heads of the Ministry of Defense, several proposals were formulated. According to these proposals, only 500 yeshiva students, intended for spiritual roles, would be completely exempt from the draft. Currently, nearly 3,000 yeshiva students are entirely exempt. For the rest, the Ministry of Defense intends to propose nine months of regular service, divided as follows: from ages 17.5 to 24, they would be called up three times, for three months each year. Those who did not serve in the IDF and are now aged 25 to 29 would be called up twice, for six months in the first year and three months in the second year. Those aged 29 and over would be required to report only for reserve duty."[9]

It seems that the heads of the yeshivas would express complete opposition to this plan. They would argue that the increase in the number of yeshiva students has not even kept pace with the natural growth of the Haredi population, and it is impossible to provide the required number of rabbis and halachic teachers for the new immigrants. The author of the article in Haaretz estimated that Agudat Israel and the heads of the yeshivas would reject Ben-Gurion's proposal, and the correspondence before us confirms that this assessment was correct.

To understand how this issue has developed throughout the years of the state's existence, it is essential to examine the nature of the arguments of each side. First, we will address the initial letter from Rabbi Herzog

---

9   *Haaretz* (5 November 1958): 6 (Hebrew).

to Ben-Gurion. In expressing his shock at the attempt to change the existing arrangement and his displeasure with it, Herzog reiterated the original claim that formed the basis of the arrangement: the Holocaust destroyed the centers of Torah learning in Europe, and today's students are the remnants of the Holocaust. On the one hand, this claim reflects the recovery and rehabilitation of Israeli society from the Holocaust, and on the other hand, it is important to emphasize that a decade had already passed since the establishment of the state, and the number of yeshiva students had increased several times over. Herzog's words also highlight that among the Torah scholars were a minority of immigrants from Eastern countries, and Torah study needs to be preserved in their communities as well. Rabbi Herzog repeated the argument familiar to us even today: Torah scholars protect the state spiritually, just as IDF soldiers protect it physically.

> Letter of Appeal from Rabbi Herzog to Ben-Gurion[10]
>
> 13 Cheshvan 5719 (November 1958)
>
> To my esteemed and honored,
>
> Mr. David Ben-Gurion, Prime Minister and Minister of Defense,
>
> Holy City of Jerusalem, may it be rebuilt and established.
>
> Honorable Prime Minister,
>
> I was deeply shocked and my heart is broken within me upon hearing the rumor that there is an intention to change the existing status of yeshiva students whose conscription is deferred as long as they are dedicated to Torah study in the courtyards of the House of God. I felt it my duty to address the following to Your Honor:
>
> Historical rights of immense significance have fallen upon Your Honor to restore the glory of freedom and

---

10 The correspondence is taken from: State Archives, Division 72.102, File 4247/21.

independence to Israel and to establish its sovereign kingdom in its homeland. As it is said, "And David was successful in all his ways" (1 Samuel 18:14). I am certain that Your Honor has seen more than anyone else the wonders of the Creator and His manifest miracles in the political arena and on the battlefields, which have brought us to this day.

With God's help, we have achieved this wondrous miracle, which heralds our redemption as promised by our prophets, traditions, and heritage. However, we did not merit that millions of our brothers and sisters from Europe should share in our joy. They were destroyed in a venomous rage; the crown was lifted, and the pleasant homes of Jacob were demolished in the furious exile of Europe. Yet, in their deaths, they commanded us to live, to build lives for our people, to rebuild both materially and spiritually.

That wicked one, may his name be blotted out, knew, as did many before him, that the soul of this nation lies in its spirit, hidden and embedded in the holy books and the written and oral Torah. Therefore, he targeted the scrolls before attacking the people. Tragically, he achieved his desire, and at the end of the war, it became clear that we suffered doubly: both physically and spiritually. Along with the destruction of Jewish communities, all the glorious centers of Torah learning in this exile were obliterated. Europe, the cradle of yeshivas, was also devastated in terms of Torah, its scholars, and its students.

Yet the mercies of God are not exhausted, and His compassions have not ended: our land, designated and prepared as a gathering place for the dispersed of Israel and the remnants of the massacre in Europe, absorbed the surviving yeshiva students and their leaders. These, one from a city and two from a family, came and rebuilt the tents of the yeshivas that were destroyed in Europe. Consequently, our holy land and we have been blessed with the return of Torah to its original dwelling, its natural place. In this respect, it has become a Torah center unparalleled in the world, something we have not achieved in many other areas.

I am confident that this was before Your Honor's eyes ten years ago when you granted yeshiva students their special status regarding conscription. This act of affection demonstrated to us all your appreciation and recognition of the remnant of Torah in Zion and its importance in our new state's life.

Now, the first decade of the state has brought the return of the exiles from various diasporas to their homeland. Hundreds of thousands of our brethren, may they increase, have returned, including many from Eastern countries, most of whom are faithful to the spirit of ancient Israel, preserving the traditions and heritage of their ancestors. However, they also brought the disheartening news that the destruction of Torah that spread in Europe did not spare these countries either, though due to different factors. By God's grace, a relative few of these immigrants have been absorbed into the yeshivas, from whom some will become pillars and cornerstones, restoring the crown of Torah to Eastern Jewry, whose great scholars illuminated the land with their Torah for centuries. If at all times our concern for the existence of yeshivas in Israel is great and intense, then how much more so in this difficult hour.

In essence, the background to this matter is much deeper and broader: the people dwelling in Zion under the skies of independence have a duty to grant yeshiva students, who are entrusted with preserving the nation's spiritual assets (and they do so with unimaginable self-sacrifice in an unbearable economic situation), exemption from any conscription obligation as long as they dwell in the tent of Torah. For they, too, are conscripted and stand for the security of the Torah of Israel and its heritage, through which we have arrived here. Both groups guard the fundamental assets of the nation, which are the Torah of Israel and the Land of Israel.

I am certain that we all firmly and unwaveringly believe that the voice of Torah emanating from the halls of Torah and the holy yeshivas is a shield against the hands of Esau and Ishmael, who plot wicked and murderous schemes against us. The closeness to God that envelops these holy places strengthens the precious defenders, and they, in turn, will plead for our peace and victory.

Therefore, I come before Your Honor with a trembling heart, yet with confidence, that Your Honor, who elevated himself to the heights of all of Israel by granting yeshiva students their special conscription status, will continue to show affection and appreciation to the sons of Torah, and no change, even the slightest, will occur in their status.

My heart is full of hope that Your Honor will understand my distressed spirit, which compelled me to write this long letter at a time of weakness and exhaustion. May the Lord's grace rest upon Your Honor to grant my request.

May the Giver of the Torah protect and guard Your Honor from all sorrow and harm, and may Your days be one hundred and twenty years of good life, all dedicated to elevating the crown of our state in holiness.

With the blessings of the Torah and the land,

and with deep appreciation,

Yitzhak Isaac Halevi Herzog

Interesting Points Emerge from Ben-Gurion's Response

Ben-Gurion's words, though assertive in tone, are neither aggressive nor confrontational. He is very careful not to attack the religious and Haredi camp, and thus he emphasizes that his statements are a proposal rather than a directive. However, he does not kowtow to Rabbi Herzog and clearly demonstrates his familiarity with halakha and the sources in general, showing that he is not an "empty cart" and is capable of arguing in the language used in the religious camp. In fact, Ben-Gurion expresses regret over the original 1948 arrangement because he has observed that the number of young men seeking to be included in the original agreement has grown significantly over the years. He argues that it is immoral to exempt them from military service while their peers risk their lives to defend the homeland. He also unequivocally rejects Rabbi Herzog's claim that spiritual sacrifice is equal in measure to that of a young soldier fighting, and he dismisses the assertion that it is thanks to Torah scholars that we are living in the days of the establishment of the state.

Response Letter from Ben-Gurion to Rabbi Herzog

Prime Minister
Jerusalem, 27 Cheshvan 5719
10 November 1958

To: The Chief Rabbi of Israel
Rabbi Yitzhak Halevi Herzog
Jerusalem—

Shalom and blessings,

I regret that I could not immediately respond to your letter from the 13th of Cheshvan 5719.

I was very sorry to hear that you are not in good health, and first of all, I want to wish you a speedy and full recovery.

Regarding the yeshiva students, the matter, I believe, is not so simple. When I exempted yeshiva students from military service ten years ago, their number was small, and as I was told then, this was the only country where there remained students learning Torah for its own sake. I am pleased to note that yeshiva students took part in the defense of Jerusalem like the other young men of Jerusalem. The situation has changed since then. The number of yeshiva students has increased. I do not know if there is any basis for the accusation that some go to yeshiva to avoid service. I want to assume that this claim is unfounded, but there is no doubt that over time the number of yeshiva students has grown, and their number has reached thousands. In foreign lands, the gentiles do not need the defenders of Israel. Here, we are all Jews, and our security depends solely on us; and this is, first of all, a great moral question: is it right that the son of one mother should die defending the homeland while the son of another mother sits safely in his room studying, while most of Israel's young men risk their lives unto death?

I do not dare to come to you with a specific law from Maimonides, that in a milchemet mitzvah (a commanded war), everyone goes out, even a bridegroom from his room and a bride from her canopy, because you, of course, are more knowledgeable in halakha than I am. However, it seems to me that in the State of Israel, "the Torah of the bow" is part of the Torah, and it is not possible that thousands of young men will be unable to handle a weapon when called upon. One cannot ignore the possibility that Jerusalem might, God forbid, be cut off and attacked by an enemy, and hundreds of young men will be unable to defend themselves, their friends, their parents, and the Holy City. The same applies to other yeshiva centers.

Therefore, I proposed (I did not command, but I proposed) that yeshiva students who dedicate their whole lives to Torah study should undergo three months of basic training, and others should serve in the army like any other young person in Israel. This proposal I presented to the Knesset members of Agudat Israel, and the Director-General of the Ministry of Defense (Shimon Peres) proposed it to several heads of yeshivas.

We must not forget that we are no longer continuing the life of the diaspora, dependent on the mercy of others, and we cannot continue to behave as a people who rely on the table of others. We stand on our own, and the burden of security rests solely on us. This is a great privilege that we have achieved after many hundreds of years, and this privilege, in my opinion, obligates every young person in Israel.

I cannot find in the Torah, or the Prophets, or the Writings, that Torah scholars were exempt from defending the homeland. We must remember that our current circumstances have changed: we have never been surrounded on all sides by enemies seeking to destroy us, and the means of warfare in our days are not the same as those in the times of the First or Second Temples. Now, it is a complex matter requiring extensive training.

I cannot agree in any way with your statement that "because of the yeshiva students we have reached this point." They did not build the land, they did not risk their lives for its independence (although some of them did), and they do not have special rights that other Jews do not have. Our Sages said: "Greater is one who benefits from the labor of his hands than one who fears Heaven." Military service does not diminish Torah study; and in independent Israel, the Torah is not complete unless it also includes the Torah of defending the people and the homeland. Without the existence of the people of Israel, there will be no Torah, and saving the nation precedes all else. Indeed, those who honor Torah scholars (and I dare say that I am among them) and wish to see them held in esteem must ensure that they do not isolate themselves from the community and do not exempt themselves from the most sacred duty — the duty to defend their parents, relatives, community, and nation.

I ask you to influence the heads of the yeshivas to demand, at the very least, that all yeshiva students undergo three months of basic training.

Again, I wish you all the best and a full recovery.

With respect and friendship,

David Ben-Gurion

As is known, the Haredi camp rejected Ben-Gurion's proposal as well as many other proposals over the years regarding changing the existing arrangement. Since then and until today, the governments of Israel have been negotiating with the Haredi parties to find a solution to the problem of the growing number of Haredi young men not enlisting and to their successful integration into Israeli society.

[This chapter is an English translation of Mirit Dinur, "From the Archive: Correspondence between Rabbi Yitzhak Isaac Halevi Herzog and David Ben-Gurion on the Question of Inducting Yeshiva Students to the IDF in Israel's First Decade," *Israelim*, vol. 4 (2012): 157-165 (Hebrew).]

Dr. Mirit Bat-Horin is a historian specializing in Israeli society, pioneering movements, and national service. She earned her PhD from Ben-Gurion University of the Negev, where her dissertation, *'We Didn't Come to Kiryat Shmona with a Help Flag in our Hands': Changes in Manifestation and Pioneering, The Shelef Project as a Case Study, 1976-1985*, examined the evolution of pioneering ideology and settlement initiatives in late 20th-century Israel. Her research explores the role of Zionist activism and grassroots initiatives in shaping Israeli society.

The Halakhic Definition of the Wars of the State of Israel in the Teachings of Rabbi Yitzhak Isaac Halevi Herzog

Neria Guttel

I. Since When Are the Modern Day Wars of Israel Categorized As Commanded Wars?

The halakhic determination that the wars of Israel in the modern era, from the establishment of the state and slightly before, are defined as 'commanded wars,' along with the resulting halakhic implications, is a widespread and recurring consensus in writings on the laws of military and warfare. This consensus is a central theme that runs through the teachings of many great and distinguished scholars, to the extent that it is rarely debated but rather explained and relied upon. This determination carries numerous and significant halakhic ramifications, and there is indeed a substantial difference between the determination that the laws of war are merely an extension and development of the laws of saving an individual or the community, and the determination that the basis of the laws of war lies in a completely different category of laws: the laws of war in general, and commanded war in particular. For instance, the question of the permissibility of violating Shabbat for preemptive defensive activities may lie at the intersection of these two approaches; similarly, the question of the permissibility of compulsory drafting of civilians for combat; the question of the permissibility, and perhaps obligation, of entering into danger for the success of a military mission; the extent of women's integration in combat processes, if at all; the question of the permissibility of cutting down fruit trees for military needs, and more.

The understanding that the wars of the State of Israel have the unique halakhic status of commanded wars is so simple and clear today, that the novelty inherent in this statement goes almost unnoticed. Moreover, many have not been exposed to the fascinating, fundamental, and important struggle that accompanied the stages of the formation of this determination. Examining the foundational elements of the issue reveals that the development of this determination was neither simple nor clear, and certainly not universally agreed upon. On the contrary, at its inception, it was subject to debate, disagreement, and controversy among some of the greatest scholars of Israel. The goal of this article is not only to expose and elucidate this confrontation but, first and foremost, to 'restore matters to their former glory'. Our interest here is to highlight the role of Rabbi Yitzhak Isaac Halevi Herzog, as the most significant, central, and decisive figure in establishing the position that all subsequent scholars rely upon, even if the 'source' of this universal contention has often been forgotten, and the appropriate attribution to the original author – lacking, thereby failing to 'bring redemption to the world'.

"Each generation and its interpreters." Rabbi Herzog was providentially chosen to stand at the foundations of the halakhic decisions needed during that critical time of the establishment of the state. This period was, of course, a complex and intricate halakhic crossroads. Two thousand years of exile had severed the nation from its state and the people from their sovereignty, with all the implications thereof. There were no halakhot for the Ministry of Defense or the Ministry of Health, nor for the Ministry of Welfare or the Ministry of Finance, not for Agriculture, nor for the Police, and so on. At this juncture, two principal approaches confronted one another:

1. The first approach can be summarized – in a nutshell – as follows: The existing halakhic literature, whether originating from the diaspora or from the early Eretz Yisrael period, is deemed insufficient to address the complexities of a modern state. On the one hand, biblical literature was partly composed during a time when the Jewish people were sovereign in their land, however Biblical literature alone cannot serve as a source of halakhic decisions. Moral guidance, and values, can surely be inferred from there, however, codified laws, judicial rulings etc. – these cannot. On the other hand, the codified formulations developed over two millennia of exile, from the Tannaim and Amoraim to the Geonim, Rishonim, and Acharonim—most notably Maimonides' Mishneh Torah and Rabbi Yosef Karo's Shulchan Aruch—are articulated in clear halakhic language but were designed for contexts vastly different from those of a modern state. As such, they do not adequately address the unique challenges posed by a sovereign state in the modern era. According to this approach, it is necessary to set aside the aforementioned literatures and develop a "new Torah" that is specifically tailored to the structure and challenges of the modern state and its implications for halakhah.

2. The second approach can be similarly summarized as follows: The principle of dimuy milta lemilta (deriving one matter from another) both permits and necessitates addressing and resolving the issues of the modern state. While the task is neither simple nor straightforward—being inherently complex and intricate,

and "not every mind can grasp it"[1]—there is a fundamental, faith-based conviction that since "this – the Torah of Moses – will never be abolished," therefore a solution will inevitably be found through proper and diligent effort.[2] It is important to note that this approach received broad support and encouragement from the rabbinic school, with Rabbi Herzog himself strongly endorsing this perspective and appreciating the clarity with which it was articulated.[3]

However, it is clear that one must identify and articulate the Talmudic source that serves as the basis for analogizing to the current matter. This principle holds true generally, and particularly in our context, when addressing war-related issues such as the defense of the inhabitants of the Land of Israel, whether before or after the establishment of the state. Similarly, in matters of conquering the Land of Israel, establishing its borders, or even expanding its territory, it is essential to pinpoint the Talmudic source that will serve as the foundation for resolving the issue. Accordingly, one approach involves adhering to well-established halakhot that have been applied for hundreds, if not thousands, of years: the laws of pikuach nefesh (saving a life) in its broadest applications,

---

1 Maimonides, *Commentary on the Mishnah, Introduction to Chapter Helek*, ed. Rabbi Yosef Kapach (Jerusalem: Mosad ha-Rav Kook, 1976), 144: "That this, the Torah of Moses, will not be annulled, and no other Torah will come from the Lord besides it, and nothing will be added to it or subtracted from it, neither in writing nor in interpretation." Also see Laws of Kings 11:6 in the uncensored editions. For questions regarding the text and its comparison with the Yigdal piyyut and with Maimonides' Thirteen Principles of Faith, see Rabbi Avraham Yitzhak Neria, *The Thirteen Principles: Explanations and Sources* (Kfar Haroeh 1992), 27-28.

2 A reflection of this perspective is articulated in Rabbi Moshe Zvi Neria, "Kuntress ha-Vikuah," in *Tzenif Melucha* (Kfar Haroeh: Khai Ro'i, 1992), 299-324.

3 For Rabbi Herzog's support of Rabbi Neria, see *Ma'asuah le-Yitzhak*, vol. 1, eds. Shulamit Eliash, Itamar Warhaftig, and Uri Desberg (Jerusalem: Yad ha-Rav Herzog, 2008), 434-435n1.

including saving an individual, the community, and the public;[4] the principle of "do not stand idly by your neighbor's blood"; the law of the rodef (pursuer) seeking to kill you or harm your fellow; and the principle of "and you shall live by them, not die by them," among others. This approach represents a policy of halakhic continuity. On the other hand, one could adhere to the laws of war, despite their being less well-known and less defined, as they have rarely been applied in practice and have mainly been discussed in abstract and academic terms. In this case, a complex task of defining, applying, and ultimately deciding and ruling on these matters becomes necessary. This approach represents a policy of innovative and creative halakhic decision-making. Naturally, the events of the War of Independence and the preceding military engagements brought these issues into sharp focus. Understandably, the Chief Rabbi of the Land of Israel was called upon to express his opinion regarding these critical matters.

Before we delve into Rabbi Herzog's responses on the matter, one last brief clarification is necessary: What constitutes a commanded war (milhemet mitzvah)? What criteria define a military action by the people of Israel as a commanded war, with all the halakhic implications that follow? From the words of Maimonides in Hilkhot Melachim uMilchamoteihem 5:1,[5] we learn that a commanded war is defined as "a war against the seven nations, a war against Amalek, and a war to assist Israel against an enemy attacking them." Two of these categories

---

4   These two matters are not identical, as many Rishonim emphasized that the principles of pikuach nefesh on a communal level are fundamentally different from, and both halakhically and practically distinct from, the principles of pikuach nefesh for an individual. See Neria Guttel, "The Halakhic Weight of the Psychological Dimension in War," *Sinai*, no. 138 (2006): 98-110.

5   For additional views by Rashi, Sefer HaHinnukh, Ra'abad, and others, see the summaries by Rabbi Shemaryahu Arieli, *Mishpat HaMilhamah* (Jerusalem: Rubin Mass, 1971), 12-13, and by Rabbi Yitzchak Kaufman, *ha-Tsava ka-Halakhah* (Jerusalem: Kol Mevaser, 1992), 1-12.

are particularly relevant to our context: the conquest of the land and the defense of Israel from its enemies.

Therefore, we shall follow the trajectory of Rabbi Herzog's halakhic responses on these matters and seek to understand the foundation he established—both for himself and for those who came after him—regarding the wars of the modern State of Israel and the halakhot that arise from them.

II. Establishing a Security Fence on Shabbat

"During the War of Independence in 1948, there was a proposal to erect a security fence around the Kiryat Shmuel neighborhood in Tiberias due to the fear of an impending Arab attack. The question arose as to whether it was permissible to continue construction on Shabbat". This is the title of a responsum that faithfully represents these two prevailing approaches: that of Rabbi Werner, the chief rabbi of Tiberias at the time, and that of Rabbi Herzog, the Chief Rabbi of the Land of Israel. Both approaches are elucidated in the course of Rabbi Herzog's halakhic response.[6]

Rabbi Werner sought to draw an analogy between the matter at hand and the law concerning the dissemination of warnings about a plague. He argued that while it is permissible to disseminate such warnings across the entirety of the Land of Israel, "which is like one province," this does not permit the desecration of Shabbat in a city where the plague has not yet spread. Rabbi Herzog responded to this restrictive interpretation by arguing that even within Rabbi Werner's framework, the decision is more nuanced. Rabbi Herzog stated, "I maintain that it depends on the expert doctors; if they say that there is a risk of the plague spreading and that the population needs to be vaccinated—even if this involves an act prohibited by Torah law—if it was not done before Shabbat, it

---

6   *Pesakim u-Ketavim*, vol. 1 (Jerusalem: Yad ha-Rav Herzog, 1989), Responsa on Orach Chaim, sec. 5 [reprinted from *Responsa Heikhal Yitzhak* (Jerusalem: Yad ha-Rav Herzog, 1972), Orach Chaim, sec. 31.

is permitted on Shabbat... In our situation, certainly, an enemy attack is considered a common danger.

Furthermore, Rabbi Werner argued that since no attack had yet occurred in Tiberias, the situation did not currently meet the criteria for pikuach nefesh (saving a life). He based his reasoning on Maimonides' language, which suggests that the desecration of Shabbat is permitted only after the gentiles "lay siege to Israel," but not before such a siege begins. Consequently, Rabbi Werner concluded that in this case, it would not be permissible to violate Shabbat. Rabbi Herzog, however, rejected this argument. He pointed out that while the language of the Sages refers to "laying siege," this is not the terminology used by the Rishonim (early commentators) or in the Shulchan Aruch (Orach Chaim 329:6), which states, "even if the gentiles have not yet come but intend to come, Shabbat is desecrated." Rabbi Herzog emphasized that "it is clear that the law applies even if they merely intend to come, for in matters of pikuach nefesh, even preparatory actions override Shabbat." In response to Rabbi Werner's concern that this reasoning could lead to permitting the construction of defensive walls in all cities across Israel "lest the gentiles come," Rabbi Herzog replied that the decision in such matters should be a carefully considered military judgment, analogous to a well-balanced medical decision. He asserted that "the decision depends on the experts' estimation.[7] If the experts in your area, based on information from those specialized in assessing the intentions of the gentiles, estimate that an attack is likely, who can take responsibility and oppose their judgment? This is the legal ruling you must follow."

---

7   This is also the reason Rabbi Herzog outright rejects rabbis raising doubts about the benefit of erecting a barbed wire fence, as well as rabbinic skepticism regarding the likelihood of an attack on the neighborhood: "Regarding the actual benefit of barbed wire fences and the reasoning that the first attack might be on the Old City, we rabbis are not experts in making such decisions, as this is a matter of strategy. (There is also a contrary reasoning, that they might specifically, God forbid, attack Kiryat Shmuel, which is more important economically, and furthermore, it is an entirely Jewish city.)"

Rabbi Herzog further informed Rabbi Werner that "here in Jerusalem, we permitted the production of armored vehicles on Shabbat, based on the military command's assessment that, according to the intelligence received, an attack on Jerusalem was imminent, either on Shabbat or immediately thereafter, and there was not sufficient time to complete the work before Shabbat."

However, it is essential to ensure that all possible measures are taken to prepare adequately during the weekdays. Rabbi Herzog emphasizes the importance of this preparation, stating, "It is necessary to add workers as much as possible and arrange for them to work in shifts during the weekdays, day and night, even though it will cost a lot of money, for Shabbat is not overridden for financial loss." And only when the desecration of Shabbat is absolutely necessary is it be permitted: "There is no wisdom, understanding, or counsel against the Lord, and it is necessary to permit it." Additionally, Rabbi Herzog advises that "to the extent possible, all work should be done by two people jointly," as this approach minimizes the extent of Shabbat desecration.

All of this was articulated by Rabbi Herzog in response to Rabbi Werner's approach and arguments. However, Rabbi Herzog concludes his response with a decisive statement that fundamentally distinguishes his own perspective:

> "I must note that I spoke only from the perspective of pikuach nefesh, but in my opinion, this struggle of ours has the status of a commanded war (milhemet mitzvah). Since the UN granted us part of the Land of Israel, if we do not defend it properly, we will lose this opportunity, Heaven forbid, and we will no longer have a secure refuge for our brethren in the diaspora in case of distress, God forbid. Our recent history suffices as evidence, as is self-evident. Also, if we lose this opportunity, it will lead, Heaven forbid, to despair among masses of Israel and, in the long run, to the nullification of our holy religion among most of the nation and to assimilation. This should suffice one wise as you. And in a commanded

war, it is permitted to begin the siege on gentile cities on Shabbat, and certainly to engage in defensive actions."

In other words, once the situation is redefined from pikuach nefesh to that of a commanded war, the entire halakhic framework shifts. Under these circumstances, it becomes permissible to besiege gentile cities on Shabbat, and certainly to engage in defensive actions on Shabbat. Thus, according to Rabbi Herzog's approach, the previous discussion about whether it is permissible to fortify the neighborhood on Shabbat becomes unnecessary, as it is clear that there is no prohibition against such actions. For our purposes, it is evident that, at that time, defining the situation as a commanded war was not universally accepted, and Rabbi Herzog had to innovate and present a compelling argument to establish this position against Rabbi Werner's more conservative interpretation.

III. Defensive and Offensive Activities on Shabbat

Similarly, Rabbi Herzog had to establish his approach in contrast to that of Rabbi Meshullam Roth. A few months before the declaration of the State (late Adar II 1948), Rabbi Herzog was approached by Mr. Tuvia Bir, a representative of the Ezra youth movement, with a series of halakhic questions. These questions included: "Is it permitted on Shabbat to volunteer for certain defense activities, or even required to do so? Similarly, regarding offensive actions taken for defense purposes; likewise, regarding purely offensive actions; is it permissible to go out on Shabbat for patrol activities within or around the city by car? Is it permissible to keep a diary on Shabbat, documenting enemy movements observed from a lookout post, as a basis for superior surveillance of personnel or weapons? Is it permitted to stop and inspect cars on Shabbat at checkpoints using flashlights that are turned on and off? Is it permissible to forcibly conscript people?" Rabbi Herzog's response to these questions, along with a copy he sent for Rabbi Meshullam Roth's review, sparked a fascinating discussion between the two, touching on both the substance of the halakhic rulings and, more importantly, the definition of the broader situation. Within less than ten days, an engaging and rapid exchange of correspondence took place between them on this subject, in which the aforementioned approaches—previously articulated in the context of Rabbi Herzog's debate with Rabbi Werner—were once again explored and revealed.

Rabbi Herzog clarified to the members of the Ezra movement[8] that first and foremost, one must generally obey the professional authority, namely the military authorities. Our case, the Israel Defense Forces, is not like the old case of a Jewish soldier in a foreign army. There, in the foreign army, it was better for the Jew to try to avoid it, and let someone else, a non-Jew, do the work on Shabbat. Not so "in a Hebrew army, which is entirely Jewish, where the permit to desecrate Shabbat is for the sake of defending Israel, hence there is no room for this question."

At this point, Rabbi Herzog himself highlights the possibility of the existence of the two principal approaches concerning the current situation's definition, while he unambiguously sides throughout the response – with the 'commanded war' approach.

> "If the permission is based solely on the principle of saving Israel, meaning pikuach nefesh for the many, it has already been ruled… that these matters are not performed by minors and women, etc., but by the great ones of Israel and their sages… And if the permission is based on a broader context, meaning that this is Israel's war in its land, a commanded or obligatory war, then there is certainly no room for this question."

From reading this paragraph alone, one might understand that Rabbi Herzog's position is somewhat uncertain, and he himself is not entirely decided on defining the situation as a mandatory war. This is also seemingly implied by the continuation of his response:

---

8   *Pesakim u-Ketavim*, Ibid., sec. 48, includes significant additions and expansions on the parallel published in *Responsa Heikhal Yitzhak*, Ibid., sec. 37. Regarding the response itself, see *Ma'asuah le-Yitzhak*, supra note 3, pp. 452 ff.

> "Although offensive actions for defense are not directly a matter of pikuach nefesh, and if the permission is based solely on the principle of pikuach nefesh, it is not so clear; however, since the expert calculated and found that through this offensive action a nearby Jewish settlement would be saved, this is a form of pikuach nefesh or saving Israel from an enemy attacking it (after all, we did not start the war, but they came upon us, and all our actions are essentially for defense)… And all the more so, when viewing this struggle from a broader perspective, that it is a commanded or obligatory war for the entire people of Israel."

And furthermore:

> "… Purely offensive actions depend on the basis of the permit, whether within the framework of saving lives or within the broader framework of Israel's war, as above. If it is within the latter framework, then one is allowed to besiege non-Jewish towns three days before Shabbat, and wage war with them every day even on Shabbat, even in a discretionary war, and all the more so in a commanded war, for in an obligatory war one is allowed to lay siege to such towns on Shabbat."

But if this is not so; the following passage leaves no room for doubt regarding his own position.

> "In my opinion, this struggle is an obligatory war, as I have explained, and although a commanded war must be declared by a king, and we have no king, the entire public, or most of it, as already explained by my predecessor, the Gaon of blessed memory in Responsa Mishpat Kohen, has the authority of the King of Israel, and this conscription was declared by the vast majority of the Yishuv in the Land of Israel, which is considered like the entire congregation of Israel… And even those

who disagree with this assumption, and think that this is not Israel's war, but a struggle to save Israel in terms of saving many lives, they must admit that any attack that truly weakens the enemy's power ultimately saves Israel. And if you say that 'reducing the number of non-Jews so they do not come upon us' is only a discretionary war, – when would this be the case, when the non-Jews are presently sitting calmly, and we go to war against them to diminish and weaken them lest they come upon us sometime in the future, – but when they have already come upon us to destroy and expel us from our holy inheritance, then all actions aimed against them are part of an obligatory war."

It is therefore clearly evident that Rabbi Herzog's own opinion is firm and resolute: we are dealing with a commanded war, and therefore the laws of a commanded war should apply.[9] One must conclude that the style of the previous paragraphs, which sought to determine the law even according to the different approach, was only to provide an answer also according to their perspective, and their method. As if to say: My own opinion is clear – this is a commanded war, with all that it entails. However, even according to your approach, scholars who do not believe

---

9 However, he seeks, as much as possible, to limit and minimize the desecration of Shabbat: "Religious Jews must demand from the command that, in any case where it decides to carry out an attack to weaken the enemy, and also for defense, it must carefully calculate in advance if this attack can be carried out before Shabbat, or if it can be postponed until after Shabbat. They must not schedule it specifically for the holy day of Shabbat. The same applies even to fortification activities and similar defensive measures. But if the order is given on Shabbat, and it is assumed that time is pressing and it is impossible not to comply, as non-compliance would undermine military discipline and jeopardize the entire struggle, they must comply. It is understood that the demand does not concern what happens after the fact but to insist with all vigor that if it is possible before Shabbat or can be postponed until after Shabbat, the command is forbidden to schedule it on Shabbat."

as I do that we are dealing with a commanded war, but rather with pikuach nefesh for the many, you too, in this case should agree that it is still appropriate to decide the matter in this manner.

In a passage – that was for some reason omitted at the time from Responsa Heikhal Yitzhak, and which was recently published in its right place – Rabbi Herzog adds, strengthens, and emphasizes his approach:

> "… Any war for the conquest of the land when given the opportunity is an obligatory war, and the opportunity was given (and although now there is a withdrawal from the United States, a disgraceful retreat, nevertheless the matter is still pending and standing). May the Rock of Israel counsel us with good advice before Him, but laxity now will surely cause us to fail completely, and we must continue, until God willing we reach a decision with good advice before Him, blessed be He.
>
> … I return to the matter of the question. As I said, if this were only a discretionary war to expand Israel's borders, there would be room to argue that one only goes out to a discretionary war according to a court of seventy-one, and today we do not have a court of seventy-one, but in my opinion, this is a commanded war, and the power of the large and decisive majority of the Yishuv is like the power of a king in Israel, see Mishpat Cohen Siman 144 (15a), and there is no need for a court of seventy-one, and thus we have the power to compel conscription, but the matter still needs clarification. But if my opinion is not accepted, even if we judge this only from the narrow perspective of saving Israel in terms of saving many lives, there is still room to argue that for such a commandment of saving the entire settlement, we coerce… But there is still no absolute decision, and therefore I refrain from deciding either positively or negatively and it still requires much study…"

It seems that this complex style well illustrates how, at that time, the matters were still unresolved and certainly not simple. This conclusion about the complexity of the matter, is not only an indirect conclusion borne out by implication from Rabbi Hezog's writing style, but it is also explicit in the responsa themselves. As mentioned, before us is the correspondence between Rabbi Herzog and Rabbi Meshullam Roth regarding the question discussed above, and their discussion clearly speaks for itself.

Rabbi Roth decisively states[10] that a permit can only be given "if it is clear that the offensive action is needed now for defense and rescue from danger." Rabbi Roth explicitly clarifies that this determination does not express only a specific, pin-pointed, disagreement but rather it is an expression of a fundamental disagreement in definition, at the very least it expresses Rabbi Roth's skepticism towards Rabbi Herzog's approach.

"Regarding the question… you have written that in an obligatory war, one initially besieges towns of non-Jews on Shabbat, and in your opinion, this struggle has the status of a commanded war, and although such a war must be declared by the king, the entire public or its majority has the authority of the King of Israel, and so forth in his response… he discusses that since it is for the conquest of the land, it is an obligatory war. This matter needs much deliberation, because Nahmanides considers the commandment to be in force for generations – to conquer the land to inherit it and to settle and establish oneself in it as owners, like in the days of Joshua. However, if now we conquer an Arab village in the Arab state, or the international area (around Jerusalem), as per the latest UN plan, which is our maximal hope and demand for now, and even if we are fortunate that the UN cancels the withdrawal and enforces the partition decision, we would still be obligated after the conquest to leave and hand over the place to others".

Moreover, even Rabbi Herzog's claim that everyone must admit, at the very least, that an attack weakens the enemy's power, and therefore it should be seen as "saving Israel", is not accepted by Rabbi Roth's view,

---

10 Rabbi Meshullam Roth, *Responsa Kol Mevaser*, vol. 1, sec. 47.

and he sees such a situation of offensive warfare as a "discretionary war." Rabbi Roth is also not prepared to accept Rabbi Herzog's permission for forced conscription – "I was very astonished… where do we find that one is forced to endanger his life for a commandment… to put oneself in danger to save his friend, we have not heard… and indeed it is very difficult, that the court would need to deal with such a question to judge actual life-and-death matters and to take upon itself the responsibility of coercion by force for conscription… and it is not clear at least that this is an obligatory war, and if so, a court of seventy-one is needed, and in cases of doubt regarding lives, one should be lenient. Certainly, if there are volunteers it is better, but not to force them according to the court's ruling." At the very most "so as not to weaken their hands" it is possible to coerce conscription for logistic positions, or for guard duty, – "but not to force by power full conscription to fight on the frontlines." As we have said earlier: Rabbi Roth did not adopt Rabbi Herzog's approach in defining the fighting as a commanded war, and as a result, he significantly limited Rabbi Herzog's practical rulings.

Rabbi Herzog did not agree with Rabbi Roth's approach and a few days later he reinforces his perspective and its implications.[11] He reemphasizes his reliance on Rabbi Kook's response "that the majority of the public is like a king… and for saving the entire or majority of the people of Israel… everyone is obliged to put themselves in danger", and a court is authorized, and even required, to enforce this commandment. He repeats – and emphasizes that his rulings are valid even for those who do not define the situation as an "obligatory war" but only as "saving many lives", but ultimately, he clearly repeats and clarifies his own approach: "In my opinion, saving the settlement in the current situation and within this historical context, is not just saving the settlement but saving the entire people of Israel and also all of Judaism. And how can there be any doubt in my eyes that one must take risks for this."

---

11 *Pesakim u-Ketavim*, Ibid., sec. 50; this responsum was not published at the time in *Heikhal Yitzhak*.

Rabbi Herzog was not satisfied with this, and sent an additional response to Rabbi Roth,[12] in which he responds in detail, point by point, to his objections. On the one hand, he substantiates the rulings he established even according to the school of thought that does not consider this a commanded war, and on the other hand, he reiterates his position that this is indeed certainly such a war: "… I stated my opinion, that this is an obligatory war for several reasons, but even for those who think that this is merely a matter of saving Israel in the sense of saving many lives…." He reemphasizes "that I rely on my predecessor, the pious and wise Gaon, in Responsa Mishpat Cohen, but I abbreviated, and even this conclusion is based on his words there… and there are two conclusions there… and there is no doubt that the truth is with the great priest among his brothers, Rabbi Avraham Yitzchak Kook, of blessed memory… and so the opinion of the Torah definitely leans", and finally his position: "This is a matter of war for all of Israel."

As for Rabbi Roth's claim that "since we cannot settle in the Arab part, etc., there is no matter of conquering the land, etc., and it is not a commanded war," this claim is decisively rejected by Rabbi Herzog, both via a return to the Halakhic foundation, and no less based on a factual, realistic description, "as I clearly know":

> "The main basis of my opinion is that this is generally a matter of aiding Israel from the enemy that comes upon them and as explained by Maimonides [Kings, Chapter 5, Law 1], this is an obligatory war, and I only used the Nahmanides as a branch. But regarding Jerusalem, this is about saving Israel from the danger of death and famine alike, as they are not allowing any food into Jerusalem, and it should be judged that those defending the Holy City, may it be rebuilt and reestablished, are fulfilling the commandment of conquest, and even if this area will not be entirely ours, nevertheless we will have great strength there since we are the majority.

---

12   *Pesakim u-Ketavim*, Ibid., sec. 49; *Responsa Heikhal Yitzhak*, Ibid., sec. 39.

And the enemies' objective, as I clearly know, is to force those who remain after they, God forbid, commit mass murder, to flee from Jerusalem. And the conquest of the Castel, etc., is to thwart their murderous plan to uproot us from here. And to fight so that there will be a settlement in the Holy City, the ultimate goal is that we remain settled there, and this is a commandment like initial conquest (and this also ensures the very existence of all of Judaism – and 'a hint to the wise is sufficient'). But here we are discussing the matter from the point of view of conquest, and I say that this is in general a matter of conquest, that is, to maintain the settlement. And especially in Zion, the house of our life, etc. And as for the conquest of Arab villages in the Arab area, if the objective is not for complete conquest, but because by doing so we weaken the enemy's forces, this itself is part of the conquest of Jerusalem, so that we can at least hold onto the part that will ultimately be ours, God willing. And in this, we must rely on the experts among those who understand warfare in its entirety."

Regarding defensive combat that pre-empts the enemy's attack, Rabbi Herzog believes that the Halakhah does not require "to limit ourselves specifically to defense, but rather any action that, according to the commanders, ultimately weakens the enemy who has already come upon us, is a continuation of an obligatory war...."

IV. Volunteering for Military Activity

Rabbi Herzog repeated these principles in another responsum,[13] answering the question "Is it permitted or obligatory to volunteer for defense activities?" First of all, Rabbi Herzog responds with surprise to the question itself: "This question I almost do not understand. In the

---

13   *Pesakim u-Ketavim*, Ibid., sec. 52.

current situation, if we did not volunteer for defense activities, isn't there, God forbid, a risk of total annihilation facing all of us, and surely we are obligated, for what choice do we have, to surrender to the enemies? If, God forbid, we surrender and are conquered under their hand, it is clear that ultimately – they will destroy us, God forbid... And there is no greater danger than this... Not to mention the desecration of God's name that would be caused by this in the eyes of the entire world... And besides, this also concerns the survival of Judaism among thousands of thousands of Israelites all over the world, after the terrible Holocaust, when all the hopes of Israel are tied to the revival of Israel in its holy land, for if the masses of Israel completely despair, the entire religion will collapse, and a hint to the wise is sufficient." As for the substance of the Halakhic definition, as mentioned, his decision is clear: "In my opinion, this is a commanded war, since the United Nations decided to return to us at least part of the land of Israel to establish an independent government, this is a war of conquest of the land", according to both Nahmanides – and even! – Maimonides.[14] And once again: "There is no doubt in my mind that this is a commanded war for the conquest of the land, aside from the reasoning of 'aiding Israel from the enemy'..."[15]

14 "...according to Maimonides... although he states (Hilkhot Melachim 5:1) that a commanded war is the war against the seven nations, his intention is clear, for his rulings are given for practical application, why, then, does he give this example of the aforementioned type of war, as these nations no longer exist? Rather, he was hesitant to explicitly define the war of conquering the land, for an understandable reason, and therefore he gave a hint, and his intention is to conquer the land when we have the opportunity to do so."

15 Regarding the need for a king, and in continuation of relying on Rabbi Kook's teachings on the matter, Rabbi Herzog defines that "although we do not have a king, the majority of the settlement combined with the institutions, the Chief Rabbinate, etc., have the status of a king..." See also *Pesakim u-Ketavim*, Ibid., sec. 115, which will be mentioned below: "...the settlement, especially when combined with the majority of Jews abroad, holds the power equivalent to that of a king..."

"... In conclusion, my opinion is that this war against the Arabs who seek to negate our right, and indirectly against Britain who is failing in her role, is an obligatory war from four aspects: A) From the perspective of saving Israel... B) On account of the commandment of conquering the land of Israel when we are given the opportunity. C) So that Israel does not fall into despair... D) ... A refuge for every trouble that should not come... Since this is the case, our struggle has the status of an actual obligatory war, and in an obligatory war, the law is to besiege the cities of the non-Jews even initially on Shabbat... This is the process of every war, even a defensive war, to launch an attack for the sake of defense...

This definition is translated by Rabbi Herzog into a series of practical rulings:

"Is it permitted or obligatory to volunteer for activities, and which ones?... Even if we do not judge this struggle as a commanded war... I wonder how the question of whether it is permitted can arise. Not only is it permitted for us, but we are obligated. But as to the matter itself, I have already expressed my opinion that this is an obligatory war, and for a commanded war, one even takes out a groom from his chamber and a bride from her canopy...

Bal Tashchit... I have explained above that our struggle is a type of obligatory war... therefore, it is obvious that it is permitted to destroy...

Hiding weapons in the ground... Driving a car before and after the attack... In my opinion that this is an obligatory war, it is permitted, even without turning to the principle of defense for saving Israeli lives....

> Using the telephone on Shabbat... According to my definition that this is an obligatory war, all this is part of the act of war, and when a war was permitted on Shabbat, not only the actual combat was permitted, but everything that is vitally necessary for the war...
>
> And you asked if it is permitted to place girls in the kitchens of the army bases to prepare meals... You have seen from the words of the Radbaz, who is strict, that this is permitted in a commanded war, and the same applies to a struggle for saving Israel...."

And so too in other responses, even those where this issue is only indirectly related, Rabbi Herzog repeatedly returns to the same definition. For example, in his discussion "regarding the oath for the military", he writes as an obvious fact that "... given the current situation, when we are forced to fight, this is indeed an obligatory war, of saving Israel...." [16] Again, in his discussion "on the establishment of the state before the coming of the Messiah," [17] Rabbi Herzog writes that:

> "... This is not a discretionary war but an obligatory war and obligation... the commandment of conquering the land which is a commandment from the Torah according to the opinion of Nahmanides, and it is an obligatory war... and know that we are not discussing this from the perspective of the law of saving lives, which obligates everyone to save Israeli lives, for if so, a situation might arise where enemies come upon us and announce that if we surrender under them they will not harm us, and if because of saving lives there is no longer an issue, but when they come upon us in the land of Israel, and we already have the right to establish our own state, this is an obligatory war... This is an obligatory war, and we

---

16 *Pesakim u-Ketavim*, Ibid., sec. 51.

17 *Pesakim u-Ketavim*, Ibid., sec. 115, and Ibid., pp. 518.

must enter a risk of lives to prevent certain destruction…
It seems to me that we have a basis to conclude that this
is an obligatory war, and that the Yishuv, and even more
so in combination with the majority of Israel abroad,
have the authority like a king to enforce conscription…"

And once again, in an additional article and in a different context: "In conclusion, in my opinion, this is undoubtedly an obligatory war and obligation… It is clear to me that the war of conquering the land and war against the non-Jews who come upon us, are wars of commandment which are obligatory."[18]

V. Halakhic Guidance for the Members of Kfar Etzion

At the same time, it appears that even Rabbi Herzog himself experienced a development in defining the situation and the practical halakhic implications derived from it. In January 1948, members of Kfar Etzion sent a letter to the Chief Rabbinate, requesting Halakhic guidance on a wide range of questions:[19] "How to behave in unloading the cargo from the vehicles? Is it permitted for us to return fuel barrels, and various packaging vessels, in the vehicles…? Is it permitted for us to distribute on Shabbat the letters that were brought by Jews on Shabbat…? Is it permitted for the members of the secretariat to open and handle on Shabbat the frequent letters sent from our members in the city…? How to behave in case there is an urgent need to respond to such a letter on Shabbat? … Is it permitted to transfer our mail by Jews

18 See *Ma'asuah le-Yitzhak*, vol. 1 (Jerusalem: Yad ha-Rav Herzog, 2008), 240, 243, 250, 261-262, 271-272; and Yitzchak Roness, "The Wars of Israel: Halakhah and Ideology in the Teachings of Rabbi Isaac Herzog," Ibid., 451-473.

19 For a comprehensive review of the security situation in Gush Etzion at that time and clarification of the background to the questions, see the letter from the group's secretary, Mr. Dov Knohl, in *Pesakim u-Ketavim*, Ibid., pp. 204-206.

on Shabbat…? Sometimes there is an opportunity to transfer our mail by non-Jews, what is the law in this case, if it happens on Shabbat…? What is the law for clothes – and objects that our wives and children left here and they frequently request to transfer them due to their scarcity… It was decided to prepare a place for aircraft landing when necessary. The people who worked with tractors in preparing the area came on Friday and said that they need another two to three days to finish the work, and asked for permission to work also on Shabbat…" and more.

Rabbi Herzog, of course, responded to their request, and replied thoroughly to each and every question.[20] However, examining the responses reveals that everything is based on the principle of saving lives and the Halakhic implications derived from it, and not at all on the definition of the fighting as an obligatory war: "In the current situation, aren't the cargoes a matter of saving lives… therefore it is permitted; … returning fuel barrels and various packaging is only a matter of muktzah or weekday activities… but returning them to the city is also a matter of saving lives… therefore the answer is permitted; … the letters reached you by Jews who performed a Torah-prohibited labor to bring them, and nevertheless there is no prohibition, as the very labor was permitted due to saving lives…; permitted, due to a doubt of saving lives… if the clothes and the like are necessary for the health protection of the women and children, such as winter clothes and they are in cold dwellings… in houses where it is impossible to warm them up, it is possible to permit…", and so on, as mentioned without relying at all upon the definition of the situation as an obligatory war, and the Halakhic implications derived from that. Therefore, it is not surprising that unlike Rabbi Roth's critical response to the above-discussed responsa, by contrast, in his response to this current one,[21] Rabbi Roth does not see fit to challenge its principles, and is satisfied with a brief discussion of various details.

It is clear that compared to the previous responses, we would expect that even if Rabbi Herzog wanted to rule in this Halakhah in a way that

---

20 *Pesakim u-Ketavim*, Ibid., sec. 46; see also *Responsa Heikhal Yitzhak*, sec. 34.

21 See Rabbi Meshullam Roth, *Responsa Kol Mevaser*, Ibid., no. 45.

would be agreed upon by everyone, including the school of thought that follows the path of saving lives and not the path of an obligatory war, he himself would still need to express his own opinion that we are dealing with an obligatory war. First of all, this was his consistent approach in the aforementioned responsa; secondly, various Halakhic implications arise from this definition, as described above! One must say that even Rabbi Herzog himself experienced a ripening and development in his views. In this relatively early response, he was still following the 'continuing path', the one based on the approach of saving lives. However, from one point to another, while his contemporaries such as Rabbi Werner and Rabbi Roth remained 'on their post' clinging to their earlier understanding and definition, Rabbi Herzog himself experienced a significant shift, leading to a sharp and clear conclusion: This is an obligatory war.

VI. Copyright Belongs to Rabbi Herzog

From then until today, this understanding that the wars of Israel in the modern era should be defined as 'commanded wars,' with all its halakhic implications, has long become a foundational principle. Rabbi Herzog's teachings on this matter have become so widely accepted that they are now regarded as basic consensus. It is worthy to bring this recognition to the world, and to restore to Rabbi Herzog his rightful honor. It is worthy that all should know that this perception was, at the time, a matter of intense debate among the great sages of Israel, and it is Rabbi Herzog who holds the 'intellectual copyright' over this crucial halakhic innovation.

Rabbi Prof. Neria Guttel, a distinguished Israeli rabbi and scholar, serves as the head of the research department at Mercaz Torah v'Medina in Nitzan and is a community rabbi at the Redlich Synagogue in the Givat Shaul neighborhood of Jerusalem. His research has significantly influenced both religious and academic circles. He has taught at various academic institutions and contributed to publications on Halakhic and Zionist thought. Rabbi Guttel is a senior member of a dedicated team in the IDF

Military Rabbinate, tirelessly involved in the sensitive and critical task of identifying victims from the October 7, 2023, massacre.

[This chapter is an English translation of Neria Guttel, "The Halakhic Definition of the Wars of the State of Israel in the Teachings of Rabbi Yitzhak Isaac Halevi Herzog," in *Ma'asuah le-Yitzhak*, vol. 2 (Jerusalem: Yad ha-Rav Herzog, 2009), 311-322 (Hebrew).]

Milhemet Mitzvah Without a King: Rabbi Yitzhak Isaac Halevi Herzog's Halakhic and Ideological Perspectives on the 1948 War of Independence

Yitzchak Avi Roness

THIS STUDY OF RABBI YITZHAK Isaac Halevi Herzog's worldview, will focus on his halakhic discussion of the status of the 1948 War of Independence. We will explore how his halakhic opinion on these matters was influenced by his views on various issues related to the State of Israel.

The establishment of the State of Israel introduced a novel phenomenon: A sovereign Jewish army fighting to conquer and defend its homeland. The underground organizations that preceded the state's establishment did not introduce the concept of a Jewish combat soldier, as many Jews had long served in the armies of various nations.[1] The novelty lay in the existence of a Jewish sovereign army.[2]

Rabbi Herzog's foundational discussions, aimed at defining the halakhic status of the battles of 1948, were written during the British Mandate period. His halakhic analysis examined both the general permissibility of warfare in modern times, as well as the specific issues raised by soldiers who sought out his halakhic guidance.

---

[1] These soldiers exerted a considerable influence on the halakhic discourse of their era. A notable example is the Machaneh Yisrael, authored by the Chafetz Chaim, which serves as a condensed Shulchan Aruch tailored for the needs of soldiers. For a comprehensive analysis of responsa pertaining to military service, see Yitzhak Ze'ev Kahana, "Military Service in Responsa Literature," *Sinai*, vol. 23 (1948): 129-161 (Hebrew).

[2] The profound sense of renewal in this phenomenon is expressed by Yehuda Amital, *Hamaalot Mimaamakim* (Jerusalem: Agudat Yeshivat Har Ezion, 1986), 20 (Hebrew):

"The very phenomenon of war is a biblical one. Throughout the two thousand years of our exile, we did not know war—we experienced many troubles and hardships, but war was not among them… In exile, there is no war; the reality of exile is 'I will bring faintness into their hearts,' and every rustling leaf will terrify them… The Psalms of David take on a meaning that is not new to them; they return to their original significance, for King David of Israel waged wars… If, after two thousand years of exile, we once again breathe an atmosphere reminiscent of the Bible, it is possible only in the light of the Messiah."

I. The Issue of Shabbat in the Military – The Response to the Ezra Organization in 1948

In a responsum dated the 28th of Adar II, 5708 (March 30, 1948), written just over a month before the declaration of the state, Rabbi Herzog responded to a series of questions posed by the Ezra Organization.[3] They sought to clarify the permissibility of participating in combat on Shabbat, and the proper conduct vis-a-vis specific military activities required at the time. In this responsum, Rabbi Herzog succinctly articulated the key principles of his approach. He submitted his response for review by his close friend, Rabbi Meshulam Roth, and following Rabbi Roth's comments, Rabbi Herzog revisited and further clarified his original statements.

The questions posed to Rabbi Herzog were as follows:

1. Is it permissible on Shabbat to volunteer for certain defensive activities, or perhaps it is even obligatory to do so?
2. The same question applies to offensive actions undertaken for defensive purposes.
3. The same question applies to purely offensive actions.
4. Is it permissible to maintain a log on Shabbat:
5. In connection with enemy movements observed from a lookout position?
6. At a base, to achieve oversight of personnel or weaponry?
7. Is it permissible to stop and inspect cars on Shabbat at checkpoints using flashlights that are turned on and off?
8. Is it permissible to forcibly recruit individuals for military service?

---

3   The questions are signed by "Tuvia Bir, Ezra Organization." For more on this figure and the Yeshiva Students' Battalion ("Tuvia Battalion") that he led on the eve of the establishment of the State of Israel, see Tom Kleifer, "The Conflict of Drafting Yeshiva Students," (MA thesis, Hebrew University of Jerusalem, 2003; Hebrew).

II. Defensive Activities on Shabbat

The questioners are well aware that pikuach nefesh (saving a life) overrides Shabbat, but they inquire whether they are permitted to volunteer for an operation that does not necessarily require the involvement of all the soldiers in the unit. Additionally, they ask how to approach combat carried out on Shabbat that does not qualify as purely defensive activity (-offensive actions undertaken for defensive purposes).

At the outset of his response, Rabbi Herzog clarifies the significant difference between soldiers in a "Hebrew army composed entirely of Jews" and Jewish soldiers who served in non-Jewish armies, regarding combat on Shabbat:

> "This question might have been relevant in a non-Jewish army... where the entire allowance for violating Shabbat is only because the Jewish soldier was coerced, and if he did not comply, he would face severe punishment, which constitutes a life-threatening situation for him. Why, then, would he volunteer?... But in a Hebrew army, composed entirely of Jews, where the allowance to violate Shabbat is for the sake of defending Israel, there is no place for this question."

A soldier who is coerced into violating Shabbat, and who also fears that refusal to act might lead to "severe punishment, thus constituting a life-threatening situation for himself,"[4] may claim that the actions he

---

4   *Pesakim u-Ketavim*, vol. 1 (Jerusalem: Yad ha-Rav Herzog, 1989), 212 [sec. 48] (Hebrew). In another place, in *Pesakim u-Ketavim*, vol. 2 (Jerusalem: Yad ha-Rav Herzog, 1989), 512 [sec. 115] (Hebrew), Rabbi Herzog explains that the conduct of an individual soldier in such situations must be considered with regard to its implications for the welfare of the entire Jewish community: "If they do not enlist, aside from the punishment they will receive, which also affects lives… they will endanger the very existence of Israel among the nations." Based on this consideration, Rabbi Herzog believes that voluntary enlistment of Jews should be encouraged even where conscription is not mandatory for everyone, as there is concern that "if Jews,

performs fall under the category of melakhah she'eina tzericha legufa (a labor not needed for its own sake). However, combat carried out within a Jewish army that protects the lives of the inhabitants of the land justifies even lechatchila (from the outset) Shabbat desecration. Rabbi Herzog thus adds:

> "If the allowance is based solely on the principle of saving Israel, meaning pikuach nefesh for the many, it has already been ruled in the baraita (Yoma 84b) and by Maimonides that such actions are not to be performed by minors or women… but rather by the greatest sages of Israel."

This is especially true in the context of a milhemet mitzvah (an obligatory war), where "there is certainly no place for this question."[5]

This dual discussion—relating first to the standard laws of pikuach nefesh, and then turning to examine the laws of milhemet mitzvah—will continue to underpin Rabbi Herzog's entire response.[6] He will later suggest that the matter be considered from the additional perspective of

> relying on their religion that forbids desecrating the Sabbath, all or the vast majority of them refuse to volunteer — this too will endanger the Jewish people in that country, and perhaps worldwide, as it will be said that Israel is not loyal to the government and is a danger to the state."

5   The unique halakhic status of "Israel's war in its land" sets the inquirers apart, even when compared to Jewish soldiers fighting as part of the Brigade against the Nazi enemy. Regarding the latter, Rabbi Herzog ruled, in *Pesakim u-Ketavim*, vol. 1 (Jerusalem: Yad ha-Rav Herzog, 1989), 255 [sec. 56] (Hebrew): "This is a war that involves the saving of Israel, but it is a war of the nations in which Jews join as their soldiers; it is not Israel's war." For this reason, Rabbi Herzog did not agree to extend to them the permission regarding forbidden foods that was granted to Israeli soldiers during their war, as he indicated in Ibid., 239 [sec. 52] (Hebrew).

6   The difference between these definitions lies in the fact that when the war itself is defined as a milhemet mitzvah or as an obligatory war, all actions necessary for the success of the war effort are permitted on the Sabbath, even if they are not directly related to saving lives.

an individual's duty to engage in the "saving of the many," a halakhic duty which differs both from the laws of war and the usual laws of pikuach nefesh.

III. Offensive Actions for the Purpose of Defense

The principle that pikuach nefesh overrides Shabbat prohibitions was originally stated to permit actions that serve to save from an immediate danger. Offensive actions, are therefore "not directly a case of pikuach nefesh," even when their ultimate aim is defensive. Therefore, "if the allowance is to be based solely on the principle of pikuach nefesh, it is seemingly not so very clear."[7]

Nevertheless, Rabbi Herzog continues to argue, that since no Shabbat prohibitions should stand in the way of any action necessary to save or prolong life, therefore even actions aimed at preventing future dangers should be permitted on Shabbat.[8] However, Rabbi Herzog limits this broad allowance to situations where there is a clear estimation of the danger being defended against. This is contingent on the professional opinion of a security expert. Once such an opinion has been received, "Since the expert has calculated and found that by this offensive action a nearby Jewish settlement will be saved, thereby this becomes a form of pikuach nefesh, or of 'saving Israel from an approaching enemy.'" However, there is no need to turn to a specialized expert opinion, as "one

---

7   *Pesakim u-Ketavim*, vol. 1 (Jerusalem: Yad ha-Rav Herzog, 1989), 213 [sec. 48] (Hebrew).

8   In *Pesakim u-Ketavim*, vol. 1 (Jerusalem: Yad ha-Rav Herzog, 1989) [sec. 45 and sec. 52], Rabbi Herzog proves that "pikuach nefesh (saving a life) is also relevant to future concerns," and he supports this with references to the law regarding a city near the border, as well as to the law stating that the "great ones of Israel" personally involve themselves in saving lives, even when the same result can be achieved with the help of a non-Jew. He also references the law that "all who go out to save return to their place," amongst other sources.

Milhemet Mitzvah Without a King

must rely on the commander in such cases, for otherwise, there would be no end to the matter, and no defensive operations could be sustained."[9]

An action involving pikuach nefesh is permitted even when the danger is not immediately apparent. Rabbi Herzog proves this contention by referencing the words of Tosafot in Pesachim, which indicate that as long as there is a concern for danger which can be defined as occurring "frequently", one may prepare for it in advance by performing activities that involve Shabbat labors. "In the current situation, the danger is indeed frequent, and therefore, the matter returns to the answer given in section A above."[10]

In this section of his discussion, as in the previous one, Rabbi Herzog reiterates that the allowance could be granted from the narrow perspective of the laws of pikuach nefesh. However, he continues, it is permitted all the more so "When viewed from a broader perspective,

---

9 In his response to Rabbi Werner, in *Pesakim u-Ketavim*, vol. 1 (Jerusalem: Yad ha-Rav Herzog, 1989), 198 [sec. 45] (Hebrew), Rabbi Herzog added a condition for the permissibility of such actions: The decision to carry out such an operation must be made with the active participation of a religious representative who understands the value and sanctity of the Sabbath. He reiterated a similar point in sec. 52 (Ibid., 233) concerning a parallel decision about the need to conduct a military raid on enemy property on the Sabbath: "It is essential that religious Jews, who are deeply aware of the gravity of desecrating the Holy Sabbath, be among those (making the decision)."

10 In his response in sec. 52 (Ibid., 233), Rabbi Herzog more emphatically permitted a 'defensive attack' even "from the narrow perspective of saving lives." He argued that the Noda B'Yehuda, who was stringent regarding postmortem examinations for saving a patient not presently before us, would agree that in the current situation, "any Jewish settlement near those positions, which is in danger from the non-Jews, should be considered as one facing imminent danger. And since, according to experts, the operation may protect them, it is permitted."

namely, that this is a milhemet mitzvah or an obligatory war incumbent upon the entirety of Israel."[11]

IV. Offensive Operations on Shabbat

The third question posed to Rabbi Herzog concerns offensive operations that do not have any defensive character whatsoever. In the previous section of his discussion, Rabbi Herzog already noted that the possibility of giving an allowance based on the criteria of pikuach nefesh (saving a life) is "not entirely clear." Therefore, regarding offensive actions, Rabbi Herzog clarifies that the matter is directly tied to "the basis of the allowance, whether it is provided from within the narrow framework of pikuach nefesh or within the broader framework of the wars of Israel, as mentioned above." From the perspective of the "narrow framework," it is not permissible on Shabbat to perform any labor which is not required for pikuach nefesh. However, the laws of war allow for much more, and from the perspective of these laws, there is no doubt that such activities should be permitted. In a milhemet mitzvah (an obligatory war), it is even permitted lechatchila (from the outset) to begin the work of laying siege on Shabbat: "For if it is within the latter framework, then we lay siege to the cities of gentiles three days before Shabbat, and wage war with them every day, even on Shabbat, even in a discretionary war (milhemet reshut), and certainly in a milhemet mitzvah, where it is permissible to lay siege on Shabbat from the outset."[12]

---

11 *Pesakim u-Ketavim*, vol. 1 (Jerusalem: Yad ha-Rav Herzog, 1989), 213 [sec. 52] (Hebrew). Rabbi Herzog does not specify which category of milhemet mitzvah he is referring to, as discussed below.

12 *Pesakim u-Ketavim*, vol. 1 (Jerusalem: Yad ha-Rav Herzog, 1989), 213 [sec. 58] (Hebrew). Rabbi Herzog repeatedly underscores the clear distinction between the laws of war and the usual Torah laws regarding saving a life (pikuach nefesh). Concerning the relationship between the permission to desecrate the Sabbath in war and the general permission due to pikuach nefesh, see Rabbi Avraham Avidan, *Sabbath and Festivals in the IDF* (Yerushalayim: Yeshivat Shaalvim and Igud Lohame Yerushalayim,

At this point in the discussion, defining the combat as a milhemet mitzvah no longer appears as an additional aspect appended incidentally to an allowance based on pikuach nefesh laws. Instead, it serves here as the fundamental basis of the allowance. Rabbi Herzog, therefore, feels the need to justify his determination that the reality of his time is indeed that of a milhemet mitzvah: "In my opinion, this struggle has the status of a milhemet mitzvah… and although a milhemet mitzvah needs to be declared by the king, and we do not have a king, the entire public or the majority of it, as my predecessor, the gaon zatzuk"al, already explained in his responsa Mishpat Kohen, has the authority of the King of Israel, and this recruitment was declared by the vast majority of the Yishuv in the Land of Israel, which is considered the entire community of Israel."[13]

However, if this is indeed a case of milhemet mitzvah, why did Rabbi Herzog bother until now to discuss whether or not the various activities would be allowed from the perspective of the laws of pikuach nefesh?[14] Does this perhaps indicate the existence of an internal personal

1990), 4-19 (Hebrew); Rabbi Eliezer Shenwald, "'Until She is Subdued': A Halakhic Source for Examining Operational Issues on the Sabbath in a Sovereign Jewish State," in Eliyahu Shenwald, ed., *Sefer Harel: Israeli Militarism through a Religious Prism* (Hispin: Yeshivat ha-Golan, 2000), 119-184 (Hebrew).

13 *Pesakim u-Ketavim*, vol. 1 (Jerusalem: Yad ha-Rav Herzog, 1989), 213 [sec. 58] (Hebrew). In the aforementioned sec. 52, Rabbi Herzog reiterates his opinion that the people are permitted to go to war even in the absence of a king, but here he introduces a new point—the consent of the rabbinate: "And even though we do not have a king, the majority of the settlement, along with the institutions, the Chief Rabbinate, etc., have the status of a king—and even Agudat Yisrael issued a proclamation in favor of conscription."

14 Although this style of discussion—presenting an idea, rejecting it, and then later on returning to and revisiting the rejected idea—characterizes Rabbi Herzog's writing, which often appears unrefined and unedited, it seems that in this specific instance, the intent was to construct an argument that would persuade even those who disagree with his fundamental approach. See his decisive wording on this very matter in sec. 52 (Ibid., 231): "There is no doubt in my mind that this is a milhemet mitzvah for the conquest of the

hesitation on the part of Rabbi Herzog? This is surely not the case! Rabbi Herzog's intention was to convince even those who disagreed with his position that the bottom line of his ruling was indeed correct. It would seem that as he penned his Tesuva Rabbi Herzog was imagining "those who disagree with this assumption and believe that this is not a war of Israel," partly because they believe that the absence of a king prevents the application of the milhemet mitzvah category here. Therefore, Rabbi Herzog continues in his response to try to base the allowance for offensive actions on the pikuach nefesh laws, without any reliance on the laws of war.

Thus, although he began this section of his discussion by clearly declaring that the permissibility of these actions "depends on the basis of the allowance," Rabbi Herzog nonetheless continues to argue that even "those who disagree with this assumption and believe that this is not a war of Israel, but rather a struggle for the saving of Israel, pikuach nefesh for the many, must acknowledge that any offensive action with real impact weakens the enemy's power and ultimately saves Israel." However, this argument is strained. In the previous section of his discussion, Rabbi Herzog wrote that permitting activities under the broader category of "pikuach nefesh to prevent future danger," can only be sanctioned when they are conducted to prevent a) a "frequent danger"; and b) when this assessment is given by an expert. It is difficult, then, to extend this allowance – as he does here – and claim that any action aimed at weakening the enemy's power would also fall under this category of "immediate rescue" from a "frequent" danger.[15]

---

land – aside from the rationale of 'assisting Israel against an enemy', and all the more so since this is a case of 'aiding Israel against an enemy', since there is no other choice."

15 In sec. 49 (Ibid., 219), Rabbi Herzog clarifies that this argument is not entirely clear to him: "If the attack is merely to generally weaken the enemy's power, there is room for hesitation – if we do not consider this struggle a milhemet mitzvah since it was not declared by a king."

This difficulty is further highlighted by the fact that in this section of his discussion, Rabbi Herzog is forced to contend with the argument that even when the matter is viewed from the prism of laws of war, this still does not automatically justify conducting offensive operations on Shabbat. The Gemara in Sotah defines a war intended "to diminish the gentiles so that they do not come against us" as a discretionary war (milhemet reshut), and as such one may not initiate such warfare on Shabbat.[16] Rabbi Herzog responds to this potential challenge by arguing that one must differentiate between an offensive war aimed solely at weakening the enemy, which is indeed defined as a milhemet reshut, and a localized offensive action taken as part of an overall defensive war: "This applies when the gentiles are currently quiet, and we go out to war against them to diminish and weaken them for the future, lest they come against us. But when they have already come against us to destroy and expel us from our holy inheritance, then all actions directed against them fall under the category of a milhemet mitzvah."[17] He reinforces this distinction in his response to Rabbi Roth: "This was said regarding the beginning of the war... but when they have already come upon us and we are in great danger, this does not mean that we must limit ourselves only to defense; rather, in such a case, any action that, according to the commanders, will ultimately weaken the power of the enemy who has already come against us is considered a continuation of a milhemet mitzvah."[18]

16 From comparing this to Rabbi Roth's critiques (as discussed below), it appears that this discussion, beginning with the words "if you conclude," was inserted into the response following Rabbi Roth's critique, as Rabbi Herzog found it necessary to mention both the question and the rejection within the body of his letter.

17 *Pesakim u-Ketavim*, vol. 1 (Jerusalem: Yad ha-Rav Herzog, 1989), 214 [sec. 48] (Hebrew).

18 *Pesakim u-Ketavim*, vol. 1 (Jerusalem: Yad ha-Rav Herzog, 1989), 222 [sec. 49] (Hebrew). Similarly, Rabbi Shaul Yisraeli wrote in his discussion of the halakhic status of a reprisal operation: "Every war has periods of pauses and reduced activity, such as at night, would anyone even raise the thought

Nevertheless, Rabbi Herzog concludes: "Religious Jews should demand from the command that in any case where they decide to conduct an offensive operation to weaken the enemy, and also for defense, a careful calculation should be made in advance to determine whether this operation can be carried out before Shabbat, or whether it can be postponed until after Shabbat. They must not schedule it specifically for Shabbat, and the same applies even to fortification activities or the like for defense."[19]

On the other hand, "if the order is given on Shabbat, and it is assumed that time is of the essence and it is impossible not to comply, for otherwise military discipline would be undermined, and the entire struggle would be compromised, one must comply."

Regarding the remaining points that appear in the original question[20]—behavior at a checkpoint, keeping a lookout journal, etc.—

---

that since the enemy is not fighting at this moment, it should therefore be categorized as merely 'to weaken the non-Jews so they do not attack'?", see Shaul Yisraeli, *Amud HaYemini* (Jerusalem: Eretz Hemdah, 1966), 5 [sec. 16] (Hebrew).

19 A similar requirement is mentioned at the end of Rabbi Herzog's response to Rabbi Werner regarding the construction of a security fence on the Sabbath. See *Pesakim u-Ketavim*, vol. 1 (Jerusalem: Yad ha-Rav Herzog, 1989), 198 [sec. 45] (Hebrew).

20 In the aforementioned sec. 52, Rabbi Herzog responded to a similar list of questions, where the fighters inquired further about harming "enemy personnel who may be innocent." Rabbi Herzog writes that if they refer to reprisal operations during wartime, intended to deter the enemy and prevent the killing of unarmed civilians, then the matter requires further consideration, "and much depends on the investigation of the issue in terms of its expected impact on the course of the war… and the matter must be carefully considered" (Ibid., 235). In that same discussion (Ibid., 234), Rabbi Herzog rejects an argument made by others in his time, who suggested learning from Maimonides' words regarding the incident in Shechem, and his claim that all enemy people deserve to be put to death because they did not protest or enforce justice against the murderers. Rabbi Herzog argues that one cannot compare the Arab inhabitants of the land and their

Rabbi Herzog responds briefly, noting that he does not know the subject in detail, but he establishes as a general rule that anything deemed essential and necessary, so that without it "the function of the base, and the defense, would suffer," is permitted, with the restriction that it be done with a modification: writing should be minimized as much as possible—done with the left hand, in Rashi script, or in non-Hebrew letters.

V. Compulsory Recruitment of Soldiers

The final question, concerning the compulsory recruitment of soldiers, does not specifically relate to the laws of Shabbat. In his response, Rabbi Herzog returns to examine the halakhic status of the combat itself. He begins by discussing the exemption of the "fearful and faint-hearted" from participating in a milhemet reshut (a discretionary war) and expands upon the conceptual and ideological value of combat within the Israel Defense Forces.

After quoting Maimonides on the prohibition of fear in battle and the soldier's obligation to rely on "the Hope of Israel and its Savior in time of distress," and to be infused with the awareness "that he is waging war for the sake of the sanctification of God's name," Rabbi Herzog elaborates on the unique nature of the Jewish people and its army:

> "When Maimonides writes 'and he should know that he is waging war for the sake of the unifying God's name'… his intent is not limited to wars against those who have decreed to make Israel forsake their faith, for he is also referring to a milhemet reshut, which is aimed

behavior towards the terrorists, with the people of Shechem, since "the Arabs, in their misguided thinking, believed that we came to steal their land from them and declared war on us; this has no relevance to Maimonides' words there." Furthermore, Rabbi Herzog asserts that it cannot be expected of the masses to stand up against the armed gangs— "The unarmed masses are powerless against the bandits of the gangs, and coercion is something for which the Merciful One pardons."

at expanding the borders of Israel. As the Zohar says, 'the Torah, Israel, and the Holy One, blessed be He, are one,' and a war to expand the borders of Israel is also considered a war for the sanctification of God's name. The more that Israel's strength, which seeks to unify God's name, especially in the land upon which 'the eyes of the Lord your God are from the beginning of the year to the end of the year,' increases in the world, the closer we come to the day of which it is said, 'On that day, the Lord will be one and His name one.'"

"... And there is no doubt, in my opinion, that the establishment of a Jewish state in the Land of Israel, as a sanctuary and refuge for the Jewish people, will be the stage marking the end of the exile, and afterward, the redemption will come. And anyone who brings the end of the exile closer also brings closer the return of Israel and the dissemination of the true unification of God's name in the world."[21]

Having made these remarks, Rabbi Herzog returns to the issue of compulsory recruitment, and once again, we encounter the difference stemming from the halakhic definition under which we approach the combat: if we determine that this is a milhemet mitzvah (an obligatory war), there is a clear basis for enforcing recruitment. However, if the obligation to fight is based solely on pikuach nefesh (saving a life) and the commandment to rescue one's fellow from danger, then there is no basis for deviating from the usual halakhic principle that a person is not obligated to endanger themselves to fulfill a commandment.

Rabbi Herzog initially reiterates his view that this is indeed a milhemet mitzvah, since "the power of the vast majority of the Yishuv (the Jewish community in Palestine) is akin to the power of the king in Israel… and there is no need for a Sanhedrin of seventy-one, and

---

21 *Pesakim u-Ketavim*, vol. 1 (Jerusalem: Yad ha-Rav Herzog, 1989), 216 [sec. 48] (Hebrew)

according to this, we have the power to enforce recruitment."[22] However, as we have seen in his discussions in previous sections, Rabbi Herzog attempts here as well to demonstrate that the allowance can be justified even if one does not accept his view in this regard.

As he proceeds to explain, indeed, from the perspective of the general duty to save lives, there is no basis for compulsory recruitment, since the halakhic authorities have ruled that a person is not obligated to put themselves in danger to save their fellow. However, this only applies when the danger threatens the lives of individuals; the situation is different when the combat aims to protect the entire Jewish settlement—"But if my opinion is not accepted, even if we consider this only from the narrow perspective of saving Israel in terms of 'pikuach nefesh for the many', it is still arguable that for such a commandment, involving the saving of the entire Yishuv, we enforce recruitment."

Rabbi Herzog clarifies his intent, and writes that he is not suggesting a distinction between saving an individual life and saving a large number who are jointly in danger, but rather a case where the danger is posing a threat to the "entire Yishuv," and therefore it is as if the "entire congregation of Israel" were in danger: "In Mishpat Kohen, my predecessor, the gaon [Rabbi Kook], ruled that for the saving of the entire Jewish people… one is obligated to place oneself in possible danger, and even in certain danger. And since the Yishuv is considered the 'entire congregation of Israel', it can be said that we enforce recruitment for this, even if there is no actual status of a milhemet mitzvah, since we do not have a king today."

Even so, Rabbi Herzog acknowledges that this last argument is not entirely clear, as "this matter depends on reasoning as to whether, the

---

22 *Pesakim u-Ketavim*, vol. 1 (Jerusalem: Yad ha-Rav Herzog, 1989), 217 [sec. 48] (Hebrew). Rabbi Herzog qualifies his statement: "However, the matter still requires further investigation." It seems that his reservation pertains to the issue of coercion, which must be understood in light of Rabbi Roth's letter, where he argues that a decision regarding coercion is akin to a ruling on capital cases, and contemporary rabbis lack the authority to issue such rulings. See note 36 below.

Yishuv is considered akin to 'the entire congregation of Israel' even for this"[23]—in other words, while it is true that we find that the inhabitants of the Land of Israel have the status of "Kehal Yisrael," it is possible that Rabbi Kook's words, and his halakhic innovation are relevant only to a situation in which the danger threatens the people of Israel as a whole (or at least a majority of the nation), and it does not apply to a case where the danger applies to those categorized as the "congregation of Israel" – a term by which the inhabitants of the Land are referred to. Without deciding this matter, Rabbi Herzog proceeds to outline his understanding of the situation, explaining how in his eyes the threat to the Jewish inhabitants of the Land of Israel constitutes a danger to the entire nation, since "the destruction of the Yishuv, God forbid, could lead to the destruction of the entire Jewish people or most of them," "the destruction of the Yishuv could lead to a movement of destruction, God forbid, for the Jewish people throughout the world."[24] Nevertheless, Rabbi Herzog writes: "I refrain from deciding either in the affirmative or the negative, and this still requires much deliberation."[25]

Rabbi Herzog concludes his remarks with a note that even compulsory recruitment must be conducted in an orderly manner— "There must be order and regulation in the enforcement of recruitment," "and it is not possible for each individual to establish the order and regulation," "and if there is a need to criticize the actions of those in

---

23 Rabbi Herzog revisited this reasoning in other halakhic contexts as well. See note 64 below.

24 *Pesakim u-Ketavim*, vol. 1 (Jerusalem: Yad ha-Rav Herzog, 1989), 217, 220 [sec. 48, 49] (Hebrew).

25 However, see the conclusion of his letter to Rabbi Meshulam Roth, written a few days later (Ibid., 224), where any tone of doubt disappears entirely: "In my opinion, the salvation of the residents of Israel in the current situation, and in the historical context under these circumstances, is not only the salvation of the settlement but the salvation of the entire Jewish people, and Judaism as a whole. How can there be any doubt in my mind that we must take risks for this?"

charge and to comment or raise concerns, the public has the right to do so, and there is independent press and public opinion."[26]

VI. Response and Counter-Response

Rabbi Herzog submitted his response to Rabbi Meshulam Roth for review, and Rabbi Roth commented on some of his statements.[27]

As previously noted, Rabbi Herzog derived from the words of *Tosafot* that *pikuach nefesh* (saving a life) permits one to prepare for a future danger only when this danger is defined as one which may be deemed to occur "frequently." Rabbi Roth understood from his wording, that Rabbi Herzog intended to permit, in the case of a "frequent" danger, Shabbat desecration through performing labors in a broad manner, without requiring a close examination of the direct necessity of each specific labor. Rabbi Roth cited the *Hatam Sofer* to argue that such an allowance must belimited in nature, and applied only to actions that

---

26 *Pesakim u-Ketavim*, vol. 1 (Jerusalem: Yad ha-Rav Herzog, 1989), 217 [sec. 48] (Hebrew).

27 Rabbi Meshulam Roth's letter was published in his book *Shu"t Kol Mevaser*, vol. 1 [sec. 47], and Rabbi Herzog's response in the following two sections of his own book [secs. 49-50]. Rabbi Herzog often submitted his responsa for review by his rabbinic colleagues. For example, he did not return his response on these issues [sec. 52] to the inquirers until he received the approval of Rabbi Tzvi Pesach Frank: "I was hesitant to rely on myself in such serious matters—Sabbath observance on one side and saving lives and Israel's wars, a milhemet mitzvah, on the other—and I handed it over to the esteemed Rabbi Tzvi Pesach Frank, who returned it to me today with his full agreement with my opinion. The condition was fulfilled regarding the point of 'until an expert rabbi joins me in this decision.'" See *Pesakim u-Ketavim*, vol. 1 (Jerusalem: Yad ha-Rav Herzog, 1989), 245 [sec. 52].

directly contribute to saving lives, as otherwise,[28] it could be interpreted as a general permission to perform labor on Shabbat.[29]

---

28 The Hatam Sofer rejected the ruling of his father-in-law, Rabbi Akiva Eiger, who allowed cooking food on the festival (specifically dried fruits) even when the foodstuff is prohibited for consumption on that same day, in reliance on the principle of *ho'il* ("since"). The Hatam Sofer explained that even though there are many ill people, and there presence is thus quite common, nonetheless it is rare to find patients who specifically require this particular dish for their recovery, and thus it should not be considered a common occurrence.

29 In *Pesakim u-Ketavim*, vol. 1 (Jerusalem: Yad ha-Rav Herzog, 1989), 195 [sec. 45] (Hebrew), Rabbi Herzog permitted the construction of a security fence around the city of Tiberias on the Sabbath due to the fear of enemy attack, arguing that "in our situation, an enemy attack is certainly considered a common occurrence." The inquirer, Rabbi Werner, the Av Beit Din of Tiberias, argued that permitting Sabbath desecration to prevent a danger that is not present and for which there is no clear evidence opens too wide a door: "If so, we should permit building a wall on the Sabbath in all the cities of Israel, for surely they want to attack us everywhere" (Ibid., 197). In response, Rabbi Herzog replied: "The law is similar to that of a dangerously ill patient, where the matter depends on the assessment of experts, and if the experts… assess that it is likely that they will attack, who can take responsibility and oppose them?" Rabbi Herzog further noted: "Here, we permitted making armored vehicles on the Sabbath based on the command's assessment, which was based on intelligence received that an attack on Jerusalem was planned for the Sabbath or immediately after." In sec. 52 (Ibid., 239), Rabbi Herzog permitted training with weapons on the Sabbath "in positions… even though it was not heard that the enemies were preparing to come and attack, in the current situation, it is as if they heard. It is well known that they are seeking every opportunity to attack us, and as long as the state of war continues, they are likely to come." Later, Rabbi Herzog issued a general directive permitting training soldiers on the Sabbath, writing: "Indeed, all our hope is in God, the God of our strength and our Rock of salvation, that He will thwart the schemes of our enemies… and only with this faith shall we act and succeed… With this hope and faith, and with the permission of the Heavenly King of Kings, who possesses power and might, who instructed us in His Torah to stand and defend

"In this case", Rabbi Roth contends, "it should only be permitted if it is clear that the offensive action is currently required for defense and saving from danger."[30]

Rabbi Herzog clarifies that his statements are aligned with the restrictive interpretation of the *Hatam Sofer*, since the current situation involves the attempt to prevent an existing danger: "An offensive action to undermine the enemy's power, who is ready at any moment to attack nearby Jewish settlements—if an offensive action against one of their positions keeps them occupied with their own defense and unable to launch an attack, this is considered *pikuach nefesh* in that very matter, even if they have not yet begun their assault."[31] However, he adds, "if the offensive action is merely to weaken the enemy's power in general, it requires careful consideration." Rabbi Herzog emphasizes that the above is based solely on the application of the criteria of *pikuach nefesh*: "If we do not consider our struggle to be a *milhemet mitzvah*, since it was not declared by a king."

The disagreement between the two rabbis, is not about the theoretical understanding of the halakhic definition, but rather relates to its practical application: how far can one stretch the definition of an "offensive action necessary for defense and saving from danger"[32]? In

> ourselves in times of trouble, we agree to permit all necessary and required actions for the future... However, our words are expressly conditional that these rulings are only as a temporary measure, and when it appears that the danger has passed, we will revoke this directive," in *Pesakim u-Ketavim*, vol. 1 (Jerusalem: Yad ha-Rav Herzog, 1989), 255 [sec. 55] (Hebrew).

30 *Shu"t Kol Mevaser*, vol. 1 [sec. 47].

31 *Pesakim u-Ketavim*, vol. 1 (Jerusalem: Yad ha-Rav Herzog, 1989), 219 [sec. 40] (Hebrew).

32 In his response, the Hatam Sofer's concern about the potential misuse of this permission is evident, as it could theoretically be extended to allow the violation of all Sabbath prohibitions. This issue is not as pronounced in discussions related to emergency situations during wartime, but it becomes sharply relevant in discussions about routine security activities. The problem

Rabbi Herzog's response on this matter, we once again see his attempt to persuade even those who disagree with the specifics of his arguments that, despite their objections, religious soldiers should be instructed to participate in the combat.

Rabbi Herzog points out that there are two reasons not to oppose the religious soldiers' participation in an offensive move on Shabbat:
1. There is a strong presumption we can follow, in order to determine that the offensive action is indeed necessary—"In most cases, forces are not wasted on an offensive action unless the purpose is to prevent an attack by the enemy on a nearby Jewish position that is in imminent danger."[33]
2. Even if the offensive action were to be conducted on Shabbat without proper justification, nonetheless the individual soldier should still be instructed to participate together with the rest of his unit: "If it has already been decided to carry out an offensive action on Shabbat, even if the commander's intention is unclear and it may be only to weaken the enemy's power in general, since the majority of the unit will certainly obey without questioning the order, then it can be said that it is a mitzvah to join them to strengthen their power, so that they do not fall before the enemy or into his hands, in which case they would surely be killed."[34]

Rabbi Roth further argues that the definition of a *milhemet mitzvah* should not apply to the offensive combat aimed at capturing Arab villages

---

with routine activities, where it is not immediately clear how each action saves lives, is particularly challenging. Indeed, Rabbi Herzog revisited this issue when discussing the operation of police forces on the Sabbath. See *Pesakim u-Ketavim*, vol. 1 (Jerusalem: Yad ha-Rav Herzog, 1989), [sec. 58] (Hebrew). In this discussion, Rabbi Herzog returns to the aforementioned words of the Tosafot and grapples with a fundamental question regarding the boundaries of this permission and its practical application.

33 *Pesakim u-Ketavim*, vol. 1 (Jerusalem: Yad ha-Rav Herzog, 1989), 219 [sec. 49] (Hebrew).

34 Ibid. 220 (Hebrew).

around Jerusalem. He explains that the capture of an Arab village in this area cannot be included in the mitzvah of conquering the Land of Israel, since the United Nations Partition Plan designates this area as one which will not remain under Jewish sovereignty after the end of hostilities.

In his response to this objection, Rabbi Herzog begins by clarifying: "My main reliance is that this is entirely a case of 'saving Israel from an enemy that has come upon them,' and it is explained by Maimonides that this is a *milhemet mitzvah*. I only cited the Nahmanides as an additional support,"[35] and in truth, the residents of Jerusalem are in danger of death and starvation.

In Rabbi Herzog's view, Nahmanides would opine that a war aimed at ensuring continued settlement in the land, even without maintaining sovereignty over it, should be seen as a war of conquest of the land:

> "Even though this area will not fully belong to us, we will still have considerable power there because we are the majority. And the enemies' goal, as I know for certain, is to force those who remain, after God forbid much bloodshed, to flee from Jerusalem… and to fight to ensure that we remain in the Holy City… is a mitzvah like an initial conquest… I say that this too is part of the conquest, meaning to sustain the settlement… by weakening the enemy's power, this itself is part of the conquest of Jerusalem, so that we can at least hold onto the part that will ultimately be ours with God's help."

These final words stem from the perspective we mentioned earlier, which contends that each individual action should not be measured in isolation but rather should be seen as part of the overall military effort. Therefore, "any action that, according to the commanders, will ultimately weaken the power of the enemy that has already come upon us is considered a continuation of a *milhemet mitzvah*."[36]

---

35 Ibid. 222 (Hebrew).

36 Ibid.

In his final comment, Rabbi Roth criticizes Rabbi Herzog's argument that it is permissible to conscript soldiers by force, even if the combat is not considered a *milhemet mitzvah*.[37] Rabbi Roth asks: "Where do we find that one is compelled to endanger their own life?" Rabbi Roth quotes from the writings of prominent halakhic authorities that a person is not obligated to put themselves in danger to save their fellow man, and "it is clear that there is no distinction in this matter between saving an individual or saving many, and I have proofs for this, but I must be brief."

In his response, Rabbi Herzog reiterates his initial claim that his statements are based on the assessment that the case at hand does not resemble the regular situation of *pikuach nefesh*, nor can it be compared to a situation in which many are in danger, but rather—"My intention was what I stated earlier, 'the *pikuach nefesh* of the entire Jewish people,' meaning that I relied on Maimonides' words in his commentary on the Mishnah (Bechorot 4:2), based on the Talmud in Horayot (3a) and the Jerusalem Talmud (Horayot 1:2), that the settlement is considered the entire congregation of Israel, and that this applies here as well… and that for the saving of the entire Jewish people, or the majority of it – which is considered as the whole – each individual is obligated to put themselves in danger, even if we assume that without a king there is no status of *milhemet mitzvah*… And since one is obligated, why should the court not compel him to fulfill this positive commandment, which is greater than all the commandments?"[38]

Rabbi Herzog concludes: "In my opinion, saving the Yishuv in the current situation and in the historical context of these circumstances is not only about saving the Yishuv but also about saving the entire Jewish

---

37 Rabbi Roth concluded that the Beit Din should refrain from ruling "to judge capital cases directly, and take on the responsibility of coercion through force for conscription. For they are acting contrary to the law by drafting from the age of 17 and up… and it is not clear that this is a milhemet mitzvah, which would require a Beit Din of seventy-one, and in cases of doubt concerning life and death, we are lenient."

38 *Pesakim u-Ketavim*, vol. 1 (Jerusalem: Yad ha-Rav Herzog, 1989), 223 [sec. 50] (Hebrew).

people and even saving Judaism itself. How then can there be any doubt in my mind that one is obligated to take risks for this?"³⁹

VII. Summary of the Response

As we have seen, Rabbi Herzog starts from the premise that the situation of a Jewish soldier serving and fighting within a Jewish army in the Land of Israel is different from any previous situation in history, and therefore requires a change in approach. This is a true milhemet mitzvah (obligatory war), and the soldier must feel as if they are fighting for the sanctification of God's name. Even if one were to argue that this halakhic status does not apply in the absence of a king, it is still a great mitzvah, greater than all other commandments—pikuach nefesh for the many.

---

39 *Pesakim u-Ketavim*, vol. 1 (Jerusalem: Yad ha-Rav Herzog, 1989), 224 [sec. 50] (Hebrew). A similar wording appears in his remarks (Ibid., 220). At the end of his response to Rabbi Werner regarding the construction of fortifications in the city of Tiberias (Ibid., 198), Rabbi Herzog wrote that in his opinion, the matter should be considered within the framework of a milhemet mitzvah and "not only from the perspective of pikuach nefesh (saving a life)." One of the reasons he gave there is that if we "miss the opportunity to establish an independent state, this would, God forbid, lead to the despair of the masses of Israel and cause, God forbid, over time, the abolition of our holy religion among most of the nation, as well as assimilation." He wrote similarly in another response to questions sent to him by the Ezra Organization: "After the terrible Holocaust, when all of Israel's hope is tied to the revival of Israel in its Holy Land, should the masses of Israel completely despair, the entire religion will collapse, and that is enough said for the discerning," in *Pesakim u-Ketavim*, vol. 1 (Jerusalem: Yad ha-Rav Herzog, 1989), 230 [sec. 52] (Hebrew). In another response, where he discussed the obligation to recite Hallel on Independence Day, he criticized those who do not acknowledge the importance of the state, and within his remarks, he wrote: 'And after the horrific Holocaust, if the salvation had not come afterward, could Judaism have managed to survive'?" in *Pesakim u-Ketavim*, vol. 2 (Jerusalem: Yad ha-Rav Herzog, 1989), 486 [sec. 105] (Hebrew).

Alongside the great hope for redemption, a hope with which Rabbi Herzog concludes his letters, he also feels the tremendous threat to Judaism worldwide, the enormous danger that could develop as a result of losing the battle. From here stems Rabbi Herzog's approach to examining the halakhic issues involved in fighting on Shabbat` he is driven by a sense of urgency and of a supreme mission thrust upon him, and by the recognition of the far-reaching historical significance of these events. The importance of success in the war, and the establishment of a state as a result, extends far beyond the present moment.[40] This state, once established, will serve as a refuge and a defensive barrier against assimilation on the one hand, and as a first step toward the final redemption on the other. With this in mind, Rabbi Herzog emphasizes in his response to Rabbi Roth that these considerations leave no doubt in his mind, and that he has no hesitation in ruling that everything

---

40 Several years later, Rabbi Herzog published the following passage: "It has become clear to me that the State of Israel is an essential and vital necessity, not only from the perspective of saving the lives of hundreds of thousands of our brethren who survived the inferno in Europe… In my heart, the conviction was firmly established that this is something that Judaism itself, from an internal perspective, greatly needs. It was as clear to me as the midday sun that the horrific Holocaust, which destroyed most of the nation along with its geniuses, its rabbis, its righteous and pious individuals, its scholars and writers, its poets and activists, caused a shift in the foundations of faith deeply embedded in the hearts of the masses of the House of Israel throughout the whole world. I feared greatly that if the dawn that began to rise in the Land of the Patriarchs and Prophets were to fade and disappear, God forbid, for a long time, the results would be exceedingly bitter, to the extent of endangering the very existence of Judaism, at least in the Diaspora… Therefore, a firm recognition developed within me that the efforts to ensure the success of our heroic struggle in the Land of Israel are something upon which the soul of the nation depends, and that this is not merely a war 'to assist Israel against an enemy' (which is certainly a milhemet mitzvah), but more than that, a war for the salvation of the soul of the nation," in Yitzhak Isaac Halevi Herzog, "Boundaries in the Law of the Kingdom," *HaTorah v'HaMedinah*, vol. 7–8 (1956): 9 (Hebrew).

necessary for the war, even on Shabbat, must be done, and this even before one turns to examine any specific halakhic considerations.

The importance and dire urgency he sees, can easily explain the consistent effort we have seen in Rabbi Herzog's words to try to persuade even those who may disagree with his fundamental assumption that the combat can be regarded as a milhemet mitzvah.[41]

After reviewing Rabbi Herzog's words in his response, we will now consider several points where it is especiallty apparent that his halakhic positions in this responsum are influenced by his ideological positions.

VIII. Halakhah and Ideology

Various scholars have noted the influence of a halakhic authority's meta-halakhic[42] worldview on their interpretation of sources, the

---

41 Although Rabbi Herzog's personal stance on classifying the war as a milhemet mitzvah is clear, he remained cautious about issuing rulings on specific halakhic details. He did not want to bear the responsibility alone and sought to include another distinguished halakhic authority in his decisions. For example, regarding the treatment of a non-critical patient: "In the current situation, where a soldier who has been wounded, even slightly, cannot effectively fight until his wound is treated, and we are deprived of this strength at that moment—who knows what the lack of that strength might cause? Therefore, it seems to me (proper) to permit any rabbinic prohibition in order to prepare him for battle. However, my heart does not allow me to permit a Torah prohibition for this reason – unless another prominent rabbi joins me in this ruling." (See Ibid., 230.) Similarly, regarding the permissibility of eating food that was heated on the Sabbath in violation of halakhah (Ibid., 239), and indeed, he wrote that Rabbi Tzvi Pesach Frank ultimately agreed with him (see Ibid., 245).

42 We use this term in alignment with Neria Guttel's broader definition, which encompasses a wide array of considerations with "social, moral, national, and ideological dimensions." For a detailed discussion, see Neria Guttel, *Hadashim Gam Yeshanim – Innovation in Tradition: The Halakhic-Philosophical Teachings of Rav Kook* (Jerusalem: Magnes, 2005), 8-10, 194 (Hebrew). Guttel underscores that these considerations are essential components of the halakhic system (Ibid, 218, 224).

definition of halakhic concepts,[43] and ultimately, their rulings.[44] Such influence is generally evident in questions that involve differing value judgments and ideological perspectives.[45] Therefore, it is reasonable to assume that a halakhic authority's response to questions arising from the existence of the State of Israel would be influenced by their views on Zionism and their theological-historical understanding of the events

---

[43] For an illustrative example of how the decisor's varying scholarly conceptions about the nature of the halakhic system itself, are translated into specific halakhic disputes, refer to Yohanan Silman, "Halakhic Determinations of a Nominalistic and Realistic Nature: Legal and Philosophical Considerations," *Dine Israel*, vol. 12 (1985): 249-251 (Hebrew). For a related discussion that contrasts the approaches of Maimonides and Nahmanides on legal reality, see David Henshke, "On the Reality of Law in Maimonides' Thought," *Sinai*, no. 92 (1983): 228-239 (Hebrew).

[44] The scholar Ephraim E. Urbach consistently integrated this fundamental insight into all his research, making it a hallmark of his scholarly work. For further exploration of Urbach's approach, see Yaacov Sussman, "The Scholarly Oeuvre of Professor Ephraim Elimelech Urbach," in David Assaf, ed., *Ephraim Elimelech Urbach: A Bio-Bibliography* (Jerusalem: World Union of Jewish Studies, 1993), 7-116, esp. 75 (Hebrew). A prime example of how a decisor's worldview can shape the theoretical foundations of their halakhic rulings can be found in Haym Soloveitchik, "Religious Law and Change: The Medieval Ashkenazic Example," *AJS Review*, vol. 12, no. 2 (1987): 205-221.

[45] Many people instinctively know when to direct a halakhic question specifically to a decisor from within their own ideological circle, and when it is possible to seek halakhic guidance from a decisor from a different ideological sector. This intuitive understanding often reflects an implicit recognition of the differing approaches and underlying values that various decisors bring to their halakhic rulings.

leading to the state's establishment[46]—a conclusion that did not escape the notice of the rabbis themselves.[47]

But how can one identify when there is indeed an ideological influence on a halakhic ruling?

Such influence may be made clearly apparent – in cases where the halakhic authority explicitly states that, due to a value-based, educational, moral, or ideological consideration, the situation should be regarded as one of sha'at hadchak (exigent circumstances), allowing the halakhah to rely on a particular opinion, or conversely, forbidding a behavior otherwise permitted by law. In such cases, the involvement

---

46   See on this matter Eliezer Goldman, *Studies and Reflections: Jewish Thought Past and Present* (Jerusalem: Magnes, 1997), 403, 407 (Hebrew).

Mordechai Breuer described it as follows: "The divergence of Torah perspectives... due to fundamental differences in outlook, leads through rationalization to the splitting of halakhah. The phenomenon of varying halakhic responses among legal authorities is not always explained by exclusive, scientific, and rational study of halakhic sources, but is sometimes conditioned by preconceived positions within the realm of Jewish thought, positions each rooted in traditional philosophy." In Mordechai Breuer, "The Debate on the Three Oaths in Recent Generations," in *Redemption and State: The Redemption of Israel* (Jerusalem: Ministry of Education and Culture, 1979), 49-57, esp. 56 (Hebrew).

See also the comments of my teacher Itamar Warhaftig regarding the background to the disputes between Rabbi Herzog and his rabbinic colleagues, in Yitzhak Isaac Halevi Herzog, *Constitution for Israel According to the Torah*, vol. 1 (Jerusalem: Yad ha-Rav Herzog, 1989), 31 (Hebrew); and *Constitution for Israel According to the Torah*, vol. 2 (Jerusalem: Yad ha-Rav Herzog, 1989), 35 (Hebrew).

47   See, for example, the words of Rabbi Shlomo Goren on the occasion of the state's tenth anniversary: "One fundamental principle crucial to understanding our approach (in resolving the state's halakhic issues)... is the basic assumption and belief in the historical and prophetic vision of the State of Israel... The key to the various solutions in the area of halakhah concerning state matters lies in the national approach of the Torah scholars to these issues," see Shlomo Goren, "State Problems in Light of Halakhah," *Ohr Hamizrach*, vol. 5, no. 3-4 (September 1958): 5-11, esp. 11 (Hebrew).

of the authority's worldview in the halakhic decision-making process is clear to all. However, this is not the case when one wishes to argue for the existence of a hidden ideological influence.

Some are of the opinion that the influence of a decisor's meta-halakhic worldview on his rulings is so decisive that it can be presumed even when it is not overt. Although halakhic reasoning is often framed in legal and conceptual terms, which by their nature, "like all legal concepts, appear in an objective guise," thereby creating the impression that the application of these concepts was not accompanied by the decisor's personal value judgment.[48] However, they would contend, this is only a partial picture. A deeper examination would reveal that the ideological assumptions underlying the formal arguments are what "guide the solution to the practical question."[49]

According to this understanding, even when the halakhic authority does not openly rely on their ideological positions, it is sufficient to reveal their ideological assumptions, which can be inferred from how the authority chose to frame the question for discussion, from "the selection of sources that form the basis for drawing conclusions," or from ideological side comments scattered throughout their writings.[50]

Others have criticized this position, arguing that anyone claiming the influence of value-based or ideological positions on the halakhic reasoning in a given case, must provide evidence from within the halakhic discourse itself. In their view, even when a clear correlation is found between the known positions of the specific halakhic authority and their ruling in a given case, one must not ignore the fact that the

---

48 See Yitzhak Englard, "The Halakhic Problem of Surrendering Territories of Eretz Yisrael: Law and Ideology," *ha-Praklit*, vol. 41 (1993): 13-34, esp. 14 (Hebrew).

49 Quotations from Itzhak Englard's language can be found Ibid., 23 (Hebrew).

50 See Ibid., 23, 28, and 33-34 (Hebrew).

halakhic conclusion is possible by virtue of the inherent halakhic rules of reasoning, without any connection to any preconceived stance.[51]

IX. The Jews in the Land of Israel Are Called the "Kahal"

This type of influence is evident, for example, in Rabbi Herzog's claim that everyone is obligated to risk their lives to save the Jewish settlement in the Land of Israel, since danger to this Jewish community is considered to be equivalent to a threat to the entire Jewish people. As we have seen, this novel halakhic assertion is based on two independent innovations. First, one must adopt Rabbi Kook's claim[52] that each and every individual is obligated to do everything in their power to eliminate and avert a danger that threatens the entire Jewish people, even if it requires putting themselves in a place of certain danger. However, in order to reach Rabbi Herzog's conclusion, one must also accept an additional premise: that this rule applies even when the danger poses a threat only to the inhabitants of the Land of Israel, since the residents of the land are considered to be the "Kahal Israel"— "I have assumed that Maimonides' statement… that the settlement constitutes the entire 'Kahal Israel,' applies to this situation as well."

At first glance, this second claim seems like a halakhic innovation lacking internal logic: the special status of the inhabitants of the land, who are called "Kahal," is mentioned in the Talmud in the context of an incorrect ruling issued by the court, one which led astray the entire "Kahal Israel" who followed their misguided directive. Does this mean that the destruction of the settlement in the Land of Israel is equivalent

---

51 Many have pointed out the need for caution in this area, see Jacob Katz, *Halakhah and Kabbalah* (Jerusalem: Magnes, 1984), 2, and 229n121 (Hebrew); Gerald J. Blidstein, *Political Principles in the Thought of Maimonides* (Ramat Gan: Bar-Ilan University Press, 2001), 12 (Hebrew); and Isadore Twersky, *Introduction to the Code of Maimonides* (New Haven: Yale University Press, 1980), 485-488.

52 *Shu"t Mishpat Kohen*, secs. 142 and 144.

to the annihilation of the entire nation?! There appears to be no basis for equating the danger pertaining to the residents of the land to a case where the entire Jewish people are threatened, such as in the days of Mordechai and Esther (this being the exact situation to which Rabbi Kook's words pertain).[53] The special "Migdar Milta" (preventive measure) that Rabbi Kook spoke of stems from the understanding that the preservation of the Jewish people is fundamental to the entire Torah of Israel.[54] But what relevance does this have to the concept of "Kahal Israel" as mentioned in the Talmud in Horayot?[55]

53   In his response there, Rabbi Kook rejects the inquirer's definition that any 'established and significant' community should be considered as 'the public,' such that the obligation to save them would differ from the duty to save an individual. Rabbi Kook argues that such reasoning should not be accepted because "in all places, it is said that the primary importance of the public is only in the entirety as a whole," in *Mishpat Kohen* (Jerusalem: Mosad ha-Rav Kook, 1966), 309 [sec. 143] (Hebrew). Rabbi Kook explains that the halakhic consideration of the residents of a particular land as a distinct public, which we find concerning the laws of prayers for rain, is merely a local ruling based on the need for each region's inhabitants to pray according to the specific climate of their land. While Rabbi Kook mentions the special halakhic status of the residents of Eretz Yisrael, "the congregation in Eretz Yisrael is considered as all of Israel," he does not claim that they are therefore subject to a special obligation in regards to the obligation to rescue them from danger. Later in that paragraph, he clarifies again that this unique ruling of saving the public applies only in cases where "the entire public, or most of it, is in danger, such as in the case of Yael and Esther."

54   "And since we act for the salvation of all Israel, which is the foundation of the entire Torah, its purpose, and its goal, this is the foundation of all forms of migdar milta (protective measures) in the world, and all is included within it," in Rabbi Abraham Isaac Hacohen Kook, *Mishpat Kohen* (Jerusalem: Mosad ha-Rav Kook, 1966), 328 (Hebrew).

55   Rabbi Herzog himself acknowledged that Rabbi Kook had not preceded him in combining these two concepts, and that in this regard, he was not relying on any prior ruling. Thus, he writes in his letter to Rabbi Roth, in *Pesakim u-Ketavim*, vol. 1 (Jerusalem: Yad ha-Rav Herzog, 1989), 223 [sec. 50] (Hebrew): "When I mentioned pikuach nefesh d'rabbim (saving the

A deeper examination of the matter reveals that this is an example of the influence of the halakhic authority's general ideological worldview on their rulings, and that Rabbi Herzog's willingness to equate these two disparate cases is connected to one of the foundational principles of his religious Zionist perspective.

This notion, that the residents of the land of Israel are considered to be "Kahal Israel," serves as a genuine halakhic consideration in several of Rabbi Herzog's responsa, and it is likely connected to Rabbi Herzog's explanation of the essence of the secret that Maimonides concealed in his words regarding the sanctification of the new month. To further understand this point, we shall examine the statements Rabbi Herzog made in a special study dedicated to Maimonides' words on this matter.[56]

Rabbi Herzog begins his remarks with the following declaration: "It is well known and widely accepted that, according to Maimonides, the sanctity of the festivals depends on the presence of a Jewish settlement in the Land of Israel." As we shall see, in Rabbi Herzog's view, this interdependency directly results from the fact that the Jewish residents in the land are considered to be the entire "Kahal Israel."

In Sefer HaMitzvot, Positive Commandment 153 – the commandment "to sanctify months and calculate years," which is the

> lives of the public), I meant pikuach nefesh of the entire people of Israel. That is, I assumed that Maimonides' words in his commentary on the Mishnah (Bekhorot 4:2), which are based on the Talmud in Horayot (3a) and the Jerusalem Talmud (Horayot 1:2) that the residents of Israel are 'the entire congregation of Israel', also apply to this matter. I have already quoted my predecessor, the righteous and pious genius, of blessed memory. See also *Mishpat Kohen* (sec. 144, 15:1), where he writes that the majority of the public is like a king and that for the salvation of the entire public or most of it, which is like all of it, everyone is obligated to put themselves in danger." In this letter, Rabbi Herzog was compelled to explain and defend the original novelty found in Rabbi Kook's words, where he distinguished between pikuach nefesh of individuals and that of the public, since Rabbi Roth did not perceive this be clear and self apparent.

56 *Pesakim u-Ketavim*, vol. 2 (Jerusalem: Yad ha-Rav Herzog, 1989) [sec. 77] (Hebrew).

mitzvah of sanctifying the new month —Maimonides states that sanctifying the month by calculation, as is done today in the absence of a Great Court that sanctifies the new month based on sighting, "can only be done in the Land of Israel." According to Maimonides, the fact that the month is sanctified according to the calculations of the inhabitants of the Land of Israel, and according to their calculations alone, encapsulates one of the fundamentals of faith:

> "And here lies a great fundamental principle of the faith, understood and recognized only by one whose understanding is profound, that today, while we are in the diaspora, we calculate the calendar and declare that this day is the new month or that this day is a festival, not because of our calculation, but because the Great Court in the Land of Israel has already established that day… And I will explain further: if we imagine, for example, that the Jews in the Land of Israel were completely absent—Heaven forbid such a thing—because He has promised that the signs of the nation will never be entirely obliterated, and there would be no court, and no court in the diaspora that had been ordained in the land, then our calculations would be of no use whatsoever."

Many commentators have attempted to make sense of Maimonides' words, and to reach a full understand of the 'great fundamental principle f the faith' that he refers to.[57]

---

[57] Rabbi Jacob Berab phrased it as follows: "The words of Maimonides are puzzling… for he seeks to deny the reality that for many years we have had no ordained authorities, so what benefit is there in the declaration of Eretz Yisrael?" And in the words of Rabbi Soloveitchik: "The words of Maimonides are *merapsin igrei* ('shatter roofs', i.e. make no sense). Who are the 'inhabitants of Eretz Yisrael' upon whose status we rely? And where have we heard that in this time there is a Beit Din in Eretz Yisrael that sanctifies months and intercalates years?" For the difficulties and resolutions offered to explain Maimonides' words, see Avraham Feintuch, *Pikudei Yesharim – Commentaries on the Sefer HaMitzvot of the Rambam* (Jerusalem: Ma'aliyot,

Some have interpreted[58] his words to mean that our current calculation derives its authority from the actions of ordained courts that established and instituted the calculation of the months for all future generations. However, since Maimonides speaks of 'the inhabitants of the Land of Israel' and not just 'ordained courts in the Land of Israel,' others have argued that he means to say that every month anew, the month is sanctified by the authority of the 'inhabitants of the Land of Israel' who reside there at that time, and that, indeed, this is the great 'secret' contained in his words. But even if this last approach can be inferred from Maimonides' wording, the logic behind such a claim remains obscure.

Rabbi Jacob Berab (in his responsa, 63) is of the opinion that Maimonides' words should be understood in light of his position on the renewal of ordination: "I say that the Rabbi follows his own view. For he believes that if all the sages of the Land of Israel gather together, they can ordain whomever they wish, and now when they declare and say that a particular day is the new month, or a particular day is a festival, it is as if they all agree that their sages be considered to be ordained for the purpose of sanctifying the new month and establishing the festivals."

The Meshech Chochmah explained the matter similarly, but in his understanding, it is not the 'sages of the Land of Israel' who sanctify the month, as if they were ordained judges for this purpose, but rather it is the calculation and determination of the 'inhabitants of the Land of Israel' themselves which sanctifies the new month. In his opinion, Maimonides believed that the power of ordination resides within the inhabitants of the land: "the authority of ordination is dependent on the

---

1992), 221-225 (Hebrew). For a comprehensive summary of all the interpretations of Rambam's words throughout the generations, see David Henshke, "The Legal Source of the Concept 'Nation': Between Maimonides and Nahmanides," *Shenaton ha-Mishpat ha-Ivri*, vol. 18-19 (1992-1994): 177-197 (Hebrew).

58 An interpretation in this direction, was suggested by the author of Megillat Esther ad loc.

inhabitants of the Land of Israel," and that "the law of ordination belongs to the collective assembly," and therefore "their calculation is equivalent to that of an ordained court."[59]

Rabbi Herzog also follows a similar path, explaining Maimonides' intent by emphasizing the power and stature of the inhabitants of the land themselves. According to Rabbi Herzog, this special status is granted to the inhabitants of the land precisely because of the halakhic definition of the concept 'Kahal Israel.' In his view, this concept refers exclusively to the inhabitants of the land, and even if only ten Jews were present in the Land of Israel, those ten would be called the 'Kahal.' He argues that this idea appears explicitly in Maimonides' words in his commentary on the Mishnah in Tractate Bechorot (4:3): "The inhabitants of the Land of Israel are called the 'Kahal,' and God called them 'the entire congregation,' even if they are only ten people, and we do not consider those outside the land."

However, Rabbi Herzog poses a question in the attempt to arrive at a deeper understanding of this principle: "What does this have to do with ordination?" – If the essence of Semicha, ordination, is the transmission

---

[59] Rabbi Joseph B. Soloveitchik, *Kovetz Chidushei Torah* (Jerusalem: Makhon Yerushalayim, 1984), 47-65 (Hebrew) explained Maimonides' words in a manner similar to the Meshech Chochmah. According to him, it is the "inhabitants of Eretz Yisrael" themselves who sanctify the month. However, in his view, the matter is understood in the opposite direction—he does not believe that the sanctification of the month depends on ordination (semicha) and that the people of Eretz Yisrael are considered as ordained. Rather, he argues that the matter depends on the power of the people, and the Beit Din have the authority to sanctify the month since their power is representative of the power of the entire nation. Rabbi Soloveitchik explained that in regard to the sanctification of the month, the Great Sanhedrin does not function as a judicial authority but rather as the nation's representatives. In his view, the sanctification of the month was entrusted to the entire people of Israel, and with the dissolution of the Beit Din, which served as the authorized representatives of the people, the responsibility reverts back to the people. When they observe the festivals according to the accepted calendar, the months are sanctified automatically.

of the tradition of Torah reception from one person to another, why cant this process be done just as effectively in the diaspora? Based on this thematic difficulty, Rabbi Herzog proposes that 'ordination' should nit be understood as an expression of the transmission of tradition, but rather as an act of consecration, in which the the ordained is sanctified with the general sanctity of the People of Israel. The one conferring ordination acts as an emissary of the entire 'Kahal Israel', endowing the ordained with the sanctity that resides within the nation as a whole. As a result, the ordained becomes known as 'Elokim' (God-like).[60]

Rabbi Herzog finds support for this concept in the original act of ordination described in the Torah, where Moses had Joshua stand before the entire congregation of Israel, and afterward, he laid his hands upon him. Rabbi Herzog suggests that Maimonides interpreted this event, "apparently based on a Midrash that is no longer in our possession," to signify that "the true conferrer of ordination is the 'Kahal Israel', meaning that the sanctity of the nation is imparted to the ordained."

This would explain why ordination can only occur in the Land of Israel, seeing as the entire 'Kahal Israel' is only considered such when they reside in the land: "But in the diaspora, even if they are tens of thousands, they are considered individuals, not a congregation; and in ordination, this is the essential point, that the sanctity of Israel as a congregation is imparted to the ordained… Therefore, there is no ordination in the diaspora."

Rabbi Herzog adds that according to Maimonides, the sanctification of the new month also requires the sanctity of the entire "Kahal Israel," – which is a sanctity that exists only in the land – and therefore if, God

---

[60] Rabbi Herzog reinforces this explanation concerning the essence of ordination, noting Maimonides' statement in *Hilkhot Sanhedrin* 4:15 that if someone who is unworthy is ordained, "it is like consecrating a blemished animal for the altar."

forbid, the Jews were completely absent from their holy land, "there would be no validity to the sanctification of the months."[61]

X. "Our Nation Is Not a Nation Except in Its Land"

As we have seen, Rabbi Herzog not only attributes a special status to those living in the Land of Israel, but he also understands that the terms Kahal (congregation), Edah (assembly), and Israel refer exclusively to those residing in the Holy Land.

This halakhic formulation appears to have a clear ideological implication regarding the inseparable bond between the people and their land. If Rabbi Saadia Gaon famously stated that "Israel is a nation only by virtue of its Torah," Rabbi Herzog here presents a different formulation: "The nation is not a nation except in its land," as he explicitly states: "Israel is only called a Kahal in the Land of Israel; but in the diaspora, even if they are numerous, they are considered individuals—not a congregation."

Rabbi Herzog bases this sharp nationalistic worldview of the nature of the connection between the people and the Holy Land, on Maimonides' halakhic writings. He does not borrow from, or rely upon, any sources of secular nationalistic thought, but rather on purely

---

61 Rabbi Herzog offers only a brief discussion on this point, yet his remarks regarding the requirement that "all the congregation of Israel" must not be absent from the land suggest a nuanced understanding of Maimonides' intent. It appears that Rabbi Herzog interprets this requirement as integrating the perspectives of both the Meshekh Hokhmah and Rabbi Joseph B. Soloveitchik. According to Rabbi Herzog, while "the sanctification of the new month" does indeed hinge on the presence of ordained individuals, the crux of this ordination is not to be understood as a form of divine inspiration or spiritual endowment uniquely bestowed upon the ordained. Rather, the essence of ordination lies in its expression of the collective sanctity of the Jewish people. This sanctity, rooted in the community of Israel residing in the land, becomes the foundation for the legal and religious authority exercised in the process of sanctifying the month.

religious and halakhic sources.⁶² Nevertheless, his perspective is not far removed from modern nationalist thinking.⁶³ He saw in these statements an expression of the importance of residing in the Land of Israel, which served as a cornerstone of his Zionist worldview regarding the strong bond between the nation and its land. This halakhic-ideological outlook, which was sharply articulated by the Hatam Sofer—"If, God forbid, no Jews remain in the Land of Israel, even if Jews reside in the diaspora, it is considered the destruction of the nation, God forbid"⁶⁴—served

62 The distinctly religious nature of his thought is particularly evident in the notion he raises —though it is ultimately rejected by Rabbi Herzog—that this fundamental principle holds true only when the land maintains its sanctity with regard to the commandments dependent on it. Should the land lose its sanctity, the designation "congregation of Israel" would then revert to its application to the majority of Jews, regardless of their geographical location. This idea underscores the profound connection between the sanctity of the land and the collective identity of the Jewish people in Rabbi Herzog's halakhic thought.

63 David Henshke, "The Legal Source of the Concept 'Nation': Between Maimonides and Nahmanides," *Shenaton ha-Mishpat ha-Ivri*, vol. 18-19 (1992-1994): 177-197 (Hebrew) argues that Maimonides' words are grounded in a comprehensive conception wherein "the national character of the public exists specifically in the residents of Eretz Yisrael... In other words: national territory is an essential component in defining national identity" (Ibid., 190). He contends that this perspective is intrinsically linked to Maimonides' fundamental understanding of Torah as a legal system designed to govern the life of a community and a nation. Thus, the unique status of the land of Israel is not attributed to its "supreme sanctity... but because it serves as the national foundation of the people of Israel" (ibid., 191). Henshke further observes (ibid., 189n34) that Rabbi Herzog's writings suggest he, too, began to adopt this line of thought.

64 This quotation is taken from the *Shu"t Hatam Sofer*, Yoreh De'ah [sec. 334], referenced in David Henshke, "The Legal Source of the Concept 'Nation': Between Maimonides and Nahmanides," *Shenaton ha-Mishpat ha-Ivri*, vol. 18-19 (1992-1994): 195-196n46 (Hebrew).

as the intellectual foundation for Rabbi Herzog's innovative halakhic conclusion.[65]

65 This principle, which identifies the inhabitants of the Land of Israel as the "Congregation of Israel," is referenced in multiple places within Rabbi Herzog's responsa. For instance, Rabbi Herzog employs this concept when asserting that the collective power of the public is analogous to that of a king in matters of authority, particularly concerning the decision to lead the nation into war. He writes, "The king derives his power solely from the people, as he is chosen by the people. Similarly, we can assert that the entire people, and primarily the people of Israel who reside in the Land of Israel, as stated above, possess the authority of a king concerning national matters," in *Pesakim u-Ketavim*, vol. 2 (Jerusalem: Yad ha-Rav Herzog, 1989), 520 (Hebrew). In a similar vein, Rabbi Herzog remarks on page 213, "This conscription was declared by the vast majority of the settlement in the Land of Israel, which is considered as the entirety of the Congregation of Israel."

In his discussion on the obligation to recite Hallel on Israel's Independence Day, in *Pesakim u-Ketavim*, vol. 2 (Jerusalem: Yad ha-Rav Herzog, 1989), 486 (Hebrew), Rabbi Yitzhak Isaac Halevi Herzog presents a compelling argument for the recitation of Hallel in celebration of a military victory. This is relevant even for those who view the establishment of the State as an act of hastening the End of Days (d'chikat ha'ketz), and who might argue that had the Jewish people remained passive, the Arab attacks against them could have been avoided. Rabbi Herzog bases his argument on the Gemara in *Moed Katan* 26a, which posits that the obligation to tear one's clothes upon hearing "bad news" includes news of the defeat of "the majority of Israel," even if the defeat occurred in a war they unlawfully initiated—a war where "they brought it upon themselves." From this, Rabbi Herzog infers that if there is an obligation to mourn in the event of a defeat, even in an unjust war, then there must also be an obligation of thanksgiving in the event of a victory. Rabbi Herzog then anticipates a potential objection to this reasoning: one might argue that the obligation to mourn was specifically due to the fact that the defeat affected a majority of the public, whereas in other circumstances, such as when only a minority is affected, the obligation might not apply. He counters this by asserting that if the events had not occurred in the Land of Israel, there would indeed be room for doubt in this matter. To support his point, he references Maimonides' commentary on the Mishnah in *Bechorot*, which suggests that saving the inhabitants of the Land of Israel is akin to saving the entire Congregation of Israel. However,

XI. A Realistic Approach to Understanding the Purpose of Torah Laws – Milhemet Mitzvah Without a King

We will now suggest an additional area in which we may, once again, witness the same phenomenon. In his above-mentioned ruling that a war can be defined as a milhemet mitzvah (obligatory war) even in the absence of a king, and that the will of the public is halakhically equivalent

> Rabbi Herzog also acknowledges a caveat: while this reasoning applies to certain halakhic issues, such as semicha (ordination) and the determination of the calendar years, it may not necessarily extend to other areas. He draws a parallel to the laws of tithes and terumot, where the commandment is contingent upon the arrival of the entire Jewish people (bi'at kulchem) in the Land of Israel (*Hilkhot Terumot* 1:26). Thus, while there is a strong basis for the recitation of Hallel in the context of a military victory, Rabbi Herzog carefully nuances his argument by acknowledging the complexities inherent in applying these principles to different halakhic contexts.
>
> Other halakhic authorities who discussed the question of reciting Hallel on Independence Day debated whether it is appropriate to view the victory in 1948 as a miracle performed for "all of Israel." See, for instance, the words of Rabbi Goren, who unequivocally supported this view, in Shlomo Goren, *Torat HaMedina* (Tel-Aviv: Hemed, 1996), 581-582 (Hebrew), as opposed to Ovadia Yosef, *Shu"t Yabia Omer*, vol. 6 (Jerusalem, 1976), Orach Chaim, no. 41 (Hebrew); and Moshe Tzvi Neria, in *Be-Tzomet ha-Torah ve-ha-Medinah*, vol. 3 (1991), 93-94 (Hebrew), who rejected this view, based on the reasoning we mentioned in Rabbi Herzog's aforementioned caveat.
>
> In another place – in *Pesakim u-Ketavim*, vol. 2 (Jerusalem: Yad ha-Rav Herzog, 1989), 515 (Hebrew) -- Rabbi Herzog mentions this principle in the context of clarifying Maimonides' opinion regarding the mitzvah of settling the Land of Israel. Rabbi Herzog raises the idea that Maimonides included in his count of mitzvot only those commandments that are incumbent upon all of Israel, "wherever they may be." He then comments that this idea should not be contradicted by the fact that Maimonides included in his count the land-dependent commandments, which are obligatory only in the Land of Israel, because "the Land of Israel is different, as its inhabitants are called the Congregation, and they are the Congregation of Israel, as explained in his commentary on the Mishnah in Bechorot (4:2)."

to the king's command, Rabbi Herzog followed the teachings of Rabbi Kook. He added the following rationale to explain why this is so: "The king's power derives only from the people as they chose him, and so we can say that the entire people... have the authority of the king in matters concerning the nation... It stands to reason that the combined power of all those who appoint – is no less than the power of the one they appointed."[66] Sovereignty does not derive its authority from Heaven, but rather directly from the people, the nation, and therefore a legitimate government has the power to lead the nation into war. The role of halakhah is to guide and regulate this earthly war.

If so, in Rabbi Herzog's opinion the "Wars of Israel" described in halakhah are not to be seen as some sort of religious or spiritual reality, which is dependent on divine approval, through a king and Sanhedrin, but rather as an earthly reality, and political entity. Thus, in his eyes, the warfare he witnessed being waged against the Arab militias in 1948 was perceived to be an embodiment of the milhemet mitzvah discussed in the Talmud and by the halakhic authorities.

Many other halakhic authorities of his day did not share this same perspective. For example, when Rabbi Elyashiv reviewed these halakhic rulings, at Rabbi Herzog's request, he wrote in support of the conclusion that the laws of war differ from ordinary pikuach nefesh (saving a life) laws, and yet at the same time he emphasized that these laws depend on conditions that do not presently exist.. He, too, concluded that when "the experts believe that attacking the enemy is the best method of defense... they may attack even on Shabbat." However, he prefaced this by stating that "it seems that this halakhic allowance depends on a ruling establishing a state of war, which depends on the Sanhedrin, etc.," and

---

66   From his article on the establishment of a state before the coming of the Messiah, in *Pesakim u-Ketavim*, vol. 2 (Jerusalem: Yad ha-Rav Herzog, 1989), 520 (Hebrew), Rabbi Herzog initially presented this reasoning as his own. Only afterward did he note that upon reviewing the writings of Rabbi Kook, "I found that the esteemed rabbi of blessed memory explicitly writes this as well."

only "if a status of milhemet mitzvah or milhemet reshut (discretionary war) is established [as above, according to the Sanhedrin]."[67]

A similar understanding of the essence and purpose of the halakhic system is also reflected in Rabbi Herzog's principled position rejecting the possibility of relying on the Ran's statements in his sermons regarding *mishpat hamelukha*, royal justice. The Ran explained the relationship between the monarchy and the Sanhedrin as the relationship between a religious institution which has spiritual, heavenly aims and goals, and a governmental institution which is focused on regulating human relations. As the state was about to be established, many thought of turning to the

---

[67] Rabbi Yosef Shalom Elyashiv, *Kovetz Teshuvot*, vol. 2 (Jerusalem: Seewald, 2006), 34 (Hebrew). See also a similar discussion in the writings of the Chazon Ish regarding the distinction between "a war involving all of Israel, a mitzvah war or a discretionary war declared by the king and the Sanhedrin" and "a force that besieges a city, and the inhabitants go out to repel them and save themselves." In the latter case, "even though their battle is a mitzvah war, it is nevertheless not included in the exemption granted to an army camp." Commentators have explained his words: "It is reasonable to assume that his intention is that while they are obligated to fight to save themselves, this situation does not carry the full legal status of a war in terms of the obligation to fight under compulsion or the duty of those not in immediate danger to risk themselves to save others," in Yitzhak Kaufman, "The Parameters of a Milhemet Mitzvah," in *Ha-Tzava ke-Halakhah* (Jerusalem: Kol Mevaser, 1992), 4-5n4 (Hebrew). There, it also cites the opinion of Rabbi Herzog on this matter. Additionally, Rabbi Moshe Shternbuch discusses this in *Moadim u-Zemanim*, vol. 4 (Jerusalem 1964), 31 (Hebrew):

> "The primary designation of 'war' applies when all of Israel is in their Land with a Sanhedrin or a king. However, without this, even if it involves life-threatening situations where it is a mitzvah for everyone to assist, as explained by Maimonides (in Hilkhot Shabbat, chapter 2), it is considered within the framework of a pursuer (rodef)... but this does not carry the full halakhic status of a war, and this is evident."

It appears that Rabbi Shternbuch here revised an earlier interpretation he suggested to explain these matters, as published in *Shu"t Seridei Esh*, vol. 2, sec. 34.

Ran's statements, seeing his comments as a basis upon which one can try to erect and fashion the new state's legal system. On various occasions, Rabbi Herzog noted this theoretical possibility, repeatedly rejecting any such proposal.[68]

The Ran explains that the reason the king must at times involve himself in matters normally relegated to the judicial system, stems from the fact that the primary concern of Torah law is the determination of absolute justice, without regard for the implications for social order throughout the land. Therefore, the Torah granted the king judicial powers parallel to those of Torah law,[69] with which he could act, when necessary, to ensure proper social order, without being bound by Torah

---

[68] For an in-depth exploration of this issue, including the various proposals put forth by Rabbi Reuven Margoliyot, Rabbi Grodzinsky, and Rabbi Goren, see Yitzchak Avi Roness, "The State of Israel in the Halakhic Thought of Rabbi Herzog," (MA Thesis, Touro College, 2005), esp. 45-60 (Hebrew). In the context of this present analysis, however, our primary focus will be on the foundational argument presented by Rabbi Yitzchak Isaac Halevi Herzog concerning the matter. Rabbi Herzog's perspective provides a critical lens through which to understand the underlying principles at stake in this discussion.

[69] This principle also underpins the concept that a Beit Din may "execute and punish extrajudicially" as an emergency measure. The Ran explains that the authority to deviate from the standard legal framework during times of crisis traditionally falls under the exclusive prerogative of the king. The king, as the supreme authority, possesses the power to act outside the usual legal boundaries to safeguard the nation and maintain order during emergencies. However, in the absence of a monarchy, this responsibility cannot simply be left unaddressed, as it could lead to a judicial void and a breakdown of societal order. To prevent such a scenario, these emergency powers are transferred to the Beit Din, allowing them to assume the king's role in maintaining order and addressing urgent situations. This transfer of authority ensures that the community is not left vulnerable in times of crisis and that there is a mechanism in place to respond to extraordinary circumstances. The ability of the Beit Din to act in this capacity reflects the broader principle that the maintenance of societal order and justice is a sacred duty, one that may necessitate extraordinary measures in extraordinary times. This ensures that

law.⁷⁰ According to the Ran, there are two parallel legal systems which exist concurrently in Israel: the first system judges all matters according to Torah law; and the second metes out 'royal justice'.

Rabbi Herzog explains that according to the Ran's description, an offender would first be judged by a religious court, and then he would be brought to a second trial before a judge appointed by the king. The justification for the existence of this dual legal system lies in the fact that each system is aimed at attaining a different goal and purpose—the judgment according to Torah law is a mitzvah incumbent upon the community, no different from other religious commandments, such as offering sacrifices in the Temple. The court fulfills its mitzvah with awareness of fulfilling the divine command, which they know will lead to dwelling of the Shechinah (Divine Presence) in Israel. Seeing as this is their goal, therefore one should not question the practical benefit derived from fulfilling the mitzvah, just as we do not seek to understand the practical benefit of offering sacrifices.⁷¹ The king, however, acts

---

the Torah's legal system remains robust and adaptable, capable of addressing the needs of the community even in the most challenging circumstances.

70 The Ran supports his view by referencing the obligation for the king to keep a Torah scroll with him at all times, "so that he does not stray from the commandments and so that his heart does not become haughty over his brothers." The Ran explains that because the king's judicial authority grants him both the right and the duty to deviate from Torah law when necessary, it is particularly crucial for him to have a constant reminder of his connection to the Torah. This requirement ensures that even when exercising extraordinary powers, the king remains grounded in the divine law, preventing any potential misuse of his authority.

71 "The submission of a legal case to a Torah court, its adjudication, and the issuance of a ruling is a divine matter, akin to the service in the Temple, intended to maintain the divine connection between God and His holy people; in other words, it is a mystical act." Rabbi Yitzhak Isaac Halevi Herzog underscores this view by drawing on the teachings of the Ran, who emphasizes that the judicial proceedings before a Beit Din (rabbinical court) should be regarded as a mitzvah act. This means that the adjudication process is not to be evaluated solely on the basis of its practical utility, but

with a worldly purpose in mind, his goal being the preservation and maintenance of social order.

Rabbi Herzog was unwilling to accept this view. He could not countenance the proposition that the Torah's legal system be seen as a spiritual system not aimed at organizing and ordering worldly life: "It seems necessary to interpret, as I have explained the Ran's view, based on his own words, that this is about fulfilling the divine command to judge according to Torah law, even though it may not have any practical effect. But how difficult this is!"[72] By contrast, Rabbi Herzog clearly believed that the Torah's laws were given to serve as a comprehensive legal system for all aspects of life: "In my humble opinion, it is necessary to assume,

---

rather as a fulfillment of a divine commandment, much like other religious observances. Rabbi Herzog further elucidates this concept by comparing the role of the Beit Din in judicial matters to its role in sanctifying the new month. In the process of sanctifying the month, the Beit Din calculates the timing of the new moon based on precise astronomical data. Even though the exact timing of the new moon is already known to them and there may be no practical necessity for witnesses, the Beit Din is still required to accept testimony in order to officially sanctify the new month. This requirement highlights the mitzvah aspect of the judicial act, which transcends mere practicality and underscores the sanctity of the process. Rabbi Herzog's analogy illustrates that, like the sanctification of the new month, the adjudication of legal cases by the Beit Din is inherently a religious duty that serves to reaffirm the divine connection between God and the Jewish people. The judicial process, therefore, is not merely a means to an end but is itself an essential part of the religious and spiritual fabric of the Torah. For a more in-depth exploration of this idea, see Yitzhak Isaac Halevi Herzog, *Constitution for Israel According to the Torah*, vol. 2 (Jerusalem: Yad ha-Rav Herzog, 1989), 78 (Hebrew).

72 Yitzhak Isaac Halevi Herzog, *Constitution for Israel According to the Torah*, vol. 1 (Jerusalem: Yad ha-Rav Herzog, 1989), 167 (Hebrew). Rabbi Herzog wrote these words in response to an article published by Rabbi Goren in 1948, several months before the declaration of the state, in which Rabbi Goren sought to rely, among other things, on the words of the Ran.

as I have said, that the fixed legal system is Torah law."⁷³ "It is impossible to say… that if Torah law would be implemented, that the political order would be destroyed, that there would be no fear of justice among those who commit wrongdoing – for most of the offenses defined by Torah law in capital cases. God forbid to say so, for the entire Torah is for the sake of the world's stability."⁷⁴

73 In *Constitution for Israel According to the Torah*, vol. 2 (Jerusalem: Yad ha-Rav Herzog, 1989), 78 (Hebrew), Rabbi Yitzhak Isaac Halevi Herzog articulates the necessity of granting judicial powers to the king, drawing on a nuanced understanding of the king's role within the governance of the nation. Rabbi Herzog posits that one of the king's primary responsibilities is to maintain and oversee the moral state of the entire nation. Citing the biblical verse, "A king by justice establishes the land," Rabbi Herzog argues that the king is likely to be more attuned to the moral and ethical needs of the nation than the Beit Din (rabbinical court), whose members, as Torah scholars, are deeply immersed in their study and may lack the practical insight necessary for governance. This perspective underscores Rabbi Herzog's view that the king, as a central figure of authority, must be equipped with the necessary judicial powers to fulfill his role effectively. See Yitzhak Isaac Halevi Herzog, *Constitution for Israel According to the Torah*, vol. 1 (Jerusalem: Yad ha-Rav Herzog, 1989), 172 (Hebrew).

74 In *Constitution for Israel According to the Torah*, vol. 3 (Jerusalem: Yad ha-Rav Herzog, 1989), 305 (Hebrew), Rabbi Herzog's rational approach to Torah law becomes evident through his openness to comparing Jewish law with other legal systems. Rabbi Herzog assumes that these systems, though different in origin, address parallel issues with similar intentions and purposes. This comparative approach reflects his belief in the universality of certain legal principles and the profound wisdom embedded in Torah law. In Yitzhak Isaac Halevi Herzog, "Introduction," in *The Main Institutions of Jewish Law* (London: The Soncino Press, 1936), Rabbi Herzog expresses his hope that the world will come to recognize the depth of wisdom inherent in Torah law. He asserts that most Torah laws are well understood by reason and that anyone who studies them will find them to be rationally sound. Rabbi Herzog further praises the intellectual depth, subtlety, and fairness of Torah rulings, likening the legal wisdom of other systems to "a monkey compared to a human" when set against the vast and profound legal wisdom of the Torah. This comparison is particularly striking given Rabbi Herzog's

This basic rationalistic understanding of the purpose of the Torah laws, and the fundamental aim of its legal system, is that which animates and underlies Rabbi Herzog's view that the Torah's laws of war refer to the reality of a this-worldly state, and he does not imagine postponing the implementation of these laws to some imagined distant future when a king, and Sanhedrin, will exist once again.[75]

> expertise in both Roman and English law. See Yitzhak Isaac Halevi Herzog, *Constitution for Israel According to the Torah*, vol. 1 (Jerusalem: Yad ha-Rav Herzog, 1989), 226, 228 (Hebrew).
> Rabbi Herzog's rational view of Torah law aligns closely with David Henshke's characterization of Maimonides' understanding of the Torah. Henshke argues that Maimonides perceived the Torah as a legal system fundamentally aimed at guiding the life of a community and a nation, emphasizing the rational and ethical dimensions of its laws. Henshke's interpretation underscores the practical and moral orientation of Torah law, mirroring Rabbi Herzog's rational approach. See David Henshke, "On the Reality of Law in Maimonides' Thought," *Sinai*, no. 92 (1983): 228-239 (Hebrew). This rational perspective on Torah law stands in contrast to the views of graduates from the Lithuanian yeshiva world, who often emphasize the uniqueness of halakhah compared to the laws of other nations. According to this view, the laws of the nations, being the product of human intellect, are primarily designed to regulate relationships between individuals and create a well-functioning society, thus being based on practical and empirical considerations. In contrast, the logic of halakhah is seen as fundamentally different, operating on a plane distinct from secular law. This distinction is poignantly expressed by Naftali Kirsch, *Studies in Halakhah: Explanations and Comments on Talmudic Topics* (Tel Aviv: Tsioni, 1961), 9 (Hebrew), where he highlights the unique nature of halakhah as transcending the practical and empirical foundations of secular legal systems.

75 Rabbi Herzog's rational understanding of the nature and purpose of Torah laws also profoundly influenced his interpretation of the halakhic distinction between a discretionary war (milhemet reshut) and an obligatory war (milhemet mitzvah). Rabbi Herzog contends that the exemption from requiring Sanhedrin approval before engaging in a discretionary war, stems from pragmatic and worldly considerations. He explains: "To avoid delay, for if the matter is presented to the Sanhedrin, there is a concern for prolonged

XII. Conclusion

In his halakhic ruling, the decisor reflects what he perceives as the proper alignment between the given reality, in all its various aspects, and the theoretical halakhic concepts and specific laws found in halakhic literature. A decisor's worldview can influence the halakhic ruling at every stage of the decision-making process: in assessing the reality before him, understanding the Talmudic sources and defining the halakhic concepts themselves, or in his consideration of educational or public policy factors that may tip the scales in favor of or against a particular ruling. In extreme cases, such as in instances of migdar milta (preventive

> discussions, and in the meantime, the nation will be endangered... Therefore, the matter was entrusted to the king to decide swiftly, and of course, because he is dedicated to this role of safeguarding the state's affairs, it is appropriate to rely on him to make the proper decision in consultation with the minister of the army and the minister of war." This reasoning is articulated in his work *Pesakim u-Ketavim*, where Rabbi Herzog emphasizes the necessity of swift decision-making in matters of war to prevent potential dangers to the nation. From this rationale, one can infer the possibility that a discretionary war might be waged even without the involvement of the Sanhedrin, as Rabbi Herzog further suggests. See *Pesakim u-Ketavim*, vol. 2 (Jerusalem: Yad ha-Rav Herzog, 1989), 523, and compare with his discussion on Ibid., 225. This pragmatic and realistic approach likely also informed Rabbi Herzog's disagreement with Rabbi Roth concerning the halakhic status of a preemptive strike within the context of a defensive war. Rabbi Herzog's position—that every action taken as part of the war effort must be assessed in light of the overall objectives of the war—underscores his fundamental belief that Torah laws are designed to regulate warfare in a manner that ensures the essential conditions for its successful execution. According to Rabbi Herzog, there is no halakhic basis for interpreting the law in a way that imposes impractical restrictions on the ability to defend against an enemy, even on the Sabbath. His approach reflects a broader principle that the laws of the Torah, particularly those related to war, should not impede the effective defense of the nation, but rather should support the overarching goal of ensuring the safety and security of the Jewish people. For further details, see Yitzhak Isaac Halevi Herzog, *Pesakim u-Ketavim*, vol. 2 (Jerusalem: Yad ha-Rav Herzog, 1989), 523 (Hebrew).

measures) and similar situations, this can even lead to a ruling that departs from the normative halakhic definition.

In this type of cases where long-term considerations outweigh the immediate halakhic calculation, the decisor's worldview is overt, and its influence on the ruling is clear. However, this is not the case when the ruling relies on an analysis of Talmudic issues and the definition of halakhic concepts themselves. In such instances, careful examination of the halakhic discourse allows one to point to places where the decisor's worldview underlies his interpretative processes and guides his preference for one interpretation over other possible explanations.[76]

Thus, it is possible to distinguish between instances where the decisor's worldview appears openly in the halakhic discussion, separate and apart from the halakhic analysis of the issues, and those where this same type of influence manifests itself in an indirect manner, and is interwoven within the interpretative discourse and becomes part of the very definition of the halakhic concepts themselves.[77]

The study and analysis of Rabbi Herzog's responsum to the questions posed by the soldiers fighting in 1948, demonstrate how his ideological positions contributed to his ruling that the War of Independence fulfilled the halakhic definition of a milhemet mitzvah, and how this influence is evident at various stages of the halakhic discussion. As someone who visited and comforted Holocaust survivors in the displaced persons camps, Rabbi Herzog viewed reality from a unique perspective: in his eyes, the establishment of the State of Israel after the horrors of

---

76   The influence of different methods of study and traditions of legal rulings significantly impacts the extent of interpretative independence that a halakhic authority may assume. It is important to remember that, often, the authority adopts these conventions as an inheritance from their teachers, which they are not permitted to deviate from.

77   For further discussion on how the ethical worldview of the halakhic authority influences their interpretation of the sources, see Avinoam Rosenak, *Aggadah and Halakhah*, in *A Journey into Halakhah: Interdisciplinary Studies in the World of Jewish Law* (Jerusalem: Beit Morasha, 2003), 285-312, esp. 305–312 (Hebrew).

the Holocaust, was seen as an existential necessity safeguarding the physical and spiritual future of the Jewish people.[78] This recognition underpinned his discussion; and realizing that his unique perspective was not universally accepted, he sought out ways to frame, and present the situation, in a manner which would allow him to justify this same halakhic ruling – from within the 'regular' parameters of pikuach nefesh.[79]

His halakhic definition of the danger to the Jewish residents of the Land of Israel as analogous to a case of pikuach nefesh for the entire

[78] This perspective on the importance of the state finds expression in other halakhic discussions as well. For instance, when addressing the halakhic feasibility of granting full and equal civil rights to non-Jews, (a discussion borne out of the realization that refusal to grant equal rights may forestall the establishment of the state), Rabbi Yitzhak Isaac Halevi Herzog asserts that "a Jewish state is tantamount to the salvation of the nation." He further contends that rejecting the opportunity to establish a state "would extinguish the ember of hope in the hearts of most of the nation and undermine the very foundation of all Judaism." This highlights the paramount historic significance Rabbi Herzog places on the establishment of a Jewish state as a fundamental aspect of national and religious identity in the immediate aftermath of the holocaust. See Yitzhak Isaac Halevi Herzog, *Constitution for Israel According to the Torah*, vol. 1 (Jerusalem: Yad ha-Rav Herzog, 1989), 18-20 (Hebrew).

[79] In certain instances, a halakhic authority's decision to employ legal mechanisms such as hora'at sha'ah (temporary legal measures) or migdar milta (preventive decrees) can obviate the need for innovative reinterpretation of traditional sources. These tools enable the authority to tailor the appropriate ruling to the specific circumstances without necessitating a fresh conceptual analysis. However, it is crucial to recognize that these mechanisms are deemed emergency measures, and not all halakhic authorities consider themselves sufficiently qualified to invoke them. Paradoxically, it is often the humility of the halakhic authority—an attribute that may deter them from employing such drastic measures—that compels them to bridge the gap through the reinterpretation of sources. This renewed interpretation, while less immediate in its application, is perceived as less intimidating and more unive]sally accessible, offering a halakhic pathway that is open to a broader range of scholars and authorities.

nation, showcased the manner in which his religious Zionist worldview enabled a halakhic analogy and formulation which might not have been possible otherwise. We also noted the connection between his general principled understanding of the realistic nature of the halakhic system, and his understanding that the halakhic reality of milhemet mitzvah could exist even in a situation where the seemingly necessary halakhic conditions (a king and Sanhedrin) are absent.

Gerald J. Blidstein pointed out that although the qualities, values, and opinions of a sage influence the halakhah he produces, this influence is inherently limited by the fact that the sage's position is built on the sources he seeks to understand and apply. We will conclude with his words:

> "Precisely because the Talmudic synthesis is expressed so massively in the interpretation of texts, the researcher will need to delve deeply into the nature of the interpretation, in identifying the motivations and pressures behind the various contextual adjustments and resolutions, and in understanding the trends guiding the discussion. However, in any case, one cannot overlook both the commitment to the text and the trends that transcend the accepted texts. And sometimes it seems that the puzzle will remain unresolved, and that it is impossible to isolate the threads that have been so intricately woven into an organic creation."[80]

Rabbi Dr. Yitzchak Avi Roness is a lecturer in various colleges (Michlala, Orot, Givat Washington) and a communal Rav in Beit Shemesh.

---

80 Gerald J. Blidstein, "Review of 'Legal Values and Judaism', by Zeev Falk," *Dine Israel*, vol. 12 (1986): 300-319, esp. 315 (Hebrew).

[This chapter is a translation of Yitzchak Avi Roness, "The Wars of Israel: Halakhah and Ideology in the Teachings of Rabbi Yitzhak Isaac Halevi Herzog," in Shulamit Eliash, Itamar Warhaftig, and Uri Desberg, eds., *Ma'asuah le-Yitzhak*, vol. 1 (Jerusalem: Yad ha-Rav Herzog, 2008), 451-473 (Hebrew), which was based on chapters in Yitzchak Avi Roness, "The State of Israel in the Halakhic Thought of Rabbi Herzog," (MA Thesis, Touro College, 2005; Hebrew), written under the guidance of Rabbi Dr. Itamar Warhaftig.]

Section II: The Religious Soldier During the Independence War

Service in the Israel Defense Forces in the Thought of Rabbi Yehuda Amital zt"l

Aaron Ahrend

Few great rabbinic leaders have consistently focused on the Israel Defense Forces (IDF) and the challenges of the religious soldier. Our revered teacher, Rabbi Yehuda Amital zt"l (1925–2010), served as the head of Yeshivat Har Etzion in Alon Shvut for approximately 40 years. From his time as a soldier in Israel's War of Independence until his passing, one of the central issues that concerned him was the service of the religious soldier in the IDF. He addressed this topic in speech and writing, engaging with a variety of associated challenges. The following outlines a small selection of his activities and perspectives on this matter.

On one Independence Day, Rabbi Amital shared in the yeshiva, "in a moment of weakness," as he put it, about the beginning of his military service. His words reflect the atmosphere of the IDF in 1948 and the lack of awareness in the military system of that era regarding the needs of the religious soldier. Here are some excerpts from his account:[1]

> "I enlisted on the 4th of Iyar, 1948, and the next day, which was Friday, I was sent to Latrun… We gathered around a cannon and prepared to sanctify the Sabbath. I asked if anyone had wine. A Jewish fellow approached me and said yes. 'Where do you have wine from?' 'I'm a wine merchant. When I got the draft notice, I was so confused that I didn't know what to pack. I threw in a bottle of Alicante wine.' 'Good, take it out and announce to the guys that we're sanctifying [the Sabbath] at this position.' Some of the Czech immigrants who had recently arrived were half-assimilated, barely knowing anything. They had heard something about 'Kiddush,' but they didn't know what kind of ceremony it was. I began reciting the Kiddush as was my custom, and suddenly I noticed that all the soldiers were standing at attention. To avoid causing a desecration of God's name, I too stood at attention…

---

[1] R. Yehuda Amital, "Shomer Yisrael, Shamur Medinat Yisrael," Alon Shevut – Bogrim, 9 (5756/1996), p. 53. He describes the Shabbat atmosphere in the camp during 1949 in his article "L'darko shel ha-Chayal ha-Dati b'Milchemet ha-Komemiyut," published in his book HaMa'alot MiMa'amakim (Jerusalem and Alon Shvut, 5734/1974), p. 100: 'The regiment has been in existence for six months, and in the mess halls there is no sign of Sabbath. On entering the mess hall you notice nothing that sets Friday night apart from any other night: the same line, the same food, the same noise, the same tables, the same hastily eaten meal. From one distant table the sigh of a soldier pierces through the weekday atmosphere, 'Believe me, I even forget which day is the Sabbath.' Such innocent sighs, expressed in simple terms, were the only sacred remnant breaking through this mundane atmosphere." See Meital Gaz, "HaShtalvuto shel ha-Chayal ha-Dati b'Ma'arechet ha-Tzva'it b'Shanim ha-Rishonot shel Tzahal (1948–1953)," (MA Thesis, Bar-Ilan University, 2004), 15–30, 67–98.

When we left Latrun, we moved to the Acre area. One Sabbath, there was an inspection. [Haim] Laskov [commander of Battalion 79] saw me and rebuked me: 'Why haven't you shaved?' 'It's the Sabbath.' 'Why didn't you shave yesterday or the day before?' 'Well, I'll try.' Laskov shouted words whose echo I hear to this day: 'In the army, you don't try; in the army, you execute.' 'Well, I didn't know'.

On another occasion, we were required to swear an oath of allegiance… to the State of Israel, to uphold its laws, etc. I informed them that I could not swear to uphold all the orders. They told me, 'We don't mean it seriously', and I replied, 'For me, an oath is an oath. I'm not willing to swear'. They said, 'Fine, you don't have to say it, but you must sign the oath'. At that moment, the 'yeshiva boy' in me ignited: 'But Rabbi Akiva Eiger says that a written oath is still an oath.[2] I refuse.' In short, rumors spread that there was a crazy person in the battalion who refused to swear. The deputy battalion commander summoned me and asked, 'What should we do with you?' I said, 'I have a suggestion: give me a declaration—I will swear allegiance to the State of Israel, and nothing more. Regarding everything else, obedience to orders, I will not swear but will promise instead.'"

A few months later, in January 1949, Rabbi Amital published an article in the Battalion 79 synagogue bulletin. In the bulletin, Rabbi Yehuda Amital dedicated an article to outlining the areas where the religious soldier should work to shape the character of the IDF in accordance with the Torah.[3] For example, he emphasized that a religious

---

2   See She'eilot u-Teshuvot R. Akiva Eiger, First Edition, sec. 29.

3   R. Yehuda Amital, HaMa'alot MiMa'amakim (cited above, note 1), 96–107; the citation below appears on p. 96.

soldier could enhance the religious atmosphere in the military camp by fostering an exemplary community around the military synagogue, by establishing a distinctive Sabbath atmosphere, and, above all, by sanctifying the name of Heaven in public. The aspiration was for the conduct of religious soldiers to permeate military culture and be embraced throughout the IDF. His words were as follows:

> "We, a small group of simple soldiers, rank-and-file privates, carried in our hearts a grand vision of the character of the Hebrew army. We took it upon ourselves to be among the architects of this vision, and we dared to believe that we… would leave our mark, the mark of Torah, on the character of the entire army."

The secular atmosphere in the early days of the IDF is also depicted in Rabbi Amital's eulogy for Rabbi Shlomo Goren (1918–1994), the first Chief Military Rabbi. In this eulogy, Rabbi Amital highlighted Rabbi Goren's contribution to shaping the IDF as a Jewish army, in his words:[4]

> "Rabbi Goren built the Military Rabbinate. But that alone was not his greatness. In those days, he succeeded in instituting regulations concerning kashrut, the Sabbath, and holidays that would bind the entire IDF. You cannot imagine what the situation was like in those days: religious soldiers were isolated. When I enlisted, I looked around to see if there was anyone else putting on tefillin besides me, and I barely found one other. There was an anti-religious struggle… In this battle, Rabbi Goren succeeded, thanks to his personality and the ideal he set forth: to ensure that every kitchen in the IDF, everywhere, would be kosher. The extent

---

4   R. Yehuda Amital, "Voi l-Ar'a de-Yisrael de-Chasra Gavra Rabba," Alon Shevut – Bogrim, 6 (5755/1995), p. 124.

of the sacrifice—and even more so, the extent of the achievement—cannot be overstated."

Rabbi Amital also recalled Rabbi Goren's dedication and courage in his role as a military rabbi:

"Rabbi Goren was courageous in every sense of the word. Courage in the simple sense, expressed in his willingness to risk himself by going to dangerous places, and courage expressed in his opinions and rulings… Out of pure faith… Rabbi Goren went to the most dangerous locations to raise the morale of soldiers stationed at the canal outposts. Senior commanders were afraid to go, but he knew no fear. To bring fallen soldiers to Jewish burial… he crossed Legion lines alone."

In the 1960s, Rabbi Amital, together with his father-in-law, Rabbi Zvi Yehuda Meltzer, initiated the idea of the *hesder yeshiva*, a program combining military service with yeshiva study.[5] His experiences in a labor camp during the Holocaust and his service in the War of Independence undoubtedly influenced his perspective on the importance of enlisting yeshiva students in the IDF.[6] Rabbi Amital spoke on several occasions about the *hesder* concept. He listed some of the ultra-Orthodox community's objections to military service, the primary one being that Torah is acquired only through uninterrupted study, and even a brief

---

5   See the words of his son, R. Yoel Amital, "Sabi ha-Rav Tzvi Yehuda Meltzer zt"l," HaMa'ayan, Tammuz 5769/2009, p. 69. He notes that the students of the seminar at Yeshivat HaDarom in Rehovot, where both his father and grandfather taught, were the first to serve in the army within the hesder framework.

6   His perspective was rooted in the teachings of the Chazon Ish, combining recognition of divine providence with human responsibility to act naturally based on available resources. See R. Yehuda Amital, "Al ha-Ge'ulah ve-al ha-Temurah," Alon Shevut (Sivan 5738/1978): 8–9.

cessation from it precludes one from becoming a Torah scholar. Rabbi Amital rejected this view:[7]

> "This ideology diminishes the honor of Torah. The State of Israel takes pride in its scientists, doctors, and intellectuals—almost all of whom served full military service. Many of them even served as officers. They have achieved impressive accomplishments in their fields, and some have gained worldwide renown. I do not accept the claim that engagement in Torah differs in this regard from other pursuits. Not all great Torah figures of the past were full-time learners (*kolelnikim*), and Rabbi Yohanan the Cobbler's profession did not detract from his greatness in Torah. I had the merit to lead a yeshiva despite 'giving' the Nazis, may their name be erased, more than half a year of my life. Afterward, in a different context, I fulfilled my IDF service obligation for about 16 months, in addition to reserve duty. Many individuals greater than me from my generation spent long and difficult years in labor and death camps and now hold prominent positions in the Torah world."

Rabbi Amital outlined two rationales for establishing the *hesder* program:

1. This framework was initially intended to develop Zionist Torah scholars, as there was concern that religious Zionism would not thrive without a layer of Torah scholars emerging from within it.
2. This initiative reflected the religious-Zionist community's involvement in the needs of Israeli society.[8]

---

7   R. Yehuda Amital, "Ra'ayon Yeshivot ha-Hesder ve-Hagshamato," Alon Shevut – Bogrim, 14 (5761/2001), p. 35.

8   R. Yehuda Amital, "Petachav shel Elul," ibid., 4 (5755/1995), p. 40; idem, "Binu Shnot Dor va-Dor," ibid., 13 (5759/1999), 137–138; idem, "Ra'ayon" (cited above, note 7), 36–37; idem, "Talmud Torah," Daf Kesher, 7 (5758–

The *hesder* model, in which each student serves approximately 18 months of active duty in the IDF, was not adopted by the ultra-Orthodox sector. At the *Merkaz Harav* yeshiva of the religious Zionist community, a different approach was followed: Rabbi Zvi Yehuda Kook determined that military enlistment could often be deferred for many years and that service should be minimal. Rabbi Kook personally decided when each student would enlist.[9]

In the summer of 1969, Rabbi Yehuda Amital established Yeshivat Har Etzion as a *l'chatchila* (*optimal*) hesder yeshiva, without any sense of inferiority toward ultra-Orthodox yeshivot.[10] As the head of a hesder yeshiva, he maintained a strong connection with the students during their military service, regularly visiting them in their army camps, offering words of Torah, and, above all, listening to and encouraging them.[11] Approximately every two months, the yeshiva sent its students in the military a collection of essays titled *Alon Shevut*, to maintain a Torah connection with them. In 1992, when Rabbi Amital was 67 years old, he wrote a letter to the students in the military, reflecting on his meetings with them:[12]

> To the company of comrades, our beloved students…
> Instead of an in-person encounter, a few lines of

5759), p. 525. See also the letter of Dov Indig hy"d from 5733/1973, in Ch. Ben-Artzi (ed.), Michtavim le-Talya (Tel Aviv, 2005), 101–105.

9 See H. Volberstein, R. S. Klein, and S. Raz, Mashmi'a Yeshuah: Le-Demuto shel ha-Rav Tzvi Yehuda Kook (Merkaz Shapira, 5770/2010), 295–302.

10 R. Yehuda Amital, "Binu" (cited above, note 8), p. 137.

11 From R. M. Wiener: At the start of the Lebanon War ("Shalom ha-Galil"), his yeshiva cohort was urgently called to enlist. Rabbi Amital gathered them and said: "'One should only part from his fellow through words of halakhah' (Berakhot 31a), and my halakhic teaching to you is: 'Guard yourselves very carefully for your lives!'"

12 A photograph of the letter appears in Daf Kesher, 4 (5752–5754), p. 16. For additional details on these visits, see E. Reichner, BeEmunato: Sippuro shel ha-Rav Yehuda Amital (Tel Aviv, 2008), 76–78, 133–134.

> greeting. I must admit, this is not an easy matter for me emotionally. As you know, in recent years, I have completely ceased visiting our students in the army. The reason for this is my decision to yield to the limitations imposed by my advancing age. Yet even so, my heart is not at peace with this decision, and I am always stirred by mixed feelings on the matter. I want to believe that you miss these encounters, as I most certainly do. The meeting of a rabbi and yeshiva head with his students in uniform, somewhere in an army camp or out in the field in the Israel Defense Forces, always evokes a special emotion in me. Something that the rabbis of Israel in past generations never experienced—I, the least of them, have merited, by the grace of the Almighty, to experience it.

Rabbi Amital succeeded in building relationships with senior officers in the military, earning their respect and an attentive ear. Over time, he was appointed as the liaison rabbi between the IDF and the hesder yeshivot.[13]

Rabbi Amital placed great importance on observing mitzvot within the framework of military life. During the ceasefire in the Yom Kippur War, he visited soldiers near Cairo. Following the visit, he shared a story during a radio interview:[14]

> A brigade commander told us: "I was facing critical decisions. I gathered the soldiers to share my assessment of the coming developments and to prepare them for difficult possibilities. The atmosphere was particularly heavy. Suddenly, a soldier stood up and said,

---

13   See BeEmunato, 77–78, 129–134. A soldier in our platoon lost his rifle during a tank exercise in the Ze'elim sands and was sent to prison, as was customary in the IDF. After four days, he returned. When asked how he was released so quickly, he replied: "Rabbi Amital intervened for my release."

14   HaMa'alot MiMa'amakim (cited above, note 1), p. 46.

'Commander! There is another problem—tomorrow night is Sukkot, and we need the Four Species.' I was stunned," the commander recounted. "When I recovered from my astonishment, I said to him, 'Fine.' I relayed my orders over the radio: I requested such-and-such vehicles, such-and-such shells, and, finally, the Four Species. I sensed the shock on the other side. 'Where are we supposed to find the Four Species here?' came the eventual response. Anyone familiar with the authoritative tone of this commander knows that his orders had to be carried out, even under impossible circumstances. Before dawn, the Four Species arrived at the front line, and needless to say, our tank crews were glad to share the mitzvah of waving the lulav with the brigade commander."

Rabbi Yehuda Amital was among the first rabbis outside the military framework to issue halakhic rulings for soldiers.[15] In his decisions, he sought to be lenient, mindful of the unique conditions of military life. For instance, when a soldier in an officer's training course told him about the difficulty of praying properly due to his exhaustion, Rabbi Amital responded:

"During wartime, a soldier is exempt from prayer. However, during training, the situation is more complex: on the one hand, he must demand true and full accommodation from the army so that he can both pray and train effectively. On the other hand, if he fails to pray properly due to exhaustion, he should not feel guilt. He must understand that the Torah's prioritization

---

15 Another rabbi involved in such issues was R. Shlomo Min-HaHar, who co-authored Dinei Tzava u-Milchamah with R. Yehuda Eisenberg and R. Yehoshua Goleman (Jerusalem, 5731/1971). See Ch. Nahari, "HaSifrut ha-Hilkhatit le-Chayal be-Hitpathutah (1880–1975)," (MA Thesis, Bar-Ilan University, Ramat Gan, 2003), 76–81.

places a *milchemet mitzvah* (commanded war) above all other mitzvot, and that preparations for such a war are considered *mekhshirei mitzvah* (facilitatory acts), integral to the mitzvah itself."[16]

Regarding prayer in general, Rabbi Amital encouraged soldiers who had to pray during the High Holy Days while in the army, saying:

"I envy you for having to pray in the army. It is no great feat to pray in the special atmosphere of the yeshiva. When I lead as a *shaliach tzibbur* and say a single 'oy,' 400 students enthusiastically respond after me."[17]

Some of Rabbi Amital's responses to soldiers' questions were given in writing, typically as brief answers spanning three to four pages. Dozens of these responses were published in the yeshiva's bulletin, primarily during the 1970s. For example, he was asked: A religious soldier shares a barrack with a secular soldier who turns on a heating stove on Shabbat. Is it permissible to benefit from the heat generated by this act of Shabbat desecration? Rabbi Amital ruled that it is permissible to remain in the room despite benefiting from the heat of the stove. However, one must not approach the stove or take any action to warm oneself deliberately. Additionally, entering the room for purposes other than its designated residence or use is prohibited.[18]

On another occasion, he was asked whether soldiers traveling three or four kilometers in a tank for training are required to recite *Tefillat HaDerech* (the Wayfarer's Prayer). Here is a brief excerpt from his response:[19]

16 See Ch. Ben-Artzi, Derekh Acheret (Beit-El, 5751/1991), 74–77.

17 See also R. Yehuda Amital's letter in Alon Shevut – Bogrim, 17 (5763/2003), 183–184.

18 R. Yehuda Amital, "She'eilot u-Teshuvot: Tanur Chimum she-Hudlak be-Shabbat," Alon Shevut, 2(6) (5731/1971), 15–17.

19 R. Yehuda Amital, "She'eilot u-Teshuvot: Tefillat ha-Derech b-Nesi'ah b-Tank," ibid., 4(1) (5733/1973), 15–17.

"Since the roads there are inherently dangerous—ascending mountains and descending valleys—and navigating those areas safely requires great expertise, as I saw with my own eyes during my last visit to you… there is strong support for reciting the *Tefillat HaDerech* with a blessing."

On one occasion, 30 brief halakhic rulings he delivered over the phone without detailed reasoning were published. Two examples include:[20]

1. Question: Is it permissible to call home before morning prayers? Answer: Not only is it permissible, but it is a mitzvah.

2. Question: Is it permissible to hold an inspection before prayer? Answer: It is not proper, but it is not critical.

Rabbi Amital opposed ideological refusal to obey military orders.[21] However, he also opposed following orders that involved a transgression of Jewish law when it was unnecessary. For example, he once told us that it was not a severe matter to spend some time in a military prison for

---

20 R. Yehuda Amital, "Teshuvot Ktzarot ba-Telephone be-Hilkhot Tzava," Siach ba-Sadeh, 2 (5750/1990), p. 110. Regarding Rabbi Amital's position on national service for women: His son-in-law, R. Shlomo Brin, noted that he supported women participating in national service, and his daughters undertook such service. He opposed the stance of rabbis who forbade it. On his opposition to female soldiers training male soldiers in professional courses, see BeEmunato, p. 133. See also Gaz (cited above, note 1), 112–131; Keren Cohen, "HaKippah ve-haKometah: HaTmodedut shel ha-Tziyonut ha-Datit im Sugyat ha-Sherut b-Tzahal," (MA Thesis, Bar-Ilan University, 2009), 140–149.

21 As recounted by R. Yehuda Amital, "Shaliach Tzibbur," Alon Shevut – Bogrim, 8 (5756/1996), p. 168: "Today, two young men came to me seeking my blessing to attend an officer's course. I asked them, 'If ordered to evacuate Jenin, would you refuse?' When they said no, I encouraged them, saying: 'Go to your commanders and tell them, in the name of your rabbis: 'I will obey the order not because it holds higher status than halakhah, but because halakhah commands me to obey it.'"

refusing an order that required desecration of Shabbat when there was no genuine need to do so.[22]

He frequently emphasized that warfare must be conducted with moral values. His opposition to the IDF's entry into Beirut during the First Lebanon War stemmed in part from moral considerations and concerns over harm to civilians.[23] In his eulogy for Daniel Moshitz, who was killed in Lebanon in 1985, Rabbi Amital shared an anecdote illustrating Moshitz' ethical character:

> "Danny called me about two weeks before his death to ask whether it was permissible to pick oranges from a non-Jewish orchard while stationed in Lebanon."[24]

Rabbi Amital repeatedly highlighted the importance of Torah study even during military service. At one memorial event, he remarked:[25]

> "'This is the Torah: When a person dies in a tent' (Numbers 19:14). The Sages interpreted this to mean: The Torah endures only in one who 'kills himself' in the tent of Torah (Berakhot 63b). This refers to one who

---

22 See also R. Y. Weiss, BeDam Libi (Tel Aviv, 5770/2010), p. 182.

23 R. Yehuda Amital, "Meser Politiy o Meser Chinukiy," Alon Shevut, 100 (5743/1983), p. 38.

24 Regarding his remarks on Rabbi Goren (cited above, note 4), p. 126: "He insisted that combat be conducted at the highest moral standard... He proves (in his writings) that according to halakhah, one must not harm a non-combatant population, and certainly must not harm women or children. Even with enemies, one may only harm to the extent necessary for victory or self-defense... These teachings are especially important in our time, when we hear from students insufficiently guided by their teachers, statements like, 'The blood of non-Jews is forfeit.'" See also R. Yehuda Amital, "Devarim she-be-Chovah ve-Chovot she-ba-Hakara," Daf Kesher, 1 (5745–5748), 29–30; idem, "Erechem shel Chayei Adam," Daf Kesher, 8 (5760–5761), 288–289.

25 R. Yehuda Amital, "Divrei Zikaron ve-Hesped" [for David Cohen and Daniel Moshitz hy"d], Alon Shevut, 113 (5746/1986), p. 4.

settles permanently in the tent of Torah and devotes all his efforts to it. Yet there are times when one must part temporarily from the tent of Torah. As it is written in Psalms (78:60): 'And He forsook the tabernacle of Shiloh, the tent He had set among men.' At times, a person must leave the *mishkan*, the house of study. But there are those who, through great effort, merit that even when they leave the tent—the tent dwells within them. They carry the tent of Torah with them wherever they go. They live in the tent of Torah and die in the tent of Torah."

In his remarks about Rabbi Goren, Rabbi Amital described his unceasing commitment to Torah study:[26]

"Even when he was already the Chief Military Rabbi, his mouth never ceased from learning. 'Between one matter and another,' between his various responsibilities, he would sit and study. His car always had a Talmud, and he used every free moment for Torah study."

Rabbi Amital was deeply sensitive to the subject of fallen IDF soldiers and maintained close relationships with bereaved families throughout the years. During the Yom Kippur War, eight students from the yeshiva were killed. In the months following their deaths, he rarely visited the yeshiva, living in a state akin to "one whose deceased lies before him."[27] In a eulogy he delivered for them on the 2nd of Iyar, 5734 (24 April 1974), Rabbi Amital described their shared qualities and then reflected on the individual traits of each student. He was meticulous in ensuring that the

---

26 R. Yehuda Amital, cited above, note 4, p. 122. See also idem, "Divrei Petichah," Siach ba-Sadeh, 1 (5747/1987), p. 5.

27 See A. Lichtenstein, "HaRav Yehuda Amital zt"l: Mish'an u-Mivtach le-Shekulim," Yeshivat Har Etzion website. See also BeEmunato, 74–77, 81.

eulogies were of equal length, so that no family would feel slighted.[28] At a memorial event marking thirty years since the Yom Kippur War, Rabbi Amital spoke about that eulogy and the indelible memory of the eight students:[29]

> "At the memorial we held at the yeshiva after the war, I made an extraordinary effort to try to characterize each of the eight friends who fell in battle. It was not easy… For hours upon hours, I worked to retrieve from my memory every detail, even a faint glimmer of a recollection, anything that would be a true and meaningful remembrance of each one. I do not know if I succeeded. However, every fragment of memory I recalled was deeply internalized within me and became an inseparable part of who I am. These eight princes—along with the other yeshiva students who fell in Israel's wars and other tragic events—live within me.
>
> The Almighty, who knows all thoughts, examines hearts, and perceives the depths, knows just how profoundly these fragments of memory have penetrated and been absorbed into my being and consciousness. Thus, they have become my teachers and mentors. My soul is bound with theirs."

In the traditional yeshiva world, the *rosh yeshiva* taught and influenced his students in a single place: the *beit midrash*. The new model of the *hesder* yeshiva, however, meant that students divided their time between the *beit midrash* and military service in the IDF. Consequently, the role of the *rosh yeshiva* changed: not only teaching Torah in the yeshiva's study

---

28 See BeEmunato, 81–83. Rabbi D. Tropper also mentioned this in his eulogy for Rabbi Amital during the shloshim. The eulogy was published in the booklet Shmoneh Nesichei Adam (Alon Shvut, 5735/1975), 7–30.

29 R. Yehuda Amital, "Mori ve-Rabbotai," Alon Shevut – Bogrim, 21 (5766/2006), p. 11.

hall but also maintaining a connection with the students during their time in the army and even in times of war.

Rabbi Amital was one of the architects of this new model. His personal example as a soldier, his greatness in Torah and thought, and his personal charm endeared him to his students both in the *beit midrash* and in IDF camps.

Dr. Aaron Ahrend, a senior lecturer in the Department of Talmud and Oral Law at Bar-Ilan University, has published many studies on Talmudic commentary and Jewish liturgy.

[This chapter is a translation of Aaron Ahrend, "Service in the Israel Defense Forces in the Thought of Rabbi Yehuda Amital zt"l," *Daf Shvui (Bar-Ilan University)*, no. 913: *Parashat Emor and Yom Haatzmaut* (7 May 2011): 1-5 (Hebrew).]

The Path of the Religious Soldier during the Independence War

Yehuda Amital

NOT IN THE WHIRLWIND IS our path, nor in the storm do we tread. Modest and quiet are the ways upon which we walk. Yet, we march with courage, for our sights are set upon greatness. A vision has cast its light upon our path, and we walk by its glow. The heart still hesitates to venture forth with clear and open words. Even now, at the conclusion of a brief period of several months—a span in which we can, with profound satisfaction, point to many significant accomplishments in our work—the inclination remains to speak in hints. There persists a reluctance to call things by their explicit names. And indeed, the hand trembles as it pens this first-fruits confession. But the words must be spoken plainly and without embellishment, clear and unambiguous:

We, a small handful of simple soldiers, ordinary infantrymen, carried within us a grand vision of the character of the Hebrew army. We took upon ourselves the task of being among the architects of this character, daring to believe that we, this small group—in our daily conduct, in small, ordinary expressions, and in elevated and rich manifestations, all of which are revelations of a single great vision—would leave our imprint, the imprint of Torah, upon the character of the army as a whole. We knew our path would not be easy, strewn as it is with obstacles and challenges, but we were fully aware of the immense strength hidden within this vision and the courage it imparts to those who bear it. We cast our reliance upon the One who grants strength to the weary.

We translated the vision into objectives, and according to them, we charted our course. Here, we wish to present these objectives in their broad outlines, as far as this framework allows.

In translating the vision into action, four goals stood before us:

1. To contribute the religious soldier's share to shaping the military tradition of the organized and structured life of the army. This contribution is expressed in practices and actions that should serve as seeds for the constitution of military governance and practice. Over time, as these practices take root in the military culture, they integrate into this constitutional framework.

2. To imprint the Torah's mark upon the military environment, beyond the framework of command and discipline, which is where the unique character of the camp finds expression and plays a significant role in shaping the military spirit.

3. To enable the religious soldier to elevate his entire way of life, deriving from an awareness of the profound sanctity inherent in the values of the Israeli army, as one who fights the battles of the Lord for His people and land.

4. And the last in enumeration but foremost in importance: the exalted, pure contribution—not for ourselves nor for others, but for His great Name, blessed be He. A contribution to God, sanctifying His Name publicly, in the land and across the globe. "You shall love the Lord your God"—that the Name of Heaven may become beloved through you. To hearken to the voice of the Holy One of Israel, who declares to us: "You are My servant, Israel, in whom I will be glorified."

Before delving into the details of these matters, we must preface with several points to clarify some of the concepts we frequently employ.

6 | The Path of the Religious Soldier during the Independence War

One of the sorrowful phenomena in the spiritual life of the Jewish people, resulting from its exile from its homeland, is the blurring of the concept of Torah among the masses. Since our dispersal among the nations, the Torah, as it were, has diminished in stature, and its place has begun to be supplanted by "religion," a concept foreign to Israel. Gradually, we have reached a state in which the terms "Torah" and "religion" are seemingly identified with one another, though they are, in truth, as distant from one another as east is from west.

While the term "religion" merely signifies an individual or communal worship of the divine, born of the psychological need to satisfy the religious sentiment—a sentiment that indeed holds an important place within the human soul, particularly the soul of the Jew—it falls far short of encompassing the entirety of one's spiritual life. In contrast, the concept of Torah conveys an entirely different message. The Torah represents the Divine way of life, a comprehensive path encompassing all aspects of personal, communal, political, and national existence. There is no physical or spiritual movement that does not find its place within this divine creation we call Torah. The essence of the Torah lies in walking in the ways of God, for just as His ways encompass all, so too does He demand of His people to know Him in all their ways: *"In all your ways acknowledge Him, and He will make your paths straight"* (Proverbs 3:6).

This quality of walking in the ways of God was instilled in the character of the nation from its inception, in the days of Abraham our forefather: *"For I have known him, that he may command his children and his household after him, that they may keep the way of the Lord"* (Genesis 18:19). The concept of Torah, in its fullness, naturally includes the narrower content encapsulated by the term "religion." Yet, it would be a grave error to equate these two concepts. This is not the place to delve into the historical causes of this development, but we must note the reality: since our exile from our land, the Torah has, as it were, contracted, reduced to the dimensions of "religion," a kind of obligatory service concerning duties between man and God.

Therefore, with the establishment of the State of Israel and the beginning of the renewal of Jewish sovereignty, it is incumbent upon us to restore the crown to its former glory—to return to a life of Torah. A life of Torah, rather than a life of religion; adherence to God's ways, rather than religiosity.

In addressing the influence of the Torah in the Israel Defense Forces, we feel compelled to emphasize repeatedly that the Torah is our banner, and our aspiration in the army is to imprint the mark of Torah, not that of religion, which is merely a diminished, exilic substitute for a sublime and encompassing national ideal. There are numerous weak points in the army where the influence of Torah is lacking, and thus, many responsibilities fall upon the religious soldier to rectify matters. It is impossible to fully elaborate on these responsibilities within the scope of this article, but we wish to provide a few markers regarding the path of the religious soldier in the effort to shape the character of the Israel Defense Forces according to the Torah of Israel.

In discussing the contribution of the religious soldier to establishing traditions within military life, we must highlight a pressing issue: the issue of *kashrut* (dietary laws). Much has been said on this subject, both by soldiers and civilians, and there is no desire here to "add straw to the bricks." Certainly, this publication is not the place to address the role of ultra-Orthodox Jewry and its leaders in resolving this matter. Our aim is merely to underscore the great importance of the stance taken by religious soldiers and to emphasize that the manner in which they stand firm will determine the outcome and bring honor to the religious soldier.

This stance must be accompanied by practical understanding and realism on the one hand, and by confidence and dedication on the other. It must draw its strength from the vision we spoke of at the beginning of these words.

A significant role in shaping military tradition is occupied by the observance of Shabbat and festivals. Here too, it is incumbent upon us to mold their character in a manner that inspires a spirit of sanctity and serves as a source of spiritual elevation. This character must manifest itself across all dimensions of camp life. The issue of Shabbat must be addressed comprehensively, not with a symbolic or compromising solution. It encompasses matters of training, work, and formations, as well as the establishment of a special Shabbat schedule, including a later wake-up time without morning exercises, festive meals with tables set with cloths and candles, *kiddush*, communal singing, and festive foods.

There is no need to emphasize that a soldier immersed in the monotonous grayness of daily military life throughout the week must experience the fullness of Shabbat on the seventh day. Shabbat, which has played such a central role in shaping the Jewish family, must also find its place in shaping the family of the Israel Defense Forces. Few things can contribute as much to fostering social cohesion among platoons and battalions as Shabbat and festival gatherings. However, vigilance is required to ensure these gatherings do not devolve into mere musical evenings with orchestral bands, from which religious soldiers would feel compelled to withdraw. The rich heritage of ancient Israel, the product of generations, is more than sufficient; we have no need to replace it with new "traditions" crafted by various cultural officers.

Our practical approach to this matter within the battalion was characteristic. The regiment has been in existence for six months, and in the mess halls there is no sign of Sabbath. On entering the mess hall you notice nothing that sets Friday night apart from any other night: the same line, the same food, the same noise, the same tables, the same hastily eaten meal. From one distant table the sigh of a soldier pierces through the weekday atmosphere, 'Believe me, I even forget which day is the Sabbath.' Only these naïve sighs with their routine expressions add a modicum of sanctity to the air so permeated with a weekday atmosphere. The suffering of the religious soldier was great. This was not the vision of Shabbat as part of his dream for the Israel Defense Forces.

Without formal deliberation, we felt the path to rectifying this distortion did not lie in petitioning the command for changes and improvements. Our path led us, utensils in hand, through the queues before the kitchen windows, and with weekday rations in hand, we headed to the synagogue. Around tables covered with white cloths and lit candles, we sanctified Shabbat, just as Joshua's soldiers sanctified it in their time. We began with a small number, but our gathering grew from Shabbat to Shabbat. Thus, we continued each week, and the effort resonated across the battalion. Awareness grew, and the need to sanctify Shabbat and distinguish it from the weekday was felt, until one day an order appeared in the daily directives requiring company commanders to arrange festive Friday night meals. Initial attempts were made, and although the most suitable and desired approach has yet to be found, there is hope it will be discovered soon.

It is impossible to overlook the challenges that arise in a large framework such as a company or battalion. The diverse makeup of soldiers cannot be compared to the socially cohesive congregation of a synagogue. Precisely for this reason, efforts in this area are vital. Blessed are the initiators, and may the grace of God be upon their endeavors.

In discussing Shabbat, we must also mention another significant and by no means trivial issue: the matter of prisoners on Shabbat. It must be remembered that the sanctity of Shabbat applies even to prisoners, as the Torah makes no distinction between a free soldier and an incarcerated one. According to Torah principles, there is no justification for keeping a soldier in closed confinement on Shabbat when he is already detained within the camp. Even the wicked in Gehinnom, according to the Sages, rest on Shabbat.

I believe we must dare to introduce radical changes to align the conduct of the Israel Defense Forces with our values, even if these changes are unfamiliar in the armies of other nations. In any case, until a comprehensive solution is found, prisoners should be allowed to participate in prayers and Shabbat gatherings without restriction.

Numerous challenges arise due to the lack of clear halakhic guidance, particularly in the radically different conditions of the front compared to those of peacetime. By the grace of God, we have encountered many halakhic dilemmas that were unknown to us during our exile. It must be emphasized that among religious soldiers there is a profound yearning to hear the Torah's guidance—clear and complete—on the halakhic issues confronting the religious soldier in combat. Often, soldiers feel abandoned in this regard, left alone to navigate these challenges.

Let me take this opportunity to voice the heartfelt plea that emerges from the hearts of thousands of religious soldiers toward the great Torah sages: Know that the religious soldier is enduring a spiritual hunger—not for bread or water, but to hear the word of God. *Bring us the word of God!* We eagerly anticipate the day when Torah wisdom will shine forth in its full, comprehensive light, not in fragmented increments, bit by bit. We hope the recently established military rabbinate will serve as the voice of Torah wisdom, articulated by its great scholars.

Among the halakhic challenges faced by religious soldiers during battle, many are particularly encountered by the religious combat commander. It is a daily occurrence that religious soldiers refrain from accepting command positions due to these dilemmas. This phenomenon must be combated, and the only viable solution seems to be the presentation of clear halakhic rulings to the community of religious soldiers.

These challenges include unique issues that arise in combat. For example, the primary question of risking soldiers' lives, which often confronts a combat commander: When is it permissible or obligatory to endanger one's subordinates, and when must the commander take on the risk himself? Similarly, regarding the evacuation of the wounded, the question arises: When is it mandatory to rescue the injured, even at the risk of others, and when is it forbidden, even to volunteer or assist volunteers? The same issue arises with respect to the retrieval of fallen soldiers' bodies, though the halakhic considerations differ in this case.

Another unresolved halakhic question pertains to *kiddush Hashem* (sanctification of God's name) and national honor: Is it permissible, for the sake of the sanctification of Israel's name—and thus God's name—to choose death, either self-inflicted or through another, as in the case of Saul and his armor-bearer at Mount Gilboa, particularly when there is no fear of torture or desecration? On this issue, does the ruling apply equally to all ranks or only to higher ranks, where capture would result in a greater desecration of God's name? While we pray fervently that such situations never arise, the soldier heading into battle must be prepared for every eventuality, without hesitation or doubt. He must have definitive answers to all potential questions.

Another significant issue is the identification of fallen soldiers and their burial in a Jewish cemetery. This is not merely a matter of sentiment or friendly kindness but a mitzvah requiring the religious soldier to display initiative, dedication, and solemnity. We must remember the halakhic principle: *"When in doubt regarding a Torah commandment, act stringently."* Accordingly, even in cases of uncertainty, the obligation of burial must be fulfilled. Racial identification alone is insufficient; maximal effort must be made to achieve personal identification. The determination of several religious soldiers in battalion support units is commendable—they opposed expert opinions on the identity of fallen soldiers, and through their remarkable dedication, the bodies were brought for burial. Two weeks later, their comrades confirmed the identification of the fallen.

From here, we turn to the treatment of enemy corpses. The recognition that every human being is created in the image of God extends even to this domain. Scripture reminds us: *"You shall not leave his corpse on the tree but shall bury him on the same day, for an impaled body is an affront to God; you shall not defile the land"* (Deuteronomy 21:23). The Sages explain that it is because the image of God is present, and defiling the human body dishonors the King whose image it bears. During the wars of King David, burying enemy casualties was customary, as attested by the verse: *"When David was in Edom, Joab the commander of the army went up to bury the slain"* (I Kings 11:15). Another verse states: *"David made a name for himself when he returned from defeating Aram in the Valley of Salt"* (II Samuel 8:13). The Sages interpret this to mean that by burying the enemy casualties, David earned a reputation as a pious king: "He buried his fallen enemies." David's renown was thus not derived from his military victory over Aram but from his deeds upon returning from battle.

Prophecies of the End of Days also recount that Israel will bury the casualties of their enemies, such as Gog, and this act will earn them a reputation: *"The House of Israel will bury them... It will bring them renown on the day I manifest My glory"* (Ezekiel 39:12-13).

One of our comrades, distinguished for his efforts in handling and burying bodies, was rewarded in this world as well. As the Sages teach: *"The reward of a mitzvah is another mitzvah."* He was instrumental in saving a Jewish life. The incident involved an unidentified body found partially clothed among the bushes by the roadside, mere hours after the area had been captured. All outward signs suggested the body was that of an abandoned enemy corpse. One soldier, on impulse, aimed his machine gun to test it on the "corpse," but the aforementioned comrade forcibly stopped him. It was later discovered that the "corpse" was a fatigued comrade who had lain down to rest after the battle.

We previously mentioned the issue of enemy casualties, but intentionally skipped over a more significant topic: the treatment of captured enemies, as well as the handling of spoils and general behavior in combat. Much has been said about the purity of Hebrew arms, but the time has come to illuminate this issue from the Torah's perspective as well. The Torah's stance on these matters must be clearly explained, as many misunderstandings arise from a superficial reading of the written Torah without considering the Oral Torah, which is intrinsically connected to it like a flame to its wick. A thorough treatment of this topic is beyond the scope of this article, but, God willing, we will return to it.

Finally, we must address an issue often overlooked in the field: the establishment of sanitation facilities outside the camp. Among the explicit commandments in our Torah regarding military encampments is: *"When you go out as a camp against your enemies... you shall have a designated area outside the camp"* (Deuteronomy 23:10-13). While this is not relevant for established bases with fixed sanitary arrangements, in combat bases, which halakhically qualify as "camps," there is a negligent disregard for this fundamental obligation. This neglect causes discomfort to the conscientious soldier and additional spiritual anguish to the religious soldier, who sees it as a deviation from an explicit Torah commandment. This issue must be rectified.

All the questions raised here could, over time, find resolution within the framework of military regulations. However, that alone is insufficient.

Fulfilling the sacred mission of maintaining the purity of our camp—in every sense—requires great diligence, commitment, and initiative. This is especially the domain of the religious soldier.

There are, of course, areas of activity beyond the purview of military regulations—matters that will never be governed by such rules. These include life in the barracks and tents during the soldiers' free time, as well as the informal aspects of military life not subject to direct command. This provides a broad field for initiatives by those committed to the ideal of achieving a level of human and social refinement befitting a Jewish army.

Specific examples are unnecessary, but certain weak points should be highlighted: interpersonal relationships, card games, inappropriate language and conversations, and the treatment and preservation of military property. Such issues cannot be resolved by orders alone. Prohibiting gambling by decree is insufficient and ineffective. We must understand the conditions of camp life and the circumstances that drive soldiers to seek release in questionable entertainments. From this understanding, appropriate alternatives must be sought to replace the trivial pursuits in which many soldiers spend their free time.

The drive to improve these conditions must arise internally, from within us. Our contribution to this effort can be made by forming an exemplary community around the synagogue—a community unmarred by blemishes, whether moral, social, or military. Within this framework, cultural activities can flourish: regular classes on all aspects of Judaism, gatherings, discussions, and study sessions on a variety of topics. The development of such activities—both in the realm of learning and in other expressions of social life—will provide a significant response to the challenges we have mentioned and inspire similar initiatives among other groups within the battalion, fulfilling the principle that *"zeal among scholars increases wisdom."* Even those who suffer from "non-religious complexes" may, through such initiatives, be motivated toward cultural and social activity.

Another purpose of cultivating an intensive cultural environment within our community is the attraction it will hold for many isolated soldiers. These individuals may be inspired to join us and enter the gates of God. Many of these soldiers, whose religiosity is concealed behind a veil of shame, can overcome this disposition—a legacy of exile from the days of unfortunate assimilation when some Jews were embarrassed by their Judaism and sought to imitate the nobleman to gain his favor. There are also many soldiers who were raised in foreign environments and lack any knowledge of Judaism. Their integration into our community represents their first encounter with a life of Torah and Jewish values. The impression left by such an initial encounter is profound and enduring, placing great responsibility on our shoulders.

Here, we must highlight one of the great foundational principles upon which the ethical teachings of the Torah are based: the recognition of the value of the individual in Israel. Humanity was created as a single individual: "...therefore, every person is obligated to say, 'The world was created for my sake'" (*Sanhedrin* 4:5). This principle must occupy a prominent place in the awareness of the religious soldier in battle.

The danger to this recognition of individual worth is particularly acute in the military, where the mistaken notion often prevails that the lone soldier is merely a number, dispensable and replaceable. This erroneous view leads, on one hand, to the harmful feeling among soldiers that victory can be achieved without the contribution of that specific individual represented by a four-digit number randomly assigned to them. On the other hand, it results in personal needs and requests—matters of significant importance to the soldier's personal or family life—being trampled underfoot by the rigid routine of military protocol. It is imperative to sound the alarm about this perilous phenomenon in a timely manner, and these words are directed toward the attention of the high command of the Israel Defense Forces.

Finally, a few words about our own community, for which this platform aspires to be a voice. We do not claim that all is perfect among us, and we are far from ignoring our own shortcomings. Indeed, we have frequently worked together to address any moral or military flaws that have emerged among our members, with the goal of rectifying every fault and misstep. It should be noted that such collaborative efforts contain a great blessing. There have even been instances when commanders sought our help to positively influence a fellow soldier who displayed negative tendencies in various military matters. From our own experience, we have seen that religious and communal life within the walls of the synagogue has aided us in upholding moral standards.

It is a great privilege for our generation to witness the fulfillment of a vision cherished for centuries: the State of Israel has risen and become a living reality. Exiles are returning to their homeland, and the borders are returning to their rightful owners. We, the soldiers of Israel, bear an additional privilege: to count ourselves among those who have helped bring deliverance to Mount Zion and to have witnessed with our own eyes the wonders wrought by the Rock of Israel, who goes before us in battle. Let us, therefore, heed the divine call issued by the first conqueror of this heritage land: *"And Joshua said to the people, 'Sanctify yourselves, for tomorrow the Lord will do wonders among you'"* (Joshua 3:5).

[This chapter is a translation of Rabbi Yehuda Amital, "The Path of the Religious Soldier during the Independence War," *Moreshet: The Journal of Battalion 79's Synagogue* (January 1949): 4-7 (Hebrew), reprinted in *Hamaalot Mimaamakim* (Jerusalem: Agudat Yeshivat Har Ezion, 1986), 96-107 (Hebrew)]

The Activities of Rabbi Abraham Isaac Hacohen Kook in Matters of Security of the Yishuv

Moshe Ehrenwald

I. Introduction

In the summer of 1904, Rabbi Abraham Isaac Hacohen Kook was appointed Chief Rabbi of Jaffa and the surrounding agricultural settlements. In this pivotal role, he shouldered the responsibility of addressing complex halakhic challenges unique to the evolving realities of the Land of Israel during a transformative era. Among these challenges were pressing security concerns arising from the resistance of the Arab population to the expanding Jewish settlements across the region. At the same time, Rabbi Kook sought to inspire and connect with the pioneering settlers, many of whom had grown distant from Torah and halakhah. His work was part of a purposeful and visionary effort to bridge the divide between the Old Yishuv and the New Yishuv in the Land of Israel, fostering unity and collaboration among rabbis and communities across ideological and spiritual divides.

This chapter examines key instances, drawn from a variety of sources, that illustrate how Rabbi Kook addressed security-related challenges and engaged in activities directly or indirectly connected to the defense of Jewish settlements in the Land of Israel.

II. Defense of a Jewish Settlement on Shabbat

On 9 October 1911, an agreement was finalized between the council of the Rehovot settlement and the leadership of the HaShomer organization. Under the terms of the agreement, HaShomer assumed full responsibility for safeguarding the homes, courtyards, and fields of Rehovot, including liability for any damages incurred during their guards' service. The agreement outlined that HaShomer would deploy seven night guards within the settlement and five mounted guards to patrol the fields year-round, bolstered by an additional mounted guard and ten foot guards during the harvest and grape-picking seasons. The cost of the security service was set at 1,600 francs per month, with HaShomer providing a bond of 1,000 francs as collateral for potential damages.[1] When Rabbi Kook learned of the agreement, he wrote a letter to the Rehovot settlement council expressing his joy at the decision to entrust the security of the settlement to Jews. However, he urged the council to make a stipulation with the guards that they not desecrate the Sabbaths and festivals in their service unless it was a matter of pikuach nefesh (saving a life). He specified:

> "…[the guards must refrain from] Sabbath desecration involving carrying, riding, kindling fires, shooting, and similar activities. And on festivals, they must avoid prohibitions specific to the festival, namely all forms of

---

1 Zalman Asushkin, "Memories from *HaShomer* in Rehovot," in *Kovetz HaShomer: Documents, Memoirs, and Words of Appreciation Written by Veterans of HaShomer* (Tel Aviv: HaShomer, 1937), 131-135 (Hebrew); "The Contract between "Hashomer" and the Rehovot Committee," Ibid., 440-443 (Hebrew); Moshe Smilansky, *Rehovot: Sixty Years of Life 1890-1950* (Tel Aviv: Rehovot Local Council and Dvir, 1950), 70 (Hebrew).

labor generally required for security work, except for carrying and kindling fire from an already lit source."²

The cooperative settlement of Merhavia was the first Jewish community in the Jezreel Valley established by Jewish pioneers. In 1910, a conquest group (*Kvutzat Kibush*) composed of members of the HaShomer organization and laborers from the Second Aliyah settled the site. A few months later, during the winter of 1911, the settlement was formally founded as a cooperative farm where each member received wages based on their contributions. During this time, the governor of Nazareth, Shukri al-Asali, began inciting opposition against the settlement to thwart the establishment of additional Jewish communities in the area. This incitement led to tensions, including disputes between the settlement's shepherds and neighboring Arab shepherds. The local Arab population employed various means to harass the new settlement, often choosing to launch thefts and attacks on Friday nights when most residents were in their homes observing the Sabbath. In response, the settlers decided to hasten their Sabbath evening meals to conclude as early as possible. On one such Friday night, when attackers arrived, the settlers mounted horses and on foot repelled them. However, word of this incident reached Jerusalem, and rumors spread that the residents of Merhavia were publicly desecrating the Sabbath. Following the advice of writer R. Binyamin, Dr. Ruppin, and Dr. Thon, the settlers invited Jerusalem rabbis to investigate the veracity of these claims. When they learned of Rabbi Kook's intention, along with other rabbis, to visit, they hired a carriage from Nazareth to transport the delegation from Afula. However, the visit was delayed several times. Finally, they received unexpected notice that the rabbis, as part of the "Rabbinic Delegation," were waiting at the Afula train station. The settlers quickly prepared a wagon, cleaned it, and brought the rabbis to Merhavia. When they apologized for the inadequacy of the vehicle, Rabbi Kook responded with

---

2   Rabbi Abraham Isaac Hacohen Kook, chief rabbi of the city and district of Jaffa. "To the esteemed committee in Rehovot" (October 1911), Rehovot Municipal Archive.

an impassioned speech, expressing his joy at the privilege of traveling in the wagon of Jewish laborers in the ancestral homeland.

The "Journey of the Rabbis" (Masa ha-Rabbanim) was an initiative led by Rabbi Kook that took place in the winter of 1913. During this journey, a delegation of rabbis visited the new settlements in the northern region of the Land of Israel. Accompanying Rabbi Kook, then the Chief Rabbi of Jaffa, and his assistant, Rabbi Moshe Ze'ev Greenberg, were Rabbi Yosef Chaim Sonnenfeld, Chief Rabbi of the Haredi community in Jerusalem, along with his son, Rabbi Eliyahu Mordechai; Rabbi Yonatan Binyamin Halevi Horowitz, a representative of the Amsterdam Committee of Officials and Administrators, which funded the expedition; Rabbi Ben-Zion Yadler, the "Jerusalem Maggid" and national overseer of agricultural mitzvot in the settlements; Rabbi Aryeh Leib Zilberman, Chief Rabbi of Safed; Rabbi Yaakov Moshe Charlap, a prominent Jerusalem rabbi of the Mercaz HaRav yeshiva; Rabbi Baruch Marcus, Chief Rabbi of Haifa; and Rabbi Moshe Kliers, Chief Rabbi of Tiberias. The journey lasted about a month, during which the delegation visited 26 settlements and met with their residents. The objective was to bridge the divide and cultivate a sense of unity between the members of the Old Yishuv and the New Yishuv, many of whom had, to varying extents, strayed from adherence to Torah and its commandments.

The rabbis participating in the journey to the agricultural settlements spent several days in Merhavia. One night, the settlement came under attack by Arabs. The residents explained to the rabbis that such attacks frequently occurred on Friday nights, necessitating their active defense of both their lives and property. Seeking guidance, they asked the rabbis whether their actions aligned with Halakhah. Rabbi Kook decisively ruled that if they were certain the attack posed a *pikuach nefesh* (life-threatening danger), they were obligated to defend themselves. The other rabbis refrained from offering their own rulings, deferring to

Rabbi Kook, upon whom the halakhic responsibility for the settlements rested.[3]

During the visit of the rabbinic delegation on 25 November 1913, devastating news reached Merhavia: Moshe Barsky of Degania and Yosef Salzman of Kinneret had been murdered in an ambush. The rabbis were called upon to conduct a memorial for the fallen. Following the evening prayer, the entire community gathered solemnly in the dining hall. Rabbi Yosef Chaim Sonnenfeld delivered a deeply emotional eulogy, mourning the tragic loss of two young lives violently cut short by Arab attackers. With tears, he extolled their profound self-sacrifice, lauding them as youths willing to give their lives sanctifying God's name in their ancestral homeland. Rabbi Kook then rose to deliver his own heartfelt eulogy, further elevating the moment of collective grief and reflection.[4]

III. Conscription into Foreign Armies

In the summer of 1914 (5674), while Rabbi Kook was abroad, World War I broke out. The disruption of Mediterranean sea routes made it impossible for him to return to the Land of Israel. By 1916 (5676), Rabbi Kook was in London, serving temporarily as the rabbi of the Machzikei HaDat community. Among those in London at the time was Shimon Glitzenstein, a student of the Chabad Yeshiva Torat Emet in Hebron, who had been expelled from the Land of Israel by the

---

3 Gershon Gefner, "In Praise of the Righteous," in Eliezer Lubrani, ed., *The Merhavia Cooperative Book* (Tel Aviv, 1961), 95-96 (Hebrew).

4 Rabbi Yonatan Benjamin Halevi Horowitz, *These Are the Journeys of the Rabbis of the Community for the Uplifting of the Religion in the Holy Land, Who Traveled to Tour the Settlements of Samaria and Galilee in the Winter of 1914* (Kol Mivaser Zemeret HaAretz, 2001), 107 (Hebrew); Yosef Rabinowitz, *Merhavia (for the 25th Jubilee)* (Tel Aviv: Omanut Press, 1937), 43 (Hebrew); and Shlomo Zalman Sonnenfeld, *The Man on the Wall: The Life, Actions, Leadership, and Historical Period of Rabbi Yosef Chaim Sonnenfeld, the Chief Rabbi of the Ultra-Orthodox Community in Israel*, vol. 2 (Jerusalem, 1973), 303-305 (Hebrew).

Ottomans as a foreign national. In London, Glitzenstein served as Rabbi Kook's personal secretary.

Years later, Rabbi Glitzenstein recounted Rabbi Kook's extraordinary dedication to preventing the conscription of Jews into the Russian or British armies during the war. Among his many efforts, Rabbi Kook succeeded in delaying a government proposal to deport Russian nationals residing in England back to Russia, where they would be conscripted into the Russian military, which was also fighting against Germany at the time. Additionally, Rabbi Kook worked to prevent the conscription of Jews into the British army by issuing certificates identifying them as religious officials, who, according to the law, were exempt from military service. As the number of such certificates grew, the authorities began to question their legitimacy. On one particular Shabbat, a police officer came to Rabbi Kook's home, summoning him to the station for an inquiry after Shabbat. That evening, Rabbi Kook was questioned about a certificate he had issued to someone whom the police had determined was not, in fact, serving in a religious capacity, as stated in the document. Rabbi Kook explained that the certificate was based on a prior document held by the individual, which had apparently been lost. The police commander informed Rabbi Kook that he was being accused of issuing a fraudulent exemption certificate, a charge treated severely by military courts, with penalties including death. However, the officer stated that he would release Rabbi Kook this time, recognizing that the action had been done innocently, but warned him against continuing such activities. As they left the station, Rabbi Glitzenstein urged Rabbi Kook to cease these efforts due to the grave personal danger involved. Rabbi Kook, however, replied that those sent to the frontlines faced real and immediate danger to their lives, while the danger he faced in issuing exemptions was uncertain. In such circumstances, he explained, he could not exempt himself from the obligation to save Jewish lives. The following day, Rabbi Kook resumed issuing exemption certificates as if nothing had happened.[5]

It is noteworthy that during the debate over the conscription of yeshiva students in the War of Independence in 1948, opponents of conscription cited a letter by Rabbi Kook opposing the drafting of Torah scholars, without providing its historical context. When Rabbi Kook's son, Rabbi Zvi Yehuda Hacohen Kook, became aware of this, he issued a public statement on 4 April 1948, clarifying:

> "I am obligated to inform, for the sake of Torah truth, that this letter was written by him in the month of Adar 5677 (March 1917) in London, advocating for the exemption of Torah scholars from England's war with Russia and Germany, etc., which had no relevance to the obligation of saving Jewish lives and in the Land of Israel."

Rabbi Zvi Yehuda further condemned the misuse of the letter, describing it as "a distortion of the worst and most disgraceful kind."[6]

IV. THE EVENTS OF 1929 AND THEIR AFTERMATH

Yitzhak Ben-Zvi, a leader of the Va'ad Leumi (National Council) in 1929, frequently recounted Rabbi Kook's activities during the tumultuous period of the 1929 riots. When the news of the disturbances broke on a Saturday morning, Rabbi Kook did not rest or remain idle. He resolved to travel to the British administrative headquarters to intervene.[7] Shlomo Ze'evi, a member of the National Council, testified

---

5   Rabbi Shimon Glitzenstein, "Learning the Self-Sacrifice of Rav Kook," *ha-Hed*, vol. 11, no. 6 (March 1936): 12 (Hebrew).

6   Gabriel Alkobi, *Tseva Hashem: Enlistment in the IDF According to Torah and Halakhah* (Kochav Yaakov 2003), 144 (Hebrew).

7   Yitzhak Ben-Zvi to Yehuda Slutzky (5 May 1957), in Yemima Rosenthal, ed., *Yitzhak Ben-Zvi, the Second President* (Jerusalem: Israel State Archives, 1998), 490 (Hebrew).

that on Saturday morning, 24 August 1929, a group of Jews, including American nationals, approached him to request the Council's approval to meet with Harry Luke, the Acting High Commissioner for Palestine, and Thomas Campbell Wasson, the American consul in Jerusalem. They sought their intervention to halt the violence. Ze'evi accompanied the group to Rabbi Kook, seeking his leadership for a delegation that would approach the British authorities draped in their prayer shawls, symbolizing the gravity of their plea. Arriving at Rabbi Kook's residence before the morning prayer (Shacharit), they presented their proposal. Rabbi Kook expressed strong support for the initiative but explained that his physical frailty made it impossible for him to undertake the journey. In response, Ze'evi suggested traveling by vehicle, invoking the principle of pikuach nefesh (preservation of life). After a brief moment of contemplation, Rabbi Kook agreed. Accompanied by Ze'evi, Rabbi Kook walked to the nearby Hadassah Hospital, where he placed a telephone call to Luke. Speaking with urgency and conviction, he implored Luke to take immediate and decisive action to end the violent riots erupting across the country.[8] In the Haganah logbook in Jerusalem, it was recorded on that same Sabbath at 7:30 AM:

> "Rabbi Kook authorized the mission and resolved to personally lead a delegation to the government offices, determined to demand bold action—deploying airplanes and [machine guns], and seizing guarantees [in the form of hostages], including the mukhtars and the mufti. Yet, before he could depart, members of his household intervened and prevented him from leaving."[9]

Another version of the events adds further details: On Saturday morning, a day after the outbreak of the 1929 riots, news reached Hadassah Hospital on HaNevi'im Street in Jerusalem about the Massacre in Hebron. Raphael Marinov, the hospital's secretary and

---

8   Testimony of Shlomo Ze'evi (1958), Central Zionist Archives, No. 3.21.

9   Labor Archive, Lavon Institute, File 13/136 IV.

administrator, conveyed the information to Rabbi Kook, whose yeshiva was nearby. Rabbi Kook went to Marinov's office and called Edwin Samuel (son of Herbert Samuel, the first High Commissioner), who was Luke's personal secretary, and later spoke directly with Harry Luke, the Acting High Commissioner for Palestine. He informed him that he was presently in a hospital where dozens of corpses were located, despite his status as a kohen, which, according to halakha, prohibits him from being there. Furthermore, he was now desecrating the Sabbath because Jewish lives were in danger. Rabbi Kook declared to the Acting High Commissioner for Palestine that the blood spilled in Hebron was on his [Luke's] hands.[10] However, Marinov seems to have been mistaken in some details. The massacre in Hebron occurred later that Saturday morning, with reports reaching Jerusalem only hours afterward. Rabbi Kook's phone call likely pertained to the ongoing riots and fatalities in Jerusalem.

In light of Rabbi Kook's intense and proactive efforts during this critical period, the Va'ad Leumi (National Council) grew concerned that he might become a target for Arab violence. To address this threat, they appointed Eliezer Hodorov, a member of the Haganah, as Rabbi Kook's personal bodyguard. Khodorovsky maintained a vigilant presence outside the Rabbi's home and accompanied him whenever circumstances required. He faithfully fulfilled this protective role for 26 consecutive days.[11]

---

10 Testimony of Raphael Marinov, Central Zionist Archives, No. 34.20. Edwin Samuel participated on the afternoon of August 22, a day before the outbreak of the riots, in a meeting held by Acting High Commissioner Luke with representatives of the Jewish and Arab sides in an effort to calm tensions. See Yemima Rosenthal, ed., *Yitzhak Ben-Zvi, the Second President* (Jerusalem: Israel State Archives, 1998), 176 (Hebrew)

11 [Ben-Zvi to Colonel Kisch, 29 December 1929], requesting payment of 6.5 lira to Eliezer Hodorov at a rate of 250 mils per day. Hodorov was a member of the Haganah's mobile "Flying Unit" during the 1929 riots in Jerusalem and later became one of the first naval captains in the Israeli Navy in 1948.

Yaakov Shmidah, a *Haganah* driver in Jerusalem during the riots, recounted that Rabbi Kook permitted him to drive on the Sabbath for security purposes, even when the actions were not directly related to immediate *pikuach nefesh* (e.g., transporting people, ammunition, or food to sites requiring defense). Rabbi Kook believed that in such situations, one must obey commanders without overanalyzing the circumstances.[12]

Immediately after the riots erupted, the British began deploying additional military forces to the region to bolster their presence. On the eve of Rosh Hashanah 5690 (1929), about six weeks after the riots, the Chief Rabbinate permitted Jewish drivers to transport British soldiers even on the High Holidays.[13]

Rabbi Kook determined that the funerals for the victims of the Jerusalem attacks should take place immediately after Shabbat. However, the procession to the Mount of Olives did not commence until midnight due to challenges in securing a British escort to ensure the mourners' safety. Ultimately, only two or three officers were assigned to provide protection. Yitzhak Ben-Zvi, who attended the funeral, later recounted that as the burial proceeded, gunfire rang out from the direction of Talpiot, sparking fears that the mourners might come under attack by Arabs from Abu Dis and Silwan. The policemen, exhausted from their

---

12 Chaim Lifshitz and Zvi Kaplan, *Shivhei ha-Re'iyah* (Jerusalem: Nezer David, 1995), 235-236 (Hebrew).

13 "Pikuach Nefesh Overrides Shabbat and Holidays," *Haaretz* (2 October 1929): 1 (Hebrew). Below is the excerpt from *Dar HaYom* (29 September 1929): 4 (Hebrew): Representatives of the drivers, Mr. Yerushalmi and Mr. Bernstein, approached Rabbi Kook regarding their work on the High Holy Days. The rabbi ruled, "A time to act for the Lord, they have voided Your Torah," the Jews will stand in prayer, and the Jewish drivers must ensure the army can move from place to place even on these days, provided they fast and pray on Yom Kippur. It can be assumed that Rabbi Kook's ruling was based on the need to secure Jewish concentrations in synagogues on the High Holy Days, given the security tensions that followed the riots in the month of Av had not yet abated.

duties earlier in the day and visibly fearful, urged the mourners to hasten. As a result, the burial was conducted hurriedly and under great tension.[14]

Survivors of the Hebron massacre were confined to the city's police station, where they endured severe and degrading conditions. On Saturday night, Rabbi Yaakov Yosef Slonim of Hebron urgently requested that local officials contact Jerusalem for halakhic guidance on the burial of the massacre victims. The British authorities referred the matter to Albert Montefiore Hyamson, a British civil servant and historian who served as the chief immigration officer in the British Mandate of Palestine from 1921 to 1934. Hyamson consulted Rabbi Kook, who provided the necessary halakhic directives, which were then relayed to Rabbi Slonim. The burial process in the Hebron cemetery continued throughout the night, as each victim was carefully identified before being laid to rest, reflecting the solemnity and care demanded by the tragedy.[15]

The tension persisted even in the period following the riots. On the eve of Rosh Hashanah 5690 (1929), David Yellin proposed to the National Committee that they request the Chief Rabbinate to issue a statement advising against prolonged prayer services during the High Holy Days. Chaim Salomon discussed the matter with Rabbi Kook, but Rabbi Kook believed that such a directive would cause unnecessary panic.[16]

At the beginning of October 1929, the leadership of the Va'ad Leumi (National Council) sent separate letters to Rabbi Kook and

---

14 "Activities of the Hadassah Medical Organization During the Riots of Menachem-Av 5689," *Hadassah News*, no. 7-12 (Tammuz 5689 - Kislev 5690): 8 (Hebrew); and Yitzhak Ben-Zvi, *Writings, vol. 1: Memories and Records* (Tel Aviv: Mitzpeh Publishing, 1936), 204-205 (Hebrew).

15 Testimony of Rabbi Yaakov Yosef Slonim, National Library Archive, 10/01/722V.

16 Report from the National Council journal (3 October 1929), Central Zionist Archives J2/150/1.

Rabbi Moshe Mordechai Epstein, head of the Hebron Yeshiva, seeking their opinions on the potential return of the yeshiva to Hebron.

Rabbi Kook, a central advocate for the restoration of the Jewish community in Hebron, replied that "this matter is entirely entrusted to the administration of the yeshiva, headed by the esteemed Rabbi Moshe Mordechai Epstein, and no one else can express an opinion on it without their involvement."

Rabbi Epstein, in turn, responded to the Va'ad Leumi (National Council) that:

> "We cannot consider this. The fathers entrust their sons into our care, and we bear responsibility for them. How can we now bring them to such a dangerous place? When we sought a location for the yeshiva, we consulted the governor of Hebron regarding the security assurances for establishing the yeshiva in a town where most residents are Arabs. He assured us the place was safe and that the government would provide full protection. Indeed, before the incitement, Hebron was a safe place. But now, with the populace in a state of chaos, it is impossible for us to return with the yeshiva to Hebron."[17]

It is reasonable to assume that this question caused Rabbi Kook considerable inner turmoil, as he understood that the yeshiva was a critical component in rebuilding the Jewish community in the city. Nevertheless, he resolved to leave the decision in the hands of the yeshiva's head.

During a meeting of the Zionist Executive on 20 November 1929, attended by both Chief Rabbis to discuss issues concerning the Western Wall, Rabbi Kook voiced grave concerns about reports of Arab

---

17 National Committee Management to Rabbi Kook (9 October 1929); National Committee Management to Rabbi Moshe Mordechai Epstein (9 October 1929); Rabbi Kook to National Committee Management (12 October 1929); Rabbi Moshe Mordechai Epstein to National Committee Management, Central Zionist Archives J111/1.

preparations for a coordinated attack on the Jewish community, allegedly planned for December 6. He called for immediate action to notify the British authorities, urging them to strengthen military reinforcements in the region or, at the very least, to ensure that no reductions in their forces occurred. Rabbi Kook also emphasized the need for moderation in the demands regarding Jewish prayer rights at the Western Wall. While asserting the necessity of standing firm on the right to pray there, he warned against elevating secondary matters—such as "making tables, chairs, or a partition into a religious matter of the highest order."[18]

Following the violent riots in Jerusalem's neighborhoods in 1929, cattle slaughter at the shared Jewish-Arab abattoir near Jerusalem came to a halt. On 10 September 1929, Rabbi Kook issued an urgent appeal to the legal committee of the Zionist Executive, demanding immediate and serious action to secure a license for a dedicated Jewish slaughterhouse within the city of Jerusalem. He underscored the severity of the situation, pointing out that for three weeks, no meat had been available for the Jewish residents of the city. He declared, "Going to the slaughterhouse, where the murderers armed with their knives are present, constitutes a clear and present danger, even if some form of guard is provided."[19]

---

18 Protocol of the Zionist Executive Meeting (20 November 1929), Religious Zionist Archives 28–b. The discussion dealt with the response to a letter from the Muslim Association for the Protection of Al-Aqsa Mosque to the Chief Rabbinate, demanding consent that Jews have only visiting rights at the Western Wall.

19 Rabbi Abraham Isaac Hacohen Kook to the Legal Committee (10 September 1929), Central Zionist Archives S2282/30.

V. Demand for the British Government to Ensure Security

In the summer of 1931, tensions between Jews and Arabs in the Land of Israel reignited following the British government's decision to arm Jewish settlements for self-defense. Later that summer, representatives of the Arab National Congress convened in Nablus to discuss opposition to this policy and potential countermeasures at what became known as the "Nablus Conference for Arming the Arabs and Addressing the Problem of Jewish Access to Weapons." Among the participants was Sheikh Sabri al-Abdine of Hebron, who proposed forming combat groups to attack Jewish settlements. The Arab press further inflamed the situation with provocative rhetoric, intensifying the already heightened tensions. Acting on his own initiative, Rabbi Kook met with the High Commissioner to inquire about the British administration's plans to maintain order and prevent security threats. The Commissioner assured Rabbi Kook that sufficient forces were in place to manage the situation and that the administration had the authority to request additional reinforcements from British troops stationed in Egypt if necessary. He also emphasized that the administration would not yield to Arab demands to disarm Jewish settlements. Additionally, the British authorities refused to permit a general Arab strike planned for 15 August 1931. Ultimately, a demonstration took place only in Nablus, which the British suppressed with force, including live fire, injuring several protesters.[20]

---

20 "The Conference in Nablus," *Davar* (2 August 1931): 1 (Hebrew); "Impressions from the Nablus Conference [for Arming the Arabs and Dealing with the Problem of the Jews' Acquisition of Weapons]," *Davar* (4 August 1931): 1 (Hebrew); "Rabbi Kook with the Commissioner," *Davar* (7 August 1931): 1 (Hebrew); "After Shechem Day," *Davar* (26 August 1931): 1 (Hebrew).

VI. Training and Service on Shabbat and Festivals

In the spring of 1931, Yaakov Pat was appointed commander of the Haganah in the Jerusalem district and began a systematic reorganization of the region's defenses. Recruitment efforts expanded significantly, including outreach to the religious community, with even students from the Mercaz HaRav Yeshiva joining the ranks.

By 1933, a contentious debate arose within the yeshiva regarding whether religious recruits could participate in training sessions typically held on Shabbat. Some opposed recruitment altogether, citing concerns over potential desecration of Shabbat. To address the issue, Rabbi Kook invited Yaakov Pat for a discussion to understand why training was conducted specifically on Shabbat. Pat explained that Shabbat offered a rare window of free time, as organizing sessions during the week was challenging. Additionally, Shabbat provided a strategic advantage, as training could be more easily disguised as sports activities to avoid detection. During their meeting, Pat shared an account of a visit he and Rachel Yanait Ben-Zvi had made to Hebron a few months before the 1929 riots. While visiting the Jewish community and the yeshiva, they spoke with students from various countries who had come to study there. When asked how they would defend themselves in the event of violence, the students replied that they would fight back. However, when pressed on how they could defend themselves without training or weapons, their response was, "God will help us." Pat noted to Rabbi Kook that had the residents of Hebron been trained and armed, the tragic events of 1929 might have been avoided.

Despite the compelling arguments, Rabbi Kook did not permit training sessions on Shabbat. Instead, it was agreed that training for religious recruits would take place in separate groups on Fridays. This compromise led to a significant increase in recruitment from the religious community into the Haganah. Pat later recalled that Rabbi Kook provided him with a signed letter granting permission to travel on Shabbat for the sake of his duties, which he used when visiting areas where Shabbat observance was strictly adhered to.[21]

The Muslim *Nabi Musa* celebrations were a notorious flashpoint for unrest, posing a serious threat to both the Jewish community and British authorities. These volatile festivities consistently coincided with or overlapped Passover, leading the British administration to deploy additional forces in the Old City of Jerusalem to maintain order. By the early 1930s, this included the stationing of approximately twenty Jewish policemen in the Old City during the holiday period. As Passover approached, the Jewish residents of the Old City invited these officers to join them for the Seder, and the preparations for the festival evoked in the policemen a profound longing to celebrate the holiday properly with their families. They appealed to their supervisor for leave to participate in the Seder night, but he refused, citing a lack of official authorization. Undeterred, the officers sought the intervention of Rabbi Kook, sending their representative, Yitzhak Cohen, to present their case.

Rabbi Kook swiftly resolved the dilemma with wisdom and sensitivity. He ruled that half of the policemen, particularly those with families, should be allowed to celebrate the Seder at home, while the remaining half would remain on duty to ensure the security of the Jewish residents. In return, those who stayed on duty for the Seder night would celebrate the last day of Passover with their families. Rabbi Kook emphasized the importance of not leaving the Jewish community in the Old City entirely reliant on non-Jewish officers during such a potentially dangerous time.

Demonstrating his leadership and influence, Rabbi Kook immediately contacted the police commissioner by telephone to secure

---

21 Testimony of Yaakov Pat, Erev Shavuot 5709, Central Zionist Archives, File No. 139.15, and undated continuation testimony, Central Zionist Archives, File No. 53.69; *Darko Shel Adam: Kovetz le-Zikhro shel Yaacov Pat*, ed. Eliezer Lubrani (Herzliya: The Committee for the Commemoration of Yaacov Pat, 1958), 102 (Hebrew); Testimony of Shimon Agassi (28 February 1957), Central Zionist Archives, File No. 84.51; Testimony of Tikvah Eldovi, Central Zionist Archives, File No. 136.27.

approval for this arrangement. The commissioner consented without hesitation, ensuring that the Jewish officers could both fulfill their professional duties and observe the festival meaningfully.[22]

VII. Support for Arabs Who Assisted the Jewish Settlement

Rabbi Kook regularly advocated for providing assistance to Arabs who worked toward peace between Jews and Arabs. For instance, on 12 January 1931, he wrote to Colonel Frederick Hermann Kisch, head of the Political Department of the Jewish Agency:

> "The bearer of this letter, the Arab Mr. Yaseef Bey Haddad, is known for his efforts in favor of peace. Notables have already testified to his character. I acceded to his request to inform Your Excellency of his commendable nature."

In another letter, dated 3 May 1931, Rabbi Kook again wrote to Kisch:

> "The bearer of this letter is one of the Arabs known for their commitment to peace. He is currently in distress. I assisted him slightly with one lira, but he is still short of the sum needed to settle his debt. I would be delighted if Your Excellency could complete this assistance for him."[23]

---

22 Yitzhak Yud Cohen, *The Hebrew Policeman in His National Home* (Jerusalem: Achiasaf, 1939), 78-80 (Hebrew).

23 Rabbi Kook to Colonel Kisch (12 January 1931). Rabbi Kook to Colonel Kisch (3 May 1931), Central Zionist Archives 26/105J.

VIII. Conclusion – Embracing the Burden of Rabbinic Leadership in the Land of Israel

Assuming the mantle of rabbinic leadership in the Land of Israel during a period of rapid Jewish settlement placed Rabbi Kook before extraordinary and often unprecedented challenges. Among the most pressing were security concerns, which demanded his intervention and halakhic guidance on issues spanning the immediate and theoretical, the individual and communal—matters that often lacked precedent in traditional halakhic texts. Rabbi Kook undertook these responsibilities under arduous conditions: a significant portion of the Jewish population adhered to an ideological secularism, and the ruling foreign colonial administration were frequently indifferent, if not antagonistic.

Throughout this chapter, key instances have been examined, drawing from a variety of sources, to illustrate how Rabbi Kook confronted security-related challenges. These examples highlight his nuanced ability to address pressing practical realities while remaining firmly grounded in halakhic and spiritual principles. His vision, as expressed in *Orot HaTeshuva*, Chapter 15, Section 11, encapsulates the broader spiritual framework that shaped his approach, grounded in the intertwined destiny of national revival and spiritual elevation:

> "Our nation will be rebuilt and restored, regaining its strength in all areas of life, through the expansion, strengthening, and refinement of its faith, its reverence, and its sacred, divine noble essence. When all the builders of the nation come to deeply understand this truth, they will declare with strength and might: 'Come, let us return to God!' This repentance will be true repentance, a repentance of strength, a repentance that will provide power and resilience to all practical and spiritual facets, to all pathways necessary for the nation's reconstruction and perfection, for its awakening to life, for the courage of its stance. Eyes will open, the soul will be purified, its light will shine, its flight will soar, and a new nation will arise—a great, mighty, and numerous people, with the light

of God upon it and the greatness of a nation to its credit. It will rise like a lion, lifting itself like a lioness."

Dr. Moshe Ehrenwald is a graduate of the Department of History of the Modern Middle East and the Department of International Relations, holding a master's degree in Contemporary Jewry from the Hebrew University of Jerusalem. His book on the Jewish Quarter of Jerusalem's Old City during the War of Independence, based on his doctoral dissertation in the Department of History at the Hebrew University, was awarded the Yitzhak Sadeh Prize for Military Literature. His book on Mount Scopus in the War of Independence received the Moldovan Prize for Military Literature at Ariel University. His 2017 book, *The Haredim During the Independence War*, was published by Modan Publishing House.

This chapter is a translation of Moshe Ehrenwald, "The Activities of Rabbi Abraham Isaac Hacohen Kook in Matters of Security of the Yishuv," *ha-Ma'ayan*, vol. 59, no. 1 (September 2018): 25-34 (Hebrew).

The Draft and Yeshiva Students

Moshe Ehrenwald

As military conscription expanded, criteria were established for exemptions or deferments for various sectors. A comprehensive network of central and local appeals committees was set up to handle exemption requests for those eligible under these criteria. One such sector included students of higher education institutions, which also served as an important recruitment pool. This sector included students of advanced yeshivas, university students, and students in teacher training seminars.[1]

In the late nineteenth and early twentieth centuries, Lithuanian yeshivas reached their peak. Thousands of young students filled their benches, many of whom became rabbis and heads of yeshivas. Others succeeded in various fields: research, literature, political activism, and public affairs. Lithuanian yeshivas served as a forge for both the religious-rabbinical elite and the cultural-political elite of Jewish society in Eastern

---

1 Moshe Sicron, "Recruitment of Manpower in the War of Independence, Chapter 5: Exemptions from Recruitment," Israel State Archives 1970/1046-159, pp. 46-58 (Hebrew).

Europe. Most of these yeshivas, along with their students and rabbis, perished in the Holocaust.[2] In Hungary, for example, there were about two hundred yeshivas before the Holocaust, attended by approximately ten thousand students. All these yeshivas were destroyed, and many of their rabbis and students perished. After the war, some yeshivas were reestablished in Hungary and Transylvania, but they only existed for a few years before their students and rabbis immigrated to Israel or the United States.[3] Due to the importance of Torah study, Agudath Israel devoted most of its efforts and financial resources during World War II to help and rescue rabbis and yeshiva students.[4]

In Israel, there were established yeshivas, some belonging to the old settlement and others to the new settlement. During World War II and the years that followed, yeshiva heads and rabbis who survived the Holocaust and arrived in Israel established yeshivas in an attempt to rebuild what had been destroyed. In 1948, three organizations united yeshivas in Israel: "The Yeshiva Committee," led by Rabbi Zalman Sorotzkin and Rabbi Herzog, which included 55 yeshivas; "The Torah Initiative," headed by Rabbi Meir Berlin and Rabbi Uziel, which included 51 yeshivas; and "The Union of Yeshivas," led by Rabbi Dushinsky, which included 15 yeshivas. Most yeshivas were located in Jerusalem and Tel Aviv. The yeshivas catered to various types of students: mature yeshiva students with families for whom this was a way of life; students of higher yeshivas mostly aged 17 and in their twenties; small yeshivas and secondary yeshivas mostly aged 14-18; and Talmud Torahs – children of elementary school age.

In 1948, the economic and material condition of the yeshivas was difficult. Regular support from the United States had ceased, and it was

---

2   Immanuel Etkes and Shlomo Tikochinsky, eds., *Yeshivot Lita: Pirkei Zikhronot* (Jerusalem: Shazar, 2004), 7 (Hebrew).

3   Abraham Fuchs, *Hungarian Yeshivot: From Grandeur to Holocaust* (Jerusalem: Kiryat Sefer, 1978), 12, 23 (Hebrew).

4   Yosef Fund, *A Movement in Ruins: Agudat Israel's Leadership Confronting the Holocaust* (Tel-Aviv: Rubin Mass, 2008), 9-10 (Hebrew).

challenging to conduct further fundraising campaigns in addition to those held to finance the war. Some yeshivas faced crises and the threat of closure. To try to save the situation, Rabbi Zalman Sorotzkin, a member of the Council of Torah Sages and head of "The Yeshiva Committee," traveled to the United States at the end of February 1948 to conduct a fundraising campaign for the yeshiva organizations that had given him authorization.[5] Rabbi Herzog requested at the beginning of July that Minister of Religions Rabbi Fishman approach Minister of Finance Kaplan for financial assistance to save the yeshivas. He also acted to release goods purchased by the Yeshiva Committee and sent to Jerusalem after receiving the appropriate licenses for the Yeshiva Committee's consumers, but which were seized by the Jerusalem Committee.[6] At the end of August 1948, Rabbi Herzog appealed to the customs director in Haifa to release shipments of food and used clothing sent on behalf of the Yeshiva Committee by friends of the yeshivas in the United States to assist yeshiva students in Israel due to their difficult economic situation.[7]

Journalist Yaakov Gelis criticized the Zionist leadership's decision to take the university under its auspices and ensure its maintenance and development, while not doing the same for the yeshivas. However, he believed that the Haredi community should be pleased that the Zionists did not, 'in their great mercy,' take care of the yeshivas, lest these foreign guardians attempt to influence them and 'extract the soul with the embrace.'[8]

There were precedents for exempting yeshiva students from conscription during both World War I and World War II. The

[5] "Rabbi Zvi Sorotzkin on a Mission for the Yeshivas in the USA," *Kol Yisrael* (26 February 1948): 1 (Hebrew)

[6] Rabbi Herzog to Rabbi Fishman (1 July 1948), Rabbi Herzog Archives/ State Archives, F-10/4247 (Hebrew).

[7] Rabbi Herzog to the Director of Customs in Haifa, 25 Av 5708 [30 August 1948], Rabbi Herzog Archives/State Archives, F-2/4247 (Hebrew).

[8] Yaakov Gelis, "Do Not Worry About Us," *Kol Yisrael* (16 September 1948): 3 (Hebrew).

Ottoman government exempted "scholars" from conscription during World War I, and a special committee was established to handle this with the competent authorities.[9] Moshe Shertok of the Jewish Agency leadership and the Chief Rabbis agreed in July 1942 to exempt yeshiva students from conscription based on practices in the United States. It was decided to regard study in yeshivas as equivalent to study in higher education institutions and to grant appropriate exemptions to their students, without imposing national service obligations on those eligible for conscription serving as rabbis.[10]

Opposition to the conscription of yeshiva students stemmed from several reasons:

1. Rabbis and yeshiva heads believed wholeheartedly that Torah study has great value, especially in times of trouble. They viewed study as having security value and importance in preserving the spirit of the Jewish people. For example, Rabbi Yaakov Friedman of the Husiatyn Hasidic dynasty stated in a sermon that engaging in Torah for its own sake is the spiritual weapon that protects the Jewish people, thus negating the need for other weapons. The true protective weapon is Torah, which is not dependent on the consent of America or Britain.[11]

   This was also the view of Rabbi Herzog, who expressed it on various occasions. For instance, in a speech delivered to a conference of industrialists in Israel in 1943:

---

9   Rabbi Yechiel Michel Tikochinsky, "Exemption of Yeshiva Students from Recruitment," *Torah ve-ha-Medinah*, vol. 5-6 (1953-1954): 53-54 (Hebrew)

10 Moshe Sharett to the Chief Rabbinate, 12 July 1942, Rabbi Herzog Archives/State Archives, F-15/4242 (Hebrew); Chairman of the Central Recruitment Committee to Rabbi Herzog, 28 August 1944, ibid.; Yoav Gelber, *Toledot ha-Hitnadvut*, vol. 1 (Jerusalem: Yad Yitzhak Ben-Zvi, 1983), 576 (Hebrew).

11 Sermon for Shabbat Parashat Ki Tisa 5708 (28 February 1948), in *Ohaley Yaakov*, ed. Yaakov Schreiber (Tel-Aviv, 1962), 252-254 (Hebrew).

2. "Those who are permanently engaged in the tent of Torah, who have no worldly considerations of career or material future, and who sacrifice themselves and their individuality for the existence of Torah in Israel, are the spiritual heroes of the nation. As Maimonides said, yeshiva students and their rabbis are called 'the army of God.' The spiritual soldiers of the people of Israel. Let us honor and glorify our soldiers serving in the army, standing in the battle lines against the nation's enemies, for the honor of Israel, for the salvation of the people of Israel and the Land of Israel, and for the salvation of justice and human freedom. They continue the chain of heroism of Israel's armies from ancient times. However, today, like in the days of Hezekiah, king of Judah, the nation needs two types of soldiers: the army standing on the battlefront and guarding the land, and the spiritual army guarding its spiritual treasures – physical heroes and spiritual heroes."[12]

---

12 Yitzhak Isaac Halevi Herzog, "The Value of Yeshivas in the Life of the Jewish People," *Shu"t Heikhal Yitzhak*, Even HaEzer Part 1 (Jerusalem: Yad ha-Rav Herzog, 1960), 22-24 (Hebrew). This matter was later discussed in a meeting between Ben-Gurion and Rabbi Avraham Yeshayahu Karelitz, the "Hazon Ish," on 25 October 1952 at the home of the "Hazon Ish": Ben-Gurion asked how Jews with different viewpoints could live together. The "Hazon Ish" replied that they should act according to the halacha (Jewish law) that gives a camel carrying a load the right of way on a narrow path where there is room for only one camel. Those who are not religious should give way to the religious, who bear the heavy burden of Torah study and mitzvah observance. Ben-Gurion said that those who settle the land and defend it bear a heavy burden. The "Hazon Ish" responded: "By virtue of our Torah study, they can exist." Ben-Gurion replied: "If these young men did not defend you, the enemies would destroy you." The "Hazon Ish": "On the contrary, because we study Torah, they can live and work and guard." See the interview with Yitzhak Navon, who was present at the meeting as Ben-Gurion's secretary, Appendix A in Benjamin Brown, "The Hazon Ish Halakhic Philosophy, Theology and Social Policy As Expressed in His Prominent Later Rulings (PhD Dissertation, Hebrew University of Jerusalem, 2003; Hebrew).

3. Some of the leading yeshiva heads were Holocaust survivors who had lost family members and their yeshivas. After successfully immigrating to Israel, they immediately began rebuilding their yeshivas and viewed them as the last fortress of Torah study in the Jewish world that must be preserved from harm.[13]

4. There was a concern about the negative influence of the military environment and the difficulties in observing commandments and maintaining a religious lifestyle among the predominantly secular population, fearing that prolonged military service would undermine students' commitment to return to the yeshivas.[14]

---

13 Yosef Fund, *A Movement in Ruins: Agudat Israel's Leadership Confronting the Holocaust* (Tel-Aviv: Rubin Mass, 2008), 295-296 (Hebrew). Rabbi Yitzchak Ze'ev Soloveitchik of Brisk managed to escape Europe after his wife and three children perished in the Brisk Ghetto. He re-established the Brisk Yeshiva in his home in Jerusalem on Press Street.

14 David Tamar, "A Camel Laden Against a Camel Laden," *Et-Mol*, vol. 22, no. 2 (December 1996): 9 (Hebrew), according to a report written by Yitzhak Navon, who was present at the meeting as Ben-Gurion's secretary. The two figures each remained in their position at the end of the meeting; Givat Haviva Archives of the Hagana, Section 42 G-23/275 (30 November 1948), Aharon Haim Cohen, "Year of Recruitment: A Brief Review of the Activities of the Recruitment Office in Jerusalem." There were similar fears about removing members of the training farms in the kibbutzim to the army camps, as the Hashomer Hatzair kibbutzim feared recruiting their members to the British army and the Palmach, lest they not return to the kibbutz or bring back "negative influences" with which the kibbutzim would have to deal. See Yair Spiegel, *On Guard: The Contribution of Hashomer Hatzair to the Defense and Security of the Yishuv, 1920–1947* (Jerusalem: Carmel, 2010), 217-218, 258-259 (Hebrew); and Alon Kadish, "The Mobilized Training Programs," in Yechiam Weitz, ed., *Palmach: Sheaves and Sword* (Tel-Aviv: Ministry of Defense, 2000), 199-201 (Hebrew).

The Attitude in Yeshivas Towards the Haganah and Underground Movements

Among yeshiva students, there was significant sympathy for the underground movements and enthusiasm for their activities, with some students even joining or assisting them when needed. Generally, yeshiva heads forbade their students from joining these underground organizations due to concerns about secularization and the potential for distractions from Torah study. However, the attitudes of yeshiva heads towards their students involved in underground activities were not uniform: some ignored the issue, some actively sought to persuade students to cease their activities, and others expelled active participants from the yeshiva.[15]

Yechiel Eliash, the security coordinator for Hapoel HaMizrachi, proposed to Yitzhak Sadeh the establishment of a sort of "Hesder Yeshiva" within the Palmach. He reached an agreement with Sadeh and Wasserman to establish a yeshiva with 25 students at one of the religious kibbutzim affiliated with the Palmach. The unit would be divided into three classes, with each class training for eight days each month, while the remaining days would be devoted to Torah study. Rabbi Raphael Tzvi Yehuda Meltzer, son of Rabbi Isser Zalman Meltzer (head of the

---

15 Yoram Sion, *From the Springs of Harod to Jerusalem* (Jerusalem: Y. Sion, 2007), 61-72 (Hebrew); Avraham Lieberman, *Tales of Warriors* (Tel-Aviv, 1991), 148-157; Naphtali Lau-Lavie, *Am ke-Lavi* (Tel-Aviv: Maariv, 1993), 185-188 (Hebrew); *Zikhram La-Netzah* (Tel-Aviv, 1959), 110 (Hebrew), a description of the explosion that caused the death of Simcha Ozer, *ha-Tsofeh* (5 September 1947): 3-4; David Harmatz, interview with Dr. Ephraim Shakh, in *Makor Rishon, Sabbath Supplement*, no. 702: *Parashat Yitro* (21 January 2011): 12 (Hebrew); Miri Paar, *The Teacher: The Life Story of Rabbi Ezra Atiya* (Jerusalem, 1990), 207-213 (Hebrew); Elyashiv Reichner, *In His Faith: The Story of Rabbi Yehuda Amital* (Tel-Aviv: Yedioth Ahronoth Sifrei Chemed, 2008), 103, 106-107 (Hebrew); Shulamit Ezrahi, *ha-Mashgiah Reb Meir* (Jerusalem: Feldheim, 2001), 277-280 (Hebrew); Ezra Yakhin, *Elnekam: The Story of a Fighter for Israel's Freedom* (Jerusalem: Yair, 1991), 87-88 (Hebrew).

Etz Chaim Yeshiva in Jerusalem), who was the rabbi of Pardes Hanna and a member of the rabbinical committee on security matters, agreed to serve as the head of the yeshiva. The proposal was presented to Rabbis Yaakov Moshe Charlap and Rabbi Natan Ra'anan-Kook, the heads of the Merkaz Harav Yeshiva in Jerusalem, who supported the idea. Rabbi Charlap expressed his willingness to deliver a weekly lecture at the yeshiva even if it were to be established far from Jerusalem. Sadeh agreed to fund the eight days of training, and for the remaining funding, Eliash was directed by Rabbi Natan Ra'anan to Rabbi Moshe Avigdor Amiel, the Chief Rabbi of Tel Aviv, who expressed his willingness to provide the necessary funding. It was decided to establish the yeshiva at Kibbutz Ramat HaSharon (today Be'erot Yitzhak). However, the plan was ultimately shelved due to Rabbi Amiel's illness and his passing on April 15, 1946, as no alternative funding source was found.[16]

In yeshivas associated with the Mizrachi movement, such as the Bnei Akiva Yeshiva in Kfar Haroeh and the Noam Seminary in Pardes Hanna, training exercises were conducted. These exercises were overseen by Tzvi Chassid, the commander of the Religious Youth Battalion in the central Galilee.[17]

YESHIVA STUDENTS AND GENERAL CONSCRIPTION IN 1948

At the start of the registration for conscription in early December 1947, rabbis demanded that yeshiva students be exempted from the draft, as they had been exempted from conscription into the British army during World War II. Ben-Gurion responded that, for the time being, students would be exempt from conscription but not from training.

---

16 Yechiel Eliash, *A Vision that Came to Pass* (Tel Aviv: Elitzur Center, 1983), 357-359 (Hebrew).

17 Palmah Information Center, "Line of the Fallen," Captain Chassid Tzvi, who fell on May 13, 1948, as a platoon commander in the attack on Tira.

Should there be a need to draft them, the decision on exemption would be revisited.[18]

During discussions between the leadership of the Yishuv, the Central Command for National Service, representatives of religious parties, and yeshiva heads, the latter demanded the formation of religious units from their students that would train at their study locations and continue discussions on their conscription.[19] Some rabbis believed that yeshiva students should be exempted from training as well. Rabbi Moshe Glickman-Porush wrote to the Agudath Israel branch in Tiberias on January 12, 1948: "Regarding yeshiva students, the opinion of the rabbis is that they are completely exempt from conscription. The enlistment committee indeed agrees to exempt them, but they want them to receive training sessions. We oppose this as well, as it is the opinion of the rabbis."[20] On January 20, Rabbi Kahana informed Mintz, who was in Paris, that the issue of yeshiva students had been resolved in principle to the satisfaction of the yeshiva heads. Nevertheless, the practical method for their exemption had not yet been finalized.[21]

Chief Rabbi Herzog began addressing the issue of yeshiva students' conscription as early as 1940. He asked Rabbi Yechiel Michel

---

18 David Ben-Gurion, *Chimes of Independence: Memoirs (March-November 1947)*, ed. Meir Avizohar (Tel Aviv: Am Oved, 1993), 482 (Hebrew).

19 David Ben-Gurion, *The War of Independence: War Diary*, vol. 1, eds. Gershon Rivlin and Elhanan Orren (Tel-Aviv: Ministry of Defense, 1982), 179 (22 January 1948), and 193 (29 January 1948); Protocol of the Meeting of the Executive Committee of the National Service Command (14 December 1947), Israel State Archives 56/679-21 (24 December 1947).

20 Moshe Glickman-Porush to Agudat Israel Tiberias, (12 January 1948), Agudat Israel Central Archive, Jerusalem.

21 Kalman Kahana to Yosef Yizraeli (19 January 1948) Israel State Archives 49/481-15; Kalman Kahana to Binyamin Mintz, Paris (20 January 1948), Poalei Agudath Israel Archive, Box 30, File 11; "Kalman Kahane to Members of the Security Council of the World Executive Committee, Jerusalem," in World Agudat Israel Archive.

Tikochinsky, the director of the Etz Chaim Yeshiva, to investigate the matter of "exempting Torah scholars from military service."[22] At the end of December 1947, he wrote a detailed halachic treatise (comprising 48 pages) on the various aspects of yeshiva students' conscription due to the prevailing circumstances. The challenge he faced was how to balance the essential need for physical defense with the essential need to protect the nation's spiritual assets. His conclusion was that this was a milchemet mitzvah (a war of religious obligation) and a war to save the Jewish settlement in the Land of Israel and the surviving remnant of the Holocaust; therefore, yeshiva students should not be entirely exempt from participating in this war. He believed, "Care must be taken not to undermine, God forbid, the existence of Torah study, even for a short time, especially in our current situation, where the Torah centers in the diaspora have been destroyed, and we have no guardian but the Torah." Yeshiva heads should reach a suitable arrangement with the command for partial conscription under certain conditions, which would include the full exemption of outstanding students. Rabbi Herzog also noted that participation in the war would benefit the yeshivas by preventing opposition and hostility towards them from the public.[23]

In a telegram to Chief of Staff Yaakov Dori, Rabbi Herzog expressed his opinion: "The holy yeshivas in Israel deserve special treatment because, after the destruction of the diaspora, they are the remnant of Torah institutions, and their students are a small minority compared to the 35,000 students who perished in the Holocaust. The existence of these institutions, without harming them, is a matter on which the soul of Judaism depends. Conscripting them into military service, even

---

22 Rabbi Yechiel Michel Tikochinsky, "Exemption of Yeshiva Students from Recruitment," *Torah ve-ha-Medinah*, vol. 5-6 (1953-1954): 45 (Hebrew).

23 Rabbi Herzog, Regarding the Yeshiva Students in Connection with the Situation, 16 Tevet 5708, Israel State Archives, F-7/4251 (Rabbi Herzog Archive); Zorach Warhaftig, in *Constitution and Law in a Jewish State According to Halakhah* (Jerusalem: Yad ha-Rav Herzog, 1989), 236 (Hebrew).

partially, could undermine them, and we must avoid this. Please continue the treatment of them by the army as it has been until now, according to an order from the Minister of Defense."[24] Rabbi Herzog made similar statements towards the end of the war in February 1949: "The Torah is what has sustained us, and preserved us, and brought us to this time, to the beginning of the growth of our redemption in our land. What a disaster, what an internal destruction it would be if, God forbid, the Torah were forgotten from Israel in the Land of Israel. This forgetfulness would mean, in a spiritual sense, a suicide, God forbid, a severing of the living connection with the nation's past in the holy land in the past, and with its wonderful past from the spiritual perspective in exile. [...] Let us diligently guard the two pillars of the House of Israel, study, the study of Torah, and action, the observance of its sacred commandments that purify Israel."[25]

Mintz, who was a member of the Religious Affairs Committee in the National Command of the Haganah, approached Yosef Yizraeli, the representative of the Haganah command in the Executive Committee of the National Service Command and chairman of the Religious Committee, and demanded the exemption of yeshiva students from conscription. He suggested meeting with the Hazon Ish, who was the most authoritative halachic figure in the Haredi community. Yizraeli agreed, and the Hazon Ish stated that he understood the need for a general conscription, but nevertheless, yeshiva students should be exempted. The Haganah understood the logic behind the request, and it was accepted.[26]

---

24 Yitzchak Isaac Halevi Herzog, Chief Rabbi of Israel, to Chief of the General Staff, Lieutenant General Yaakov Dori, undated, Israel State Archives F-7/4251 (Rabbi Herzog Archive).

25 From remarks made by Rabbi Herzog at a party held in honor of his 60th birthday on 14 February 1949, The Message of the Chief Rabbi of Israel, Rabbi Yitzchak Isaac Halevi Herzog.

26 Yosef Izre'eli, *Bi-Shelihut Bithonit* (Tel-Aviv: Am Oved, 1972) 81 (Hebrew). Avraham Lieberman, a Lehi member residing in Bnei Brak, was responsible

In mid-February 1948, Rabbi Kahana drafted an agreement, approved by the head of the National Command, Israel Galili, and by the Chief Rabbis and other rabbis. The agreement stated: "Yeshiva students, according to the lists approved by three yeshiva heads, are exempt from military service (in full or partial conscriptions). Yeshiva administrations should provide capable students with training for self-defense in place, under the command and guidance of the supreme command. This agreement will be considered a temporary arrangement for the year 1948 and will be reconsidered at the beginning of 1949. It cannot be canceled except by a new agreement." Three representatives of the yeshiva heads signed the agreement: Rabbi Reuven Katz, Rabbi Yosef Kahaneman, and Rabbi Shabtai Yagel. Rabbi Katz was the Chief Rabbi of Petach Tikvah, a member of the Chief Rabbinate Council, head of the Lomza Yeshiva, and a member of the Executive Committee of the Yeshiva Council. Israel Galili, head of the National Command of the Haganah, also signed the text.[27]

On March 9, Israel Galili forwarded the text of the decision to the regional brigades and the Palmach, requesting that "the training of yeshiva students be arranged in such a way as not to disrupt the study regimen in the yeshivas. Therefore, contact should be made with yeshiva heads to ensure that vacation times are utilized for training, coordinating the dates, and so on. This directive means that yeshiva students will only be included in the non-recruited Home Guard." The exemption applied to yeshiva students who began their studies before November

for a Lehi weapons depot and also hid weapons in the yard of the Hazon Ish.

27 Israel State Archives 49/481-15, 19 February 1948, the text with the signatures of the three representatives of the heads of the yeshivas to Rabbi Kalman Kahane; ibid., 20 February 1948, Kalman Kahana to Israel [Galili]. Rabbis Kahaneman and Yigal were Holocaust survivors who served as heads of yeshivas in Europe and re-established their yeshivas in Israel, which were destroyed in the Holocaust.

1947 and were approved by the yeshiva heads.[28] The exemption also included rabbis and yeshiva heads who were actually serving, provided they obtained approval from the Chief Rabbinate.[29]

Yeshiva heads committed not to prevent their students from volunteering for conscription, and indeed, there were many who enlisted despite the temporary exemption they received.[30] For example, eight students from the Bnei Akiva Yeshiva in Kfar Haroeh, who trained on-site, went to reinforce the force holding Birya in the Galilee. On the last Sabbath of their stay at the yeshiva, a farewell party was held in their honor, attended by the yeshiva rabbis who blessed them.[31]

There were actually two agreements, one for Jerusalem and another for all other places. As described by Yehuda Bloy from the Agudath Israel Center in Jerusalem in a letter to his party's branch in Tiberias: "According to the agreement between Agudath Israel and the National Service Command Center in the new settlement, yeshiva students are not completely exempt. They receive blue cards and train within the

---

28 Israel State Archives, 49/959-117, March 1948, Head of National Command to Golani, Carmeli, Alexandroni, Kryati, Givati, Etzioni, Bulgarians [Palmach]; Tsvi A. Tal, "On the Issue of Drafting Yeshiva Students," in Michael Corinaldi, Moshe David Herr, Rivka Horwitz, and Yochanan David Silman, eds. *Studies in Memory of Professor Ze'ev Falk* (Jerusalem: Mesharim, 2005), 355 (Hebrew). The Haim-Guard Corps, consisted of older recruits and mainly engaged in static guard duties, with personnel partially mobilized or serving as reserves; Golani Brigade Commander to Battalion Commanders, District Commanders, regarding the training of yeshiva students, 17 March 1948, Israel State Archives 49/5205-55.

29 National Service Command / Instructions and Summaries, Section 5 (14 March 1948), Israel State Archives, GL-4/46642.

30 "85 percent of Jerusalem youth enlisted," *Davar* (9 March 1948): 6 (Hebrew).

31 *Fifty Years of an Israeli Religious Youth Movement: Bnei Akiva 1929–1979*, eds. Mordecai Bar-Lev, Yedidya Cohen, and Shlomo Rosner (Tel Aviv: Bnei Akiva Movement, 1987), 77 (Hebrew).

yeshiva walls. In Jerusalem, we made a different agreement, according to which yeshiva students are completely exempt until Lag B'Omer [May 27, 1948], and after Lag B'Omer, if the situation does not improve, God forbid, they will reconsider. You must negotiate with the recruitment offices in your place, and if you need our help, we will fulfill it."[32] Rabbi Herzog noted in a booklet that included responses to questions he was asked in the field of security that "regarding yeshiva students, so that the Torah is not forgotten, God forbid, from Israel, since those in the Land of Israel are the surviving remnant – special arrangements have been made separately for the new settlement and separately for Jerusalem."[33] It seems that Rabbi Herzog, who was highly respected both in the leadership of the Yishuv and among most of the spiritual leaders of the religious and Haredi community, was the key figure who succeeded in bridging everyone and bringing about the agreement in Jerusalem.

Yeshiva Students in Jerusalem

The involvement and participation of yeshiva students in Jerusalem's security affairs were of particular importance due to the severe manpower shortage in the city. For many years before the war, yeshiva students participated in Haganah operations as members of the organization or ad-hoc supporters.[34]

---

32 Yehuda Blau on behalf of Agudat Israel to Agudat Israel, Tiberias (3 March 1948).

33 Rabbi Yitzchak Isaac Halevi Herzog, *Pesakim u-Ketavim: Orach Chaim*, vol. 1 (Jerusalem: Yad ha-Rav Herzog, 2989), Section 52, p. 236 (Hebrew).

34 Testimony of Nehemia Rabin, *ha-Haganah bi-Yerushalayim*, vol. 1 (Jerusalem, 1975), 9 (Hebrew); Avraham Halperin, "From Those Days," ibid., 169 (Hebrew); Yaakov Pat, "Contacts with Rabbi Kook," *Alon le-Haverim* (1971): 14 (Hebrew); Shimon Agasi, "The Religious Defense Units," ibid., 15 (Hebrew); Yaakov Zoltak, "Organization of the Religious Unit in Jerusalem," ibid., 17 (Hebrew); *Darko Shel Adam: Kovetz le-Zikhro shel Yaacov Pat*, ed. Eliezer Lubrani (Herzliya: The Committee for the Commemoration of Yaacov Pat, 1958), 102, 215 (Hebrew); *ha-Haganah*

The onset of hostilities and general conscription created a new situation. Some yeshivas located in the northern part of the city were affected early in the conflict. For example, the Beit Yosef Tzvi Yeshiva, headed by Rabbi Dushinsky and located at the end of Shmuel HaNavi Street opposite Sheikh Jarrah, had 150 students, some of whom were Holocaust survivors, who had to leave the yeshiva and their residences to find alternative accommodations.[35] Similarly, the yeshiva in the Mekor Chaim neighborhood in the south of the city had to vacate its premises due to the siege and attacks on the neighborhood, with its students moving from place to place in the city. A similar situation occurred in yeshivas farther from the front, especially during periods of shelling.[36]

The request of Haredi organizations to exempt yeshiva students from enlistment was accepted by the leadership of the National Service Command in Jerusalem. Each student had to provide a certificate from the head of the yeshiva and one of three yeshiva organizations. On December 31, 1947, Rabbi Moshe Glickman-Porush approached the heads of yeshivas in Jerusalem, requesting lists of their students aged 17-25 "so that we can be sure that only yeshiva students receive exemptions."[37]

    bi-Yerushalayim, vol. 1 (Jerusalem, 1975), 169 (Hebrew), testimony of Avraham Halperin; Shimon Agassi, "Organization of Religious Units," Alon la-Haverim (Jerusalem: Havrei Hahaganah, 1971): 15 (Hebrew); and ha-Haganah bi-Yerushalayim, vol. 1 (Jerusalem, 1975), 214-215 (Hebrew).

35 Avraham Yochanan Blumenthal and Rabbi Yosef Tzvi Dushinsky to Rabbi Moshe Porush in New York (17 February 1948), Agudat Israel Central Archive, Jerusalem.

36 Rabbi Baruch Yitzchak Levin, "Introduction," in Divrei Levi (Jerusalem, 1948). Rabbi Levin served as the head of the Mekor Chaim Yeshiva; Naftali Kravitz, ed., Achar Ha'Asaf (Jerusalem 1970), 451, from a letter by Rabbi Sarna dated Sivan 5708; and Interview with Rabbi Eliyahu Grossberg (February 26, 2008), who studied at the Mir Yeshiva in the Beit Yisrael neighborhood.

37 Menachem Glickman-Porush to Rabbi Moshe Glickman-Porush (22 January 1948); Moshe Glickman-Porush to the heads of the yeshiva (31 December 1947), Agudat Israel Central Archive, Jerusalem; Organization

The commander of the religious youth battalion "Modi'in," composed of students from religious schools, members of religious youth movements, and working youth aged 15.5 to 17.5, approached Rabbi Herzog on January 1, 1948, proposing that due to the needs of the time, the arrangement should also apply to yeshivas with students of these ages serving in his battalion, to train them and minimize disruption to the yeshiva's educational and social activities. He proposed that:

1. Yeshiva students be recruited by their yeshiva administrations into a special unit within the religious battalion. If feasible, classes would be composed according to yeshivas based on the number of recruits.

2. Their battalion activities would be coordinated with yeshiva heads according to the conditions of each yeshiva.

3. Unit commanders and instructors would be from the battalion's command staff until yeshiva students were trained as commanders and instructors.[38]

However, yeshiva heads and leaders of Haredi parties opposed the conscription of young people under the age of 18, especially those studying in yeshivas.[39] It should be noted that recruits of the religious Gadna battalion also encountered difficulties in religious matters.[40]

---

of Young Haredim by Agudat Israel, Tiberias, "list of 15 yeshiva students from Torah Or in Tiberias, aged 17-25," (5 January 1948), Talmud Torah and Yeshiva Chayei Olam, "list of 62 students from Yeshiva Chayei Olam, aged 17-25," (12 January 1948), Agudat Israel Central Archive, Jerusalem.

38 Battalion Commander to Rabbi Yitzchak Halevi Herzog, 19 Tevet 5708 [1 January 1948], State Archives / Rabbi Herzog Archive F-28/4247.

39 Remarks of Rabbis Levin and Fishman (Maimon), Protocol of the Government Meeting on 26 May 1948, pp. 6-7, Minutes of the Meetings of the Provisional Government, Volume A.

40 Mordechai Reichman [from the Intelligence Battalion Staff] to the Mizrachi World Center, attention M. Shapira, 7 May 1948, Religious Zionism Archives, File 286.

The executive committee of the National Service Command in Jerusalem negotiated with the heads of yeshivas and other religious institutions in the city, as well as with the national center of the National Service Command in Tel Aviv. An agreement was reached on February 12, 1948, and sent by the National Service Command to yeshiva organizations. The main points were: understanding the reasons for the yeshiva heads' demand to postpone the conscription of yeshiva students. The executive committee believed that yeshiva students, like all young people in Jerusalem, were obligated to train for self-defense, with the understanding that they would be deployed only in cases of necessity and mortal danger. If the yeshiva heads did not accept this, the executive committee agreed to grant yeshiva students for whom Torah study was their primary occupation a three-month deferment, until Lag B'Omer – May 27, 1948. After this period, the issue would be reconsidered. The yeshiva heads promised not to oppose their students' volunteering and would not interfere with the rights of volunteers. The list of those eligible for these certificates would be determined by the yeshiva heads and approved by a committee composed of representatives from the yeshiva organization, the National Service Command, and the religious department of the security forces.[41]

As was their custom, Neturei Karta vehemently opposed the agreement and harshly criticized Agudath Israel for agreeing to negotiations on this issue and for agreeing to submit the names of yeshiva students. "By doing this, we will, God forbid, be handed over to them for punishment or mercy." Therefore, "none of us will go, nor will we give our names to a group of blood traders and sellers of our holy

---

41 Y. Sternowitz and Ze'ev Epstein, Central Recruitment Command Jerusalem to the Yeshiva Committee, Torah Enterprise, United Yeshivas Jerusalem, copies to the Chief Rabbinate of Israel and the Central Agudat Israel, 12 February 1948, Israel State Archives, Rabbi Herzog Archive F-7/4251; "Yeshiva Students Exempt from Recruitment," *Hayom* (13 February 1948) (Hebrew).

8 | *The Draft and Yeshiva Students*

Torah for money."⁴² They consistently opposed all conscription, not just that of yeshiva students.

In early January 1948, the HISH battalion "Michmas" was unsure what to do with five of its recruits who were students of the Hebron Yeshiva in Jerusalem. It was agreed to check whether they had enlisted voluntarily. If they had been drafted, they were to be released to continue their yeshiva studies and subsequently drafted according to the agreement with the yeshiva heads.⁴³ Ze'ev Falk, who studied at the Hebron Yeshiva, also studied law at the university and was active in the Haredi youth organization "Ezra." He requested a temporary release to study for his midterms and fulfill his educational role in "Ezra." Falk was temporarily transferred to a non-conscripted HISH company that served as a reserve.⁴⁴

Elimelech Mintzberg, a 36-year-old yeshiva student and father of three who also worked several hours a day to support his family, asked Rabbi Reuven Bengis, head of the rabbinical court of the Haredi community, if he should enlist and serve the number of hours he stopped studying to work. After Rabbi Bengis confirmed that Mintzberg returned to his studies after finishing work "and did not waste time idly, it was determined that even during his work to support his family, he was still considered a yeshiva student and exempt from service like all those who

42 "Neturei Karta to the Students and Scholars of the Yeshivas!" *HaChoma*, no. 37 (22 January 1948): 1 (Hebrew).

43 Israel State Archives, 49/2644 – 455 (9 January 1948), Addressed to David L'Daromi. Student names: Aharon Freund, Pinchas Bumzao, Binyamin Epstein, Shaul Barzel, and Shmuel Kalman Kook.

44 Israel State Archives, 49/2644-455, 21 January 1948, National Board of "Ezra" to the local commander of Jerusalem; ibid., 19 February 1948, "Ezra" Jerusalem branch administration to the Jerusalem District Commander, regarding our member Ze'ev Falk; ibid., 25 February 1948, Ze'ev to David L'Daromi, regarding temporary release; ibid., 49/2644-456 (22 February 1948), David L'Daromi to Company A Commander, regarding Ze'ev Falk. Ze'ev Falk later became a professor of law at the Hebrew University of Jerusalem.

bore the yoke of Torah like the other yeshiva students, for without flour, there is no Torah."⁴⁵ Elimelech Mintzberg was killed on July 14 by a shell that hit his home.

On February 22, after the explosion of car bombs on Ben Yehuda Street in central Jerusalem, yeshiva students were sent by their rabbis to help clear the debris to search for survivors. Yeshiva students worked for several consecutive nights clearing the rubble.⁴⁶

In March, when students began transferring from the HISH battalions to the HIM units, where service was partial, the "Michmas" battalion requested guidance from the district headquarters regarding yeshiva students, asking if they should be treated like students. The response they received was that they should not be drafted for full service and should be placed in the HIM [Home Guard].⁴⁷

Despite the possibility of exemption, hundreds of yeshiva students preferred to leave their yeshivas and voluntarily presented themselves at recruitment offices in Jerusalem. Yaakov Tchernovitz, who reported on the state of recruitment in Jerusalem in early March 1948, noted that "the number of yeshiva students is also significant."⁴⁸ Many students from the Kol Torah Yeshiva enlisted, and 12 of the 83 students in the

---

45   Zelig Reuven Bengis, Head of the Rabbinical Court of the Orthodox Community in Jerusalem, (30 January 1948).

46   Givat Haviva Archives of the Hagana, Section 42 G-23/275 (30 November 1948), Aharon Haim Cohen, "Year of Recruitment: A Brief Review of the Activities of the Recruitment Office in Jerusalem."

47   Israel State Archives, 49/2644-455 (12 March 1948), Mikmash to Mar, regarding students; ibid., 17 March 1948, Tan to Amir Mikmash, regarding students.

48   Yaakov Tchernowitz (Tsur), *Battle of the Day: Pages of the Past* (Jerusalem: Keter Publishing, 1977), 241 (Hebrew). Yaakov Tchernowitz (Tsur) was responsible for recruitment in Jerusalem, see "Recruitment in Jerusalem is Satisfactory," *HaBoker* (8 March 1948): 3 (Hebrew).

yeshiva were killed in battles.[49] Chaim Grove, a resident of Kfar Ata, born in August 1931, studied at the Shfat Emet Yeshiva of the Gerrer Hasidim in Jerusalem. In June 1947, as a faithful member of Agudath Israel, he filled out a form to leave the national committee of the Knesset of Israel. When hostilities began, he enlisted with a group of friends from Agudath Israel and was sent for training at Arza, without his parents and teachers at the yeshiva knowing. He was seriously injured in the battle for the children's farm in Motza on April 5, 1948, and died of his wounds the following day. His parents learned of his enlistment only when they were informed of his death in battle. His yeshiva mate Yosef Kovlevitz from Tel Aviv, who was injured in the same battle, also enlisted with him.[50]

Instructions were sent to the commanders of the battalions in the Jerusalem district to facilitate the integration and service of religious soldiers. It was determined that religious soldiers would be concentrated in special companies, provided with a kosher kitchen, and given conditions to maintain the unique character of their unit by setting times for prayer and Torah study. Battalion commanders were asked to appoint commanders for these companies who were "especially understanding and tactful [as] this will determine the number of recruits in the future."[51]

Journalist Gershon Swat, from the Haaretz newspaper, who met in early March 1948 with Rabbi Yaakov Moshe Charlap, one of the heads

---

49 "The Reflection of the Yeshiva Over the Years," *Pamei Kol Torah* (September 1959): 2 (Hebrew).

50 List of departures from the National Committee to the Knesset of Israel, 13 Sivan – 13 Tammuz 5707, Central Zionist Archives 8830 1J; Shamai Ginzburg, *A Chapter of Memories from the Last Years of Our Master the Rebbe, the Imrei Emes of Blessed Memory* (Jerusalem, 1988), 29-30 (Hebrew); David Ben-Gurion, *The War of Independence: War Diary*, vol. 1, eds. Gershon Rivlin and Elhanan Orren (Tel-Aviv: Ministry of Defense, 1982), 364 (22 April 1948) (Hebrew); Ministry of Defense Yizkor website.

51 Private Archive, Bir family, and Israel State Archives, 49/2644-455 (25 March 1948), Rubin, Inspector and Standards Officer of the Brigade to Moriyah, Michmas, Beit Horon, Metzudah. Subject: Religious Soldiers.

of the Merkaz HaRav Yeshiva and the rabbi of the Shaarei Chessed neighborhood, wrote on March 8:

> "The exemption of yeshiva students from conscription until Lag B'Omer [May 27] does not mean exemption from night and day guard duty. In Shaarei Chessed, the young men from the yeshivas hurry to their posts at dusk. At dawn, the student returns to study in his yeshiva, and no one shirks, for being a 'guardian of Israel' is a duty, and yeshiva students fulfill their duty with Hasidic enthusiasm."[52]

Shulamit Ezrahi described in her book about her father, Rabbi Meir Chadash, the supervisor of the Hebron Yeshiva in Jerusalem, the atmosphere in the yeshiva during those days. Among the yeshiva students were those who could not find peace of mind and sought to join some activity. Some thought they should undergo training to know how to handle a weapon in times of trouble. In contrast, her father believed that yeshivas were the last fortress left to the Jewish people in the struggle for the nation's character, against the secularism and atheism that had taken over the settlement in the land. The yeshivas preserved the nation's spiritual future. He believed that leaving the yeshiva would disconnect them from its atmosphere. He also did not trust the leaders of the settlement, knowing their attitude toward the Torah and its scholars. He argued that if they knew that yeshiva students were trained, they would exploit them continuously for various military missions, which would harm the continuation of the yeshivas. Rabbi Chadash acted to quell the unrest in the yeshiva to continue the studies as usual. However, during the shelling period, he turned a blind eye to the young men who

---

52 "Release of Young Yeshiva Students until Lag B'Omer," *Haaretz* (8 March 1948): 2 (Hebrew). The interview with Rabbi Yaakov Moshe Charlap was conducted on the occasion of his departure to the USA for a yeshiva fundraising campaign.

volunteered temporarily to guard.⁵³ Nevertheless, when the "Tuvia Battalion" of yeshiva students was established, both Aharon, Rabbi Chadash's son, and Yaakov Chaim, the son of Rabbi Yechezkel Sarna, head of the Hebron Yeshiva, enlisted, along with dozens of Hebron Yeshiva students.⁵⁴

At the end of March 1948, discussions about the conscription of yeshiva students reopened. The recruitment authorities in Jerusalem sent a letter to the presidency of the Yeshiva Council and the administration of the Torah Initiative, informing them:

> We regret to inform you that due to the worsening security conditions in Jerusalem and its surroundings, we are compelled to cancel all exemption certificates, including temporary exemption certificates. Yeshiva students will be called, therefore, in the coming days, to enlist for the defense of Jerusalem. We will try to integrate those students for whom Torah study is their primary occupation into partial service. Please contact us to arrange suitable conditions.⁵⁵

Unit commanders began implementing the new order. For example, the commander of District 3, responsible for northern Jerusalem, ordered the yeshiva students to be enlisted and integrated into work

---

53   Shulamit Ezrahi, *ha-Mashgiah Reb Meir* (Jerusalem: Feldheim, 2001), 282-285 (Hebrew).

54   List of soldiers in the battalion, Bir Family Archive.

55   Central Zionist Archives, 14 3J (29 March 1948), Dr. M. Simon and Aharon Haim Cohen to the Presidium of the Yeshiva Committee and the management of the 'Torah Enterprise,' 29 March 1948, copies were also sent to the Chief Rabbis of Israel and Dr. M. Buxbaum [representative of Agudat Israel], State Archives F-8/888, and Central Zionist Archives J3 14.

with partial conscription.⁵⁶ They are exempt from full conscription. This caused misunderstandings and confusion. The commander of District 5, responsible for central Jerusalem, contacted the Yeshiva Council on April 22 after one yeshiva student summoned to report on April 25 claimed he was exempt from conscription. The Yeshiva Council was asked to clarify to that yeshiva student that his exemption had expired. Rabbi Moshe David Tennenbaum, secretary of the Yeshiva Council, replied that it had been agreed with the National Service Command that as long as discussions regarding yeshiva students' conscription were ongoing, no actions would be taken in this area, and therefore, the exemption card should be honored until decisions were made.⁵⁷

In mid-April 1948, a meeting was held in Rabbi Herzog's office, attended by almost all the yeshiva heads, and a committee was elected, consisting of Moshe Shapira from the Jewish Agency, Zorach Warhaftig from the National Committee, and two yeshiva representatives, to investigate and arrange the conscription of yeshiva students. However, the National Service Command in Jerusalem continued its intention to conscript yeshiva students despite requests to continue operating under the agreement. On April 25, the heads of the Jerusalem recruitment center responded to the Yeshiva Council's request, stating:

> Despite our desire to consider the important reasons presented in your letter, we face only the harsh reality of a war for the existence of the Jewish people in the Land of Israel as a whole and the Jerusalem settlement in particular, a war that stands on the brink of decision in the coming days and requires the mobilization of all

---

56   Israel State Archives 1949/840 – 9 (31 March 1948), Day Order by Gotfried [codename of the district 3 commander]; similarly in district 5: see Israel State Archives, 49/2644 – 319, 31 March 1948, Levanon to district commanders: Ziv, Shahar, Avner, Yelik, Oh, Integration of Yeshiva Students in the Heim (Home Guard).

57   Halevi to the Committee of Yeshivas in Israel (22 April 1948), Israel State Archives 49/2644 – 310.

8 | *The Draft and Yeshiva Students*

human resources we can enlist in the campaign. Under these conditions, the center cannot exempt any sector or individual in the Jerusalem settlement from the obligation to participate in the war effort. We are prepared to fulfill the promise of the Haganah forces commander in the Jerusalem district and employ yeshiva students only in the municipal guard. The General Staff will empower us to require yeshiva students to appear as stated above, and instructions have been given to the inspection committee and the military police to implement this decision. We hope that the yeshiva heads will assist us in fully implementing the decision and alleviate the situation of the yeshiva students by encouraging them to voluntarily report to the recruitment stations.[58]

Shmuel HaKohen Weingarten, an active member of the Haganah who joined a group of HIM personnel, mostly from the Shaarei Chessed neighborhood, in assisting the military police in searching for draft dodgers, recounted in his memoirs that they were sent on the first day of Passover on April 24, 1948, to conduct inspections among moviegoers in Jerusalem. One of the three apprehended near the "Eden" cinema was a yeshiva student. When asked who permitted him to go to a movie while the yeshiva student exemption agreement was intended to allow them to study, he had no answer. He was put on trial, and it was decided to enlist him. When his yeshiva head learned of the circumstances of his arrest, he was unwilling to intervene or handle his release. His family tried to

---

58 Yaakov Tchernowitz (Tsur), Chairman, and Aharon Haim Cohen, Honorary Secretary to the Committee of Yeshivas in Israel, copies to the two Chief Rabbis of Israel, to the Commander of the Defense Forces in the Jerusalem District, to the Audit Committee, and to the Military Police, 25 April 1948, State Archives, F-8/888.

appeal the decision, but the young man accepted his conscription and became an exemplary soldier.[59]

Ben-Gurion complained to a delegation from Agudath Israel that visited him on April 22 about the lack of conscription of yeshiva students. They replied that there were only 300 eligible students for conscription "and this is the only remnant, and their study is required for salvation." They added that one student from the Shfat Emet Yeshiva of the Gerrer Hasidim who enlisted was killed in early April defending Arza, and another was injured.[60] On April 27, a meeting of yeshiva students was held at the Etz Chaim Yeshiva in Jerusalem, attended by yeshiva heads and their rabbis. All speakers emphasized the importance of continuing yeshiva studies at this time, after the Holocaust and during the current danger.[61]

The exemption also included yeshiva rabbis, neighborhood rabbis, and synagogue rabbis. Lists of their names were sent to the National Service Command by the Chief Rabbinate. Some synagogue rabbis were officially appointed by Rabbi Uziel during April 1948. Those listed were asked by the National Service Command to contact their office on Ben Yehuda Street to fill out appropriate forms and receive exemption certificates (white cards).[62]

---

59 Shmuel Hacohen Weingarten, "The Military Police of the Haganah," *Alon la-Haverim* (Jerusalem: Havrei Hahaganah, 1976): 27 (Hebrew).

60 David Ben-Gurion, *The War of Independence: War Diary*, vol. 1, eds. Gershon Rivlin and Elhanan Orren (Tel-Aviv: Ministry of Defense, 1982), 364 (22 April 1948). The deceased was Chaim Grob, born in 1931, who was part of the Agudat Israel recruits platoon and was killed in the battle for the children's farm in Motza in early April 1948, along with three comrades. This group had eight additional wounded in that battle.

61 "Assembly of Yeshiva Students," *HaYoman* (28 April 1948) (Hebrew).

62 Requests addressed to Rabbi Uziel for appointing rabbis to Sephardic synagogues in Jerusalem: Mishkenot neighborhood, Nachlat Zion, Mor Baruch Tel Arza, Ruchama, and more, Nisan 5708 [April 1948]; Rabbi Uziel to the National Service Command Center (11 April 1948), request

8 | *The Draft and Yeshiva Students*

The exemption also included yeshiva students who were veteran recruits of the Haganah and trained, causing difficulties in their units. Hanoch Tempelhof, responsible for the unit defending the Jewish Quarter in the Old City, tried at the end of April to get approval from the adjutant of the Jerusalem district to reinforce the besieged force in the quarter with 12 yeshiva students who served in Company C of the HISH battalion "Moriah" until their release, but this was not within the adjutant's authority as the exemption was granted by the high command.[63]

In early May, as part of the preparations for the anticipated Arab armies' invasion, full conscription was extended to older ages, and the issue of yeshiva students' conscription arose again.

On May 1, the Jerusalem district commander issued a general conscription order stating:

> "All Home Guard and People's Guard members up to and including the age of 40 [...] are required to enlist fully. [...] This order applies to all institutions and employers. They must release their conscripted employees according to this order and preserve their

---

to release Rabbi Meir Benayahu appointed as the rabbi of the Ruchama neighborhood and the 'Shaarei Rachamim' synagogue in the neighborhood; Dr. M. Simon, Head of Operations at the National Service Command Center to Rabbi Uziel, 7 May 1948, State Archives / Rabbi Uziel Archive F-8/888.

63 Israel State Archives, 1948/670 – 54 (18 April 1948), Hanoch to Yaakov [Moshe Rusnak, commander of the district]; 22 April 1948, Hanoch to Gold [Yehoshafat Harkabi, commander of Company B 'Moriah'] (23 April 1948), Hanoch to Rubin [district adjutant]. Hanoch's list included six students from Merkaz Harav and six from Hebron Yeshiva. Hanoch described them as "trusted and capable, especially suitable for the Old City." The only one from this group who reached the district in early May was Rabbi She'ar Yashuv Cohen, who was wounded in the fighting in the district and went into captivity with the fall of the district. The others from this group fought elsewhere, one of them, Yosef Nadav, was killed on July 18, in battles in the Mandelbaum sector.

full rights at their workplaces. This directive takes effect on Sunday, May 2, 1948, at 0600." A special appeals committee was established.[64]

Despite the state of emergency, the new conscription order met with widespread and vigorous opposition from the Haredi community leadership and yeshiva heads. Opponents viewed this conscription order as a tangible threat to the continuation of the yeshivas, violating the agreement regarding yeshiva students unilaterally by the military system.

Rabbi Yosef Tzvi Dushinsky, the Chief Rabbi of the Haredi community in the Land of Israel and the rabbinical court of the Haredi community, issued an instruction to yeshiva students stating:

> "Any yeshiva student, one who sits and learns in the Beit Midrash, must not appear, report, or register for any conscription or similar matters, even for a short time [...] and a double and multiplied duty is upon every yeshiva student now to strengthen and exert themselves in studying and diligence in Torah study with greater intensity and vigor."[65]

Rabbi Karelitz, the "Hazon Ish," opposed any conscription of yeshiva students, even partial and temporary conscription, and even for a few days for training purposes only. He viewed the conscription order as a severe decree endangering all of Israel.[66] Rabbi Isser Zalman Meltzer, head of the Etz Chaim Yeshiva, issued a similar directive.[67] This was

---

64 Central Zionist Archives, 10 3J, 1 May 1948, recruitment order signed by the district commander. And Yarkoni's [Meir Sharvit] instructions, commander of the Fortress [Home Guard].

65 *The Torah Book of Rabbi Amram: The Neturei Karta Method* (Jerusalem: Neturei Karta, 1976), 116 (2 May 1948) (Hebrew).

66 Zevi Yavrov, *Sefer Maaseh Ish* (Bnei Brak, 1998), 57.

67 Yedael Meltzer, *On the Way of the Tree of Life* (Jerusalem: Erez HaHen Publishing, 1986), 24 Nisan 5708 [3 May 1948]; and Rabbi Aryeh Leib Shteinman, *Da'at Torah* (1967), 443-444.

8 | *The Draft and Yeshiva Students*

also the view of Rabbi Tzvi Pesach Frank, the Chief Rabbi of Jerusalem. Rabbi Frank, who had supported the Haganah in various areas since the 1930s, saw the struggle for Jerusalem as a matter of life and death, as reflected in his halachic rulings on security matters. Nevertheless, he opposed conscripting those whose primary occupation was Torah study, stating, "Heaven forbid to remove them and disconnect them from the tent of Torah and enslave them to the army of war, training, or other tasks, and know with certainty that anyone who devoted his soul and life to Torah study is a soldier in the legion of the King of the Universe, defending our people and our land."[68]

Agudath Israel attacked the National Service Command for unilaterally canceling the agreement to exempt yeshiva students without any prior consultation and without official notification of the cancellation, and for instructing the military police not to honor exemption certificates. Mordechai Buxbaum, Agudath Israel's representative in the National Service Command, announced that the Haredi community would not agree to abolish the yeshivas, which also have a role in the redemption of the people, as Torah study is the "apple of the eye" of the Jewish people, and it would do everything to preserve the flame of Torah from being extinguished. Buxbaum recalled that at the first meeting of the executive committee of the National Service Command, he read out the five conditions decided by the Council of Torah Sages for the conscription of Haredim, among them the condition that yeshiva students be exempt from conscription and training. He demanded that the agreement not be changed and that all negotiations regarding yeshiva students be removed from the agenda until Lag B'Omer (May 27, 1948).[69]

---

68 Shabbetai Rosenthal, *Holocaust for a Generation: Rabbi Zvi Pesach Frank, His Life and Teachings* (Jerusalem, 1972), 107 (Hebrew). For example, he permitted work on the Sabbath to produce armored vehicles.

69 M.H., "Recruitment Issue," *HaYoman* (2 May 1948); "On the Recruitment of Yeshiva Students," *HaYoman* (3 May 1948) (Hebrew); "On the Exemption of Yeshiva Students from Recruitment," *Kol Yisrael* (13 May 1948): 4 (Hebrew). Representatives from approximately 15 synagogues in Mea Shearim and its surroundings signed a letter to Rabbi Herzog, urging

Negotiations with the National Service Command were difficult, and there were even threats of sanctions against the yeshivas. Rabbi Herzog responded harshly to these threats in a letter to the National Service Command on May 7, 1948:

> "I am very sorry that the proposal I presented to you was not accepted, and I am still trying to reach a compromise. However, I must tell you that in the event of a final failure, God forbid if you treat those who are fixed in the tent of Torah, the soul of Israel and the foundation of its eternity, as mere draft dodgers and cut off their food, whatever your reasons may be, I will publicly protest against you, sharply, in the eyes of all Israel. You have no right to use such drastic coercive measures against the remnant of the observants of our holy Torah in Jerusalem, our holy city, from which Torah will go forth to the Land of Israel and all Israel."[70]

Presumably, due to Rabbi Herzog's status, the threat worked, and the issue of sanctions was removed from the agenda.

In discussions between security officials on one side, and the Chief Rabbinate and yeshiva heads on the other, Moshe Shapira and Zorach Warhaftig also participated. Warhaftig noted in his memoirs that Rabbi Herzog, who was the founder and president of the Yeshiva Council, and

---

him to secure the full exemption of all yeshiva students in Jerusalem, "the remaining remnant from all over the world, and not to disturb them from their studies." See to the letter from Chief Rabbi Yitzhak Isaac Halevi Herzog from representatives of synagogues, after the Sabbath of Parashat Acharei, 1 May 1948, Israel State Archives, F-4251/7, Rabbi Herzog Archive.

70 Israel State Archives, F-4251/7 (Rabbi Herzog Archive); and Zorach Warhaftig, in *Constitution and Law in a Jewish State According to Halakhah* (Jerusalem: Yad ha-Rav Herzog, 1989), 232, 519; 28 Nisan 5708 [7 May 1948], Chief Rabbi Yitzhak Isaac Halevi Herzog to Mr. Yaakov Tchernowitz (Tsur), etc., heads of the National Service Command.

all yeshiva heads "opposed any form of military conscription, even just for weapon training. They feared a breach that could widen. My opinion was that yeshiva students should agree to weapon training, even in the yeshiva courtyards. I saw this as a moral obligation for the recruits in the Haganah and even a matter of life and death for the yeshiva students themselves. However, the opinion of the Chief Rabbinate prevailed."[71]

In Yeshivat Mercaz HaRav, which was not Haredi, there were differences of opinion. The majority supported conscription, including the yeshiva head, Rabbi Zvi Yehudah Kook, who published his opinion in the pamphlet "Lemitzvot Haaretz." Rabbi David Cohen, one of the heads of Yeshivat Mercaz HaRav, ruled that it was a milchemet mitzvah in which everyone must participate. He believed arrangements should be made "so that the Torah institutions and yeshivas are not disrupted, Heaven forbid, but rather supported and aided by arranging companies alternately and considering different situations. And they helped their brothers in the war, in prayer, to the Rock of Israel and its Redeemer." Rabbi Shear Yashuv Cohen, son of Rabbi David Cohen (the Nazir), who was a student of Yeshivat Mercaz HaRav, belonged to the "Moriah" battalion and was temporarily released as part of the yeshiva students' exemption arrangement. Rabbi David Cohen supported his son's conscription and asked him to enlist after the Seder night [April 25, 1948]. Indeed, Rabbi Shear Yashuv Cohen returned to service, joined the fighters in the Jewish Quarter in the Old City, was wounded there in battle, and was taken captive to Jordan after the quarter's surrender. The yeshiva director, Rabbi Shalom Nathan Ra'anan, also supported this view. Opponents included Rabbi Charlap and some of his students, who believed that Torah study should continue despite their positive attitude towards the establishment of the state and Zionism.[72]

---

71 Zorach Warhaftig, in *Constitution and Law in a Jewish State According to Halakhah* (Jerusalem: Yad ha-Rav Herzog, 1989), 231-233 (Hebrew).

72 *Megillat Milchama ve-Shalom, From the Archives of Rabbi David Cohen ZT"L* (Jerusalem: Nezer David, 1974), 25-30 (Hebrew). Published in a letter to yeshiva students, Iyar 5708; Rabbi She'ar Yashuv Cohen, "Thus

Some opponents of conscription used a section of a letter written by Rabbi Avraham Yitzchak Kook to the Chief Rabbi of the Jews of Britain on March 14, 1917, asking him to intervene with the authorities to exempt yeshiva students in Britain from military service. Rabbi Kook, who was then in England serving as the rabbi of the Machzikei HaDath community in London, actively helped yeshiva students obtain military exemptions by generously granting rabbinical ordination certificates. In 1948, Rabbi Kook's words against the conscription of yeshiva students were published without noting their context. When his son, Rabbi Zvi Yehuda Kook, learned of this, he was very angry and called it a forgery, publishing the pamphlet "Lemitzvot HaAretz" and later a proclamation explaining the correct context of his father's words written in London in 1917, to exempt yeshiva students from a war that had no vital interest requiring saving lives in the Land of Israel.[73]

We Established the First 'Fighting Yeshiva,'" (March 2006), online here (https://www.yeshiva.org.il/midrash/4562); and Rabbi Zvi Yehuda Kook, "For the Commandments of the Land," in *Torah Study and Military Service: Collection of Articles* (Jerusalem: Hakibbutz Hadati, 1980); S. Daniel, "The Student and the Rabbi Await Redemption," *Et-Mol*, vol. 7, no. 3 (January 1982): 19 (Hebrew). Rabbi Charlap, a scion of a prominent Jerusalemite family, received his early education at the Etz Chaim Yeshiva. His father served as a judge in the rabbinical court of Rabbi Yehoshua Leib Diskin. Rabbi Charlap first encountered Rabbi Abraham Isaac Hacohen Kook during the latter's visit to Jaffa in 1904 and subsequently embraced his teachings, particularly the notion that the building of the Land of Israel is a pivotal step in the process of divine redemption. He later joined the Merkaz Harav Yeshiva, becoming one of its leaders while also serving as the rabbi of the Shaarei Chesed neighborhood. Notably, Rabbi Charlap viewed the United Nations' decision to establish a Jewish state as the beginning of the redemptive process, marking the occasion with a religious dance performed in festive holiday attire.

73 Neria Guttel, "'Freedom for our Yeshiva Students' or the Mitzvah of Their Recruitment: Rav Kook's Letter and the Debate on Its Interpretation," in Moshe Rachimi, ed., *The Kipa and the Helmet* [=*Amadot*, vol. 1] (Elkana: Mikhlelet Orot, 2009), 25-39 (Hebrew).

Some rabbis did not view the overall opposition to conscription favorably and believed that a way should be found to conscript yeshiva students while finding arrangements to minimize the impact on the yeshivas. Rabbi Shlomo Yosef Zevin, a rabbi of Mizrachi, who published his opinion under the name "one of the rabbis," ruled that Torah scholars must also participate in the milchemet mitzvah, as it was a matter of life and death and saving thousands of Jews. He asked the yeshiva heads, "You must also urge the Torah scholars, those qualified by age and body, to participate in the campaign, to do so. Will your brothers go to war, and you will sit here?" In conclusion, he added, "Practically speaking, there may be concern that the yeshivas will empty out as most students leave the study institutions, and what will become of the Torah? But for this purpose, we must enter into negotiations with the recruitment institutions on known practical arrangements, and there is always a way to find relief and limitations. As far as I know, there was such a willingness on the part of those institutions. But to decide decisively not to participate at all, not to register and not to be counted, no and no and no – where do you get this?"[74]

Other factors and individuals in the religious community believed there was no justification in Jerusalem's security situation at the time to demand the exemption, including the Center for Religious Workers and the geographer and historian Dr. Abraham Jacob Brawer.[75] Yitzhak Rafael, one of the leaders of Hapoel HaMizrachi, who was a member

---

74 Yehezkel Cohen, *Giyus Ke-Halakha - Conscription according to Halakha* (Jerusalem: Hakibbutz Hadati, 1993), 217-220 (Hebrew); in the Poalei Agudath Israel publication – *She'arim*, this opinion was criticized. See P. Borovsky, "Those Who Put Themselves to Death," *She'arim* (15 July 1948): 1 (Hebrew).

75 Archive of Religious Zionism, File 286, 10 March 1948, Y. Leibowitz to Rabbi Meir Berlin, see Michael and Abraham Jacob Brawer, *Memoirs of a Father and His Son* (Jerusalem: Mosad ha-Rav Kook, 1966), 667 (Hebrew); Menahem Zvi Kadari, *Stations in the Days of My Life*, ed. Michal Franz-Kadari (Tel-Aviv: The Family, 2011), 41 (Hebrew). From a personal diary he wrote during his stay in besieged Jerusalem.

of the Jerusalem Committee, sharply criticized the Haredi community and yeshiva students at his party's executive committee meeting on June 15: "It cannot be denied that there were also disgraceful manifestations, unfortunately, among the Haredi community, and there were draft dodgers. Even yeshiva students, hundreds of them, congregate without any justification, without any substantial participation in battle, while Jerusalem stood to the test."[76]

Various factors tried to influence the yeshiva heads to change their stance against conscription. In discussions held by the Information Department and the district commanders of the "People's Guard" on May 4 and 5, it was discussed that a delegation should be sent to the Chief Rabbis and other important rabbis to ask them to support conscription and also to take measures against those disguising themselves as Torah scholars to cover up their draft evasion.[77]

The common understanding among all the rabbis was the obligation for everyone to participate in the security effort while finding a way to minimize the impact on yeshivas and their students. There was a debate about the extent and nature of the arrangement that would ensure this. After much deliberation and discussion, an agreement was signed on May 10, establishing the status of yeshiva students in Jerusalem. It was agreed that, in principle, yeshiva students were exempt from conscription, but due to the severe situation in Jerusalem, a temporary directive was established:

1. Yeshiva students aged 17-22 (inclusive) will receive concentrated training, within a special framework established for this purpose, for no more than three days of concentrated training and up to 24 hours per month for knowledge renewal. Upon receiving the

---

76 *Panim*, no. 17 (15 June 1948): 5-6 (Hebrew), Archive of Religious Zionism, 7/85, 124-5-3. Later, Yitzhak Rafael noted the active participation of the Mizrachi Workers' members in the campaign.

77 Central Zionist Archives, 107 /3J (4 May 1948), Protocol of Weekly Information Assembly; ibid., 4 /3J (5 May 1948), Protocol of District Commanders' Meeting.

training, they will be exempt from any conscription, neither full nor partial. The training location will be chosen with the consent of the yeshiva heads.

2. Yeshiva students aged 23 and older will receive training in the manner mentioned above, and after Lag B'Omer [May 27, 1948], they will be required to enlist in the municipal guard, solely for guard duties, for no more than 12-15 hours per week. They will be under religious command, and their duties will be concentrated only in specific areas where they live and their surroundings, and they will not be sent to frontline positions. The service will be conducted with strict adherence to religious and moral laws.

3. Exceptionally outstanding yeshiva students will be exempt from any conscription duties (they will receive special approval from the Chief Rabbis).

4. Teachers, instructors, and spiritual supervisors will be exempt from any conscription duties.

5. A thorough personal review will be conducted among the yeshiva students to determine those eligible for the aforementioned rights.

6. The yeshiva heads agree and commit not to interfere with any students who voluntarily wish to participate in more active service forms. These students will retain all their rights in the yeshiva without discrimination.

7. All yeshiva students will report to a special enlistment station, undergo a medical examination, and receive an appropriate card.

8. The yeshiva heads commit not to accept students of conscription age, except for those transitioning from a Talmud Torah to a yeshiva or from one yeshiva to another.

9. To implement the above arrangement, a joint and permanent committee of yeshiva heads and the National Service Command will be established under the leadership of the Chief Rabbis.

10. The aforementioned agreement cannot be altered without the committee's consent.

The agreement was signed by the two Chief Rabbis of Israel (Herzog and Uziel), Rabbi Dushinsky, the Chief Rabbi of the Haredi community, and the heads of the main yeshivas in Jerusalem.[78] On behalf of the district command, the agreement was signed by Meir Rabinowitz-Batz, commander of the district engineering unit. Aharon Haim Cohen, secretary of the Jerusalem National Service Committee, forwarded the main points of the agreement proposed by the yeshiva heads for prior approval by the National Service Command Center.[79]

On May 16, the heads of the National Service Command Center in Jerusalem informed the Yeshiva Council, the Chief Rabbis, and the Agudath Israel Center of their agreement to the proposed agreement and announced that the authorized institutions would strictly adhere to its clauses and finalize with the yeshiva representatives the conditions for the enlistment and training of yeshiva students. The rabbis who signed the agreement were asked to issue a public call for volunteering and general enlistment to defend the people at this critical hour.[80]

Some tried to persuade Rabbi Dushinsky not to participate in the negotiations for the exemption of yeshiva students, as it would signify

---

[78] Religious Zionism Archives, File 287 (10 May 1948), Arrangement and Agreement. Yeshiva heads who signed: Rabbi Isser Zalman Meltzer, head of the Etz Chaim Yeshiva, Rabbi Yaakov Moshe Charlap, head of the Merkaz Harav Yeshiva, Rabbi Yechiel Michel Tikochinsky, director of Etz Chaim, Rabbi Eliezer Yehuda Finkel, head of the Mir Yeshiva, Rabbi Yehezkel Sarna, head of the Hebron Yeshiva, Rabbi Yaakov Hanoch Sankovich, head of the Sfas Emes Yeshiva (Gur Hasidim).

[79] Aharon Haim Cohen, Honorary Secretary to the National Service Command Center, undated, Poalei Agudath Israel Archive, Box 20, File 7.

[80] Y. Tchernowitz, Chairman, Dr. M. Simon, Head of Operations, Aharon Haim Cohen, Honorary Secretary, to the Yeshiva Committee, Torah Enterprise, and for the attention of the Honorable Chief Rabbis of Israel, Central Agudat Israel, 16 May 1948, State Archives F-8/888.

recognition of the secular government. He did not accept their opinion, saying that without an agreement with the Israeli government, it would lead to the closure of yeshivas and the cessation of Torah study. He was more cautious about causing a cessation of Torah study than entering disputes. He supported Rabbi Herzog, who led the negotiations, and signed the agreement himself.[81]

A severe shortage of weapons and the fighting in the city, which broke out immediately after the British left on May 14 in the afternoon, limited the possibilities for absorbing and training a large number of new recruits. The National Service Command decided to operate on a limited basis until the storm passed. Among other things, it was decided, for the time being, to register yeshiva students in preparation for their partial conscription. Amid the intense battles and shelling of the city, a special enlistment office for yeshiva students was opened in central Jerusalem on May 25. The office operated until May 30. According to the mobilization report for May 23-28, 217 yeshiva students enlisted, and half were exempted for medical reasons. M. Simon, one of the heads of the recruitment center, noted in the report that "it is self-evident that their military value is not very high [...] but the matter has a public-national value that cannot be underestimated."[82]

A military doctor who examined the yeshiva students informed Yaakov Tchernowitz (Tsur), the recruitment officer in Jerusalem, that

81 Raphael Katzenellenbogen, "Rabbi Dushinsky Thirty Days After His Passing," *She'arim* (18 November 1948): 2-3 (Hebrew).

82 Immediate demand from Etzioni for 600 weapons. See Israel State Archives 48/500– 48 (7 May 1948), 30:19, Etzioni to Yadin, Avidar. This telegram was sent after the recruitment of Heim personnel was almost complete, and it became clear there weren't enough weapons to equip them, Central Zionist Archives, 9380 /S25 (25 May 1948), National Service Command to Brigade Commander, Deployment Movement on 16-20 May 1948; ibid., ibid., 31 May 1948, Deployment Movement on 23-28 May 1948; *Ha Yoman* (27 May 1948) (Hebrew); *Ha Yoman* (28 May 1948) (Hebrew); "Inside Jerusalem: Yeshiva Students Reporting for Service," *Ha Yom* (26 May 1948): 2 (Hebrew).

many yeshiva students suffered from malnutrition, lung diseases, and especially tuberculosis.[83] Yaakov Tchernowitz (Tsur) wrote about this in July 1948: "The yeshivas present a particular problem: After the agreement was reached for their students' enlistment, a medical examination was conducted on those who enlisted, as required by law. It was found that more than half of the yeshiva students in Jerusalem were disqualified for health reasons due to their general weakness or severe organic diseases they were afflicted with. This poor health is an inevitable result of these boys' harsh living conditions, characterized by semi-starvation and exhausting spiritual work."[84] It should be noted that some yeshiva students were Holocaust survivors and still suffered from what they experienced several years earlier.

THE TUVIA BATTALION

In the special recruitment office for yeshiva students, about 900 people enlisted within two weeks, about 270 of whom were exempted

---

83 Yaakov Tchernowitz (Tsur), *Battle of the Day: Pages of the Past* (Jerusalem: Keter, 1979), 241 (Hebrew). This situation greatly concerned the Chief Rabbi, Rabbi Herzog, who wrote about it to the President of the Mizrachi, Rabbi Meir Berlin, on 1 June 1948:

> "The examination proved that about 35% of them [from the yeshiva students] are utterly weak and suffer to some extent from internal illnesses! This is a horrifying situation... This is a tragedy! The reasons are simple: lack of sufficient nutrition for the young who constantly tire their minds. And lack of air and cleanliness in their homes." Rabbi Herzog wanted to address the issue in cooperation with the Yeshiva Committee and in consultation with doctors. See Religious Zionism Archives, File 287, 23 Iyar 5708 [1 June 1948], Rabbi Herzog to Rabbi Berlin, ibid., ibid., [3 June 1948], Rabbi Herzog to Rabbi Berlin.

84 Yaakov Tchernowitz (Tsur), "Fighting Unity of Communities and Neighborhoods," *Davar Yerushalayim (Journal of Jerusalem Workers)*, no. 10 (23 July 1948): 3 (Hebrew).

for health reasons. About 260 rabbis, teachers, and outstanding students were also exempted per the agreement. About 370 students were found fit for conscription according to the terms of the agreement. On June 2, Yaakov Tchernowitz (Tsur) informed the Yeshiva Council that:

> "Due to the seriousness of the situation in the city, we are currently unable [...] to conduct regular training for yeshiva students. Preparing these trainings will require an additional two to three weeks. Since during the negotiations, the yeshiva heads informed us [...] that the yeshivas are ready, regardless of weapon training, to send their students within a special framework for fortification work. And since the fortification issue is very serious and urgent, and every Jew in Jerusalem is obliged to contribute to this work due to pikuach nefesh (saving lives), we propose that yeshiva students be directed during these days to fortification work, according to a special arrangement, within their groups. [...] It is self-evident that the agreement remains in force in all its clauses. The training will be implemented immediately when it is possible, and the young men will be directed to it."

With the district commander's, David Shaltiel's, consent, the yeshiva students were drafted into a religious unit called the "Tuvia Battalion," named after its commander, Tuvia Bir, who was previously a squad commander in the HISH battalion "Michmas." The unit also included yeshiva students from the Haredi community, except for members of "Neturei Karta." Due to a lack of trainers and weapons, the unit members were not trained but engaged in fortification work, contributing over 4,000 workdays until the end of November 1948.[85]

---

85 Aharon Haim Cohen, Year of Recruitment: A Brief Review of the Activities of the Recruitment Office in Jerusalem, 30 November 1948, State Archives Section 42, G23/275; Yaakov Tchernowitz (Tsur), Chairman of the

Yeshiva students were divided into three groups:

1. Blue cardholders tasked with fortification work in organized units under military command.
2. Gray cardholders exempt from conscription and fortification work.
3. White cardholders exempt from conscription and fortification work for medical reasons.[86]

Tuvia Bir appointed six company commanders, each appointing a deputy and three platoon leaders.[87] For example, he approached Avraham Zelushinsky, a Hebron Yeshiva student who was already enlisted in the Haganah and was known to him previously, and appointed him responsible for the recruits from his yeshiva.[88]

Tuvia Bir approached the Chief Rabbis and yeshiva heads, proposing to employ even those with gray and white cards in the following roles:

1. Guarding the bodies and casualties from the shelling.
2. Supervising kashrut in military kitchens.
3. Assisting the wounded in hospitals.
4. Youth guidance.
5. Cultural activities among religious soldiers.[89]

Executive Committee of the National Service Command to the Yeshiva Committee, 2 June 1948, ibid., Rabbi Herzog Archive F-9/4247.

86 Bir Family Archive, 17 June 1948, Aharon Haim Cohen, National Service Command Center to all concerned.

87 Tuvia Battalion Day Order from 24 June 1948, Section E; Day Order from 2 July 1948, Bir Family Archive.

88 Telephone interview with Avraham Zlushinsky, 6 and 11 June 2007.

89 Bir Family Archive, 13 July 1948, Tuvia Bir to Rabbi Moshe Tenenbaum [Secretary of the Yeshiva Committee], regarding yeshiva students with white and gray attendance cards.

These proposals were apparently only partially accepted.

Bir sought the approval of the joint committee of yeshiva heads and the National Service Command Center to train the yeshiva students in his battalion.[90] At the end of July, Levi Rahmani, a squad commander in the Gadna "Yonatan" company, who had been fully enlisted since early December 1947 and participated in many battles, was assigned to the "Tuvia Battalion" to train the unit's members. The main intention was for yeshiva students to be able to defend themselves when necessary and continue with fortification work in the meantime. In practice, few training sessions were conducted.[91] Some students received theoretical lessons in using a rifle and a hand grenade in a room in the Beit Yisrael neighborhood.[92]

The unit operated as a military unit in every way, and service in it was mandatory. Some battalion members had to leave their permanent residences in the frontline neighborhoods due to fighting and shelling, and the battalion headquarters had to issue instructions to its recruits in the "Journal" – the Agudath Israel bulletin. For example, on July 12, 1948, unit members who moved were asked to submit their new address to their company commanders or battalion headquarters "or else measures will be taken against them."[93]

It was determined that yeshiva students serving in other units and not subject to full conscription were allowed to transfer to the yeshiva students' unit and enjoy their rights. Some took advantage of this and requested transfers.[94]

---

90   Bir Family Archive, 19 July 1948, Tuvia Bir to Rabbi Moshe Tenenbaum.

91   Interview with Levi Rahmani, 25 February 2008.

92   Telephone interview with Avraham Zlushinsky, 6 and 11 June 2007.

93   *Ha Yoman* (12 July 1948). And also in *Ha Yoman* (23 June 1948) (Hebrew); for yeshiva students with white attendance cards, *Ha Yoman* (3 August 1948) (Hebrew).

94   Order and Standard for the Recruitment of Yeshiva Students, undated, Bir Family Archive; To Company Commander V of Battalion 3 from Tuvia

Bir was very strict about ensuring that the battalion's activities were carried out in accordance with the agreement. When he learned that Rabbi Yechezkel Sarna, the head of the Hebron Yeshiva, instructed his students serving in the battalion not to go out to work more than once a week, he informed him that this was against the agreement, and if his students did not show up for work twice a week, he would consider it a breach of the agreement, and his students might lose their rights as yeshiva students.[95] Rabbi Eliezer Yehuda Finkel, head of the Mir Yeshiva, also approached the National Service Command through the yeshiva students' battalion commander, Tuvia Bir, on August 3, demanding that yeshiva students not be employed more than once a week.[96] In his response, Bir suggested to Rabbi Finkel not to forward the letter to the National Service Command, as the representatives of the yeshiva heads were supposed to meet with the representatives of the National Service Command anyway, and it would be better for them to handle the matter.[97] On the same day, he informed Dov Tzwobner of the Mir Yeshiva that his platoon members and other students from his yeshiva should report immediately upon receiving the order to the battalion headquarters. Bir added that violating this order would be

---

Battalion Commander of Yeshiva Students, 4 July 1948, regarding the transfer of a yeshiva student from your company to my battalion, ibid.

[95] Bir Family Archive, 2 August 1948, Tuvia Bir – Battalion Commander to Rabbi Yechezkel Sarna, head of the Hebron Yeshiva. Tuvia Bir heard about the head of the yeshiva's instruction to his students from Chaim Yaakov Sarna, the head of the yeshiva's son, who served as a squad leader in his battalion. He prepared a written response but eventually conveyed its content orally. Rabbi Sarna recounted in his memoirs that he urged his students, including his son and son-in-law, to fortify Jerusalem against the danger. See Rabbi Yechezkel Sarna, *Memoirs*, p. 27.

[96] Bir Family Archive, 3 August 1948, Rabbi Eliezer Yehuda Finkel to the National Service Command in Jerusalem via the Battalion Commander of the Yeshiva Students, regarding the recruitment of yeshiva students.

[97] Bir Family Archive, 4 August 1948, Tuvia Bir to Rabbi Eliezer Yehuda Finkel.

considered a breach of the agreement between the yeshiva heads and the National Service Command, and as a result, he would take the measures he deemed necessary.[98]

Most fortification work by yeshiva students was carried out within the battalion framework. Local commanders sometimes approached yeshivas directly. For example, the commander of District 5 of the People's Guard, responsible for the city center, directly approached the head of the Shfat Emet Yeshiva (of the Gerrer Hasidim), which was within the district, and asked him on June 1 to mobilize his students who were not in combat roles for fortification work in the district area.[99] Local commanders sometimes independently "drafted" yeshiva students, including those exempt for medical reasons, and employed them in fortification work without authorization from the competent authorities. Tuvia Bir demanded they cease this as it violated the agreements and disrupted his unit's activities.[100]

Fortification work also involved young yeshiva students not subject to the conscription order. On June 2, 15 students aged 14 from the Kol Torah Yeshiva participated in fortification work that lasted all night.[101] Walter Katz, the commander of the Kiryat Shmuel and Rehavia area, needed to reinforce a position that had been damaged. He did not want to burden his few men busy with guard duty further. Katz approached Rabbi Ephraim Offenberger, the director of an Agudath Israel dormitory,

---

98 Bir Family Archive, 4 August 1948, Tuvia, Battalion Commander of Yeshiva Students to Dov Zwebner, regarding appearance.

99 Central Zionist Archives 64 3J, 1 June 1948, National Guard in Jerusalem to Rabbi Sankovsky [correct name: Sankovich], head of the Sfas Emes Yeshiva: Yeshiva Sfas Emes to fortify Jerusalem.

100 Tuvia Bir to Gershon Company Commander G Battalion 5, 1 July 1948; Tuvia Bir to Dr. Bamberger, Division Officer in Battalion 65, 8 July 1948, Bir Family Archive.

101 Central Zionist Archives 64 3J, 4 June 1948, Intelligence and Information Officer of District 4 to Commander of District 4: Fortifications – Information.

who was a Haganah member, who immediately provided him with 20 boys who stood in a long chain and passed the heavy bags to one another. Within two hours, the renewed position was standing.[102]

Eli Zohar-Lichtenstein, a platoon commander in the Gadna "Yonatan" company, replaced the "Moriah" battalion members who captured the Notre Dame building opposite the Old City walls. Yeshiva students helped fortify the building during the night. Yerach Etzion, one of the fortification coordinators in the city, recounted that yeshiva students worked on fortifications in the Notre Dame building, including the son-in-law of Amram Blau, the leader of Neturei Karta. Their task was to transport a pillbox at night under fire from the Notre Dame courtyard to St. Paul's Street at the intersection of the road descending into the Musrara neighborhood, overlooking the Damascus Gate square. They were also tasked with setting up positions inside the Notre Dame building. These positions were destroyed daily by the Legion's artillery positioned opposite them.[103]

Haganah member Avraham Zuchovitzky recounted in his memoirs that on one night, he was assigned urgent fortification work in the Sanhedria neighborhood. He was provided with groups of yeshiva students of different ages from Jerusalem's established yeshivas. When he saw them, he wondered whether these "workers," unaccustomed to physical effort, could handle the urgent task. But when they began work, the picture changed, as he described: "I couldn't believe my eyes when I saw these young men approach their task as a sacred mission. They approached their work with vigor and dedication, with picks and hoes [...] Hour followed hour, and the fortification work neared completion. The young men did not disappoint. They worked truly to sanctify the

---

102 *ha-Haganah bi-Yerushalayim*, vol. 2 (Jerusalem, 1975), 35 (Hebrew), Testimony of Walter Katz; Walter Katz, "Facing the Buffer Neighborhoods in the South – Kiryat Shmuel," *Alon la-Haverim* (Jerusalem: Havrei Hahaganah, 1976): 16 (Hebrew). Rabbi Offenberg was later appointed as the Religious Officer of the Jerusalem District.

103 *ha-Haganah bi-Yerushalayim*, vol. 2 (Jerusalem, 1975), 239 (Hebrew).

Name, the land, and the people. In my heart grew the conviction that we could overcome our enemies."[104]

Avraham Zelushinsky was responsible for a group of yeshiva students brought to the police school in Sheikh Jarrah on May 18 in the evening to fortify the place. The Etzel unit commander present ordered them to stay in the building, handed them Molotov cocktails, and instructed them to stop the Legion's armor with them if attacked. Zelushinsky was aware that his men, who were untrained, could not carry out the task. After hours of arguments and persuasion, the commander agreed to release his men, and they left the place.[105]

By the end of 1948, the district commander saw no military benefit in maintaining the unit. On November 2, 1948, Bir approached the Chief of Manpower and proposed immediately training all yeshiva students in Jerusalem and deploying the young men aged 23 and older for guard duties, thus creating a reserve battalion composed of young manpower. His proposal was not accepted, and the unit was disbanded.[106] On December 9, 1948, the Jerusalem district headquarters informed the "Tuvia Battalion" commander of the battalion's dissolution and the transfer of those who served fully to the district's 164th battalion.[107]

Yeshiva students were sometimes also employed in additional auxiliary roles, besides fortifications. After the Palmach withdrew from Zion Gate on May 19, several attempts were made in the following

---

104 Avraham Zukhobitsky, "In Those Days," *Alon la-Haverim* (Jerusalem: Havrei Hahaganah, 1971): 19 (Hebrew); Telephone interview with Rabbi Eliyahu Grossberg, 26 June 2008. He studied at the Mir Yeshiva.

105 Telephone interview with Avraham Zlushinsky, 6 and 11 June 2007.

106 Israel State Archives, 959/1949 – 110, 2 November 1948, Tuvia Bir, Commander of Tuvia Battalion to Head of Personnel 1, Regarding: Yeshiva Students Battalion in Jerusalem. A handwritten note dated 17 December 1948 on the document states that the battalion was disbanded.

107 Private Archive, Bir Family, 9 December 1948, Ze'ev Feldman, Administration Officer of the Jerusalem District Headquarters to Tuvia Commander, Regarding: Yeshiva Students Battalion 'Tuvia'.

nights to break into the Jewish Quarter through Zion Gate. Dr. Rudolf Wert, responsible for medical services in the Jerusalem area, enlisted a group of yeshiva students who waited night after night, for several nights, in the Mount Zion area, to serve as stretcher-bearers to evacuate about 50 wounded hospitalized in the Misgav Ladach Hospital in the Jewish Quarter.[108] In contrast, when two soldiers arrived at the Hebron Yeshiva and requested 40 volunteers to help evacuate the Jewish Quarter residents after the Palmach breakthrough, no volunteers were found among the yeshiva students. Rabbi Yosef Brandwein, who was in the yeshiva shelter at the time, banged on the table and demanded that the yeshiva students volunteer. Some yeshiva managers told him that if they knew the students would return to the yeshiva after completing the task, they would allow them to go, but they feared they would keep them there, and eventually, no students would remain in the yeshiva.[109] On the Sabbath night of May 28, 1948, yeshiva students from the "Tuvia Battalion" went up to Mount Zion to welcome the Jewish Quarter residents after the surrender. They carried the quarter's children and elderly down Mount Zion to the buses waiting for them. After the quarter's refugees were transported to the Katamon neighborhood and settled there, the yeshiva students prepared for the Sabbath evening prayer.[110]

108 *ha-Haganah bi-Yerushalayim*, vol. 1 (Jerusalem, 1975), 57, Testimony of Dr. Wert, who noted their great willingness, along with a group of girls from the Irgun, to carry out this mission; Dr. Wert, S.R. – The Medical Service, "On the Walls," *Alon la-Haverim* (Jerusalem: Havrei Hahaganah, Independence Day 1962): 91-92 (Hebrew).

109 Menahem Barash-Ro'i, *Be-Sodam shel Yakirei Yerushalyaim*, vol. 2 (Jerusalem: Rubin Mass, 1982), 214-215 (Hebrew). Rabbi Brandwein studied in the yeshivas of Jerusalem and Safed, was ordained as a rabbi by Jerusalem's chief rabbis, and belonged to the Stratin and Lelov Hasidism; his sons and daughter served in the Haganah and Irgun.

110 Hanina Schiff, "Letter to Editor," *Hamodia* (23 Iyar 5755) (Hebrew): "The Yeshiva Students Risked Their Lives for Rescue in the Old City." Schiff, a Gerrer Hasid and student of the Sfas Emes Yeshiva, participated in the

8 | *The Draft and Yeshiva Students*

A unit commanded by Netanel Lorch blew up the Beit El Maal building (the treasury of the Arab Higher Committee), located in no man's land near the road from Jaffa Gate towards Bethlehem Road. The goal was to block the road with the collapse caused by the explosion, preventing Legion reinforcements from arriving. Several yeshiva students were recruited for the operation to carry explosives into the building.[111] During the intense fighting in the Mandelbaum – Hungarian Houses sector in mid-July 1948, yeshiva students from the "Tuvia Battalion" in the sector were employed in fortification work and also in evacuating casualties from the front line.[112] When the new cemetery was established in Sheikh Bader, after it was impossible to bury on the Mount of Olives and in Sanhedria, yeshiva students were taken with a work manager to the lumber warehouses of Mann and Berman near the Shaare Zedek Hospital and built coffins for the bodies accumulating in the city. These bodies were buried for two days by workers building the airport in the nearby Valley of the Cross.[113] Among the workers paving the "Burma Road," which supplied Jerusalem starting from the first ceasefire, were yeshiva students from the "Tuvia Battalion." Due to the work's necessity, Rabbi Herzog granted a work permit for the Sabbath.[114] Before Passover 1949, the military rabbinate managed to kasher almost all the

operation. Before ascending Mount Zion, they received the blessing of the Gerrer Rebbe and permission to travel on the Sabbath from the Brisker Rav (Rabbi Yitzchak Ze'ev Soloveitchik) due to the danger of walking because of the shelling.

111   Netanel Lorch, *ha-Yom Yifneh* (Tel-Aviv: The Ministry of Defense, 1997), 124 (Hebrew).

112   Bir Family Archive (20 July 1948), Communications Order.

113   Meron Benvenisti, *Jerusalem's City of the Dead* (Jerusalem: Keter, 1990), 77 (Hebrew), according to the memoirs of Yerachmiel Etzion.

114   Testimony of Meir Batz, *ha-Haganah bi-Yerushalayim*, vol. 2 (Jerusalem, 1975), 281-282 (Hebrew).

army kitchens overnight with the help of over 500 yeshiva students who volunteered for the operation.[115]

Organizing the fortification work encountered many problems, affecting those employed in these tasks. Some issues arose from inefficient organization and some from the supervisors' attitudes toward the workers. For example, on June 2, a group of 56 people, including 15 students from the Kol Torah Yeshiva, began their work very late. There was insufficient food and tools, and only at 5:00 AM was a vehicle sent to bring them back. The group's supervisor noted in his report that the work was inefficient and the workers' morale was very low.[116] Another group was hastily mobilized in the midst of the Shavuot holiday and waited until evening in the Givat Shaul neighborhood, dressed in holiday attire, for the vehicles to take them to the Beit Mahsir (Beit Meir) area. There was insufficient water, and the food was not kosher. The group's supervisor noted in his report that people could not be summoned from their homes at 2:00 PM for work that was supposed to start at 8:00 PM. He added that "it is no wonder that the people swore never to go out again for fortification work."[117] Other complaints referred to mistreatment and disrespect towards yeshiva students when the work supervisor spoke to them harshly, saying that anyone who did not work would get a bullet in the head and that he would treat them like dogs. One of them was hit with a Sten gun, and they did not receive food as usual.[118]

---

115 Israel State Archives, 50/1308– 417 (13 April 1949), Shlomo Goronchik (Goren), Chief Rabbi of the IDF to Chief of Staff Lieutenant General Yaakov Dori, "Operation 'Kosher for Passover."

116 Central Zionist Archives 64 3J, 4 June 1948, Intelligence and Information Officer of District 4 to Commander of District 4: Fortifications – Information.

117 Central Zionist Archives 64 3J, 15 June 1948, District Commander 8 to Commander of District 3.

118 "Hatred of the Common People for the Scholar," *HaYoman* (18 June 1948) (Hebrew); Moshe Akiva Druck, "Jerusalem Notes: Disgraceful Abuse," *Kol Yisrael* (1 July 1948): 3 (Hebrew).

8 | *The Draft and Yeshiva Students*

The recruitment of yeshiva students sparked a public debate, including a "poster war" for and against it.[119] The press also occasionally addressed the issue. For instance, John Kimche, in his article "The Morale in Jerusalem" in Haaretz on July 5, 1948, noted that the yeshiva students in Jerusalem had gained a reputation as defeatists, demonstrating with signs reading, "We do not want a state; we want challahs and fish." Only after they were taken from their homes on the Sabbath and the religious sector commander spoke to them alongside military police did they begin working on the fortifications. Kimche noted that afterward, he saw these young men working diligently and faithfully, and their commander praised them as the best among his men.[120] The Haredi public was hurt by the portrayal of yeshiva students in the article. The article sparked reactions in the Haredi-religious press. M. Morozov wrote an article in Agudath Israel's "Journal" titled "In Hatred and Lies, They Loved." "The Tzofeh" presented clarifications from the Jerusalem recruitment center, mainly that the demonstration mentioned was not carried out by yeshiva students but by a fanatical and marginal group. The recruitment of yeshiva students was arranged between the recruitment center and the Chief Rabbis and yeshiva heads. The duty to participate in the defense of Jerusalem was clear to everyone, and the agreement was meant to preserve the yeshivas' existence while ensuring that the students fulfilled their duty to defend Jerusalem.[121]

---

119   Netanel Lorch, *ha-Yom Yifneh* (Tel-Aviv: The Ministry of Defense, 1997), 105 (Hebrew), according to his father Mordechai's personal diary on May 13, which stated: "The Poster War for and Against Yeshiva Students' Recruitment Annoys Many."

120   Yitzchak Ben-Aharon, "Letter to the Editor," *HaYom* (17 May 1948): 2 (Hebrew); and Jon Kimche, "The Morale in Jerusalem," *Haaretz* (5 July 1948): 3 (Hebrew).

121   M. Maorzon, "They Loved Hatred and Lies," *HaYoman* (16 July 1948): 3 (Hebrew); "Open Questions to Mr. Kamhi," *HaYoman* (22 July 1948) (Hebrew); and "Against John Kamhi's Slander of the Yeshiva Students in Jerusalem," *ha-Tsofeh* (21 July 1948): 4 (Hebrew).

Digleinu, the Young Agudath Israel bulletin, published "A Letter from a Soldier to a Yeshiva Student," in which a recruit from the Young Agudath Israel critically described his experiences since he parted from his yeshiva student friend six months earlier. He noted that he agreed with the decision of the Torah leaders that only young Haredim who were not yeshiva students should enlist, while yeshiva students should continue their studies. He wrote that despite his request to serve in a religious unit, he was assigned to a regular unit whose commanders and most members were secular, describing the difficulties faced by religious soldiers. "Our spirits were not very high, but we had no free time for thoughts, as we were tasked with fighting and winning." Later in his letter, he mentioned the support they received from the religious officer and his movement. At the end of his letter, he posed several questions that troubled the recruits, which he wanted to present to the yeshiva students:

> "I understand that the study period is entirely sacred for Torah, but there are also interim periods and free hours from study on holy Sabbaths, and we hoped that while we were in the army, you would care for us and the Talmud Torah children we cared for, educated, and guided—that you would feel responsible for these children, feel responsible for our soldiers, visit them in their camps once on the Sabbath, once on a holiday, to encourage, influence, and strengthen our spirits. But it became clear that this was not the case, because when I visited our settlement during a break and asked the children I had guided if anyone was looking after them, organizing them, they answered no, and I was simply embarrassed. And when I met fellow soldiers and asked if any yeshiva students had visited to give a Torah lecture or a moral conversation or to participate in a Sabbath gathering, they answered no, and again I was embarrassed. I decided to awaken your heart that this is not right, and you must correct it. Forgive me for

a simple soldier like me daring to awaken the yeshiva students who sit all day in the tent of Torah, because rebuke is customary even for a student regarding his rabbi, and better is open rebuke than hidden love. I await your response."[122]

It soon became clear that religious soldiers encountered severe problems maintaining their religious lifestyle during their military service. This ongoing problematic situation, which remained unresolved, strengthened the position of those opposed to the conscription of yeshiva students. Neturei Karta mocked Agudath Israel, whose newspapers complained about the problems of religious recruits, as they could have foreseen this in a "state of Sadducees." In an article directed at a "Yeshiva Student," the writer emphasized that the struggle for the exemption of yeshiva students from conscription is not the main issue, but rather "no Haredi Jew has a part or inheritance with this state of Sadducees, nor, therefore, in their war. On the contrary, it is forbidden for any Haredi Jew to participate in this war." However, if there is a special obligation imposed on yeshiva students, it is a holy war against these heretics, a sacred war to save the Torah and Judaism from their persecutors.[123]

In early October 1948, Dov Lipov, the director of manpower in Jerusalem, issued another conscription order for essential work, including all those not enlisted in full conscription. The Chief Rabbis and yeshiva heads reached a special agreement with Lipov allowing all yeshiva students to continue their studies as usual until after the holidays on October 26, 1948. The names of all yeshiva students were gathered at the Yeshiva Council office on October 8 to arrange their exemption. On October 24, a notice was published by the "Tuvia

---

122 Deglenu La'Meguysim, bulletin of the Youth Movement of Agudath Israel – Agudist Youth in Eretz Yisrael, Legion 8 (December 2, 1948): 3 (Hebrew), Bimat HaChayal (The Soldier's Platform), a letter from a soldier to a yeshiva student, signed Yitzchak.

123 Ch. M., "Letter to a 'Yeshiva Student,'" HaChoma, no. 48 (23 September 1948): 4 (Hebrew).

Battalion" that all yeshiva students not exempted by the battalion doctor from fortification work must report on October 26 at 7:15 AM to the battalion headquarters. All yeshiva students subject to the essential work order reported as required and were organized into work groups to begin work the next day. On October 29, the commander of the "Tuvia Battalion" announced that all yeshiva students who had not yet reported for essential work must do so by 12:00 PM, or they would be considered draft dodgers. Lipov stated at a press conference on December 2 that all 300 yeshiva students drafted for essential work reported to work alongside the rest of Jerusalem's residents.[124]

In late October 1948, the Chief Rabbinate sent the Yeshiva Council a list of over 50 rabbis in yeshivas, neighborhood rabbis, and synagogue rabbis who received certificates of their actual positions to obtain exemption certificates from the manpower director.[125]

Yeshivas Outside Jerusalem

Even in yeshivas outside Jerusalem, outstanding students who devoted themselves entirely to Torah study were exempted. The recruitment center reviewed the exemption requests. A request from the

---

124 "Notice from the Yeshiva Committee Office," *HaYoman* (8 October 1948): 4 (Hebrew); "Important Notice to the Yeshiva Students in Jerusalem," *HaYoman* (24 October 1948): 1 (Hebrew); "Yeshiva Students for Essential Works," *HaYom* (26 October 1948): 2 (Hebrew); "Notice from the Human Resources Coordinator," *HaYom* (27 October 1948): 2 (Hebrew); "Yeshiva Students Went Out for Fortifications," *HaYoman* (28 October 1948) (Hebrew); "Notice to Yeshiva Students," *HaYoman* (29 October 1948): 4 (Hebrew); "Essential Work Recruits Fulfilled the Commandment of Saving Lives," *HaYom* (2 December 1948): 4 (Hebrew).

125 Rabbi Shmuel Aharon Shazuri, Chief Secretary of the Chief Rabbinate to the Yeshiva Committee (28 October 1948) and (31 October 1948), Israel State Archives GL-2/8553.

Chief Rabbinate of Tel Aviv on May 2 for the exemption of rabbis was only partially granted and according to the agreement's criteria.[126]

Tel Aviv yeshiva students trained in early May 1948. Before heading to training, they gathered on the roof of one of the yeshivas, and David Bernholtz, head of the security department of the Workers' Council of Agudath Israel, explained their role. Rabbi Shraga Grossbard of Agudath Israel bid them farewell, saying he hoped the order and discipline they would learn in their training would later assist them in their studies.[127] Tzvi Ze'ev Friedman, a Belz Hasidic yeshiva student, recounted in his memoirs that due to the security situation in Tel Aviv, which suffered constant sniper fire from Jaffa, the Tel Aviv Haganah headquarters approached the Yeshiva Heads Council and requested to recruit 100 yeshiva students for guard duties and to man positions. It was agreed that the young men would undergo partial training and guard twice a week at night to not harm their studies. He and his friends were trained for two days in operating a Sten submachine gun and throwing grenades, but only theoretically, without firing. After the capture of the Manshiya neighborhood and the Hassan Bek Mosque at the end of April 1948, Tel Aviv's security situation improved, and they were not used for their intended role.[128]

Binyamin Mintz noted in a letter to Ben-Gurion in mid-June 1948 that at the time, 312 yeshiva students were approved for full exemption, 45 of whom were exempted due to their medical condition, leaving only 267 yeshiva students whose Torah was their craft from yeshivas outside Jerusalem. Mintz requested the approval of more than twenty additional yeshiva students that the yeshiva heads forwarded to him. Most were new immigrants who studied in yeshivas abroad before immigrating

---

126 P. Globman to the Chief Rabbinate of the Jaffa-Tel Aviv District (4 May 1948), Poalei Agudath Israel Archive, Box 20, File 7.

127 "Yeshiva Students for Training," *Gesher* (6 May 1948): 1 (Hebrew).

128 Tsvi Zev Friedman, *Zekhor Yemot Olam* (Bnei Brak, 2012), 92-93 (Hebrew). According to him, on the third day of training, they were photographed for recruitment propaganda.

to Israel, and a minority were yeshiva students from Jerusalem who arrived during the truce to their homes outside Jerusalem. Mintz noted that although the exemption agreement included new immigrants, the recruitment center did not approve their exemption and, in addition, ordered exempted yeshiva students to obtain call-up cards obliging them to partial conscription, contrary to the March 9 agreement applicable to the entire year of 5708. Mintz added that the training of Tel Aviv yeshiva students was carried out, but the training of yeshiva students in the Tel Aviv area was not carried out, despite the yeshiva heads demanding it, due to difficulties from the security forces.[129]

In mid-July 1948, the recruitment center for the Tel Aviv and South district informed the Bnei Brak Security Committee that all rabbis who received full exemption from military service were also exempt from partial service, such as fortifications, guard duties, etc.[130] Various yeshivas submitted data on their students to the recruitment and exemption bodies in July 1948. On July 15, the recruitment center discussed how to treat them. Binyamin Avniel reported that at the time, 312 yeshiva students were exempted, and now an additional list of 80 people who moved from Jerusalem to Tel Aviv was submitted. Agudath Israel approached Ben-Gurion, who contacted the recruitment center and requested approval of their exemption. Various proposals were raised during the discussion, and it was decided to approve their exemption but require them to undergo training for two months and conduct a check to see if all those exempted were indeed studying.[131]

---

129 Binyamin Mintz to Prime Minister David Ben-Gurion, "Regarding: Yeshiva Students Recruitment" (15 June 1948), Poalei Agudath Israel Archive, Box 7, File 9.

130 Ministry of Defense, Recruitment Center for the Tel Aviv and Southern District to the Security Committee of Bnei Brak, "Regarding: Release of Rabbis from Partial Service" (13 July 1948), Poalei Agudath Israel Archive, Box 21, File 3.

131 Details of the Recruitment Center meeting on 15 July 1948 Section 7, Israel State Archives File 56/679 – 21.

Rabbi Levin and Rabbi Fishman approached Ben-Gurion and complained that yeshiva students were being recruited contrary to the agreement. Rabbi Levin discussed this on July 22 with Dr. Avniel after yeshiva heads and his party activists approached him. Avniel said that all those on the lists would be completely exempt, even from partial conscription, and tried again to convince Rabbi Levin to agree to train them in weapon use for emergencies. Rabbi Levin replied that for the time being, the agreement should not be changed for several weeks, after which the rabbis and yeshiva heads would discuss the matter again.[132]

The pressure to increase the number of exemptions continued. Ze'ev Fischer-Schein of the Poalei Agudath Israel, who was a member of the recruitment committee, reported at a meeting of the executive committee of Poalei Agudath Israel on July 21 on the development of events in handling the exemption of yeshiva students. He noted that "until now, I was the final arbiter of who is a yeshiva student. Now that a new list of 27 new immigrants has been submitted (some of whom were genuinely only yeshiva students). I brought the matter before the executive committee, and they rejected the approval. Then the students of the Hebron Yeshiva came (about 22). Then more students came. I demanded approval from the three yeshiva heads, but they refused to sign. They went to Rabbi Yitzhak Meir Levin, who went to Ben-Gurion. Ben-Gurion called Avniel, and it was decided at the executive committee to approve up to 380 [exemptions]. They submitted more than the above number to me, and I saw that there were things that were not straight here, and I refused to deal with it further." Mintz said: "We see that the Torah leaders demand, and even Ben-Gurion accepts. Therefore, we must also accept, we labored, and it no longer matters

---

132   Y.L. Cohen Fishman to David Ben-Gurion, 24 Sivan 5708 [1 July 1948]; D. Ben-Gurion to Rabbi Y.L. Cohen Fishman, 4 July 1948, Ben-Gurion Heritage Archive, Sde Boker; Rabbi Yitzhak Meir Levin to Dr. Avniel (20 July 1948), Israel State Archives GL-1/44806; Yitzhak Meir Levin to the Heads of Yeshivas, 20 July 1948; Rabbi Yitzhak Meir Levin , Protocol of Conversation between Rabbi Levin and Dr. Avniel (22 July 1948), ibid.; Yitzhak Meir Levin to the Heads of Yeshivas, 22 July 1948, ibid.

what each of us thinks about it. We all share responsibility, together with the comrade [Fischer-]Schein. I suggest demanding from Comrade Schein to continue arranging the matter." It was decided to task Fischer-Schein with continuing to handle the matter despite his reluctance. The Poalei Agudath Israel movement did not want to appear as the cause of the conscription of yeshiva students.[133]

On July 23, a concluding meeting was held between the committee of yeshiva heads and members of the executive committee of Poalei Agudath Israel, and positions regarding the conscription of yeshiva students were agreed upon. Ze'ev Fischer-Schein undertook to handle the matter.[134] On July 25, Rabbi Levin was informed by the recruitment center that it had been decided to approve the exemption of 124 new yeshiva students in addition to the 436 yeshiva students already approved and that the list should be considered closed.[135] On July 29, Rabbi Fishman and the head of the manpower division, General Moshe Tzadok, held a discussion with Ben-Gurion regarding yeshiva students. Following the discussion, the head of the manpower division informed the brigades, the ministers of defense, and religion that "yeshiva students should not be conscripted for full or partial conscription." This refers to those exempted as outstanding students whose Torah is their craft, whose names were

---

133   Protocol of the Executive Committee meeting (21 July 1948), Poalei Agudath Israel Archive, Box 30, File 8; Rabbi Yitzhak Meir Levin to Kalmer, Recruitment Center (23 July 1948), Israel State Archives GL-1/44806. Rabbi Levin's request to the Recruitment Center to add 22 students from the Hebron Yeshiva to the exemption list.

134   "Poalei Agudath Israel for the Sake of the Yeshiva Students," *She'arim* (29 July 1948): 1 (Hebrew).

135   Recruitment Center to Rabbi Yitzhak Meir Levin, Minister of Welfare, "Regarding: New Yeshiva Students, 25 July 1948," a photocopy of the document in Leader in the Storm of the Period: Commemorating the 35th Anniversary of Rabbi Yitzhak Meir Levin's Passing, *Special Edition of the Newspaper Hamodia* (10 August 2006): 21 (Hebrew); Secretary of the Minister of Welfare to the Yeshiva Committee (1 August 1948), Israel State Archives GL-1/44806.

8 | *The Draft and Yeshiva Students*

approved by three yeshiva heads. The yeshiva administrations were requested to train capable yeshiva students for self-defense within the yeshiva grounds "by order under the guidance of the supreme command. This agreement will be considered a temporary arrangement for the year 5708 and will be discussed anew at the beginning of the year 5709. It cannot be canceled except by a new agreement."[136] In a discussion held by the recruitment center on August 2, it was decided to exempt yeshiva students from partial conscription and require them to undergo training and guard duty for 24 hours a week.[137]

In time, Rabbi Yitzhak Meir Levin recounted his persuasion efforts for the exemption of yeshiva students. At one of the meetings of the temporary government held in Tel Aviv, a delegation of yeshiva heads arrived wanting to meet with Ben-Gurion regarding the exemption of their students from conscription, but Ben-Gurion refused to meet them. Rabbi Levin sent Ben-Gurion a note during the meeting requesting an urgent conversation with him, but Ben-Gurion replied that he had to leave immediately after the meeting to the general staff and had no time. Rabbi Levin did not give up and wrote another note that he had to meet him regarding a battalion of trained soldiers equipped with the most advanced weapons, with whose help we would win. Ben-Gurion agreed to meet him for a few minutes after the meeting. At the end of the meeting, Ben-Gurion asked Rabbi Levin nervously what battalion he had. Rabbi Levin replied that there were about 400-500 yeshiva students in the country who sit and study Torah, who are the remnants of the

---

136 David Ben-Gurion, *The War of Independence: War Diary*, vol. 1, eds. Gershon Rivlin and Elhanan Orren (Tel-Aviv: Ministry of Defense, 1982), 625 (29 July 1948); Head of the Division General Staff/Personnel/1, to Shach [Recruitment and Absorption Service], Brigades, Minister of Defense, Minister of Religion, 29 July 1948, Regarding: Recruitment of Yeshiva Students, Poalei Agudath Israel Archive, Box 21, File 3; Y.L. Cohen Maimon to the Central Agudat Israel in the Land of Israel, Tel Aviv, 29 July 1948, State Archives G-4767/4.

137 Details of the Recruitment Center meeting on 2 August 1948, Israel State Archives 697/56-21.

magnificent yeshivas of Europe that were destroyed in the Holocaust, and we must keep them in the yeshivas, and without a doubt, through their Torah and prayers, we will win. Ben-Gurion asked Rabbi Levin if he truly believed this. Rabbi Levin replied with tears in his eyes that he believed it with complete faith. Ben-Gurion thought for a moment and then said he was convinced and agreed to give Rabbi Levin a letter instructing the recruitment center to defer the conscription of yeshiva students.[138] During a discussion in the Knesset on the Security Service Law in October 1958, Ben-Gurion referred to the exemption of yeshiva students during the War of Independence, saying: "When the state was established, one of the greats of Judaism and Torah in our time, Rabbi Maimon [Fishman] and also Rabbi Yitzhak Meir Levin spoke to me. They said: since all Torah centers in the diaspora were destroyed and this is the only land where yeshivas remain and the students are few, they should be exempt from military service. Their words were accepted by me. It seemed to me they were right, and I gave an order to exempt yeshiva students."[139]

There was still a difference between the yeshivas in Jerusalem and those in other parts of the country. Rabbi Levin wrote to Rabbi Moshe Glickman-Frosh at the end of August in response to his appeal regarding a change in the conscription policy for yeshiva students: "It was determined here [in Tel Aviv] according to the agreement to exempt them from any conscription until the upcoming holidays [starting on October 4—Rosh Hashanah and ending on October 25—Simchat Torah]. If you [in Jerusalem] have been informed that they must perform guard duty for 24 hours a week, perhaps this is only done in the Jerusalem area, and you must insist on this. In general, the more firmly we stand by our opinion, the better." Rabbi Glickman-Frosh replied that

---

138 Y.Ts. Govitz, Condemned to Life, pp. 220-223. Govitz, an activist of Agudat Israel, recounted in his memoirs that he personally heard the story from Rabbi Levin.

139 Protocol of Discussion No. 513 on 13 October 1958, Knesset Records, Volume 25, p. 13.

they were indeed informed in Jerusalem that yeshiva students would be completely exempted from the month of Elul [starting September 5].[140]

A particular issue was whether to grant new immigrants who studied in yeshivas abroad the right to exemption. Rabbi Levin forwarded to Dr. Avniel on September 1 a list of nine yeshiva students who had arrived from abroad (born between 1902 and 1928) and requested that they be added to those exempt from conscription. The recruitment center did not comply with the request, stating that the exemption from conscription only applied to yeshiva students currently in the country, not new immigrants arriving from abroad, and that the list was now closed. Nonetheless, the actual number of exemptions had already reached around 550.[141] The Yeshiva Council submitted another list to Rabbi Levin at the end of November 1948, including six yeshiva students who had arrived from abroad. Rabbi from Brisk approached Rabbi Meir Karlitz at the end of December 1948, informing him about 19 yeshiva students and their rabbi who had arrived on a ship from Romania and asked him to ensure that the Yeshiva Council would handle their spiritual absorption.[142] Ben-Gurion opposed their exemption. In early February 1949, he wrote to Rabbi Herzog that despite highly appreciating his

---

140   Moshe Glickman-Porush to Yitzhak Meir Levin, 15 Av 5708 [20 August 1948], Agudat Israel World Archive; Yitzhak Meir Levin to Rabbi M. Glickman-Porush, Jerusalem, 27 August 1948; Moshe Glickman-Porush to Rabbi Yitzhak Meir Levin, 29 Av 5708 [3 September 1948], Central Agudat Israel Jerusalem Archive.

141   Rabbi Yitzhak Meir Levin to Dr. Avniel, Chairman of the Recruitment Center (1 September 1948), Israel State Archives GL-1/44806; Galia Hertz to Rabbi Levin, undated, Levin Family Archive; Recruitment Center to Rabbi Yitzhak Meir Levin, 15 September 1948, ibid.

142   Yeshiva Committee in the Land of Israel, List of Yeshiva Students Who Came from Abroad, 22 Cheshvan 5709 [24 January 1948], Levin Family Archive; Rabbi Yitzhak Zeev Soloveitchik to Rabbi Meir Karelitz (15 Tevet 5709 [28 December 1948], in Shimon Meller, *Iggerot Maran ha-Griz* (Jerusalem: Meller, 2008), 353-354.

reasons for exempting immigrant yeshiva students, "there is a risk of misuse of this right, and there have been cases confirming this concern."[143]

Another problem arose when it was decided to conscript those born in 1931. At a meeting of the temporary government on May 26, Rabbi Levin asked why the conscription had to start from the age of 17, a practice not common in any army. After discussion, it was decided to accept Minister Aharon Zisling's wording: "In an emergency, compulsory conscription will be instituted for the Israel Defense Forces in all its services. The conscription age will be determined by the State Council or the temporary government."[144]

At the government meeting on June 6, it was decided to conscript 17-year-olds for two months, provided they would not be sent to the front without an explicit government decision. In mid-June 1948, the

143   David Ben-Gurion to Chief Rabbi Herzog, 8 February 1949, Ben-Gurion Heritage Archive; From time to time, there was still a need to intervene to uphold the agreements. For example, Rabbi Levin approached Ben-Gurion at the beginning of November 1948 to prevent the recruitment of yeshiva students from Petah Tikva and Tel Aviv for guard duty on outposts and to Minister Bentov to exempt them from picking work. See Yitzhak Meir Levin, Minister of Welfare, to D. Ben-Gurion, Prime Minister (5 November 1948), Israel State Archives, GL-1/44806; David Mushin from the Prime Minister's Office to Rabbi Levin, 10 November 1948, Levin Family Archive; Secretary of the Minister of Welfare to Rabbi Kahaneman, Rabbi M. Karelitz, and others, 14 November 1948, ibid., ibid.; Major Ezra Omer, Chief of Staff to Rabbi Herzog, 16 November 1948, State Archives/Rabbi Herzog Archive F-4247/29. District Commander of the Eye to Rabbi Katz Petah Tikva, Regarding: Yeshiva Students, 12 November 1948; Commander of the Heim in the Petah Tikva area requested to receive the order of the Minister of Defense in writing; Gedalia Hertz to Rabbi Yitzhak Meir Levin , 9 November 1948, Levin Family Archive; Yitzhak Meir Levin to Rabbi Gedalia Hertz (29 November 1948), Israel State Archives GL-1/44806; Rabbi Yitzhak Meir Levin , Minister of Welfare to M. Bentov, Minister of Labor and Construction, 1 December 1948, ibid.

144   Minutes of the meetings of the Provisional Government, Volume 1, Protocol of the meeting on 26 May 1948, pp. 6 and 10.

8 | *The Draft and Yeshiva Students*

recruitment center determined that all young people born in 1931, whether already in service, in one of the pre-military frameworks, or not in any framework, should undergo training for two months. After the training, the trainees would return to their previous studies and duties and not be conscripted for full or partial military service.[145]

Due to the fierce fighting and losses during the invasion month, there were many plans to use the 17-year-olds to fill the ranks. The head of the Manpower Directorate, General Moshe Tzadok, reported on June 11 that 3,000 17-year-olds could be conscripted for training. According to the government's decision, they were conscripted for training under the command of the Gadna and trained near Kfar Yona and Camp 80 near Pardes Hanna. Acting Chief of Staff Yigael Yadin demanded on July 5 that the 17-year-olds be placed in the artillery. On July 18, it was agreed to establish reserve units, including two battalions of 1,300 Gadna personnel who had been training for two weeks in Pardes Hanna, and to allow their use for the defense of the northern coastal plain. In a discussion on July 23 about filling positions in various units, it was revealed that 24,500 men were missing. Among the sources to fill the gap, General Tzadok also suggested 3,500 from the Gadna. On August 6, he proposed sending the 17-year-olds, who were due to complete their training in two weeks, to the artillery, the Air Force, the Armor, the Navy, and the Signal Corps.[146]

---

145 David Ben-Gurion, *The Restored State of Israel*, vol. 1 (Tel-Aviv: Am Oved, 1969), 157; Ministry of Defense/Recruitment Center, Instructions and Summaries, Supplement No. 12, 16 June 1948, Training of 1931 Births, Israel State Archives, GL-4/46642.

146 David Ben-Gurion, *The War of Independence: War Diary*, vol. 2, eds. Gershon Rivlin and Elhanan Orren (Tel-Aviv: Ministry of Defense, 1982), 504 (11 June 1948), 576 (5 July 1948), 599 (18 July 1948), 619 (23 July 1948), and 634 (6 August 1948) (Hebrew); David Ben-Gurion, *The Restored State of Israel*, vol 1 (Tel-Aviv: Am Oved, 1969), 237 (Hebrew); and David Dayan, *Yes, We Are Youth!* (Tel-Aviv: Ministry of Defense, 1977), 130-132 (Hebrew).

Agudath Israel expressed its opposition to Conscription Order No. 3, published in early July 1948, which included compulsory conscription for all those born in 1931 and for men aged 36-45, as well as for women. Agudath Israel claimed that this order exceeded the agreement made between Agudath Israel and the Central Command for National Service, and therefore could not obligate Agudath Israel's members. This opposition was published in the "Journal."[147] In response, Yaakov Tchernovitz, chairman of the Jerusalem recruitment center, reacted sharply the following day in a letter to the "Journal" editorial board. He stated that the agreement signed with Agudath Israel did not specify any age limitations and added that the ad's publishers and the newspaper in which it was published would be held accountable for this.[148] Tchernovitz also contacted the Jerusalem District Commander and the Attorney General, asking them to investigate whether there were grounds for a lawsuit against the "Journal."[149]

Not everyone shared Agudath Israel's opposition to the conscription of those born in 1931. Among them was Tuvia Bir, commander of the Yeshiva Students' Battalion, who sought to recruit them into his battalion.[150] David Goldberg, head of the Jerusalem branch of the Young Agudath Israel, approached the Jerusalem Agudath Israel Center on July 20, after they published that the conscription order for those born in 1931 did not obligate them, noting that the national leadership of the Young Agudath Israel had decided that those born in 1931 should enlist for training, and those born in 1932 should enlist for essential work. He announced that the movement would ensure that they would be

---

147 "Announcement of the Central Agudat Israel regarding Recruitment Order No. 3," *Ha Yoman* (8 July 1948): 1 (Hebrew).

148 Yaakov Tchernowitz (Tsur), Chairman of the Jerusalem Recruitment Center to the Journal Editorial Board, 1 Tammuz 5708 [8 July 1948], State Archives G-276/7; *Ha Yoman* (9 July 1948) (Hebrew).

149 Yaakov Tchernowitz (Tsur) to the Jerusalem District Commander and the Attorney General, 8 July 1948, State Archives G-276/7.

150 Tuvia Bir to Rabbi Tenenbaum, 11 July 1948, Bir Family Archive.

8 | *The Draft and Yeshiva Students*

concentrated in religious units and that the Jerusalem branch intended to act according to this decision. However, he requested to hold an urgent meeting within 24 hours to clarify the matter, or they would act according to their movement's national leadership decision. The person in charge of the Jerusalem Agudath Israel Center, Rabbi Moshe Glickman-Frosh, requested in early August 1948 from the leadership of the Agudath Youth Association not to publish the announcements sent to the Jerusalem branch calling for the conscription of 17-year-olds, because the Agudath Israel Center had decided against conscription and it might cause a rift with the party and youth center in Jerusalem.[151]

On August 31, Rabbi Levin approached Ben-Gurion, writing that it seemed clear to him that the agreement regarding the exemption of yeshiva students also included those born in 1931, and that the conscription authorities did not want to release them without explicit instruction from him [Ben-Gurion]. Levin requested that Ben-Gurion issue this instruction promptly.[152] At the meeting of the Executive Committee of the Recruitment Center on September 9, it was determined to approach all relevant parties to obtain the number of yeshiva students born in 1931 and to refer the matter to the Defense Minister for a decision. Ultimately, it was determined that regarding yeshiva students born in 1931, a special committee would determine the list of institutions whose students were eligible to be defined as yeshiva students, and those who began their studies in these yeshivas before November 1947 would be entitled to receive exemption from conscription as yeshiva students.[153]

---

151   David Goldberg, Branch of Tze'irei Agudat Yisrael, Jerusalem, to the Central Agudat Israel in Jerusalem, 20 July 1948; Moshe Glickman-Porush to the Agudati Youth Movement, Tel Aviv, 1 Av 5708 [6 August 1948], Central Agudat Israel Archive, Jerusalem.

152   Yitzhak Meir Levin to David Ben-Gurion (31 August 1948), Israel State Archives GL-1/44806.

153   Secretary of the Minister of Welfare to the Yeshiva Committee (3 August 1948), Israel State Archives GL-1/44806; Protocol of the Executive Committee Meeting of the Recruitment Center, 9 September 1948, Israel

In accordance with the agreement, the recruitment center provided detailed lists with the names of yeshiva students born in 1931 to the recruitment offices with instructions to defer their conscription until January 1, 1949.[154]

The total number of exemptions for yeshiva students, according to a report from the recruitment center as of November 1, 1948, was approximately 800, of which 312 were in Jerusalem, 177 in Tel Aviv, and 149 in the Dan region, including Bnei Brak.[155]

Yeshiva students were part of a list of sectors that various entities or the students themselves believed should be exempt from general conscription duties. The sector closest and most similar to yeshiva students were the students and teacher seminar students, who also received special conditions.

Recruitment and Exemptions for Students of Higher Education Institutions

The question of whether to continue teaching and studying at the university while the Jewish community was fighting for its existence and the realization of its vision for a Jewish state was a pressing issue. This question concerned everyone: the political leadership, the military command at various levels, the university administration, faculty, and students. It involved practical and moral aspects, immediate and future considerations, as well as objective and subjective perspectives. Should the immediate and urgent needs of the war take precedence, halting studies until the conflict's end? Should priority also be given to

---

State Archives 679/56 -21; Copy of Instructions and Summaries from 4 November 1948, Poalei Agudath Israel Archive, File 21, Box 3. Committee members were: M. Idelberg, M. Kalmer, and Z. Fisher-Shain.

154 Recruitment Center to the Tel Aviv Recruitment Office (4 November 1948), Poalei Agudath Israel Archive, File 20, Box 9.

155 Recruitment of Manpower in the War of Independence, Israel State Archives 1046/1970 – 159, pp. 54-55.

other needs of the soon-to-be-established state by continuing to train individuals essential for its various functions? Should personal interests be favored over national ones? Could students continue their studies while their peers were fighting and sometimes being injured?

Ben-Gurion's opinion was clear and decisive, as expressed in his meeting with a delegation from the university administration on February 16, 1948. He stated that any student engaged in scientific work for security purposes should not be released from this work nor transferred to another service location. Other students would not be completely exempt, but efforts would be made to allow them to continue their studies as much as possible. On that same day, Ben-Gurion sent written instructions to the Jerusalem District Commander, Shaltiel, noting, among other things, that:

> "It is essential to ensure that, even in times of emergency, studies at the university continue as much as possible, and that this esteemed institution is not closed under any circumstances. Jewish scientific forces, especially in the fields of physics, chemistry, and medicine, have a valuable role in the defense services and homeland security. Any student or teacher of conscription age, recruited for scientific work for security needs, is considered to be working in the service. Concentration of students in one department or unit sent to the front should be avoided, and they should be dispersed as much as possible among different units. For students nearing the end of their studies, it is important to allow them—without causing significant harm to security services—to continue their studies, and for this purpose, to arrange their work in the security service intermittently, as much as possible. Students in the Etzion Bloc should be given free time to refresh their studies."[156]

156 David Ben-Gurion, *The War of Independence: War Diary*, vol. 1, eds. Gershon Rivlin and Elhanan Orren (Tel-Aviv: Ministry of Defense,

These instructions implied a certain reduction in military service in favor of studies. This decision was not easy, especially in the Jerusalem district, which constantly suffered from a manpower shortage and pressure from Ben-Gurion and the high command to receive reinforcements. Several attempts were made to combine military service with studies, but the problem remained unsolved.

David Shaltiel, the Jerusalem District Commander, began to implement Ben-Gurion's instructions, which implied a certain concession on quality personnel for the district's combat units, already suffering from a manpower shortage. On February 25, he sent written orders to the commanders of the two Haganah battalions in Jerusalem. The order stated that the competent authorities had decided that to "preserve the spark of culture in the country," it should be:

> "Communicated to all concerned that any student-soldier not holding a special position is permitted to return to their studies, according to the conditions set by the competent authorities and academic institutions, and for this purpose, they will be promptly transferred to the Haim [Guard Corps]. The Haganah units have room only for fully conscripted individuals. This information should also be communicated to the students in the Haganah units in the Etzion Bloc. Those among them who claim their rights will be promptly replaced and transferred to city units in the Haim. This right is available to claimants until the 28th of this month at midnight. You must ensure that these instructions are conveyed to nearby bases via wireless."[157]

1982), 248-249 (16 February 1948) (Hebrew).

157 AAJ, 06/48, 25 February 1948, David [Shaltiel] to Shadmi [Moriah], David L'Daromi [Mikmas], copy to Yarkoni [Commander of the Heim in the Jerusalem Area], University Administration; Israel State Archives, 1950 / 553 – 57, 28 February 1948, "Daily Order from Gold [Harkavi] Commander of Company B in Battalion 1" [Moriah].

8 | *The Draft and Yeshiva Students*

The student platoon of the Haganah Battalion 'Mikmash' in the Etzion Bloc decided at the beginning of March that all but one would take advantage of the right to transfer to the Haim and continue their studies.[158] By the end of March, students at the Hebrew University were divided into three groups: those fully conscripted who had stopped or never started their studies; those who could partially study in Jerusalem; and a new group beginning to organize to ascend Mount Scopus and combine studies with guarding the place.

In early April, the Jerusalem District's quartermaster instructed that Bezalel students not belonging to the Haganah battalions, Moriah and Mikmash, be transferred to the Haim. The student list included eight in the Haganah battalions and 20 transferred to the Haim.[159]

A similar arrangement existed for students at the Technion in Haifa. Members of the student platoon responsible for securing transportation lines were recruited for month-long periods based on their academic year.[160] After completing the recruitment period, they returned to their studies, replaced by students from another year. The final decision regarding Technion students was communicated on March 31 to Dr. Ben-Yehuda, head of the National Committee's Education Department: on April 1, 1948, all first-year course students were required to enter service. On April 15, 1948, fourth-year course graduates entered full service. On April 20, 1948, second and third-year course students entered service, thereby halting studies at the Technion.[161]

---

158 Monia [Menachem Richman, company commander] to Shura [his brother Yaakov] (10 March 1948). Menachem Richman, *Youth in the Shadow of the Storm, 1924-1948*, ed. Ami Shamir (Tel-Aviv: Ministry of Defense, 1996), 90 (Hebrew).

159 Israel State Archives, 49/2644 – 456 (5 April 1948), Adam, Battalion Adjutant, to Fortress, Subject: Bezalel Students.

160 Zadok Eshel, *The 'Carmeli' Brigade in the War of Independence* (IDF Ma'arachot and Ministry of Defence, 1973), 53 (Hebrew).

161 P. Globman, Commander of the Recruitment Service to Dr. Ben-Yehuda (31 March 1948), Israel State Archives 1956/679– 34.

Special accommodations were also made for students studying abroad. The conscription order applied to single and married men without children aged 18-35 abroad, calling them to return to the country immediately in early April 1948. Students studying abroad were granted an extension until the end of the semester in June 1948. Those with only one year remaining after this semester were granted an additional year of extension. Outstanding students, with exceptional talents studying in fields important to the country, were allowed to remain abroad until completing their studies.[162]

At a meeting on February 1, after coordinating with the Youth Education Committee of the National Service Center, the status of teacher seminar students was determined:

> "A seminar student will not be recruited unless his departure is essential for a special assignment. Each case will be reviewed individually by the department manager. If the department manager determines that the student's departure is essential and the student has no examination obligations from the seminar, the departing student is entitled to receive a graduation certificate along with his classmates and must be placed in a teaching framework upon return from service. If the manager finds the student's departure essential, but the student has an examination obligation from the seminar, the student will be recruited with examination leniencies assured… In any case of a student's recruitment request, the department manager must first receive the student's grade transcript, and only after the manager communicates his opinion in writing does the seminar

---

162 Recruitment Order for Citizens Abroad, Commander of the Recruitment Service / Instructions and Summaries, Section 5, Israel State Archives, GL-4/46642; Commander of the Recruitment Service / Instructions and Summaries, Supplement No. 1 (15 April 1948), ibid.

administration inform the student of his examination exemption status."[163]

In the later stages of the war, the seminars began the academic year while the war was still ongoing on many fronts. At the David Yellin Teachers' College in Jerusalem, students were called to resume their studies on June 15.[164] At the Levinsky Teachers' College in Tel Aviv, studies for two sixth-grade classes [second-year] began on July 22, 1948.[165] The Teachers' College in Beit HaKerem, Jerusalem, announced the opening of the upper class on August 10, 1948, the preparatory class on September 19, and the first class on September 23, 1948.[166]

[This chapter is an English translation of Moshe Ehrenwald, "The Draft and Yeshiva Students," in *The Haredim During the Independence War* (Moshav Ben Shemen: Modan Publishing, 2017), 281-323 (Hebrew).]

Dr. Moshe Ehrenwald is a graduate of the Department of History of the Modern Middle East and the Department of International Relations, holding a master's degree in Contemporary Jewry from the Hebrew University of Jerusalem. His book on the Jewish Quarter of Jerusalem's Old City during the War of Independence, based on his doctoral dissertation in the Department of History at the Hebrew University, was awarded the Yitzhak Sadeh Prize for Military Literature. His book on Mount Scopus in the War of Independence received the Moldovan Prize for Military Literature at Ariel University. His 2017 book, *The Haredim During the Independence War*, was published by Modan Publishing House.

---

163 Protocol of the Committee Meeting on Youth Studies by the Central Recruitment Service (1 February 1948); Protocol of the Discussion in the Education Department (1 February 1948), Israel State Archives, GL-8/1728.

164 "Inside Jerusalem: At the Teacher's Seminary," *HaYom* (15 June 1948): 2 (Hebrew).

165 Advertisement in *Haaretz* (21 July 1948): 4 (Hebrew).

166 *Haaretz* (10 August 1948); and *Haaretz* (17 September 1948) (Hebrew).

The Recruitment of Haredim

Moshe Ehrenwald

Recruitment Before the War of Independence

The Arab attacks in the years 1920, 1929, and 1936-1938 against the Old Yishuv and Haredi community, and the heavy losses in life and property they suffered, led many of them to realize that their opposition to Zionism did not protect them from the Arab nationalists and the masses. Some understood that they needed to organize to defend themselves and joined the Haganah, including a group of young men associated with Agudat Yisrael.[1] Religious-Haredi youth enlisted in the Irgun and Lehi during the 1940s, some coming from the B'rit

---

1   Rabbanit Avitzedek (Rakovsky), *Alon la-Haverim* (Jerusalem: Havrei Hahaganah, 1974): 34–35; *Alon la-Haverim* (Jerusalem: Havrei Hahaganah, 1976): 26; Yaakov Orlovsky, "Remembering Friends 'from Those Days,'" *Alon la-Haverim* (Jerusalem: Havrei Hahaganah, 1968): 7; Eliezer Deutsch z"l in *Kol Yisrael* (27 November 1947): 1; David Dayan, *Yes, We Are Youth!* (Tel-Aviv: Ministry of Defense, 1977), 110–111. An agreement was also made with the Ezra youth movement associated with Poalei Agudat Yisrael; Chaim Hoyzman, *Avraham Leib Hoyzman, Hy"d: His Life and Work* (Jerusalem 1949), 6–8, 12, 15–18. The agreements between Agudat Yisrael Youth and the Haganah were verbal and never documented in writing.

HaHashmona'im youth movement and others independently.² During the recruitment for the war effort in World War II, it was agreed to include a religious unit in the Coastal Guard, which included non-party-affiliated Haredim and members of HaPoel HaMizrachi.³

Bnei Brak was founded in 1924 by a group of Chassidim from Warsaw who aspired to engage in agriculture. After the 1929 riots, the Haganah recruited young people from the community and trained them to defend the area. Later, representatives from Bnei Brak residents were integrated into the Haganah command in the Dan region.⁴ Bnei Brak's orchards served as training grounds for the Dan area, and arms caches were built in the city for storing weapons.⁵

Recruitment According to the Mandate of the Yishuv Institutions in 1948

The United Nations partition plan and the hostilities that erupted immediately afterward necessitated the expansion of recruitment and the imposition of compulsory service for the entire Jewish population. The national institutions, the Jewish Agency, and the National Committee published a mobilization order at the beginning of December 1947, stating that all men and women aged 17 to 25 were required to register

---

2   *Lehi Anashim: An Encyclopedia of Lehi Members* (Tel-Aviv: Yair, 2003), vol. 1, 317; and vol. 2, p. 785; Interview with Yehonatan Yulis-Yuval, April 7, 2008; *Nahalat Shlomo: le-Zikhro shel Shlomo Elbeh* (Jerusalem: Elbeh Family, 1997), 183; Moshe Rivlin, *2004-1925* (Jerusalem: The Zionist Library, 2008), 130–131.

3   A. Halevi, "A Chapter in the History of the Movement: The Poalei Agudat Yisrael Notrim Platoon in Atlit," *She'arim* (28 August 1947): 3.

4   Yitzhak Meir, *Al Homotayikh Bnei Brak*, vol. 1 (Bnei Brak: The Society for Research on the History of Bnei Brak, 1988), 298–305. The representatives of Bnei Brak in the Gush Dan headquarters were the head of the local council, Yaakov Farbstein, Yehezkel Arieli, and Rabbi Yitzhak Meir.

5   Shaul Biber, From Darkness to Daylight, pp. 194–204.

and make themselves available for security roles and essential work, starting December 9, 1947.⁶ Activists and organizations of Agudat Yisrael began organizing for recruitment. Rabbi Moshe Glickman-Porush, head of the Agudat Yisrael center in Jerusalem, invited several party activists to a meeting on December 4, 1947, to discuss the current situation and the questions that would arise.⁷

On December 10, the Workers' Executive Committee of Agudat Yisrael issued guidelines for their members regarding the mobilization order: to register and request at the recruitment offices to be placed in religious units, and for women to request exemption from training on religious grounds. Members were asked to inform party branches of their enlistment, and the branches were to forward lists of recruits to the Executive Committee. It was further stated that negotiations on religious issues had not yet concluded and the Executive Committee was in contact with the movement's rabbi and other Torah scholars on this matter.⁸

Recruitment and its implications were discussed in various forums of Haredi party members and rabbis in Tel Aviv and Jerusalem. Security agreements with the Yishuv's recruitment institutions in Jerusalem were generally made independently by Haredi activists and local rabbis, with only partial coordination with their colleagues outside Jerusalem. Similarly, their counterparts in the Tel Aviv area acted independently.

As noted, on November 4, 1947, the Executive Committee of the Council of Torah Sages decided to approve the inclusion of Agudat Yisrael representatives in the Yishuv's Security Committee, arguing

---

6 "Service to the People Headquarters Declaration No. 2," *She'arim* (11 December 1947): 1.

7 Moshe Glickman-Porush to Rabbi Avraham Yochanan Yadler Blumenthal, 19 Kislev 5708 [December 2, 1947], Agudat Yisrael Center Archives, Jerusalem.

8 "Poalei Agudat Yisrael Executive Committee Instructions – On the Service to the People Census, Urgent Circular No. 2 from December 10, 1947," *She'arim* (11 December 1947): 1.

9 | The Recruitment of Haredim

that it was a matter of security and salvation. However, they decided not to send representatives to other institutions until another meeting was dedicated to the issue.[9] This decision marked the beginning of the cessation of separatism in the security domain. Rabbi Moshe Glickman-Porush understood the decision as "security yes, recruitment no," meaning involvement in security matters without conscription.[10] The partition plan, the onset of hostilities, and the recruitment order from the national institutions led to a change in this decision.

A partial composition of the Council of Torah Sages of Agudat Yisrael debated whether to permit recruitment and under what conditions. The Haredi parties received a written opinion from their rabbis on December 12, 1947, regarding the recruitment conditions their representative on the recruitment committee should demand:

1. There should be no compulsory recruitment of women and girls.
2. Yeshiva students should be exempt from recruitment and training.
3. Kosher food should be provided in all camps.
4. There should be no training on Shabbat and holidays.
5. Religious units should be organized separately (as was customary in the Haganah).

The opinion further stated: "If they do not agree to any of these conditions, the Agudat Yisrael representative should not be part of the recruitment committee." The letter was signed by members of the Council of Torah Sages, Rabbi Avraham Yaakov Friedman, the Admor

---

9 Protocol of the Executive Committee Meeting of the Council of Torah Sages, 21 Cheshvan 5708 [November 4, 1947], Agudat Yisrael World Archive. The decision was accepted by all six members of the Executive Committee present at the meeting. The seventh member, Rabbi Weidenfeld, did not attend the meeting.

10 Moshe Glickman-Porush to the Young Haredi Organization, Tiberias, 24 Kislev 5708 [December 7, 1947], Agudat Yisrael Center Archives, Jerusalem.

of Sadigura, and Rabbi Meir Karelitz, who lived in Tel Aviv. They noted that they received this halachic ruling from Rabbi Zalman Sorotzkin, a member of the Council of Torah Sages and the director-general of the Yeshiva Committee, on behalf of Rabbi Isser Zalman Meltzer, a member of the Council of Torah Sages and head of the Etz Chaim Yeshiva in Jerusalem. Rabbis Friedman and Karelitz stated that they agreed with this halachic ruling.[11]

Rabbi Moshe Glickman-Porush commented on this decision, noting that due to the difficulty of travel, not all members of the Executive Committee of the Council of Torah Sages convened to discuss it, and not all signed the change. He added:

> "It is regrettable that only three members of the Executive Committee of the Council of Torah Sages signed. To my knowledge, they did not consult with Maran Shlit"a [Rabbi Dushinsky], and I do not know if they consulted with the Chazon Ish Shlit"a [Rabbi Avraham Yeshayahu Karelitz]. The Gaon Av Beit Din of Brisk Shlit"a [Rabbi Yitzchak Zev Soloveitchik] did not respond at all."[12]

On December 11, 1947, the Agudat Yisrael Center in Tel Aviv decided, among other things, to publish a proclamation regarding the recruitment, which they distributed to all cities in the country except Jerusalem. A copy of the proclamation was sent to the Agudat Yisrael Center in Jerusalem on December 15.[13]

---

11 Avraham Yaakov from the Sadigura Rebbe and Meir Karelitz to the World Agudat Yisrael Organization, Executive Committee, Jerusalem, Friday, Hanukkah Eve 5708 [December 12, 1947], Poalei Agudat Yisrael Archives, Box 38, File 1.

12 Moshe Glickman-Porush to Agudat Yisrael Tiberias, 5 Tevet 5708 [December 18, 1948], Agudat Yisrael Center Archives, Jerusalem.

13 M. D. Levenstein and Y. M. Abramowitz to Agudat Yisrael Center in Israel, 2 Tevet 5708 [December 15, 1948], Agudat Yisrael Center Archives, Jerusalem.

9 | The Recruitment of Haredim

The recruitment system began to operate. In a proclamation issued by the Youth of Agudat Yisrael, the members were called to recognize "the responsibility of the hour" and to appear united for the registration, "to ensure the conditions that would allow our full participation in the security service." The members were urged to insist "strongly" on serving in concentrated religious units. An Agudat Yisrael street advertisement published in December 1947 stated: "God has granted us the recognition of our right to independence in our state in part of the Land of Israel. As a result, the entire Yishuv, in all its layers, is prepared for extensive preparation and defense against rioters and attackers. May God strengthen the hands of Israel's defenders who stand in the battle."[14]

Members of the Agudat Yisrael Center in Jerusalem claimed at a meeting held on December 24 that without their opinion on the ruling signed by only three of the seven members of the Executive Committee of the Council of Torah Sages, it could not be considered a decision of the Council of Torah Sages according to its procedures. Therefore, it was premature to call for recruitment until the conditions set by the rabbis were agreed upon and accepted. Additionally, although signed on behalf of the Agudat Yisrael Center in Israel, it was drafted in Tel Aviv without coordination with the Jerusalem Center members. If they had been consulted, they would have had comments on the publication and the wording, as Rabbi Glickman-Porush wrote: "Agudat Yisrael has never used the term 'Yishuv institutions' for the Jewish Agency and the National Committee as 'authorized institutions.' For us, the Jewish Agency and the National Committee are not 'authorized institutions.' We fight against the authority they have taken for themselves. The phrase 'Daughter of Israel, do your duty for your people, for your land' enlist

---

14 "Agudat Yisrael Youth Movement Recruitment Circular," *She'arim* (11 December 1948): 1; "To the Haredi Public, Agudat Yisrael Center in Israel," Tevet 5708, Fund, Separation or Participation, p. 154, according to the Archive of the Institute for Diaspora Studies, Tel Aviv University, Section A 2, File 113.

'for the service of the people' is not successful [...]. The simple public does not read details, only the last line."[15]

Despite the criticism, those who advocated separatism and non-recognition of national institutions also enlisted. It seems that the approval of the spiritual leadership matched the atmosphere prevalent at least among the majority of the younger generation of the Haredi public. The decision to call on all members of the Haredi parties to enlist in the general recruitment announced by the Yishuv institutions can be seen as a fundamental and perhaps even revolutionary change: the spiritual and political leadership of the vast majority of the Haredi public called on all those eligible for recruitment to fight for the Jewish state about to be established in the Land of Israel and to defend it—to be willing to sacrifice their lives for something they had opposed or at least not supported until recently.

The political and spiritual leadership of Agudat Yisrael, in its various factions, understood the severity of the situation immediately after the outbreak of hostilities, and the movement's publications explained the situation to the public. For example, the headline in *Kol Yisrael* on January 1, 1948: "Chanon, gaze from above at the outpouring of blood. A flood of blood sweeps our land. The terrible events in the Holy Land. Ninety victims this week." Hence came the call for involvement "in the face of the bloodshed that has engulfed all the cities of Israel in the Holy Land and Jerusalem, and in the face of the worsening dangers day by day by enemies who said let us wipe them out as a nation." The Agudat Yisrael Center in Israel, after hearing the opinions of "great rabbis" in the land, declared at the beginning of January the duty of service for those aged 17 to 25 and for the People's Guard for those aged 26 to 46 in religious units and the condemnation of any form of evasion. The youth were called to integrate into the Yishuv's defense system and to maintain "the purity of action and the sanctity of the camp, as instructed by the Torah scholars." For "the murderers' hand threatens anyone who

---

15   Moshe Glickman-Porush to Agudat Yisrael Center, Tel Aviv, 12 Tevet 5708 [December 25, 1948], Agudat Yisrael Center Archives, Jerusalem.

bears the name Israel. Therefore, no person of Israel is exempt from defending life and property." The circular further stated: "Only builders' sons who were educated in Torah and mitzvah are worthy that Israel's salvation will come through them. They can also impart their spirit to many others."[16]

However, Binyamin Mintz and Rabbi Kalman Kahana demanded in contacts with Yosef Yizraeli from the Haganah's national headquarters, and later from Ben-Gurion, to establish a mechanism responsible for their people's service conditions, to train instructors and commanders from their movement, and to involve representatives from their movement in local headquarters.[17]

The Haredi organizations did not wait for full compliance with their demands and began to organize the recruitment of their people, cooperating among the various organizations on recruitment matters, dealing with recruits, and security issues. In the early period following the outbreak of hostilities, the treatment was local and improvised, not systematic. For example, on January 20, 1948, representatives of the Jerusalem Workers' Union of Agudat Yisrael and the Youth of Agudat Yisrael were called by Yehuda Blau from the Agudat Yisrael Center in Jerusalem for a joint consultation to resolve misunderstandings related to the recruitment of girls.[18]

16 "Service to the People Announcement," *Kol Yisrael* (1 January 1948): 1; Decisions of Agudat Yisrael Center on January 13, 1948, Poalei Agudat Yisrael Archives, Box 62, File 2; Agudat Yisrael Protest Against the Authorities, HaBoker, p. 7, January 16, 1948; Internal Circular to All Youth and Haredi Public Circles in Israel, Service to the People Committee of Agudat Yisrael Center in Israel, Shevat 5708, Poalei Agudat Yisrael Archives, Box 20, File 4; "Agudat Yisrael Commanded Its Members to Enlist – Condemn Any Evasion," *HaBoker* (18 February 1948): 4.

17 David Ben-Gurion, *The War of Independence: War Diary*, vol. 1, eds. Gershon Rivlin and Elhanan Orren (Tel-Aviv: Ministry of Defense, 1982), 193 (January 29, 1948).

18 Yehuda Blau to Agudat Yisrael Youth Movement, Jerusalem Branch; Yehuda Blau to Poalei Agudat Yisrael, Jerusalem Branch, 9 Shevat 5708 [January

On January 13, 1948, a joint recruitment committee was established with the following composition: two from Agudat Yisrael, two from the Workers' Union of Agudat Yisrael, two from the Youth of Agudat Yisrael, a representative of the Ezra youth movement, and a representative of the Agudat settlements, under the authority of the Admor of Sadigura, Rabbi Avraham Yaakov Friedman, Rabbi Yosef Shlomo Kahaneman, and Rabbi Meir Karelitz. A security committee was also established, consisting of members of Agudat Yisrael, the Workers' Union of Agudat Yisrael, and the Youth of Agudat Yisrael, headed by the Admor of Sadigura-Pshmishel, Rabbi Mordechai Shalom Yosef Friedman. Financial and economic committees were also formed. The committees began operating in Tel Aviv in February 1948. All branches were asked to establish local committees to care for movement members, inform the central committee of the committee members' names and addresses, and submit all names of registrants and recruits with all their details by February 29. The central committee members were David Bernholtz of the Workers' Union of Agudat Yisrael, Yitzhak Meir of the Youth of Agudat Yisrael, the Agudati youth, and Raphael Levi of the "Ezra." The Jerusalem local committee held its first meeting on March 7.[19]

In early March, Bernholtz explained to representatives of the Haredi organizations how to organize the religious units and prepare the

20, 1948], Agudat Yisrael Center Archives, Jerusalem.

19 Kalman Kahana to Binyamin Mintz, January 20, 1948, Poalei Agudat Yisrael Archives, Box 30, File 11; Agudat Yisrael Center, Tel Aviv, News, Issue No. 2, 21 Shevat 5708 [February 1, 1948], Poalei Agudat Yisrael Archives, Box 30, File 12; The Joint Committee for All Poalei Agudat Yisrael Branches, Agudat Yisrael Youth Movement and "Ezra," Adar Aleph 5708, Poalei Agudat Yisrael Archives, Box 21, File 1; Kalman Kahana to Members of the Security Council of the World Executive Committee, February 24, 1948, Agudat Yisrael World Archive; Shlomo Zalman Druck to the Central Committee for the Treatment of Recruits, March 10, 1948, Poalei Agudat Yisrael Archives, Box 21, File 3.

9 | The Recruitment of Haredim

kitchens.[20] Bernholtz reported in a meeting with the rabbinical committee at the joint recruitment department in mid-March, attended by Rabbi Kalman Kahana, Rabbi Shmuel Shzadrovitzky, and Rabbi Lamberger, on the actions of the religious service, the situation of the recruits, and the issues at hand. Yitzhak Meir reported on the kosher arrangements in the camps and the preparations for the Passover holiday.[21]

RECRUITMENT IN JERUSALEM

In Jerusalem, the behavior and enlistment of the Haredi population were crucial to the city's overall resilience. This was due to the large size of this population, a significant portion of which lived in frontier areas and combat zones. However, the leadership of the Jerusalem Haredi population was more conservative, and the tendency towards separatism remained strong, as did opposition to Zionism and the establishment of a Jewish state. The UN resolution that granted Jerusalem international status seemed to align with their perspective: complete submission to the Jewish state, international recognition, and the possibility of being excluded from the fighting.

Nevertheless, the Jerusalem Haredi leadership aligned with the new direction. A proclamation issued by the Mobilization Committee of the Agudat Yisrael Center in Jerusalem called for all 17 to 25-year-olds to report "each to his post."[22] In the initial stage, a census was conducted in which those liable for conscription between the ages of 17 and 25 were required to report and register at the centers of the People's Service

---

20 Recruitment Matters Meeting, She'arim, p. 4, March 11, 1948. Participants included Rabbi K. Kahana, R. Aharonowitz, and D. Bernholtz from Poalei Agudat Yisrael; Avraham Rein and Yitzhak Meir from Agudat Yisrael Youth Movement; Raphael Levy from the National Administration of "Ezra." Representatives from Poalei Agudat Yisrael branches in Jerusalem, Haifa, and Kfar Ata also participated.

21 "The Movement in the Recruitment System," She'arim (18 March 1948): 1.

22 Flyer reproduction, undated, A"Z Disk 31.

Mobilization Center, established by the Jewish Agency and the National Committee. On December 14, 1947, activists from various factions of Agudat Yisrael in Jerusalem began distributing questionnaires to their members and preparing lists of those eligible for recruitment up to age 35 from among the residents of the city's Haredi neighborhoods.[23]

The first meeting of the Jerusalem Recruitment Committee, headed by M. Eisenstadt and including members such as Yaakov Tchernowitz (Tsur), Aharon Haim Cohen, and attorney Dr. Mordechai Buxbaum, who served as a representative of Agudat Yisrael and the Old Yishuv, was held on December 24, 1947. At this meeting, action lines were set for Jerusalem, where an estimated 15,000 were liable for conscription. Due to the city's population's unique nature and composition, it was deemed necessary to secure the cooperation of Agudat Yisrael, Sephardim, and other elements to assist in the success of the recruitment.[24] Dr. Buxbaum told committee members that the Haredi rabbis had agreed to assist in the defense but had not yet consented to recruitment, adding that he had requested an immediate gathering of the rabbis to decide on the matter. He proposed exempting 400 yeshiva students in Jerusalem, thereby obtaining "numerous concessions from the rabbis." Buxbaum requested the establishment of a special office to handle Haredim so as not to create the impression that recruitment was placing them under the auspices of institutions they did not wish to belong to.[25] This demand points to the difficulties in adapting to the increasing involvement of the Haredi leadership in activities led by the Yishuv institutions; even

---

23 Reports on Activities on 1-3 Tevet 5708 [December 14-16, 1947], Agudat Yisrael Center Archives, Jerusalem. Among the prominent activists involved were: Shlomo Zalman Druck, Fishel Gelernter, Yaakov Schnitzer, and Shmuel Rozovsky.

24 Z. Epstein to the Service to the People Headquarters, December 28, 1947, A"Z 49/2644 – 359 B.

25 A"ZM, 124 3 J (24 December 1947), Protocol of the Executive Committee Meeting of the Recruitment Operation Committee.

9 | The Recruitment of Haredim

after agreeing to enlist, they wanted to maintain their independence, especially in Jerusalem.

At the end of December 1947, the People's Service Mobilization Center in Jerusalem approached all local institutions to assist in conducting the census.[26] At a press conference on December 31, 1947, committee members provided details of the recruitment plans. Buxbaum highlighted the promise given to religious recruits that they could maintain their religious lifestyle during their service and called on the Haredi public to enlist to protect lives and property. Of the 16 recruitment stations opened, four were specifically for Agudat Yisrael members.[27]

The Agudat Yisrael Center in Jerusalem held discussions on recruitment, and after consultations with Torah leaders, it was decided to respond to the call. In early January 1948, Agudat Yisrael newspapers published notices calling on "all our young people from all sectors of the Haredi community in Jerusalem, to come and take their positions and fulfill their duty to protect lives and property." The notices stated that special units would be established for Haredi soldiers and that all demands for the observance of religious commandments by the recruits had been met. It was also noted that the duty to report applied only to men and that yeshiva students were exempt from the census. Special enlistment stations for Haredi youth were opened. Israel Meir Kleiner, chairman of the Poalei Agudat Yisrael branch in Jerusalem, was appointed, in coordination with the People's Service Mobilization Center, as a representative on the Jerusalem Recruitment Committee, but his appointment was delayed. Meanwhile, he was appointed

---

26 A″Z 49/2644–390, December 26, 1947, M. Eisenstadt, Chairman, Aharon Haim Cohen, Honorary Secretary of the Service to the People Headquarters, Jerusalem, to the Jewish Agency and the National Committee.

27 "Jerusalem Awaits Ten Thousand Recruits Within Two Weeks," *HaBoker* (1 January 1948): 3. Agudat Yisrael's recruitment stations were at the Beit Yaakov Girls School on David Yellin Street, the Agudati Youth Organization in the Even Yehoshua neighborhood, the Horev Synagogue on Ibn Gabirol Street, and the Rehavia Gymnasium.

chairman of the census committee at the station where Agudat Yisrael members registered at the Beit Yaakov school on David Yellin Street in Jerusalem. Rabbi Moshe Glickman-Porush instructed him on January 1, 1948, to report there between 4:00 p.m. and 9:00 p.m. until January 8. Another station was opened at the Yemenite Talmud Torah.[28] Agudat Yisrael continued to encourage the enlistment of Haredi youth in all its publications: "After exhaustive considerations, discussions, and clarifications by the great Torah leaders—register en masse."[29] Amram ben Moshe Blau wrote in the weekly "Kol Yisrael" against the complacency of the Diaspora towards the situation in Jerusalem and criticized the complacency within the Jerusalem Haredi community, despite the events affecting each individual. He called for financial assistance from movement members abroad and the unification of all forces as befits an emergency.[30]

On January 1, 1948, 16 stations for enlisting in the People's Service were opened; at the Agudat Yisrael station in the Eben Yehoshua neighborhood near Mea Shearim, both national and Agudat Yisrael flags were flown. This station continued to operate even after the number of stations was reduced at the end of the first recruitment phase.

---

28 "Agudat Yisrael Center Calls on Every Individual in Jerusalem Aged 25-17," *Kol Yisrael* (1 January 1948): 1; "Notice to the Service to the People Headquarters," ibid., ibid.; "In the Agudat Yisrael Center," ibid., ibid.; Moshe Glickman-Porush to Y. M. Kleinlehrer, 19 Tevet 5708 [January 1, 1948], Agudat Yisrael Center Archives, Jerusalem; Kalman Kahana to the Service to the People Headquarters, Attn: Globman, 19 Tevet 5708 [January 1, 1948], Poalei Agudat Yisrael Archives, Box 30, File 11; "The Registration Continues," *Kol Yisrael* (8 January 1948): 1; "To Register," *Kol Yisrael* (22 January 1948): 1; Yehuda Blau to the Yemenite Talmud Torah Administration, 24 Shevat 5708 [February 5, 1948]; Agudat Yisrael Center Archives, Jerusalem.

29 *Kol Yisrael* (22 January 1948): 1, "On Reporting."

30 Amram Blau, "Chaos," *Kol Yisrael* (8 January 1948): 2; Editorial, "Mobilizing Our Forces," ibid., p. 1.

9 | The Recruitment of Haredim

On Shabbat, January 3 and 9, rabbis delivered sermons in dozens of synagogues in the city about the duty to enlist.[31]

The Jerusalem Mobilization Center made the necessary arrangements to allow yeshiva students to register without interrupting their Torah study. In a report issued in mid-January, it was stated that the number of recruits from among Haredi youth had increased over the past week. The People's Service Mobilization Executive in Jerusalem decided that the census would continue until the entire operation was completed, and the notice of the census's conclusion did not apply to Jerusalem. Five active recruitment stations were maintained, including two for Agudat Yisrael.[32] By the end of the first recruitment phase at the end of January, only three stations remained open in Jerusalem, including one at the Poalei Agudat Yisrael center on Geula Street 24.[33]

The Jerusalem Agudat Yisrael was dissatisfied with their treatment by the Yishuv institutions and the need to cooperate with them. Yehuda Blau, Rabbi Moshe Glickman-Porush's deputy after his departure abroad, addressed recruitment and defense in a letter written on January 20, 1948, to the Agudat Yisrael Youth Center in New York: "Even though we reached an agreement in this matter with the consent of all Torah leaders, since they have the money and organization, their hand is stronger, and through all kinds of tricks and cunning they bypass us and increase their influence. If it were not a matter of life and death, we would have already withdrawn from this agreement."[34] He requested urgent financial assistance to maintain their independence and avoid dependence on Zionist institutions.

---

31 *Haaretz* (January 4 and 11, 1948)

32 "The Recruitment Stage is Complete," *HaBoker* (16 January 1948): 7; "Another Week of Recruitment in Jerusalem," *HaBoker* (19 January 1948): 4. Agudat Yisrael stations were in the Reshkes School in Shaarei Chesed and the Agudati Youth Club in the Even Yehoshua neighborhood.

33 "Recruitment Stations Did Not Disappoint," *Ha Yom* (30 January 1948): 6.

34 Yehuda Blau to the Young Agudat Yisrael Movement Center, New York, 9 Shevat 5708 [January 20, 1948], Agudat Yisrael Center Archives, Jerusalem.

Agudat Yisrael established a security committee in Jerusalem, which appointed among its members an "Agudat Command" intended to coordinate all its members who had previously enlisted in the Haganah and those who reported for the People's Service in the current census. It was determined that the Agudat Command would maintain constant contact with the general headquarters to coordinate defense and training activities. The committee was headed by David Goldberg of the Agudat Yisrael Youth. The committee was formally subordinate to the Agudat Yisrael Center in Jerusalem but operated almost independently. Representatives were appointed in all neighborhoods to maintain contact with the public. The Agudat Yisrael Security Committee in Jerusalem operated even during the difficult fighting days, and its offices in the Sarsour Building on Ben Yehuda Street in the city center were open to the public every day between 11:00 a.m. and 1:00 p.m. In the city's major synagogues, it was announced in the middle of the Shabbat prayer on behalf of the Agudat Yisrael Center to report for service, except for women and yeshiva students. However, the tendency towards separatism had not yet dissipated. Menachem Glickman-Porush noted that the independent Agudat Command's role was to organize young Haredim under "military discipline" and added: "We prevent our youth from being subject to commanders foreign to our spirit and foreign in their actions and tactics. We prevent such commanders from coming near us whom we do not approve."[35]

---

35 "News from the Situation Committee of Agudat Yisrael Center in Jerusalem," *Kol Yisrael* (29 January 1948): 1; Menachem Glickman-Porush, "Independent Agudati Command," ibid., p. 2; Kol Yisrael, "The Situation Committee of Agudat Yisrael Center, Jerusalem," *Kol Yisrael* (5 February 1948): 1; "To the Haredi Public," *HaYom* (17 May 1948): 2; David Goldberg, Agudat Yisrael Organizations Security Committee, Jerusalem, to Agudat Yisrael Center in Israel, Jerusalem, 10 Elul 5708 [September 14, 1948], request for financial support; Moshe Glickman-Porush to the Security Committee of Agudat Yisrael Organizations, 8 Cheshvan 5709 [November 10, 1948], Security Committee's request to submit reports on their activities, Agudat Yisrael Center Archives, Jerusalem.

9 | *The Recruitment of Haredim*

Poalei Agudat Yisrael, as was their way, tended to cooperate more with the Yishuv institutions. A special committee of four members for security affairs was established in the party branch in Jerusalem, encouraging branch members to fulfill their duty and enlist. By December 21, 1947, 30 members had expressed their willingness to enlist, in addition to many who had already enlisted in previous years. Yisrael Meir Kleiner was appointed as the branch representative on the local recruitment institution and was a member of several of its committees. On January 13, 1948, the branch transferred the names of 150 of its members subject to conscription by order of the institutions to the People's Service Mobilization Center.[36] Shlomo Zalman Druck, secretary of the Poalei Agudat Yisrael Jerusalem branch, demanded that his party's executive work to have their representative appointed as a member of the city headquarters.[37]

Haredi party leaders and spokespersons frequently encouraged increased recruitment through ideological and practical explanations of its importance and the benefit Haredi recruits would bring to the campaign and its character. Menachem Glickman-Porush wrote in January 1948: "The census has gone beyond certain circles and has taken on a general Yishuv character that does not allow room and an opening for evaders." He further noted that Agudat Yisrael had brought the issue of the census and recruitment before the Council of Torah Sages, which approved its position. Agudat Yisrael obtained an exemption from the

---

36   Shlomo Zalman Druck, Jerusalem Branch to Poalei Agudat Yisrael Union, Executive Committee, Security Department, Attn: B. Mintz, December 21, 1947, Poalei Agudat Yisrael Archives, Box 21, File 1; Poalei Agudat Yisrael, Jerusalem Branch to the Service to the People Headquarters, January 13, 1948, List of Our Members Subject to Recruitment by Supreme Institutions' Decree, Poalei Agudat Yisrael Archives, Box 21, File 1; Shlomo Zalman Druck to Poalei Agudat Yisrael Executive Committee, Attn: Rabbi Kalman Kahana, January 16, 1948, Poalei Agudat Yisrael Archives, Box 21, File 1.

37   Shlomo Zalman Druck to Rabbi Kalman Kahana, January 22, 1948, Poalei Agudat Yisrael Archives, Box 21, File 1.

census for yeshiva students and religious girls, so "it is not possible for us to sit complacently in our places and leave the task to others. [...] This obligates those of us who do not spend all day in the tent of Torah to fulfill our duty in this serious hour."[38]

Yaakov Landau, one of the leaders of Poalei Agudat Yisrael, saw the decision to enlist as a significant turning point and described the situation in mid-January 1948 with optimism, while also addressing the issues:

> "The participation of 'Agudah' en masse in the recruitment presented the Yishuv institutions with significant challenges, as they stood firm on their Torah-based demands. It must be acknowledged that the Yishuv institutions showed understanding for these demands. Matters of kosher food, Shabbat observance, and creating a Torah-based atmosphere in training camps gained more prominence with the mass enlistment of 'Agudah' members. Arrangements are now being made which, if successful, will have a decisive impact on shaping the character of the regular Hebrew army in the Jewish state. Agudat Yisrael sent representatives to the Yishuv Security Committee, and the Haredi community in Jerusalem, known for its extremism within 'Agudah,' is also represented in the city's Security Committee, with its members playing an active role in the defense ranks. Agudah's representatives sit in the People's Service Mobilization Center, at local headquarters, and its members, in the hundreds and thousands, are training for security needs. Everyone is now in a single battle, the

---

38 "Members of the 'Association' in Security Service," *HaBoker* (21 January 1948): 2, Quote from Kol Yisrael, Agudat Yisrael Weekly.

defense and preparation campaign of the Yishuv and the nation."³⁹

Meanwhile, as the recruitment of young Haredim increased, issues related to their service began to arise. In early March 1948, a committee on religious matters in the security service was established in Jerusalem, initiated by recruited members from various circles, to address the assurance of kosher food, Shabbat observance, and the religious needs of the recruits. The committee comprised representatives from HaPoel HaMizrachi, Poalei Agudat Yisrael, HaOved HaDati, Bnei Akiva, the Agudati Youth, Ezra, B'rit HaHashmona'im, and others.⁴⁰

The Executive Committee of the Mobilization Center was still debating whether and how to establish religious units.⁴¹ In a discussion on February 17, it became clear that the necessary arrangements had not yet been made. It was decided to task Executive Committee member Levi Shkolnik-Eshkol with pressing for the conclusion of this matter.⁴² Raphael Singer, from Company B of the 'Mikmas' Battalion (of the 'Etzioni' Brigade), who reported to the Agudat Yisrael recruitment office, requested a transfer to an Agudat Yisrael unit at the end of February 1948 due to his religious difficulties. The welfare officer recommended approving the request. After an investigation, it was found that there

---

39 Yaakov Landau, "What Does Orthodox Judaism Say? 'Agudat Yisrael' in Battle," *HaBoker* (16 January 1948): 3.

40 Committee Members to the Home Guard Headquarters in Jerusalem, March 8, 1948, A"Z 3/76J. The establishment of the committee was brought to the attention of all relevant military and civilian authorities, who were requested to assist its activities in achieving its goals.

41 A"Z 679/56 – 21, Protocol of the Discussion on January 11, 1948, Section C.

42 Protocol of the Executive Committee Meeting of the Recruitment Center, February 17, 1948, p. 3, A"Z 679/56-21.

was no unit where all the members were from Agudat Yisrael. He was permitted to transfer to any company of religious soldiers he wished.[43]

Agudat Yisrael also called on its members who had reported to general stations to register with the organization's offices 'so they could uphold their rights in all activities.' Towards the end of February 1948, when it seemed that the agreed-upon conditions for Haredi recruitment were not being implemented, recruits aged 17 to 25 were asked 'to wait before leaving until explicit instructions were received from the Agudat Yisrael Recruitment Committee.'[44] At the end of February, misunderstandings were resolved, and all those who had reported to the Agudat Yisrael offices in Jerusalem and were found fit for full or partial service (holders of red and green cards) were called to report on February 29.[45]

The Jerusalem District Brigade prepared to absorb religious and Haredi recruits. Initially, difficulties arose because religious recruits and their commanders were unclear about which activities were permitted on Shabbat according to Halacha. Noam Grossman, commander of the Hish Company in the 'Moriah' Battalion, reported to his commander in January: 'The religious unit in our company complains about their work on Shabbat, such as patrols, training, and the like. It reaches absurdities like not touching weapons on Shabbat, etc. If possible, it is worthwhile to obtain a letter signed by Rabbi Herzog. This may eliminate this issue once and for all. If such a letter exists, it would be good to send us a copy.' The battalion commander, Zalman Mart, recommended that Jerusalem District Commander Shaltiel address the matter, and if Rabbi Herzog's

---

43   A"Z, 49/2644– 456, February 22, 1948, Request by Raphael Singer; ibid., February 22, 1948, Transfer of the Request from Company B to Battalion Adjutant Amutz; ibid., February 24, 1948, Approval by Battalion Commander and Adjutant.

44   "In the Home Guard of Agudat Yisrael," Kol Yisrael (19 February 1948): 1; "The Situation Committee – From the Situation Committee Announcements," ibid. (26 February 1948): 1.

45   HaYom, February 27, 1948, Announcement by Agudat Yisrael Recruitment Office.

letter to Kfar Etzion was general, it should be printed and distributed to the units.[46] In a daily order from the 'Mikmas' Battalion at the end of February, kitchen workers were asked to strictly observe kosher laws, noting that 'many expenses are incurred due to carelessness in this matter.[47]

The Agudat Yisrael Youth Movement announced in early March 1948 that only after all their demands regarding religious matters were met did they agree to send their members to the camps.[48] However, issues of kosher food and Shabbat encountered by the first recruitment cycles caused further delays in recruitment until a temporary arrangement for providing kosher food was found, and the Haredi organizations approved the recruitment of their members on March 11.[49]

Nataniel Behiri, responsible for recruitment in the Jerusalem District, informed the head of the training department responsible for the training about organizing a religious training camp. He noted that about 40 people were invited on March 7 to go for training, and he estimated that the number of participants would reach 70 according to the number of registrants. Behiri noted that the Haredi leadership's demands, including maintaining a kosher kitchen in the camp, allowing public prayer, and Torah study in the evenings, were agreed upon. He emphasized that it was essential to meet these demands; otherwise,

---

46 Noam [Grossman], "Subject: Religious People in the Company," undated, A"Z 49/2644– 402; ibid., Shadmi to Ben-Yehuda, January 18, 1948. Noam Grossman was killed in early March 1948 near Atarot.

47 Machmas Battalion, Daily Order from February 27, 1948, Section 4, A"Z 49/959– 219.

48 "Agudat Yisrael Youth Movement News – Recruitment of Agudat Yisrael Youth Members," Kol Yisrael (11 March 1948).

49 "Correspondence between Rabbi Meir Karelitz and Dr. Aaron Barth, Fundraising Campaign for Recruitment," HaYom (10 March 1948; "To All Members of Poalei Agudat Yisrael, Agudat Yisrael Youth Movement, and Ezra: Poalei Agudat Yisrael Union Announces," ha-Tsofeh (11 March 1948).

it would ruin the chances of recruiting the many Haredi youth in Jerusalem.⁵⁰

After questions arose regarding the employment of members of the religious youth battalion of the Gadna in Jerusalem ('Modi'in' Battalion), district commander David Shaltiel instructed Yehoshua Arieli, the city's Gadna commander, not to require any member of the religious youth battalion to perform any work on Shabbat, except 'in cases where their lack of employment could lead to human casualties or military failure (not administrative failure—arrangements). In such a case, David [the district commander] must be notified immediately of the need for an order and prove that there was no other way in the given situation except to require the religious members to work on Shabbat.'⁵¹

The needs of religious soldiers still did not receive adequate attention from lower levels. In daily orders from the commander of District 3, responsible for northern Jerusalem, dated March 15 and April 11, it was stated that religious people should not be sent to courses for post commanders starting on March 21 and April 18, as Shabbat was included in the training schedule.⁵²

Agudat Yisrael prepared to address the halachic and ongoing religious needs of its recruits. In mid-February, Yehuda Blau approached Rabbi Henich Padwa and asked him to assume the responsibility of ruling on halachic questions that arose among the recruits.⁵³ Ephraim

---

50 A"Z, 49/959 – 216, March 3, 1948, Menachimi to Ein, Subject: Training Camp for Religious People (Agudat Yisrael, etc.).

51 District Commander to Arieli, March 16, 1948, A"Z 49/959 – 282. Instructions in response to Arieli's request from March 5, 1948.

52 A"Z 49/840– 9, Daily Orders from Gottfried, Commander of District 3. It should be noted that in northern Jerusalem there were large concentrations of religious and Haredi populations, which constituted a significant portion of the recruits in District 3.

53 Yehuda Blau, Agudat Yisrael Center to Rabbi Henich Padwa (19 February 1948), Agudat Yisrael Center Archives, Jerusalem. Rabbi Padwa was a rabbinical authority for the Haredi community in the Mishkenot and

Offenbach was appointed by Agudat Yisrael 'to oversee religious matters,' and David Eisen was appointed to oversee religious and kosher matters for a group of recruits that went for training on March 7 in Arza.[54] This group consisted of 'Jerusalem youth, immigrant youth, and youth from boarding schools.' According to one of its recruits, Aharon Mertzbach, they hardly encountered any religious problems thanks to the understanding shown by the company's commanders to which their section belonged. They also received support from an old religious section from the reinforcements sent from Tel Aviv that belonged to their company and already had extensive experience in religious matters. This framework was maintained until the start of the second ceasefire in mid-July 1948. They enjoyed public prayer, a daily Daf Yomi class, and a kosher kitchen from the first day of their service.[55] Agudat Yisrael appointed representatives in mechanisms related to the recruitment system. Moshe Weinberg was appointed as a member of the Appeals Committee of the People's Service Mobilization Center in Jerusalem. Abraham Jacob Brawer was appointed as a member of the committee for the oversight of travelers abroad at the People's Service Mobilization Center.[56]

Keneset neighborhoods and taught at the Shaagat Aryeh Yeshiva in Shaarei Chesed.

54 Agudat Yisrael Center Security Department, Appointment (7 March 1948), Agudat Yisrael Center Archives, Jerusalem.

55 Aharon M., "The Soldier's Stage – The Road of Valor," *Digleinu for Recruits*, no. 9 (15 Kislev 5709): 3 (Hebrew). This unit fought in the Motza-Arza area, where four of its members were killed in early April, and later in other areas around Jerusalem. The company commanders were Nachum Shoshani, who was killed on April 1 in the Tzova Quarry area, and Meir Hefetz, who was killed in August at the Government House. The veteran religious platoon returned to its parent unit in the 33rd Battalion of the Alexandroni Brigade, and most of its members were killed in Hanukkah 5709 in the battle for Iraq al-Manshiyya [Kiryat Gat].

56 Yehuda Blau to the Service to the People Headquarters Center, Jerusalem (27 February 1948); Aharon Haim Cohen, Secretary of the Headquarters

Meir Avniel-Elstein, commander of the training camp in Arza, noted in his memoirs that four cycles of yeshiva students [meaning religious-Haredi] trained there until the training camp was transferred to the Schneller camp in Jerusalem. Among the trainees were members of the Old Yishuv with beards and payot; others were new immigrants and Holocaust survivors. They took the training very seriously. The conditions and atmosphere in the camp were adapted to their lifestyle: strict observance of kosher laws, a daily Talmud class, cessation of training on Shabbat dedicated to prayer, Torah study, and lectures. Even the locals respected the boys and ceased their farm work on Shabbat.[57] On March 25, there were 42 men in the training unit in the Arza-Motsa area, apparently along with staff members.[58] On April 9, the 'Diary' published an article about "our boys in the training camp." The article described the recruits as young men with beards and payot in their traditional dress, new immigrants, and Holocaust survivors who enlisted and were undergoing two weeks of training. These young men changed the camp's character.[59]

Center to Agudat Yisrael Center, Jerusalem (29 February 1948); Yaakov Tchernowitz (Tsur) and Aharon Haim Cohen, Headquarters Center to Abraham Jacob Brawer, February 29, 1948, Agudat Yisrael Center Archives, Jerusalem.

57 Meir Avniel (Elstein), "Yeshiva Students Training Base in Arza," *Alon la-Haverim* (Jerusalem: Havrei Hahaganah, 1976): 20 (Hebrew).

58 A"Z 49/6774– 132, March 25, 1948, Rubin, Inspection and Standard Officer to David, Field Corps Personnel.

59 HaYom, April 9, 1948, p. 3, "Our Boys in the Training Camp" – Signed by Meir Elstein, Camp Commander; Interview with Aryeh Munzon, January 18, 2009; Interview with Yehuda Rider, June 24, 2009; Interview with Meir Zusman, January 7, 2010, and July 7, 2010; Interview with Shalom Ezra, June 1, 2010, and June 3, 2010; Interview with Aryeh Hefetz, August 1, 2010.

9 | *The Recruitment of Haredim*

This first organized recruitment was done with enthusiasm and raised great expectations. Agudat Yisrael's Jerusalem publication reported:

> "Today, the first organized groups of hundreds of Jerusalem boys, faithful to the word of God, are setting out on their mission, within special divisions. In these divisions, these young men will have the opportunity to see for themselves and show others the power of God's ways for those who follow them, not only in times of peace but also especially in times of struggle and trial. Our goal is not only to ensure kosher matters but a higher goal: to restore to our people the power of faith and unity to which our nation has long aspired."[60]

The religious platoon training in the Motza Illit – Arza area participated in a battle that developed there on Shabbat, March 20. One of the instructors, Avraham Bokser, was killed in this battle. After the training, 14 of them were stationed at the children's farm in the lower part of Motza Illit. On April 5, Arabs from Kolonia attacked the place. In the ensuing battle, four from the platoon were killed, and eight others were wounded.[61]

At the beginning of March 1948, the HaBoker newspaper published an enthusiastic letter from a recruit from Poalei Agudat Yisrael describing the religious and social atmosphere in his company: the prayers, Torah

---

60   Editorial: "Today They Go Out on Duty," *Ha Yom* (29 February 1948): 1

61   Yitzhak Levi, *Jerusalem in the War of Independence* (Tel-Aviv: Ma'arakhot, 1986), 148-149; Aryeh Munzon, *The Munzon Family Through Generations in Jerusalem* (Jerusalem, 2003), 92-91; Mishal Mizrahi, *The Kastel and the Struggle for the Road to Jerusalem* (Jerusalem, 1987), 190-191, Testimony of Reuven Agmon, Commander of the Arza-Motza Area; Funeral Description: "On Your Heights Slain," *Ha Yom* (8 April 1948). Names of the fallen: Chaim Grob, born 1931, student of the Shfat Emet Yeshiva of the Ger Hasidim, Tzvi Hirschler, born 1928, Reuven Hartom born 1928, Shamai Weinberger born 1930.

study, and the good and cordial relations with the villagers near their base.[62] The situation and recruitment demands were met with enthusiasm by some of the Haredi population. The enthusiasm led to some boys under 17 reporting for recruitment against their parents' wishes, even though they were not subject to the draft. Yehuda Blau had to instruct their representative in the appeals committee, Moshe Weinberg, that in any case where an appeal was brought before him regarding the recruitment of someone under 17, he must insist on their release.[63]

One question that arose among young Haredim was whether it was permissible for someone who had married to enlist in the first year after their wedding. Rabbi Elkana Weissenstern, a rabbi of the Beit Yisrael neighborhood, ruled that this law, which allows a groom to enlist in the first year of marriage, applies to a Milchemet Mitzvah (a commanded war), 'but as long as there is no full draft up to age sixty, then even in the first year of marriage, one is exempt and prohibited from serving in the army and any military-related activity.' Rabbi Reuven Zelig Bengis, head of the Haredi community's rabbinical court, also ruled this way. Following this halachic ruling, Agudat Yisrael requested the recruitment center exempt those meeting the criterion of being married in the first year from enlistment.[64]

Some members of Agudat Yisrael saw recruitment as part of building the party's strength and reinforcing its status, enabling it to instill its ideology among its supporters and the broader public in Israel and

62 Y. M. A., "Rejoice, Righteous Ones," *HaBoker* (1 March 1948): 2.

63 Yehuda Blau to Moshe Weinberg, Representative in the Appeals Committee on Recruitment Matters, 20 Adar I 5708 [March 1, 1948], Agudat Yisrael Center Archives, Jerusalem.

64 Yehuda Blau, Agudat Yisrael Center to Rabbi Chaim Meir Unger, 22 Adar I 5708 [March 3, 1948]; Elkana Weisenshtern to Agudat Yisrael Center Management, 24 Adar I 5708 [March 5, 1948]; Yehuda Blau to the Appeals Committee for Service to the People, 24 Adar I 5708 [March 5, 1948]; Rabbi Bengis to Agudat Yisrael Center, 29 Adar I 5708 [March 10, 1948]; Agudat Yisrael Center Archives, Jerusalem. It is unknown whether there was an agreement to this request.

the Jewish world. In January 1948, a reader of Kol Yisrael wrote to the editorial board that they joined the People's Service Mobilization due to the severe situation, but with a heavy heart and hesitations. However, this recruitment is an opportunity given to us 'to educate our youth for the service of the people according to our understanding. We now have the opportunity to start establishing a legion of defenders, not only for life and property but also for the soul of the people and its Torah image. [...] From the bitter comes the sweet.' The People's Service Mobilization Committee near the Agudat Yisrael Center issued an internal circular to the youth circles and the Haredi public in February 1948, calling for enlistment because 'only sons educated in Torah and commandments are worthy that the salvation of Israel should come through you. They can also impart their spirit to many others and remove the barrier between them and our Father in Heaven until God has mercy on His people and brings us from distress to relief.'[65] In an article by S. Arieli, published in HaYom on March 12, 1948, he argued that even if the religious situation in the religious units is satisfactory, it does not absolve responsibility concerning all other units regarding issues related to Shabbat observance and kashrut. All who are in the battle are emissaries of the entire Yishuv, entrusted with responsibility for the entire community, and no one can absolve themselves from the responsibility of spiritual hindrance. Moreover, in the campaign, the character of the independent state about to be established is shaped.[66]

Moshe Shenfeld, one of the leaders of the Agudat Yisrael Youth, expressed this in an article he published in Digleinu in May 1948, entitled 'The Recruitment to Zion.' He called on all Agudat Yisrael youth worldwide to come to Israel and enlist: 'Shall your brothers go to war, and you remain here?' He emphasizes that Agudat Yisrael members are lovers of Zion, but opponents of Zionism, and so they

---

65 L. A., "Religious Platoons," *Kol Yisrael* (15 January 1948): 2; "Agudat Yisrael Ordered Its Members to Enlist – Condemn Any Evasion," *HaBoker* (18 February 1948): 4.

66 S. Arieli, "With What We Did Not Agree," *HaYom* March 12, 1948, p. 4,

will remain even in the State of Israel. The struggle is over the character of the Yishuv and the character of the entire Jewish people. 'A double war is imposed on the faithful of the Torah, particularly on the younger generation of the faithful: standing on the state's borders for its security and standing guard over the sanctity of the state within its borders.' He saw the mass immigration of Agudat Yisrael youth not merely as a solution to individual distress but primarily as a solution to the distress of Judaism in the Land of Israel and 'the salvation of the Torah in its land.' [...] The right of Agudat Yisrael members to the Land of Israel was earned through fulfilling the commandments tied to the land and the blood covenant that hundreds of our members standing on the front line are renewing with it today. Our members [...] will return from the war upright, free from the inferiority complex that most Torah keepers suffered from, imbued with self-awareness that they sacrificed all they had for the land and the Yishuv. Even after the physical war ends, they will remain in their role as divisions fighting the spiritual battle.'[67]

In early April 1948, Y. N. Levy described the situation in Mea Shearim in the HaYom newspaper:

> "These days, the barriers separating the residents of the neighborhood have almost disappeared. Everyone is taking part in the guarding and defense, including members of Agudat Yisrael. Only the members of Neturei Karta do not participate in the defense activities and even disrupt them. In the evening, you will encounter many young men dressed in khaki clothes with wool blankets on their backs. They go for night guard duty and perform their tasks with love, diligence, and perseverance. Many of them have long payot and beards, and there is no small number of yeshiva students among them. Even the old women, for whom Zionism was considered 'treif' just a few months ago, accompany

---

67 Moshe Schenfeld, "Recruitment to Zion," *Digleinu* (3 Iyar 5708): 1.

the young men going to fulfill their duties with blessings from the depths of their hearts."[68]

Members of Poalei Agudat Yisrael Group (PAG"I), who split from Poalei Agudat Yisrael and eventually from Agudat Yisrael, also enlisted and participated in the defense of their area in the PAG"I neighborhood in Sanhedria.[69]

In mid-March, the second stage of recruiting men aged 26-35 began. Recruitment in Jerusalem was concentrated in two central recruitment stations, at the Lemel School and the Eshkol School. Special sections were opened at the stations for Agudat Yisrael members, and the People's Service Mobilization Center asked them to report promptly and go to these sections.[70]

On April 7, ages 17-35 were required to fulfill their duty to the People's Service immediately, and those already in service were asked to register again to ensure religious requirements. The Agudat Yisrael Security Committee in Jerusalem called on the public to donate funds to supply the religious needs of religious recruits.[71]

Simultaneously, the Haganah prepared to place religious recruits in special units. In a daily order from March 30, 1948, of the Hish 'Mikmas' Battalion, company commanders were asked to submit lists of religious recruits by April 2 to establish religious sections in the companies where members would receive all conditions allowing them to maintain their

---

68   Y. N. Levi, "Meah Shearim in Battle," *Ha Yom* (2 April 1948): 3.

69   "Agudat Yisrael to the Right of the Settlement," *Ha Yom* (4 May 1948): 2; Among the neighborhood defenders was Rabbi Yaakov Blau, son of Yehuda Blau, later a member of the rabbinical court and responsible for the kashrut system of the Haredi community in Jerusalem. See Yosef Klein, *Halom Yosef* (Jerusalem, 1989), 245, 248.

70   Bulletin No. 106, "To Members at the Bases: The Voice of the Hebrew Defender Broadcast Tonight," March 16, 1948, A"Z 8735 1J; "The Youngsters Are Reporting in Droves," *Davar* (19 March 1948): 7.

71   Ha Yom (6 April 1948); "Agudat Yisrael Security Committee Appeal to the Public," *Ha Yom* (7 April 1948).

lifestyle. Company commanders were asked to appoint 'understanding and tactful' commanders to these sections, as this would determine the number of religious recruits in the future.⁷² The People's Service Mobilization Center announced on Kol HaMagen HaIvri on April 7 that those who want to join religious companies and go for concentrated training should report to the recruitment station at the Eshkol School on April 12 or 14.⁷³

A similar order to concentrate religious recruits in subunits was given to the Haim members. For example, the District 5 headquarters, responsible for central Jerusalem, gave specific placement instructions on April 23 on where to place religious recruits from the new draft.⁷⁴ On May 2, a full draft of Haim members and the People's Guard in Jerusalem was announced. The Haim commander in the district instructed sector commanders in the city to include an Agudat Yisrael representative in the recruitment committee in areas with religious people and reiterated the order to concentrate recruits in certain subunits in each area so they could maintain their religious lifestyle.⁷⁵

Many young Haredim also enlisted independently without the sponsorship of the Haredi parties. For example, in the Kiryat Shmuel and Shaarei Chesed neighborhoods in Jerusalem, which belonged to District 4, a religious section of about 40 people operated under Yehoshua Vorker. Yosef Zaltzberg-Ami, District 4 commander, described them as operating in kapotas and exemplary bravery. Ami greatly admired

---

72 A"Z 49/959 – 219, March 30, 1948, Daily Order from the Commander of Battalion No. 15, Section C.

73 Service to the People Headquarters Center Announces, "To Members at the Bases: Hebrew Defender Voice Broadcasts," April 7, 1948, A"Z 8735 1J.

74 A"Z, 49/2644– 319, April 23, 1948, HaLevi to Ziv, Subject: Concentration of Religious Members in Specific Units.

75 A"Z, 49/2644 – 308, May 2, 1948, Fortress – Yarkoni to Mahbim 5,4,3,2 Father, Subject: Recruitment of Haim and the Home Guard; ibid., May 3, 1948, Yarkoni to Mahbim, Concentration of Religious Members in Specific Units.

Vorker, who excelled in his courage, and said he saw him command his men to eat and fight on Yom Kippur (with rabbinical approval).[76]

Zalman Aharonowitz-Aran, a Histadrut activist on behalf of Mapai, who was in Jerusalem until the first ceasefire, wrote on May 14 to the central committee of the Executive about the situation in Jerusalem, noting that:

> 'the plague of evasion has fundamentally affected the old Ashkenazi Yishuv (so far, the heads of yeshivas and rabbis do not allow thousands of yeshiva students to enlist), and there is also evasion among the Sephardic communities.' In a briefing he gave to the Mapai secretariat upon his return to Tel Aviv on June 8, 1948, about the situation in Jerusalem, he also mentioned the contribution of the Haredim: 'On Friday night, after Ramat Rachel was conquered [May 21, 1948], I was asked to come to Talpiot with officers to persuade the Ramat Rachel people to return to the kibbutz. [...] On the way to the regional headquarters, I saw [...] the Haganah sappers going out to their duties [...] platoons of religious Jews, adults, and youth - long beards, payot, and tallit katan - faithfully engaged in building fortifications.'[77] However, he continued to talk about 'the organized evasion by the Haredi community in Jerusalem, led by certain rabbis and yeshiva heads (these finally allowed recruitment for fortifications only).'[78]

---

76 *ha-Haganah bi-Yerushalayim*, vol. 2 (Jerusalem, 1975), 33, Testimony of Yosef Ami (Salzberg).

77 Z. Aharonovich to the Central Committee of the Executive, May 14, 1948, Israel State Archive F-2/2878; Labor Archive at Beit Berl, June 8, 1948, Zalman Aharonovich's Review at the Mapai Secretariat, p. 4.

78 Ibid., p. 7.

Gabriel Tzafroni, a journalist for HaBoker in Jerusalem, who toured the northeastern front of Jerusalem on Shabbat, June 5, visited an extreme outpost and described what he saw: 'Standing on the front, the guards changed, and long lines of yeshiva students came. They stand with their curled payot beside the sandbags. Unconsciously you come across an extreme outpost on a rooftop with a silk-clad man, his yarmulke glued to his hair, standing silently, the rifle tightly against his shoulder. [...] A foreign journalist with me couldn't hold back his smile. Don't laugh at him—the commander remarked to us—he's Nathan the sharpshooter.'[79]

Eliezer Sirks, a member of Gerrer Hasidim and the World Executive Committee of Agudat Yisrael, stayed in Jerusalem during the fighting, siege, and shelling. In a letter dated June 14, 1948, to his daughter living in Tel Aviv, he described the difficulties and concerns. He informed her that her son, Yaakov Vidislavsky, one of the commanders of the religious platoon in Hish Tel Aviv, who arrived with reinforcements in Jerusalem at the end of January 1948 and served as a platoon commander in the Talpiot area in the city's south, visited him every Monday. Another grandson, Yitzhak Sirks, belonged to the Hish Tel Aviv platoon, which defended Ben Shemen, besieged opposite Ramla and Lod, for months. His son Peretz, drafted in May 1948, served on the front in the Kakkon area. In a letter to his grandson, he wrote, 'My dear grandson, do not forget that even though you stand in battle to save our people and our land—do not forget God because only He can save.'[80]

Y. Yardeni described in HaYom the situation in Old Beit Yisrael facing Sheikh Jarrah, that despite the great suffering, life there continues almost as usual; women take care of order and cleanliness, and men say Psalms. Yardeni added, 'But not only in saying Psalms are the yeshiva students and young Haredim engaged. They are now an organic part of the defense system and not just the weak link in it. Not only do they know a chapter in the Mishnah, but their hand is in everything under

---

79 Gabriel Tzafroni, "Tour of the Jerusalem Front," *HaBoker* (14 June 1948): 3, from his diary on June 5, 1948.

80 Pinchas Sirkis, *Ish ha-Emunah* (Tel-Aviv, 1979), 206-208.

9 | The Recruitment of Haredim

the outer shell of the kapotas and shtreimels, suddenly revealed to the outsider's eyes a juicy, clever, and warm Judaism, the familiar Jew from yesterday, who seemed to be your opponent, extends a warm brotherly hand to you.'[81]

The description of an anonymous Haredi fighter appeared in Davar Yerushalayim, the newspaper of the Jerusalem Workers' Council, under the title "Zmirot" ("Hymns"):

> "On Friday night, July 16, he entered the post, wearing a shtreimel on his head and a long kapote. His eyes shone like two coals. He took off the shtreimel, set it aside, and left his kippah on his head. Then he tucked the corners of the kapote into his belt and his payot behind his ears. All this calmly, as if he did not feel or hear the whistling bullets. Then he approached the machine gun, relieved the one before him, and said, 'Well, friends, let's sing them Shabbat hymns, but hymns until their ears ring.'[82] And indeed, the residents of Mea Shearim testify that they had never heard such hymns. At dawn, when the legionnaires retreated, the post commander, 'the Sabra,' patted him on the back and said, 'What can I tell you, the hymns were iron.'"

Sh. Ben-Horin from the Jerusalem newspaper HaYom, who visited the Notre Dame sector at the end of September 1948, described the commander who came to guide them as "a young man with a beard and payot in brigade uniform," who had rescued one of his men who was wounded in the street near Notre Dame. He went on to note the appreciation of his men for his leadership qualities.[83]

---

81 Y. Yardeni, "In Besieged Jerusalem," *HaYom* (11 June 1948): 3.

82 Ephraim Katz, "Zmirot," *Davar* (20 August 1948).

83 S. Ben-Horin, "Notre Dame," *HaYom* (1 October 1948): 3. Despite the integration of many Haredim in the defense of Jerusalem, the appearance of four of them with long beards and side locks in full Hasidic dress with

The challenges faced by religious soldiers persisted in later stages of the war. In October 1948, the Security Committee of Agudat Yisrael organizations in Jerusalem requested from Welfare Minister Rabbi Levin to establish religious units in the army. They justified their demand by citing the difficulties faced by religious soldiers serving in mixed units and as isolated soldiers in bases, which led them to compromise their religious lifestyle. For example, the issue of non-kosher kitchens forced them to subsist on dry food only.[84]

Neturei Karta's publication HaChoma also harshly criticized Agudat Yisrael's recruitment system:

> "Let us describe the issue of recruitment, in which Agudat Yisrael dared to engage in negotiations with the heretics without consulting our leaders and rabbis, may they live long. This led to many innocent young men being dragged into the recruitment system, as the spirit of war beats in every young man, and here they found an opportunity to be counted among the soldiers of heresy. What does the 'simpleton' have to think about, since Agudat Yisrael widely campaigned in the streets, hardly missing a day to publish recruitment notices, and even arranged a series of sermons in synagogues and every opportunity, and they did not stop at that but continued their propaganda in the streets and markets. And the

---

rifles on Ben Yehuda Street in August 1948 attracted considerable attention among passersby. See Menahem Zvi Kadari, "Diary on August 10, 1948," in Menahem Zvi Kadari, *Stations in My Life* (Tel-Aviv: Kadari Family, 2011), 76-77.

84 David Goldberg, Agudat Yisrael Organizations Security Committee, Jerusalem, to Rabbi Y. M. Levin, Minister of Welfare, October 11, 1948, and December 6, 1948, Levin Family Archive; Minister of Welfare Secretary to Rabbi S. Shchedrovitzki, Director of the Kashrut Department, Ministry of Welfare, December 24, 1948, Israel State Archive GL-2/44806.

9 | *The Recruitment of Haredim*

proclamation was heard, 'Hurry and report! Agudat Yisrael calls you! Agudati youth calls you!' and so forth."[85]

Their criticism clearly indicates the extensive positive activity of Agudat Yisrael in recruitment matters.

THE PEOPLE'S GUARD

"The Haganah Command in Jerusalem established the People's Guard in mid-September 1947 as an overt arm of the Haganah, intended to organize the public, activate the civilian system in emergencies, and assist combat forces, assuming other civilian systems (police, municipality) would struggle to function during transitional stages. The organization was structured militarily: with a central headquarters and command and five sectors according to city areas. Recruitment stations were opened in public places, schools, synagogues, and the like. Recruitment announcements appeared legally on behalf of the Community Committee."[86]

Most of the Haredi population living in northern Jerusalem belonged to Sector 3. The sector headquarters convened for the first time on October 15, 1947, to prepare for volunteer registration and management.[87] Agudat Yisrael, which had no representation on the Community Committee, managed its members' recruitment independently and called on January 1948 for those aged 26-40 to register at special offices for the People's Guard.[88] On February 12, a list

---

85 R.H.T., "Our Duty at This Time," *HaChomah*, no. 48 (September 23, 1948): 3 (Hebrew).

86 Shmuel Arnon, *Collection of the Home Guard in Jerusalem*, p. 23.

87 Protocol of the meeting on October 15, 1947, A"Z 4 3J.

88 "Registration for the Security Headquarters," *Kol Yisrael* (8 January 1948): 1 (Hebrew); "To Register," *Kol Yisrael* (22 January 1948): 1 (Hebrew).

of registration stations in religious neighborhoods was published. All who registered at the general stations were asked to register by February 15 at the Agudat Yisrael Center to ensure their rights.[89]

On February 12, the Agudat Yisrael Security Committee in Jerusalem appointed six representatives to various departments at the Jerusalem District People's Guard headquarters.[90] Neighborhood managers were appointed to report the names of People's Guard recruits and identify those wishing to be under Agudat Yisrael's authority.[91] The extreme factions of Agudat Yisrael were opposed to this organization. At the end of February, Amram ben Moshe Blau accused the People's Guard of lacking kashrut, desecrating Shabbat, and serving the Zionist institutions 'to conquer the stubborn Haredi Judaism.' He proposed that the People's Guard in Jerusalem be transferred from the Community Committee's responsibility, which Agudat Yisrael did not participate in, to the general authority of the Yishuv or that Agudat Yisrael establish its own People's Guard under its command, but the Community Committee's leadership did not agree to this.[92]

---

89 "Situation Committees of the Haredi Community and Agudat Yisrael in Their Work," and "In the Home Guard of Agudat Yisrael," *Kol Yisrael* (19 February 1948): 1; and "Notice to the Haredi Public," *Ha Yom* (12 February 1948).

90 HaYom (13 February 1948); A"Z 3 3J, February 12, 1948, Protocol. From the full meeting of the Home Guard Headquarters in Jerusalem. The six representatives were attached to the following departments: Training, Legal Affairs, Organization and Recruitment, Intelligence Office, Public Relations, Finance, Supply.

91 Agudat Yisrael Center, Security Department, to Shimon Menachem Bergman, 26 Adar I 5708 [March 7, 1948]; Agudat Yisrael Center Security Department Home Guard to Shimon Menachem Bergman, 28 Adar I 5708 [March 9, 1948], Agudat Yisrael Center Archives, Jerusalem. Shimon Bergman was responsible for the Shaarei Chesed neighborhood.

92 Amram Blau, "The Security Issue and the Home Guard," *Kol Yisrael* (26 February 1948): 2 (Hebrew).

9 | The Recruitment of Haredim

At the Agudat Yisrael Center members' meeting on March 8, the issue of whether to join the Community Committee's Situation Committee, which the People's Guard was subordinate to, was on the agenda, contrary to the position of the Haredi community, Agudat Yisrael's partner in the Situation Committee. After debates, it was decided to participate in the Situation Committee on the condition it be called the Agudat Yisrael and Community Committee Situation Committee. Two activists were chosen to represent Agudat Yisrael on the local Situation Committee.[93] On March 18, Poalei Agudat Yisrael representatives also joined the People's Guard headquarters in Jerusalem. At the headquarters meeting on March 18, an Agudat Yisrael representative noted that in Sector 6, where they organized recruitment alone, they succeeded in recruiting about 200 people. He added that after the clarification scheduled at the Agency on March 19 regarding the conflict between Agudat Yisrael and the defense forces about burial in Sanhedria, he hoped cooperation would be full and fruitful. In the Shaarei Chesed neighborhood, about 300 people were waiting for the clarification to conclude, then they would join the activities, 60 of them in Haim.[94]

The People's Guard prepared for activity among the religious-Haredi population, understanding its uniqueness. On Shabbat in the first half of March 1948, informational meetings were held in synagogues. On one Shabbat, 17 meetings were held, and over 20 on another, with plans to establish a trustee board in each area to build more trust. Agudat Yisrael members also participated in the People's Guard's circle of explainers.[95]

---

93 Yehuda Blau to Agudat Yisrael Center in Tel Aviv (8 March 1948), Agudat Yisrael Center Archives, Jerusalem.

94 A"Z 3 3J, March 19, 1948, Home Guard Jerusalem, Headquarters, Memorandum from Headquarters Meeting on March 18, 1948.

95 A"Z 3 3J, March 18, 1948, Protocol of Headquarters Meeting, Propaganda Matters; Moshe [responsible for the Explainers Team]: "The Mood of the Home Front in Jerusalem," ibid., 94/3J, March 23, 1948; "The Department M. Fotoritzky, Home Guard Information and Propaganda Department,

Agudat Yisrael occasionally directly addressed its recruits. For example, all People's Guard members in the Beit Yisrael, Mea Shearim, Beit Ungarin, Beit Naitin, Beit Warsaw, and Geula neighborhoods were required to assemble on April 4 at the new building of the Yavne Talmud Torah.[96] People's Guard commanders, members of Agudat Yisrael, were called to a meeting at the movement's office on June 24 'for important information.'[97] Agudat Yisrael also worked to establish religious sections in the People's Guard. At the end of April, all those interested in joining these sections were asked to report to People's Guard stations or Agudat Yisrael offices, at the Beit Yaakov School, or at the Kol Torah Yeshiva.[98] Agudat Yisrael did not always meet its commitments. On May 31, the Agudat Yisrael Center promised to send 250 people for fortification work without coercion, but only 150 arrived. The next day, actions were taken against them.[99]

Agudat Yisrael appointed its members as commanders of the People's Guard units it established.[100] On August 18, 1948, Rabbi Moshe Glickman-Porush complained in a letter to Dov Rosen, People's Guard Commander in Jerusalem, that no Haredi was appointed to a responsible position in the organizational restructuring of the People's Guard despite their participation in the organization's activities. He

---

Report on the Activities of the Home Guard Information and Propaganda Department in February-March 1948," Israel State Archive, G-7/276.

96 "To the Home Guard Members from the Home Guard Jerusalem," *Ha Yom* (4 April 1948).

97 "Announcement," *Ha Yom* (4 June 1948).

98 "Announcement – Home Guard by Agudat Yisrael," *Ha Yom* (28 April 1948).

99 A"Z [Biderman], June 6, 1948, Aba [Home Guard] to Hezekiah [Engineering Unit Jerusalem District], Subject: Fortification Works.

100 A. Weingarten to Agudat Yisrael Center Management, Jerusalem, 13 Tammuz 5708 [July 20, 1948]; "To Shmuel Schulberg," 14 Tammuz 5708, [July 21, 1948], Agudat Yisrael Center Archives, Jerusalem.

demanded appointing Haredim to all positions because 'we will not agree for our members to be second-class citizens in the Jewish Yishuv in Jerusalem.'[101]

Yitzhak Avrahami, commander of North Jerusalem, testified that 'most of the People's Guard members in this sector were religious, many with beards and curled payot, and although they had no idea what military discipline was, they fulfilled every role willingly and with exceptional dedication. They defended the city, held positions, and guarded roadblocks. One of the headquarters members was Rabbi Zelig Heine, grandson of the Gerrer Rebbe, notable for his long beard and payot. This dear Jew was completely immersed in his role from morning until after midnight.'[102]

Yehuda Klein-Amitai, who fought in the Independence War in the 79th Battalion of the 7th Brigade, wrote an article in January 1949 published in his battalion's synagogue bulletin, summarizing the journey of a religious soldier in the IDF. He described the vision of a group of religious soldiers in his battalion to influence the character of the Hebrew army, comprising four goals: participating in determining the military tradition of regular army life, leaving a mark of Torah on military culture, elevating the holy values of military service in the eyes of the religious soldier, and most importantly, sanctifying God's name in Israel and worldwide.[103]

---

101   Moshe Glickman-Porush, Agudat Yisrael Center, to Dov Rozen, Home Guard in Jerusalem, 13 Av 5708 [August 18, 1948], Israel State Archives G-1/273.

102   *ha-Haganah bi-Yerushalayim*, vol. 2 (Jerusalem, 1975), 73, Testimony of Yitzhak Avrahami.

103   Yehuda Amital, "Our Path (Notes on the Path of the Religious Soldier in the Israel Defense Forces)," *Morasha: The Synagogue Bulletin in the 79th Mechanized Reconnaissance Battalion, 7th Brigade* (Tevet 5709): 4-7; Elyashiv Reichner, *In His Faith: The Story of Rabbi Yehuda Amital* (Tel-Aviv: Yedioth Ahronoth Sifrei Chemed, 2008), 102-127. Yehuda Amital was a Holocaust survivor who arrived in Israel in December 1944, began studying at Hebron Yeshiva in Jerusalem, and joined the Haganah. In May

Recruitment in Other Parts of the Country

After the recruitment decision, Agudat Yisrael and Poalei Agudat Yisrael branches nationwide began preparing to manage their members' recruitment. Names of candidates from Haredi parties were submitted to municipal and district headquarters after agreement with the national Haganah headquarters about their inclusion. Poalei Agudat Yisrael led this activity, with its members appointed to local recruitment committees in cities and councils: Ramat Gan, Petach Tikva, Haifa, Netanya, Raanana, Rishon Lezion, Rehovot, Kfar Ata, Bnei Brak, and Hadera.[104] Attendance also began according to orders: by January 8, 1948, 59 members of Poalei Agudat Yisrael aged 17-25 and additional girls reported at the Petach Tikva branch. In the Bnei Brak branch, 25 reported, three in Nachalat Ganim, and 11 in Tiberias.[105]

In early February, religious recruits were asked to delay their attendance until agreed service conditions were established. Some recruits were returned after starting service. Recruitment resumed only at the end of February, when a religious department was established

---

1946, he moved to study at the Kletzk Yeshiva, which was re-established in Rehovot and led by Rabbi Tzvi Yehuda Meltzer, son of Rabbi Isser Zalman Meltzer, who headed the Kletzk Yeshiva in Poland until he immigrated to Israel in 1925. In July 1947, Yehuda Klein-Amital married Miriam, daughter of Rabbi Tzvi Yehuda Meltzer. He later founded and led the Yeshivat Har Etzion in Alon Shvut and served as a minister without portfolio in Shimon Peres' government in 1995.

104 Binyamin Mintz to representatives on the local recruitment committees, December 17, 1947, Poalei Agudat Yisrael Archives, File 21, Folder 1; Kalman Kahana to the Central Recruitment Committee of Agudat Yisrael Organizations in Haifa, 23 Tevet 5708 [January 5, 1948], ibid., File 21, Folder 3.

105 Yisrael Edelman, Poalei Agudat Yisrael Petah Tikva, to the Poalei Agudat Yisrael Center Tel Aviv, January 8, 1948, Poalei Agudat Yisrael Archives, File 21, Folder 1.

to meet recruits' religious needs.[106] All who delayed their attendance were required to report, demand placement in religious units, and inform party branches. On March 8, 1948, Agudat Yisrael announced in its publication that those who had not yet reported for their duties for any reason must report by March 11, and 'those who do not report by this date will face severe measures.'[107] Recruitment resumed in all settlements, and farewell parties were held for recruits. At these parties, representatives of various Agudat Yisrael organizations, rabbis, and representatives of Haredi parties in local councils gave blessings.[108]

Following an agreement between Agudat Yisrael Center leaders in Tel Aviv and Dr. Binyamin Avniel, Chairman of the People's Service Mobilization Center, and Avraham Ahituv, Commander of the Tel Aviv Civil Guard, the Agudat Yisrael Center Recruitment Committee in Tel Aviv approached their movement members who met the following criteria on January 21, 1948: those who once served in any army role; those trained in first aid; those over 25; to urgently contact the Agudat Yisrael Center Recruitment Committee in Tel Aviv. The agreement included Shabbat observance, kashrut, and the establishment of religious units.[109]

106 Ze'ev Fischer-Schein to Katz, Secretary of the Mizrachi Workers Kfar Saba, February 5, 1948, Poalei Agudat Yisrael Archives, File 38, Folder 11; Kalman Kahana to Alter Tana, Rishon LeZion, February 5, 1948, ibid., File 30, Folder 12; David Bernholtz to the Situation Committee by Agudat Yisrael Organizations, February 17, 1948, ibid., File 21, Folder 1; Kalman Kahana to branches of Poalei Agudat Yisrael, February 23, 1948, ibid., File 21, Folder 3; David Bernholtz to all branches of Poalei Agudat Yisrael, February 24, 1948, ibid., File 21, Folder 1; "In the Recruitment of the Religious Brigades," *Ha Yom* (4 March 1948): 4.

107 "Last Chance for Recruits," *Ha Yom* (8 March 1948).

108 "Our Recruits Go to Defend the Land. Farewell Party for Our Recruits in Bnei Brak. Farewell Party for Our Recruits in Rishon LeZion," *She'arim* (24 March 1948): 1.

109 Agudat Yisrael Center Tel Aviv, News Issue 2, 21 Shevat 5708 [February 1, 1948], Poalei Agudat Yisrael Archives, File 30, Folder 12; M. D.

The Agudat Yisrael Youth Movement expanded its apparatus and moved to new offices in Tel Aviv due to widespread recruitment.[110] Menachem Talmi, who toured the front-line neighborhood positions in Tel Aviv in early March 1948, encountered a young man 'with long payot, a black hat on his head, and glasses on his eyes, all looking like a Jerusalem yeshiva boy.'[111]

Similar activities occurred in Haifa. Poalei Agudat Yisrael member Moshe Blitental served as a member of the district recruitment office, and Dr. Avraham Cohen served at the Hadar HaCarmel recruitment office. Poalei Agudat Yisrael members and members arrived at the recruitment office in December 1947, demanding to serve in a religious company. The female members requested not to be drafted for active service for religious reasons and expressed their willingness to fulfill any essential role according to the movement's orders.[112] The list of Poalei Agudat Yisrael and Agudat Youth recruits from Haifa in early January included 35 people.[113] In early February 1948, a joint Situation Committee of all organizations was elected: Agudat Yisrael, Poalei Agudat Yisrael, Agudat Yisrael Youth, and women's organizations of Agudat Yisrael and Poalei Agudat Yisrael. This Situation Committee formed a recruitment committee that registered all youth intended for recruitment in early February and awaited party headquarters instructions regarding their

    Levenstein and Y. M. Abramowitz to all members of Agudat Yisrael and ZAY, Subject: Service to the People, Circular No. 17, Agudat Yisrael Center Archives, Jerusalem; *Kol Yisrael* (5 February 1948): 1 (Hebrew).

110 Agudat Yisrael Youth Movement – Agudat Yisrael Youth, HaYom, April 16, 1948.

111 M. T., "In the No Man's Land" in Neve Shalom, Davar, p. 5, March 5, 1948.

112 "Recruitment of Our Members in Haifa and Kfar Ata," *She'arim* (1 January 1948): 4 (Hebrew).

113 Daniel Hartman, Secretary of the Poalei Agudat Yisrael Branch in Haifa, to the Executive Committee Tel Aviv, January 12, 1948, Poalei Agudat Yisrael Archives, File 21, Folder 1.

recruitment.[114] Three members of the Agudat Yisrael organizations' Situation Committee deliberated on whether to enlist or be released due to their committee role. One of the three, Daniel Hartman, approached Rabbi Kahana on February 17 and requested checking if they could be exempted from recruitment to continue their role on the Situation Committee. He noted that he did not want to be a draft dodger, so if he did not receive an official exemption, he would enlist on February 20.[115]

In Haifa, fulfilling religious requirements was difficult as religious organizations had no representation in 'Haifa Security Services.' There was no supervision of kashrut in training camps. The Situation Committee in Haifa requested that the Joint Security Affairs Committee near Agudat Yisrael organizations act to regulate recruitment and manage religious recruits in Haifa. The kashrut issue was brought to the attention of the Haifa area commander, who promised to address it immediately.[116] However, the issue was not resolved. At the end of January, ten Agudat Yisrael members from Haifa were drafted into a regular company despite their request to join a religious company. A request to the recruitment center did not change the decision. Yaakov Katz, a Poalei Agudat Yisrael leader in Haifa, blamed their

---

114 Secretariat of the Situation Committee by Agudat Yisrael Organizations in Haifa, to the Central Recruitment Committee of Agudat Yisrael Organizations Tel Aviv, February 8, 1948, Poalei Agudat Yisrael Archives, File 21, Folder 1; "In Agudat Yisrael Haifa," *Kol Yisrael* (12 February 1948): 1 (Hebrew); Avraham Cohen to Rabbi Dr. Kalman Kahana, (15 February 1948), Poalei Agudat Yisrael Archives, File 21, Folder 1.

115 Daniel Hartman, Haifa, to Rabbi Kalman Kahana, Tel Aviv (17 February 1948), Poalei Agudat Yisrael Archives, File 40, Folder 15.

116 "Haifa in the Situation Committee," *She'arim* (26 February 1948): 4 (Hebrew); David Hartman and Nissim Levatov to the Joint Committee on Security Matters by Agudat Yisrael Organizations Tel Aviv, (30 March 1948), Poalei Agudat Yisrael Archives, File 21, Folder 1; "The Joint Committee on Recruitment Matters by Poalei Agudat Yisrael, ZAY, and Ezra to the Situation Committee in Haifa," (31 March 1948), Poalei Agudat Yisrael Archives, File 21, Folder 1.

representative at the national recruitment center, Ze'ev Fischer-Schein, for the mishap.[117] Agudat Yisrael organizations had to announce at the beginning of April that their members should not go for training until kashrut was guaranteed in the kitchens.[118] On April 18, Agudat Yisrael Center in Tel Aviv informed Ben Gurion, as Chairman of the Yishuv Security Committee, that training camp kitchens in and around Haifa were still not kosher and that the military police threatened Agudat Yisrael members with measures if they did not immediately report. Ben Gurion was asked to order ensuring kashrut in all camps and instruct the military police not to act against those refusing to go to camps with non-kosher kitchens.[119]

Farewell parties were held in Haifa for recruits. Among the rabbis who blessed the recruits were Rabbi Baruch Markus, Chief Rabbi of Haifa, and Rabbi Avraham Yitzchak Klein, a member of the Council of Torah Sages. Rabbi Baruch Hager, the Seret-Viznitz Rebbe, a Council of Torah Sages member of Agudat Yisrael living in Haifa, was among those blessing the farewell party at the branch in his city on March 9. His eldest son, Eliezer Hager, enlisted and served as a fighter in the religious company of Platoon B, Battalion 22 of the Carmeli Brigade, participating in all battles in Haifa and Galilee with his unit until the war's end. Rabbi Eliezer Hager was appointed Rebbe in 1964 after

---

117 Yaakov Katz to Z. Fischer-Paine, Executive Committee of Poalei Agudat Yisrael Tel Aviv (20 February 1948), Poalei Agudat Yisrael Archives, File 38, Folder 11.

118 Situation Committee by Agudat Yisrael Organizations Haifa to the Joint Recruitment Committee Tel Aviv (5 April 1948), Poalei Agudat Yisrael Archives, File 21, Folder 4; Announcement: Statement of the Chief Rabbinate of Haifa, *She'arim* (8 April 1948): 4 (Hebrew); "On the Supervision of Kashrut in Haifa," *She'arim* (15 April 1948): 1 (Hebrew).

119 M. D. Levenstein and Y. M. Abramowitz to David Ben-Gurion, Chairman of the National Security Committee (18 April 1948), Israel State Archive, F-1/1056.

his father's death.[120] Haifa hosted gatherings of religious and Haredi soldiers, such as the opening ceremony of the camp for religious soldiers belonging to CHA'ATZ (Military Labor Corps) in Haifa Bay at the end of June 1948. This camp housed over 200 soldiers from HaPoel HaMizrachi and Poalei Agudat Yisrael. On December 5, 1948, a conference of religious soldiers organized by the Poalei Agudat Yisrael Security Department was held in Haifa, attended by about 300 soldiers from units around Haifa. The conferences also featured Rabbi Baruch Hager, the Seret-Viznitz Rebbe, and Rabbi Yosef Kahaneman, head of the Ponevezh Yeshiva in Bnei Brak.[121]

In the Poalei Agudat Yisrael branch in Kfar Ata, 60 people, 45 young men, and 15 young women, reported by mid-January 1948. On January 18, they wrote to the People's Service Mobilization Center in Haifa and requested establishing a religious unit for them or alternatively placing them in another religious company. The letter protested that some people received recruitment orders on Shabbat itself and therefore refused to accept them. The fact that religious items were not included on the list of items recruits were to bring, such as tefillin, a siddur, and the like, raised concerns about the treatment of religious recruits. As a result, it was decided to delay the organization's members' attendance until religious matters were arranged. The demand was also raised to include

---

120 "ZAY News," *Kol Yisrael* (11 March 1948): 4 (Hebrew); "Farewell Party for Our Recruits in Haifa," *She'arim* (11 March 1948): 4 (Hebrew); "The Movement in the Recruitment System," *She'arim* (18 March 1948): 4 (Hebrew); *ha-Tsofeh* (12 March 1948)(Hebrew); Yoav Rosenblum, *Stories of Grandpa Yoav* (Haifa: Rosenblum Family, 2005), 18-19 (Hebrew); "Farewell Party for Recruits to the Religious Platoon," *Davar* (9 March 1948): 5 (Hebrew); Haggai Huberman, "The Rebbe Who Fought for the Liberation of Haifa and the Galilee," *Matzav Ruach* (20 April 2012): 20-22 (Hebrew).

121 "The Religious Battalion of Army Opened in Haifa," *ha-Tsofeh* (30 June 1948): 1 (Hebrew); "Gathering of Religious Soldiers in Haifa," *She'arim* (9 December 1948): 1 (Hebrew); "Gathering of Religious Soldiers in Haifa," *HaYom* (13 December 1948): 2 (Hebrew).

a permanent representative of Poalei Agudat Yisrael at the Mobilization Center to care for recruits' religious needs.[122] Similar security activities also took place in Tiberias.[123] About 40 people trained in two training cycles from the Petach Tikva branch. With older recruits who enlisted during the 1936-1939 events, the number exceeds one hundred. About 40 members participated in the third training cycle.[124]

Hundreds of Bnei Brak residents were recruited to the Haganah, many from the Haredi community. A company of Gerrer Hasidim stood out for their distinctive clothing: long coats, trousers tucked inside their socks, payot, and beards. This company trained and was sent for operations and assistance to settlements outside Bnei Brak.[125] A cohesive group of about 25 people joined the religious company in Battalion 33 of the Alexandroni Brigade, primarily composed of Bnei Akiva and HaPoel HaMizrachi members. They participated in many battles: in Tel Litvinsky (Tel HaShomer), Kula, Lod, Sakia, Khiriya, Arab Kfar

---

122 A"Z 49/481– 15, January 18, 1948, Poalei Agudat Yisrael in Eretz Yisrael Kfar Ata Branch to the Service to the People Headquarters Haifa. Subject: Reporting of Recruits Aged 25-17. Attached to the letter was a list of 60 names of recruits with their health classification.

123 Zusha Luria to Agudat Yisrael Center Jerusalem (14 November 1947), Agudat Yisrael Center Archives, Jerusalem; Moshe Glickman-Porush to the Organization of Young Haredim Tiberias (7 December 1947), ibid.; Agudat Yisrael Tiberias to Agudat Yisrael Center Jerusalem (2 January 1948), ibid.

124 "On Guard for Security Matters in Petah Tikva," *She'arim* (12 February 1948): 2 (Hebrew); Shimon Katz to the Central Recruitment Committee (13 February 1948) (Hebrew), Poalei Agudat Yisrael Archives, File 21, Folder 1; *ha-Tsofeh* (18 February 1948) (Hebrew); *HaYom* (19 February 1948) (Hebrew); Tzohar [Natan Gardi] "ACI Religious Department to Hillel [Galili] (18 February 1948) (Hebrew), A"Z 49/481– 15; "Poalei Agudat Yisrael – Petah Tikva Branch, Spiritual Committee," *She'arim* (4 March 1948): 4 (Hebrew).

125 Yitzhak Meir, *Upon Thy Walls, O Bnei Brak*, vol. 2 (Bnei Brak: The Society for Research on the History of Bnei Brak, 1993), 316-318 (Hebrew).

9 | *The Recruitment of Haredim*

Saba, Kakun, Tantura, and more. Most of the company was killed on December 28, 1948, in a battle against the Egyptian army in Iraq al-Manshiyya (Kiryat Gat). About 20 of the company's fallen, throughout its activities in the war, were Bnei Brak residents. Other recruits were sent to accelerated cook courses and attached to the Givati and Kiryati brigades as cooks and kashrut supervisors.[126]

Halachic issues were brought before the 'Chazon Ish,' who was asked, among other things, who should be released first in wartime from the front to join a non-combat unit—a family man or a single man? He replied that the single man had priority for release because he had not yet produced offspring.[127] The council head, Rabbi Gerstenkorn, cooperated with the Haganah, and his office also served as a local Haganah headquarters activity room. Immediately after the partition decision, he made a blessing and a Shehecheyanu blessing over a microphone operated in the city center and ordered drinks to be distributed to all in need.[128]

In Bnei Brak, a party was held in honor of the recruits on March 16, 1948, at the religious soldiers' home. Rabbis, the council head, and Haredi organization leaders in the city participated and blessed.[129]

126 Shaul Biber, *From Darkness to Daylight Haganah in Tel Aviv* (Tel-Aviv, 1995), 210 (Hebrew); Yosef Tzvi Govitz, *ha-Nidon le-Hayyim* (Jerusalem: Feldheim, 2000), 218-220 (Hebrew). Govitz, who had health problems, was assigned to serve in the regiment workshop, while his comrades served as fighters, some of whom fell in battle.

127 According to the testimony of Yehoshua Zaltsberg, Commander of the Haganah in Bnei Brak from 1944 to 1948, in Shaul Biber, *From Darkness to Daylight Haganah in Tel Aviv* (Tel-Aviv, 1995), 202 (Hebrew); Shlomo Cohen, *Pe'er HaDor*, vol. 3 (Bnei Brak: Netzah, 1970), 188-189 (Hebrew).

128 Shaul Biber, *From Darkness to Daylight Haganah in Tel Aviv* (Tel-Aviv, 1995), 204, 207 (Hebrew).

129 "Farewell Party for Agudat Yisrael Recruits in Bnei Brak," *ha-Tsofeh* (16 March 1948): 3 (Hebrew); Yitzhak Meir, *Upon Thy Walls, O Bnei Brak*, vol. 2 (Bnei Brak: The Society for Research on the History of Bnei Brak, 1993), 428 (Hebrew).

Recruits were attached to the religious company in Battalion 33 of the Alexandroni Brigade.[130]

The local headquarters were reluctant to include Haredi representatives. On April 22, Rabbi Kahana complained to Yisrael Galili that their representatives were only included in the headquarters of Petah Tikva and Bnei Brak 'after much running around' and asked Galili to arrange this, stating that the Haredi community should not remain unrepresented 'just because it does not please someone.'[131] Rabbi Shimon Katz complained at a Petah Tikva City Council meeting in July 1948 that since two members were added to the regional headquarters, the headquarters had ceased to convene. The mayor promised to intervene, but it was to no avail.[132]

The issue of religious soldiers reporting for activities on Shabbat occasionally arose. In July, Poalei Agudat Yisrael's Security Department announced to those called to report on Shabbat that they should only report on Sunday.[133] In November, an attempt was made to find a solution to the problem of Haim members from the Tel Aviv district going out for training and activities on Shabbat. The Tel Aviv District Commander explained that these were individuals released from full recruitment because they were tied to their jobs in essential factories, and additional workdays could not be canceled for training. The agreement was that religious soldiers would not be forced to travel on Shabbat to

---

130 Yitzhak Meir, *Upon Thy Walls, O Bnei Brak*, vol. 2 (Bnei Brak: The Society for Research on the History of Bnei Brak, 1993), 425-426, 429-430 (Hebrew); and "List of Fallen in the War of Independence," in *Bnei Brak: Thirty Years* (Bnei Brak: published by Bnei Brak Municipality, 1955), 42-47 (Hebrew).

131 Kalman Kahana to Yisrael [Galili] (22 April 1948), Poalei Agudat Yisrael Archives, File 21, Folder 3.

132 "On Guard for Security Matters in Petah Tikva," *She'arim* (22 July 1948): 1 (Hebrew).

133 "Security Department Announcement," *She'arim* (15 July 1948): 1 (Hebrew).

the guard and training locations but would go there on Friday and wait there for the rest of the soldiers. Later, the order was changed, and the Tel Aviv district instructed not to send religious soldiers for training on Shabbat, but they were to train on other days.[134]

Members of the Poalei Agudat Yisrael settlements in the frontier areas were recruited locally to defend themselves and the area they resided in. Kibbutz Hafetz Haim recruits were occasionally called to operations in other settlements in their district: assisting Nitzanim in March 1948, participating in the conquest of Arab villages in the south (Marar, Beit Daras – Operation 'Barak') in May, and assisting Kibbutz Negba. The kibbutz truck with two drivers was mobilized to transport supplies to Jerusalem. In October 1948, the kibbutz commander received an order to organize a platoon from their members to reinforce the southern front in preparation for Operation 'Yoav'. On the eve of Yom Kippur, 35 members of Hafetz Haim reported to Kibbutz Yavneh, were equipped with new weapons from Czechoslovakia, trained in shooting, and went to the front. Along with them were two additional platoons from Givat Brenner and Kibbutz Yavneh. They were initially stationed in the Julis sector and then opposite Iraq Suweidan (Negba). A kibbutz member, Yeshayahu Spitzer, was killed by a shell fired at the stronghold where he was.[135]

In June 1948, the European center of Poalei Agudat Yisrael in Paris called on the youth of all Jewish community centers in Europe: 'Come to Israel! Take up the rifle and help drive the enemy from the land of

---

134 Commander of Tel Aviv District to IDF General Staff/ICA/Military Rabbinate Main Office, Subject: Haim Domestic Training on Shabbat, November 29, 1948, Poalei Agudat Yisrael Archives, File 21, Folder 2; Administration Officer of Tel Aviv District to Regiments 1, 2, 3, 4, Subject: Departure of Haim Personnel on Shabbat, December 30, 1948, ibid., File 20, Folder 12; Administration Officer, to the Regiment Commanders, Subject: Training on Shabbat, January 12, 1949, ibid., ibid.

135 Nechama Marcus, *To Work and to Preserve: The Story of Kibbutz Hafetz Haim* (Kibbutz Hafetz Haim, 1992), 263-245; Meier and Miriam Schwarz, *Mi-Dor le-Dor* (Jerusalem: Schwarz Family, 2005), 142-144.

Israel! Enlist! As our brothers are doing—the youth in the Yishuv.' The preference was to enlist abroad only in the IDF and not the Palmach. The European center in Paris was also asked to report immediately on any group of recruits expected to arrive to organize their instruction and inclusion in religious companies.[136]

Agudat Yisrael members, who made up about six percent of all illegal immigrants in the Cyprus camps, participated in the 'Guardian Line' training conducted by Haganah and Palmach members, sent members to instructor courses, and declared themselves as future citizens of the state and fighters for its establishment, even though this was not yet seen as the steps of the Messiah.[137]

Recruitment for Essential Work on Shabbat

Members of the Haredi community, like other Yishuv citizens who were not drafted, were called for essential work. In this area, similar problems arose to those encountered by Haredi recruits. On September 30, 1948, Dov Yosef, the military governor of Jerusalem, and Dov Lipov, human resources coordinator for the Jerusalem district, issued a mobilization order for essential work for October 7 for all those born from 1900 to 1930. All economic exemptions were canceled, and a special appeals committee was established. The order emphasized that although 'the work is very essential, no work will be done on Shabbat

---

136 "Call of the European Center of Poalei Agudat Yisrael for Recruitment for the Defense of the Land," *She'arim* (24 June 1948): 1; Poalei Agudat Yisrael Executive Committee to the European Center Paris, July 16, 1948, Poalei Agudat Yisrael Archives, File 21, Folder 1. At this stage, there was no separate recruitment for the Palmach, probably because the publishers of the call did not know this.

137 Nahum Bogner, *The Deportation Island: Jewish Illegal Immigrant Camps on Cyprus 1946-1948* (Tel-Aviv: Tel-Aviv University, 1991), 270; and David Shaari, *The Cyprus Deportation, 1946-1949* (Jerusalem: Hasifria Hatsionit, 1981), 228, 230, 259, 271, 276, 277, 291.

9 | The Recruitment of Haredim

and holidays.'[138] It was promised that workers would return home on Fridays before Shabbat, and during Sukkot, efforts would be made to build kosher sukkot for them to eat during their work.[139] Dov Yosef announced at a press conference on October 8 that public reporting was satisfactory, with even a surplus of those who reported and were sent home.[140]

On October 12, an alert was declared in the Jerusalem district in preparation for the possible resumption of fighting. Leaves were canceled, and Haim members and services under partial mobilization were transferred to full mobilization and required to stay on bases. Arrangements were made to reinforce the battalions with service unit members, and the transport officer was instructed to put the entire vehicle and driver array on alert.[141] On October 15, Operation 'Yoav' began in the south, and on October 18, Operation 'HaHar' began, aiming to seize control of northwestern Judea and widen the western corridor to Jerusalem. There was concern that the fighting would spread to the Jerusalem sector. Indeed, these days saw fierce battles, especially on Mount Zion.

On Thursday, October 14, in the evening, it was announced on the radio that it was decided that due to their essential and urgent nature, work would be needed on Shabbat. The two chief rabbis, Herzog and

---

138 Dov Lipov, Human Resources Coordinator Jerusalem District to Agudat Yisrael Center Jerusalem, September 30, 1948, Agudat Yisrael Center Archives, Jerusalem; "IDF Rule in Jerusalem, Essential Work Order 5708," *Ha Yom* (1 October 1948): 1; *Ha Yom* (3 October 1948): 6.

139 "Manpower Order to Be Activated Today," *Ha Yom* (7 October 1948): 2.

140 "On Jerusalem Issues – Press Conference with the Governor," *Ha Yom* (10 October 1948): 1.

141 Administration Officer Headquarters of Jerusalem District Administrative Order No. 1 and 2, A"Z 49/959– 163, October 11 and 12, 1948; Transport Officer Headquarters Jerusalem District, Instructions from the Transport Officer, October 12, 1948, ibid.; Administration Officer, Administrative Order No. 4, October 14, 1948, ibid.

Uziel, gave a halachic permit for this. In response, the Agudat Yisrael Center in Jerusalem announced via a notice on the front page of HaYoman that the Haredi public would not participate in these works as long as there was no agreement from the rabbis of Haredi Judaism. The Agudat Yisrael Center in Jerusalem informed Dov Yosef on October 15 that he should communicate with the Haredi rabbinate, as only if a permit were received from them would the Haredi public participate in work on Shabbat. Welfare Minister Rabbi Levin complained to Ben-Gurion that 'people are rebelling, and there will be beatings,' and was told that the work was essential and could not be postponed, and the chief rabbis permitted it. Ben-Gurion asked Rabbi Levin to contact his people in Jerusalem and inform them to check the matter with Rabbi Herzog.[142]

On Friday, October 15, Agudat Yisrael Center members went to Rabbi Dushinsky, who was hospitalized at Shaare Zedek Hospital, to ask if there was room to permit work on Shabbat. Rabbi Dushinsky ruled that there was no permit. Agudat Yisrael members went to the Human Resources office and reported the decision. Rabbi Moshe Glickman-Porush and Dr. Ephraim Prader went together to speak about it with Rabbi Dushinsky, but due to his physical weakness, he referred them to the head of the Haredi community's rabbinical court, Rabbi Bengis, who heard the arguments and also ruled that the work should not be permitted on Shabbat. He declared that he would issue an order to the Haredi public in Jerusalem that they were commanded to work on these tasks during the intermediate days of Sukkot. The Haredi public did not report for work, but many who were not from the Haredi sector went out to work. HaYoman praised the 'work inspectors who

---

142 "Today, Reporting for Essential Work," *HaYom* (15 October 1948): 4; "Jerusalem Will Not Desecrate Shabbat," *HaYom* (15 October 1948) 1; and Announcement from the Agudat Yisrael Center in Jerusalem," *HaYom* (15 October 1948): 1; Agudat Yisrael Center Jerusalem to Dov Yosef, October 15, 1948, World Agudat Yisrael Archives; David Ben-Gurion, *The War of Independence: War Diary*, vol. 1, eds. Gershon Rivlin and Elhanan Orren (Tel-Aviv: Ministry of Defense, 1982), 746 (15 October 1948).

treated courteously and did not force those who did not want to work.'[143] The censorship prevented HaYoman from expressing its opinion on the order for work on Shabbat and holidays.[144] Rabbi Levin approached Ben-Gurion following Agudat Yisrael's request from Jerusalem to cancel work on Shabbat and holidays in Jerusalem and succeeded in convincing him.[145]

The chief rabbis announced on October 21 in the evening the cancellation of the temporary permit they gave for work on Shabbat and holidays, and if further need arises, a special notice will be made. The human resources coordinator announced the change, noting that canceling the obligation to work on Shabbat and holidays would increase Haredi public attendance for this work on weekdays.[146] Dov Yosef believed that the people of Jerusalem contributed more than enough to security matters, and the solution should be to bring in additional people from outside Jerusalem.[147] Essential work continued in Jerusalem on weekdays with the participation of the Haredi public,

---

143 "The Order to Desecrate Shabbat in Jerusalem Causes a Stir," *HaYom* (17 October 1948): 4 (Hebrew); Moshe Glickman-Porush to the Presidium of the Union of Orthodox Rabbis of the United States and Canada (October 21, 1948), Moshe Glickman-Porush to the Agudat Yisrael Center in France (October 23, 1948) Agudat Yisrael Center Archives, Jerusalem.

144 "Rabbi Levin with Ben-Gurion," *HaYom* (19 October 1948): 2; "On Freedom of Expression – Editorial," *HaYom* (20 October 1948): 1.

145 Yitzhak Meir Levin to Menachem Glickman-Porush, October 21, 1948; Yitzhak Meir Levin to David Ben-Gurion, October 24, 1948, State Archive GL-1/44806 and Agudat Yisrael Center Archives, Jerusalem.

146 "Order to Work on Shabbat and Holidays Canceled," *HaYom* (22 October 1948): 1; "Rabbinical Announcement on Work on Shabbat," *HaYom* (22 October 22, 1948): 4; *Haaretz* (24 October 1948).

147 *ha-Tsofeh* (24 October 1948).

and on Shabbat, October 30, sermons were given in many synagogues to encourage participation in essential work.[148]

The Jerusalem District Commander sent a letter to the two chief rabbis with his perspective on the controversy:

> "I read with great sadness the defamatory words published in HaYoman about the essential and urgent fortification works done on the holiday. I note that the description in this newspaper is distorted, lacking understanding and responsibility. Recent days have clearly proven that our assessment of the situation was accurate, and the threat of the fighting flaring up on the Jerusalem front was highly substantiated and authoritative. I gave clear instructions that only the urgent and essential work on the front lines, which are a matter of saving lives, be done on Shabbat, while work that can be postponed is postponed to weekdays. As proof, many of those who reported for work on Shabbat were released after it was determined there was no urgent need due to saving human lives. Be assured, dear rabbi, that we know how to honor the nation's sanctities and religious feelings, and in this spirit, I gave the orders to the fortification officers. In the brutal war imposed on us by the enemy, we must do everything, all Jerusalem residents together, to strike the enemy and liberate our eternal city."[149]

---

148 "Announcement of the Human Resources Office in the Jerusalem District," *Haaretz* (1 November 1948); Moshe Glickman-Porush to the Human Resources Coordinator, 23 Tishrei 5709 [October 26, 1948], Agudat Yisrael Center Archives, Jerusalem; "Sermons in Synagogues for the Sake of Essential Works," HaYom (31 October 1948): 2.

149 Commander of the District to the Chief Rabbi of Eretz Yisrael, Rishon LeZion, Rabbi Ben-Zion Meir Hai Uziel, October 1948, A"Z 49/959–110.

9 | The Recruitment of Haredim

This chapter is an English translation of Moshe Ehrenwald, "The Recruitment of Haredim," in *The Haredim During the Independence War* (Moshav Ben Shemen: Modan Publishing, 2017), 223-257 (Hebrew).

Dr. Moshe Ehrenwald is a graduate of the Department of History of the Modern Middle East and the Department of International Relations, holding a master's degree in Contemporary Jewry from the Hebrew University of Jerusalem. His book on the Jewish Quarter of Jerusalem's Old City during the War of Independence, based on his doctoral dissertation in the Department of History at the Hebrew University, was awarded the Yitzhak Sadeh Prize for Military Literature. His book on Mount Scopus in the War of Independence received the Moldovan Prize for Military Literature at Ariel University. His 2017 book, *The Haredim During the Independence War*, was published by Modan Publishing House.

The Involvement of Jerusalem's Rabbis in Security Matters During the War of Independence

Moshe Ehrenwald

RABBIS, IN THEIR VARIOUS ROLES, are part of the civic leadership at both national and local levels. In intercommunal or total wars, when civilians are in conflict and fighting zones, civic leadership becomes crucial. The rabbis who served during the War of Independence were not monolithic: some belonged to the "Old Yishuv," others to the "New Yishuv"; some held Zionist views, while others were part of the Haredi sector that opposed Zionism. They held official positions at various levels within the Jewish community, gaining authority from their communities due to their personalities and knowledge. There were Ashkenazi and Sephardi rabbis, Hasidic rebbes, and yeshiva heads. Some rabbis from the Haredi "Old Yishuv" had Zionist views, while some from the "New Yishuv" opposed Zionism. Research on the War of

Independence has not yet focused on the role played by spiritual leaders such as rabbis and yeshiva heads throughout the country, compared to the research focus on commanders, fighters, politicians, and party leaders. In recent years, the study of the involvement of civil society in the war has begun to develop.

This article will focus on the activities and contributions of Jerusalem's rabbis from various circles during the War of Independence.[1]

Rabbis from all circles, those with official positions in the Jewish community's establishment and those who served as religious-spiritual leaders of their communities, were involved in security matters, and sometimes even in the political affairs of the Jewish community in the country during the War of Independence. They addressed the halakhic and moral aspects of security problems presented to them and assisted their community members and the community's security forces in various areas, even in matters not necessarily arising from their defined roles.

Connections between the rabbis and security personnel began in the late 1920s when the Jewish community's security forces began to organize against the challenges posed by the Arabs and the British authorities. Rabbis in official positions and those serving in mixed cities and frontier neighborhoods of the Jewish community were directly involved in security events. During these events, they became acquainted with the community's security personnel. The rabbis dealt with fundamental and specific issues presented to them by various bodies and individuals. Their opinions and halakhic rulings were primarily the domain of the religious-traditional population and religious recruits. However, the heads of the Haganah upper command, who were interested in recruiting members of the religious-Haredi sector into the organization, understood that these recruits must be allowed to maintain their way of life during their security activities.

1 The article focuses solely on the activities of rabbis residing in Jerusalem during the War of Independence, and does not address related issues, such as the enlistment of yeshiva students or the recruitment of the Haredi sector into the war effort.

Among the rabbis, disagreements arose over security matters due to differing worldviews and approaches. When the question of whether to restrain or respond to Arab aggression in the 1930s was discussed, the Chief Rabbinate supported the policy of restraint advocated by the Jewish community's leadership. In contrast, Rabbi Yehuda Leib Fishman-Maimon, a leader of the Mizrachi, was against restraint. Both supporters and opponents of restraint found halakhic sources to support their positions. The Ashkenazi Chief Rabbi, Yitzhak Isaac Halevi Herzog, who supported the principle of restraint, addressed concrete questions, such as that of Yechiel Eliash, responsible for the Mizrachi defense department. Eliash asked if the field units (the "Field Companies") could act to close the exits from Arab villages at night. He was told that if the commander defined this action as an effective defense, it was permissible.[2] In September 1939, the Chief Rabbis Yitzhak Isaac Halevi Herzog and Ben-Zion Meir Hai Uziel issued halakhic guidelines on how to operate on the Sabbath for the guard unit that included religious recruits from the Haganah.[3]

A rabbinic committee, chaired by Rabbi Moshe Sternberg, the rabbi of Kfar Pines,[4] was authorized to address both the fundamental and daily halakhic questions faced by religious members of the Haganah. For instance, the issue of how to respond to the struggle against the

---

2 Hilda Schatzberger, *Resistance and Tradition in Mandatory Palestine* (Ramat-Gan: Bar-Ilan University, 1985), 101-105 (Hebrew); and Shulamit Eliash, "The Chief Rabbinate, Terror, and the Revisionists," in Hayyim Genizi, ed., *Religion and resistance in Mandatory Palestine* (Tel Aviv: Morasha, 1996), 115-131 (Hebrew).

3 "Rabbi Uziel to the HaPoel HaMizrachi Association in Tel Aviv" (27 September 1939), in Shmuel Katz and Ezra Barnea, eds., *Sefer Mikhmanei Uziel*, vol. 6 (Jerusalem: The Committee for the Publication of the Writings of Rav Uziel, 2004), 224 (Hebrew).

4 Other members of the committee included Rabbi Zvi Yehuda Meltzer, rabbi of Pardes Hanna; Rabbi Shaul Yisraeli, rabbi of Kfar HaRoeh; Rabbi Eliezer Shimshon Rosenthal, rabbi of Kibbutz Rodges (Kvutzat Yavneh); and Rabbi David Solomon, rabbi of Ein Ganim and Kfar Avraham.

decrees of the White Paper was brought before Rabbi Herzog. He involved in the deliberation his colleague, Rabbi Uziel, along with Rabbi Moshe Yaakov Charlap, one of the heads of the Mercaz HaRav Yeshiva, and Rabbi Reuven Katz, the Chief Rabbi of Petach Tikva and a member of the Chief Rabbinate. Since the matter also had political dimensions, the rabbis consulted Moshe Shapira from the leadership of the Jewish Agency. After thorough deliberations and consultations, the rabbis determined that the fight against the White Paper and the Land Laws constituted a milchemet mitzvah. This classification carried practical implications regarding the scope of permissible actions and exemptions, such as the extent of permissible activities on Shabbat, the scale of recruitment, and who could be exempt from conscription.[5]

There were rabbis who assisted underground prisoners in the years preceding the establishment of the State of Israel. Rabbi Aryeh Levin, who served as a spiritual supervisor at the Etz Chaim Yeshiva in Jerusalem, volunteered for many years as the rabbi for Jewish prisoners, both security-related and criminal, who were incarcerated at the Russian Compound prison in Jerusalem. His activities extended beyond addressing the religious needs of the prisoners. In his role at the prison, he provided significant assistance to members of all the underground movements, to their families, and even, to some extent, to their organizations, earning great respect for his efforts.[6] Rabbi Dov Eliezerov, a resident of Mea Shearim, performed a similar role for approximately five years at the Atlit detention camp. During his tenure, he spent his Sabbaths under difficult conditions in the detention camp. Despite the strict British surveillance over his activities at the camp, he managed to establish connections with the detainees and provided valuable support

---

5 Yechiel Eliash, *A Vision that Came to Pass* (Tel Aviv: Elitzur Center, 1983), 315–321 (Hebrew).

6 "Expression of Gratitude," *HaYom* (24 February 1948): 4 (Hebrew).

to them and their organizations. Rabbi Eliezerov described his activities in his memoirs:[7]

> "I never returned empty-handed from a trip to the camp. I always came back with a significant load, containing greetings, questions, and essential information on both family and non-family matters—on detention issues, legal counsel, coordination of actions, efforts for release, and much more. Needless to say, all this information could never, Heaven forbid, be recorded in writing, not even in the slightest hint. For had I been caught with such materials, Heaven forbid, the outcome would have been arrest or even deportation to Asmara in Africa or similar consequences."

The involvement of rabbis was expanded within their designated roles and in other areas necessitated by the circumstances of the war and the Zionist challenge of establishing the Jewish state.

JERUSALEM'S RABBIS IN THE WAR OF INDEPENDENCE

The unique situation of Jerusalem during the War of Independence also influenced the activities of the city's rabbis. According to the United Nations Partition Plan, Jerusalem was intended to be an international city with a connection to both states—the Jewish and the Arab—serving as a kind of bridge of peace between them. However, only the Jewish side was willing to accept the Partition Plan. The Arab side opposed it, the British did not cooperate, and the United Nations failed to take the necessary steps to implement its decision regarding Jerusalem. As a result, Jerusalem became one of the main arenas of the war. By the end of 1947, approximately 95,000 Jews—one-sixth of the Jewish population of the Land of Israel—lived in Jerusalem. The city was under siege, and its residents found themselves on the front lines, enduring heavy shelling

---

7   Dov Eliezerov, *Sha'ali Tzion* (Jerusalem: Mosad ha-Rav Kook, 1979), 7-8 (Hebrew).

that caused significant casualties and extensive damage to property and infrastructure. Of the approximately 5,500 fatalities in the War of Independence (soldiers and civilians), 1,082 soldiers and 420 civilians were killed within the boundaries of Jerusalem.[8]

In the struggle for Jerusalem, military, political, and civilian matters were intricately intertwined. Given the city's dire situation, it was not always clear to all observers that it would manage to withstand the siege. The resilience of the civilian population played a critical role in Jerusalem's ability to endure the campaign. The civilian leadership, including the rabbis among them, held a significant role in organizing the population to cope with the difficult and dangerous circumstances. The rabbis were part of this leadership, with many of them standing out in shouldering this responsibility. The challenging conditions created by the War of Independence compelled these rabbis to act in areas related to security and to assist military authorities in various capacities. The rabbis made it a point to remain among their communities, particularly at the frontlines, to serve as personal examples. Zionist rabbis sought to be involved in shaping the new state, its institutions, and its army, viewing it as their duty to voice their opinions and influence areas they deemed important. Non-Zionist rabbis understood that this was a war of survival and a matter of *pikuach nefesh* and contributed to the public, which regarded them as spiritual and communal authorities. The rabbis also sought to influence the future of Jerusalem, whose international status was fraught with political uncertainty.

THE CHIEF RABBIS

The Chief Rabbinate was one of the official institutions of the Jewish community in the country. The two Chief Rabbis, Rabbi Yitzhak Isaac Halevi Herzog and Rabbi Ben-Zion Meir Hai Uziel, stayed and operated for most of the war in Jerusalem due to the siege, which disconnected

---

8   Yitzhak Levy, *Tisha Kabin* (Tel Aviv: Ministry of Defense, 1986), 379 (Hebrew).

them for most of the war from other parts of the country. They were well-versed in the situation, and there were beneficial working relations between them and the military and civic leadership in the city. They met with officials for discussions and consultations; visited military units; were invited to military ceremonies and civic events; and encouraged the community's security forces and the city's residents during difficult times. In late January 1948, a rabbinic gathering was held in Tel Aviv with rabbis from various circles across the country to discuss matters related to the future Jewish state, current affairs, and the state of religious Jewry. Rabbi Herzog presented his view on the situation in his speech to the attendees:[9]

> "We did not want war. We did not want confrontation with our neighbors; on the contrary, we sought peace. [...] We do not rush to battle. But on the other hand, after we were attacked, we will know how to engage in a fierce war. In this regard, it must be emphatically said that this is not just a defensive war but also a war of initiative. [...] This is a mitzvah war, God's war against Amalek. We do not believe that the simple Arab masses [...] want war. But there are inciters who ignite this blaze, and it is our duty to repel the wild attacks by rioters and murderous inciters. We will not allow Jewish blood to be shed with impunity. We have already sacrificed millions of our brothers in the Diaspora saturated with this. [...] This is a mitzvah war in which we are commanded to marshal all our forces to succeed in the battle. [...] We must not rely on miracles alone. A miracle from heaven is sudden, hidden, and for now, we must organize Jewish defense [...] and not be deterred by enemy attacks."

As mentioned above, defining the war as a mitzvah war had practical halakhic implications. At the conference, it was determined

---

9   Rabbi Yitzhak Isaac Halevi Herzog, "Shema Yisrael (Speech Delivered at the Rabbinic Conference)," *ha-Tsofeh* (5 January 1948): 2 (Hebrew).

that Jerusalem would be the "capital city" of the Jewish state and that the Chief Rabbinate would remain there. The conference sent a 'Chizku Ve'imtzu' (Be Strong and Courageous) blessing to all responders and a protest to the British authorities about the siege imposed on the Old City and the inability to reach the Western Wall. Rabbi Herzog used the platform to call for adherence to interpersonal mitzvot, especially in this difficult time, and to act against the scourge of price gouging by interested parties in the community.

By remaining in Jerusalem during the siege and fighting, the two Chief Rabbis practically expressed their opinion on Jerusalem's place and status in the State of Israel, something not self-evident given the UN's decision that the city would have an international status. Their stay in Jerusalem was not a given because the central leadership of the community chose to operate in Tel Aviv. Some leaders stranded in Jerusalem due to the siege were resentful and frustrated about this, and most left the city when the road to Tel Aviv was opened during the first truce. At a government meeting on October 26, 1948, it was proposed to hold a joint meeting of the Jewish Agency executive and the government in Jerusalem. Ben-Gurion responded by saying, "I must express my regret that the Jewish Agency executive members, whom I was sure would sit in Jerusalem, are not sitting there. I saw them in Jerusalem; after returning from Jerusalem, I saw them in Tel Aviv."[10]

The convoy returning Rabbi Herzog to Jerusalem after the rabbinic gathering was attacked three times at different points along the road from Tel Aviv to Jerusalem.[11] At the beginning of February 1948, Rabbi Uziel's house was severely damaged by the explosion of an Arab car

---

10 "Minutes of the Provisional Government Meeting, 26 October 1948," in *Protocol of the Provisional Government Meeting*, vol. 9, p. 36, Israel State Archives.

11 "Among the Attacked Convoy Was His Honor, the Chief Rabbi," *ha-Tsofeh* (23 January 1948): 1 (Hebrew).

bomb near the building of the "Palestine Post" newspaper.¹² About three weeks later, on February 22, a bomb blast on Ben Yehuda Street shook the windows of Rabbi Uziel's office, and he wrote in his diary: "Great sorrow accompanied by anger against the bombers took away my desire to work."¹³ At that time, Rabbi Uziel's children lived in Tel Aviv, and he and his wife remained alone in Jerusalem, unable to visit their children.

On January 7, 1948, Ben-Gurion instructed Israel Amir, the commander of the Jerusalem district, to have the Chief Rabbis, through the Jewish Agency's political department, initiate a call from all religious leaders for a ceasefire in Jerusalem in general and in the Old City in particular.¹⁴ Attempts to contact the representative of Islam did not succeed. Rabbi Herzog often handled matters that required contacts with the British government heads in the country due to his position and good acquaintance with the British.¹⁵ A diplomatic mission to London, initiated in December 1947 by Rabbi Isser Zalman Meltzer, head of the Etz Chaim Yeshiva, and Rabbi Yaakov Moshe Charlap, one of the leaders of the Merkaz Harav Yeshiva, did not materialize.¹⁶ On January 26, Rabbi Herzog discussed the situation of the Jewish Quarter in the Old City with Sir Henry Gurney, the secretary of the Mandate government. Rabbi Herzog explained that the residents of the Jewish

12 *The Diary of Rabbi Uziel*, entries from 21 and 24 Shevat 5708; "A Bomb Explosion at the Palestine Post Building in Jerusalem," *ha-Tsofeh* (February 1948): 2 (Hebrew).

13 *The Diary of Rabbi Uziel*, entry from 22 February 1948.

14 David Ben-Gurion, *The War Diary*, vol. 1 (Tel-Aviv: Ministry of Defense, 1984), 121-122 [7 January 1948] (Hebrew); and Yisrael Amir, *On an Unpaved Path* (Tel Aviv: Ministry of Defense, 1988), 151 (Hebrew).

15 Rabbi Herzog earned a doctorate from the University of London. Before his election as Chief Rabbi of Eretz Israel in 1936, he served for many years as the rabbi of Belfast and later of Dublin in Ireland.

16 Letter from Isser Zalman Meltzer and Yaakov Moshe Charlap to Rabbi Isser Yehuda Unterman, 26 December 1947, file 287, Religious Zionism Archive.

Quarter in the Old City are representatives of the entire Jewish people to guard the holy places. It is the Haganah's role to protect them, and therefore the defenders will not leave the Jewish Quarter, as the British suggested-demanded. He suggested that Gurney mediate with the Islamic leaders to agree on the terms of a ceasefire in the Old City. He noted that he would recommend to the Jewish Agency's executive to remove the Haganah men from the quarter if the ceasefire holds and it becomes clear that the Arabs can be trusted not to harm the quarter's residents.[17]

A large convoy from Jerusalem to the Etzion Bloc on Saturday, March 27, was blocked and attacked on the outskirts of Bethlehem in the Neve Daniel area. Rabbi Herzog joined efforts to persuade the British to hasten and rescue the convoy before it was too late. He called the High Commissioner, Sir Alan Cunningham, on that very Sabbath day, urging him to send military forces to rescue the convoy.[18] The British eventually responded and rescued the convoy members the following day. On April 4, he met with the High Commissioner and protested the British soldiers' attack on the "Hurva Rabbi Yehuda HeChasid" synagogue in the Jewish Quarter of the Old City. He also conveyed a strong protest about the attack to the British Prime Minister and the United Nations. The meeting also discussed the future of Jerusalem and the international activities of the churches concerning the peace of Jerusalem.[19]

---

17 "Conversation of Rabbi Yitzhak Isaac Halevi Herzog with Sir Harold Grieve, 26 January 1948," in Gedalia Yogev, ed., *Political and Diplomatic Documents: December 1947 – May 1948* (Jerusalem: Israel State Archives and the Central Zionist Archives, 1980), 228-237 [document 139] (Hebrew).

18 The convoy members were only rescued the following day in the early afternoon. Dominique Lapierre and Larry Collins, *O Jerusalem*, trans. Ehud Amiad (New York: Simon & Schuster, 1972), 192.

19 "Rabbi Herzog Protested to the High Commissioner About the Harm Done to the 'Hurvah,'" *Haaretz* (6 April 1948): 6 (Hebrew); and *ha-Tsofeh* (6 April 1948)(Hebrew).

In mid-May 1948, Rabbi Uziel called on the Jews of Jerusalem and the entire State of Israel who were of military age to join the fighting forces: "At this great hour, when the kings of the Arabs and their mighty forces are attacking us with their armies and weapons, and Jerusalem, our holy city and our glory, and its besieged residents within its walls and suburbs are continuously attacked by our mighty enemies,"[20] to hasten the arrival of the final victory.

On May 14, the Jerusalem district headquarters declared a state of emergency in Jerusalem and a full mobilization of all men and women aged 16-48. This followed the fall of the Etzion Bloc and the fear that Legion forces would attack from there the southern approaches to Jerusalem, which were not fortified. The district commander, David Shaltiel, explained the situation to the two Chief Rabbis, Herzog and Uziel, who allowed work on fortifications even on the Sabbath. Shaltiel later recounted that on that evening, as he toured the city, he saw an old man carrying a large stone at one of the entrances. When he approached, he saw it was Rabbi Uziel. When Shaltiel asked him why he was doing this, Rabbi Uziel replied: "Today, I permitted work on the Sabbath. If the Jews do not see me really working on the Sabbath, they may not believe that today desecrating the Sabbath is sanctifying the Sabbath."[21] In a speech given by Rabbi Uziel at a party of the Jerusalem Community Committee for members of the Jerusalem district headquarters in early July 1948, he said that if he could, he would go out and fight himself, and if the danger increases, everyone would have to go out to fight, including "the bridegroom from his room and the bride from her chuppah."[22]

---

20 "The Mitzvah of the Moment," in Shmuel Katz and Ezra Barnea, eds., *Sefer Mikhmanei Uziel*, vol. 6 (Jerusalem: The Committee for the Publication of the Writings of Rav Uziel, 2004), 220 (Hebrew); "The Chief Rabbi Calls for Arms," *HaYom* (21 May 1948)(Hebrew).

21 David Shaltiel, *Jerusalem 5708* (Tel Aviv: Ministry of Defense, 1981), 164 (Hebrew).

22 "The Commander of the Jerusalem District Promises a Complete Victory," *HaYom* (8 July 1948): 4 (Hebrew).

Rabbis Herzog and Uziel were involved in establishing the military rabbinate and invested significantly in detailed halakhic rulings on matters presented to them by various parties, including religious settlements, the military rabbinate, religious youth movements, and others. Opinions were usually written after consulting with other rabbis and were the basis for the relationship between religion and the military in the State of Israel. Several principles underpinned these halakhic rulings:

1. The struggle with the Arabs for the Land of Israel is a mitzvah war.[23]

2. The military commander is the professional authority to determine what is essential for war preparations or the war itself. In the instructions for Yom Kippur of 5709 (October 1948), it was written:[24]

   > "If the Chief of General Staff determines that there are fairly well-founded concerns that the outbreak of battles so close to the holy day may mean that not taking action in works directly and vitally related to battle preparations could seriously negatively affect the course of battles, these works should be permitted within the absolute necessity for battle preparations. The sole authority to determine which works are directly and vitally related to battle preparations is the Chief of General Staff."

3. One Army - The Jerusalem district examined in April 1948 the possibility of opening non-kosher kitchens for soldiers who do not observe kashrut laws. Rabbis Herzog and Uziel noted that

---

23 Rabbi Yitzhak Isaac Halevi Herzog, *Pesakim u-Ketavim*, vol. 1 (Jerusalem: Mosad ha-Rav Kook and Yad ha-Rav Herzog, 1989), 198 [no. 45] (Hebrew).

24 Rabbis Herzog, Uziel, and Rabbi Shlomo Gorenchik (Goren), "The Instruction of the Chief Rabbis Regarding Yom Kippur in the Army," 8 Tishrei 5709, IDF Archive, file 121/50, p. 169.

"there is no place [...] to divide and distinguish between Jews and Jews regarding kashrut matters, and there is no possibility or way of permitting the establishment of two types of kitchens for units of the Israel Defense Forces."[25]

Rabbi Tzvi Pesach Frank, Chief Rabbi of Jerusalem

Rabbi Tzvi Pesach Frank, who served as the Chief Rabbi of Jerusalem,[26] maintained a close relationship with the Haganah. During the tumultuous events of 1929, while residing in the Batei Mahase complex in Jerusalem's Old City, he actively supported the Haganah's efforts to defend the Jewish community. Under the leadership of Yosef Avidor, Haganah soldiers organized within the Jewish Quarter, with Rabbi Frank hosting them in his home. Demonstrating remarkable courage, his wife concealed the soldiers' weapons in their home after they fired upon Arabs attempting to breach the Jewish Quarter.[27] In the early 1930s, Rabbi Tzvi Pesach Frank relocated to Malachi Street in the Kiryat Moshe neighborhood, where he continued his support for the Haganah. His basement served as a hiding place for grenades, and his telephone was made available for the organization's use. Two of his sons, Yaakov and Avraham, were deeply involved in the Haganah's activities.

---

25 Letter from Rabbis Herzog, Uziel, and Shmuel Aharon Weber, the Chief Secretary, to the Chief Command for the Jerusalem District, file 959/49–180, 27 Nisan 5708, Israel State Archives.

26 Rabbi Zvi Pesach Frank, born in 1873, immigrated to Eretz Israel in 1892. In 1918, he was appointed Av Beit Din (head of the rabbinical court) and in 1936, he was appointed Chief Rabbi of Jerusalem.

27 Yosef Avi-Ron, *On the Way to the IDF* (IDF: Maarachot, 1970), 33-34 (Hebrew); testimony of Yosef Avi-Ron, in Rachel Yanait, et al., eds., *The Defense in Jerusalem*, vol. 1 (Jerusalem: Havrei Hahaganah, 1973), 58 (Hebrew); Avraham Frank, *Tov va-Hesed Yirdefuni* (Jerusalem: Author's publication, 2007), 48-49 (Hebrew); Avraham Frank, interview conducted by Tsippa Wodislavsky, April 2006, *The Haganah Historical Archives*, CD50/122, digital recording.

Yaakov, one of the commanders of the religious company stationed in the Jewish Quarter during the 1936 disturbances, faced exposure due to his involvement and was forced to leave the country temporarily. Upon his return, he became a senior commander in the Air Force during the War of Independence. Avraham joined the Haganah in 1934, participating in training and operations in Jerusalem and its surrounding areas. He attended courses at various locations, including Ein Harod and Givat Shmuel, and was actively involved in Wingate's night squads. With his father's permission, Avraham operated on Sabbaths and holidays when necessary. Later, he established a spring factory, using it to assist underground movements by producing and repairing springs for weapons, thereby further contributing to the defense efforts.[28]

In January 1948, during the critical months leading up to the establishment of the State of Israel, Rabbi Tzvi Pesach Frank was approached to permit Sabbath work at the Tchorz Brothers factory in Jerusalem. The factory was engaged in armoring buses, which were essential for maintaining the connection with the settlements in the Etzion Bloc, an area under constant threat. Recognizing the urgency of the situation, Rabbi Frank issued a letter to the factory workers, stating:

> To the workers in the armoring [factory], greetings:
>
> Given that the situation in Kfar Etzion and its surroundings is extremely dangerous, and in order to save lives it is urgent and necessary to provide them reinforcements immediately, and any delay in this matter endangers the lives of Jews—

---

28 Avraham Frank, *Tov va-Hesed Yirdefuni* (Jerusalem: Author's publication, 2007), 61 (Hebrew); testimony of Avraham Halperin, in *The Haganah in Jerusalem: Evidences and Reminiscences as Told by Members*, vol. 1 (Jerusalem: Havrei Hahaganah, 1973), 52-70 (Hebrew); Avraham Halperin, *Alon la-Haverim* (Jerusalem: Havrei Hahaganah, 1971), 18 (Hebrew); and Shmuel Hacohen Weingarten, "Rabbi Frank and the Haganah," *Alon la-Haverim* (Jerusalem: Havrei Hahaganah, 1971): 14-15 (Hebrew).

> In response to your inquiry, I hereby inform you that it is permitted, and indeed mandated by the principle of pikuach nefesh, to work and immediately prepare armored buses, even on the holy Sabbath. Whoever hastens to do this is praiseworthy.
>
> May the Blessed Name in His mercy have compassion on His people, deliver them from the cruel enemy, and swiftly rescue us from the clutches of all those who rise against us. May He avenge before our eyes the spilled blood of His servants.
>
> Awaiting imminent salvation,
>
> Tzvi Pesach Frank[29]

Rabbi Frank emphasized that the workers should focus solely on tasks directly related to the bus armoring and avoid unnecessary Sabbath desecration. He entrusted his close associate and Haganah member, Shmuel Hacohen Weingarten, to relay this directive to the workers, urging them to perform their work with diligence and care, ensuring that their efforts were strictly aligned with the life-saving mission.[30]

Rabbi Yosef Tzvi Dushinsky, Chief Rabbi of the Edah HaChareidis

Rabbi Dushinsky, the Chief Rabbi of the Edah HaChareidis,[31] was accepted by Agudath Israel and the members of the Edah HaChareidis,

---

29 Avraham Frank, *Tov va-Hesed Yirdefuni* (Jerusalem: Author's publication, 2007), 20-21 (Hebrew), which includes a photograph of Rabbi Frank's handwritten letter.

30 Shmuel Hacohen Weingarten, "Rabbi Frank and the Haganah," *Alon la-Haverim* (Jerusalem: Havrei Hahaganah, 1971): 15 (Hebrew).

31 Rabbi Yosef Tzvi Dushinsky, born in 1868 in Paks, Hungary, immigrated to Eretz Israel in 1933 after being appointed as the successor to Rabbi Chaim Yosef Sonnenfeld as Chief Rabbi of Haredi Jewry in Eretz Israel and

including Neturei Karta. During the siege and fighting, he remained in Jerusalem until his passing near the end of the war. His yeshiva was located in a building on Shmuel HaNavi Street, near Mandelbaum House, at the border of the Jewish territory facing Sheikh Jarrah. Rabbi Dushinsky had to leave his apartment in the yeshiva building and the yeshiva itself shortly after hostilities broke out in December 1947. He and his family moved to live in a room in the basement of the Babad Hotel, near the Sefra printing house, where Agudath Israel's newspaper, *Hayom*, was printed.[32]

His presence on the front lines led to his involvement in issues arising from the situation, according to his path and worldview. Despite Rabbi Dushinsky's opposition to recruiting yeshiva students, he compromised and signed, with the Chief Rabbis and other yeshiva heads, an agreement with the "Central Command for National Service" which outlined the rules for the recruitment and exemption of yeshiva students in Jerusalem;[33] for example, the encouragement call from Rabbis Herzog and Dushinsky to the city's residents after the security situation worsened with the Arab Legion joining the campaign on May

---

head of the rabbinical court for the Ashkenazi congregations in Jerusalem. He oversaw the institutions of the Edah HaChareidis in Jerusalem and represented both Agudath Israel and the Edah HaChareidis in dealings with the British authorities. In 1937, he was elected to the Moetzes Gedolei HaTorah (Council of Torah Sages). See Moshe Blau, *Upon Thy Walls, O Jerusalem* (Tel Aviv: Netzah Press, 1946), 98-99 (Hebrew); Avraham Fuchs, *Hungarian Yeshivot: From Grandeur to Holocaust* (Jerusalem: Kiryat Sefer, 1979), 485-486 (Hebrew); Aharon Sorasky, *Demuyot Hod* (Jerusalem, 1978), 133-138 (Hebrew); and, most recently, Menachem Keren-Kratz, "'From Watch to Watch': Rabbi Yosef Tzvi Dushinsky," in Benjamin Brown and Nissim Leon, eds., *The Gedolim: Leaders Who Shaped the Israeli Haredi Jewry* (Jerusalem: Magnes, 2017), 337-367 (Hebrew).

32 Menachem Porush, *The Chain of Generations in Turbulent Times*, vol. 4 (Jerusalem: Author's publication, 2001), 251 (Hebrew).

33 As noted earlier, this chapter does not address the discussion regarding the enlistment of yeshiva students.

19.³⁴ Rabbi Dushinsky was involved in discussions in various forums about Jerusalem's security and political status.

Rabbi Dushinsky, who opposed Zionism, expressed his opinion on the status of religion and the ultra-Orthodox in the State of Israel in mid-June 1948. He believed that given the balance of power, there was no chance that the state would accept the Torah as the basis for its life, and therefore, every effort should be made to convince its leaders to allow all religious communities to operate wherever they wish according to Torah laws and commandments and to maintain the traditional way of life. These communities should be clearly recognized and protected by the state's laws, as is the case in some European countries.³⁵ He worked to restore peace and quiet to Jerusalem. For this purpose, he met in mid-February 1948 with the Anglican bishop in Jerusalem in an attempt to draft a joint proclamation for the three religions.³⁶ On July 2, 1948, Rabbi Dushinsky held a meeting with Count Folke Bernadotte, the United Nations mediator, in Jerusalem. The meeting was also attended by two activists from Agudath Israel, Rabbi Moshe Glickman-Porush and Rabbi Yehuda Blau. Rabbi Dushinsky spoke with Bernadotte in German and asked him to act so that Jerusalem would be placed under international control as soon as possible, and for the fighting ceasefire to continue, thus saving the city from destruction and ruin. The delegation members left the meeting encouraged. Bernadotte referred to this meeting in his diary:³⁷

---

34 "The Call of Rabbis Herzog and Dushinsky," *HaYoman* (20 May 1948): 1 (Hebrew).

35 *HaYoman* (18 June 1948): 1 (Hebrew).

36 "Agudath Israel and the Bishop," *HaYom* (2 February 1948): 4 (Hebrew). Rabbi Dushinsky maintained good relations with the Anglican bishop as early as the 1930s. See Moshe Blau, *Upon Thy Walls, O Jerusalem* (Tel Aviv: Netzah Press, 1946), 112-113 (Hebrew).

37 *ha-Tsofeh* and *HaYoman* (4 July 1948); and Folke Bernadotte, *To Jerusalem* (Jerusalem: Achiasaf, 1952), 116-117 (Hebrew).

> "At around five in the morning, a delegation of rabbis with white beards came to see me. Their main wish was to convince me how important it was for Jerusalem to become an international city in the future. They spoke mostly in a pleasant manner - the ultra-Orthodox Jews are by no means as fanatical as, for example, the extreme Zionists. Since in my proposal I recommended making Jerusalem an Arab city, with the right to self-determination for the residents of the Jewish quarter, I did not see at that moment an opportunity to expand on this issue. I had to limit myself to merely expressing gratitude to the delegation for the information they provided me."

This meeting was contrary to the position of the Executive Committee and the National Center of Agudath Israel. Rabbi Yitzchak Meir Levin said at the meeting of the Provisional Government on July 4 that he had forbidden Gurman, the political secretary of Agudath Israel, to meet with Bernadotte. He read about the meeting of Rabbis Dushinsky, Moshe Glickman-Porush, and Yehuda Blau in the press, but he was confident that they only discussed the issue of Jerusalem and did nothing that could cause harm.[38] Dov Yosef, who was appointed in August 1948 as the military governor of Jerusalem, visited Rabbi Dushinsky on the 9th of the month and reported to him about his contacts with Bernadotte regarding the future of Jerusalem. The Rabbi raised the issue of electricity supply on Shabbat and the possibility of renewing burials on the Mount of Olives. Dov Yosef promised to look into these matters.[39]

---

38 "Minutes of the Provisional Government Meeting, 4 July 1948," in *Protocol of the Provisional Government Meeting*, vol. 4, pp. 27-28, Israel State Archives.

39 *HaYoman* (10 August 1948)(Hebrew).

Rabbi Avraham Mordechai Alter, the Rebbe of Ger

The Rebbe of Ger immigrated to the Land of Israel in 1940 and stayed in Jerusalem until his death in June 1948. Due to his illness and weakness, his involvement in public affairs was limited. His Hasidim, who were drafted, would seek his blessing before setting out on operational activities. The Rebbe asked his personal assistant, Shamai Ginzburg, to inform him before going on a mission so that he could pray for him.[40] On May 28, 1948, the residents of the Jewish Quarter in the Old City of Jerusalem surrendered. It was on a Friday afternoon, close to the start of Shabbat. The surrender agreement stipulated that the civilian population, which did not participate in the fighting, would be evacuated from the Old City to the New City through Zion Gate. During the evacuation, Shabbat began. Chanina Shiff, a Ger Hasid and Holocaust survivor, who was then a student at the Sfat Emet Yeshiva of Ger Hasidism and belonged to the yeshiva student battalion, "Tuvia Battalion" – assisted the refugees from the quarter. In a letter to the editorial staff of the newspaper HaModia, he described what happened:[41]

> "The yeshiva students, who belonged to the 'Tuvia Battalion,' went up to Mount Zion on Friday evening, in Shabbat clothes, to rescue the elderly and children who were transferred from the Old City. I still remember being sent by a student to enter the inner sanctum, at the holy residence of our master and teacher, the Rebbe of Ger, the 'Imrei Emet,' Rabbi Avraham Mordechai Alter, of blessed memory, to remind him that we are going to Mount Zion, which is a place of danger, and he blessed us with success. Likewise, we entered to the great genius, the rabbi from Brisk, Rabbi Yitzchak

---

40 Shammai Ginsburg, *Pirkei Zikhronot: From the Final Years of the [Gerrer] Rebbe, the Author of Imrei Emet* (Jerusalem, 1988), 28–29 (Hebrew).

41 Hanina Schiff, "Letter – Yeshiva Students Risked Their Lives for Rescue in the Old City," *HaModia* (23 May 1995)(Hebrew).

Ze'ev Soloveitchik, of blessed memory, who then lived near the 'Sfat Emet' Yeshiva, at his relative Reb Chaim Kronchik's house, of blessed memory. We asked if we were permitted to travel on Shabbat by buses, and he replied that it was permissible to also return by buses, as walking posed a danger due to the heavy shelling. When we arrived at Mount Zion, we discovered that there was no paved road to ascend the mountain. We had to almost crawl. Upon reaching the summit of the mountain, the residents joyfully welcomed us, knowing that we had come to assist them in reaching the city. We, the yeshiva students, carried the small children and the elderly in our arms and carefully led them down the mountain, lest they fall, Heaven forbid, because the treacherous path was extremely dangerous. With God's help, we were there for about two hours, as that was the agreement with the Legionnaires - a two-hour ceasefire. From there, we transferred them, also by vehicles, to Katamon, which was then empty because everyone had fled. Among them were the scholars Rabbi Velvel Mintzberg, of blessed memory, Rabbi Attiya, of blessed memory, and the elderly Hasid Reb Hersh Dudel, of blessed memory, and the righteous Hasid Reb Chanoch Yaakovowitz, of blessed memory, and others. Afterward, we returned to the yeshiva to pray the Shabbat prayer."

It should be noted that Rabbi Baruch Yitzchak Levin, the rabbi of the Mekor Chaim neighborhood in Jerusalem and head of the yeshiva located in the neighborhood, put the yeshiva building and the dormitory at the disposal of the Haganah forces stationed in the neighborhood to defend it. The Haganah men lived in the yeshiva, ate there, and the religious among them prayed there and received a daily Torah lesson from the rabbi. Weapons were hidden in caches in the yeshiva building and its surroundings.[42]

Involvement of Jerusalem's Rabbis in the War

When the war broke out, the rabbis were called upon to address the new security circumstances due to their spiritual leadership. This involvement stemmed from the expectations placed upon them by their communities and the need for religious guidance, including their self-perception regarding their role in leadership. Naturally, the rabbis' involvement in conflict settlements, especially in Jerusalem, was highly influential, and their voices were inscribed in the national narrative. Their activities were reflected in civil and military leadership discussions, personal assistance, halakhic guidance, and providing spiritual support. Their most interesting and prominent activities were in the Jewish quarters of mixed cities, where fierce fighting took place: the Jewish Quarter in Old Jerusalem, the Jewish Quarter in Safed, and the Jewish neighborhoods in Tiberias. In this article, the extensive and unique activities of Rabbi Avraham Dayrah Hald of Safed, the Hakham Bashi Rabbi Abulafia of the Old City in Tiberias, Rabbi Yitzhak Yedidya Frankel, Rabbi of the Florentin neighborhood, the Shapira neighborhood, and other neighborhoods on the border of Jaffa, will not be detailed.

The Chief Rabbis, Herzog and Uziel, Rabbi Dushinsky, and other rabbis who stayed in Jerusalem during the siege and fighting, were involved in dealing with the city's security, political, and civil issues. Rabbis from all sectors regularly addressed synagogue congregants on Shabbat about current matters, some on behalf of the Public Information Department

---

42 Yitzhak Kopp, *The 'Michmash' Battalion in the Battles for Jerusalem during the War of Independence* (Jerusalem: Ammunition Hill National Memorial Museum, 2003), 60-63 (Hebrew).

of the People's Guard.⁴³ On January 7, 1948, a discussion on Jerusalem's problems took place at Rabbi Herzog's home. Participants included Rabbi Uziel and members of the committee dealing with Jerusalem's affairs at the time: Moshe Shapira and Dov Yosef from the Jewish Agency's leadership, Yitzhak Ben-Zvi from the National Committee, and Chaim Salomon, head of the Jerusalem Community Council. The discussion focused on the situation of the Jewish Quarter in the Old City and the possibilities of assisting its besieged residents.⁴⁴ On January 29, 1948, Rabbi Uziel convened another discussion on Jerusalem's issues in his private office on HaSolel Street, to which representatives of all the political parties in Jerusalem were invited.⁴⁵

The management of Jerusalem's affairs by the Government of Israel, which sat in Tel Aviv, and by the "Jerusalem Committee," which served as its representative in Jerusalem, sparked widespread opposition among many circles in Jerusalem. These circles believed the city should be managed by its residents, who would better attend to its matters. The Chief Rabbis were among the initiators of this activity, driven by their desire to play an active role in managing Jerusalem differently. On June 21, Minister Rabbi Yitzchak Meir Levin of Agudath Israel, Rabbi Berlin and Rabbi Kowalski of the Mizrachi, and Minister Moshe Shapira, a member of the "Government Committee for Jerusalem," met at Rabbi Herzog's home, with Rabbi Dushinsky also attending. The meeting discussed the absence of a central and authorized authority to address Jerusalem's affairs and the need to establish a Supreme Council for

---

43 "In the Synagogues," *HaYom* (20 February 1948): 4 (Hebrew); "This Shabbat in the Synagogues," *HaYom* (12 March 1948): 5 (Hebrew); and *HaYom* (19 March 1948): 4 (Hebrew).

44 *ha-Tsofeh* (11 January 1948)(Hebrew).

45 Letter from the Sephardic Community Council in Jerusalem to the Mizrachi World Center in Jerusalem, "Discussion and Consultation on Jerusalem Affairs," 27 January 1948, The Archive of Religious Zionism, Folder 287.

Jerusalem under the Chief Rabbis' authority, which would determine the city's future.[46]

During the first truce, the two Chief Rabbis traveled to Tel Aviv, seizing the opportunity to vigorously promote Jerusalem's critical interests and future status. As the truce neared its end, they returned to Jerusalem.[47] On June 28, a pivotal gathering convened at the home of Rabbi Meir Berlin, the president of the Mizrachi movement, drawing approximately 50 individuals from diverse sectors of the city. The attendees included prominent rabbis from Agudat Yisrael and Mizrachi, representatives of political factions and communal organizations, institutional leaders, and influential figures in the economic sphere. Rabbi Berlin opened the assembly by reporting on his discussions with the Chief Rabbis and Rabbi Dushinsky, all of whom staunchly maintained that surrender was unthinkable, and that the fight for Jerusalem must continue. They expressed their unwavering commitment to actively shaping the city's future. The assembly reflected a clash of convictions. Some advocated for recognizing Jerusalem as an international city, while others vehemently opposed such a concession. Many placed their hopes in the strength of the security forces, but a vocal minority revealed alarming defeatist sentiments. For example, Aharon Chayot, a leading member of the importers' and wholesalers' organization in Jerusalem and the treasurer of the Etz Chaim Yeshiva, declared the war to be lost and urged negotiating with the Arabs to save even a single Jewish life. Rabbi Tikochinsky, head of the Etz Chaim Yeshiva, warned of a growing inclination among the Haredi public to capitulate and raise a white flag if the city faced renewed bombardment. Rabbi Berlin, however, fiercely denounced such defeatism, proclaiming that he would not even sit in

---

46 "In the Matters of Jerusalem: A Meeting on Jerusalem Affairs," *HaYom* (2 June 1948): 2 (Hebrew); *HaYoman* (22 June 1948)(Hebrew); "The Future of Jerusalem," *Kol Yisrael* (24 June 1948)(Hebrew); "Rabbinical Committee on Jerusalem Affairs," *Davar* (28 June 1948)(Hebrew).

47 "In the Matters of Jerusalem: Encouragement," *HaYom* (5 July 1948): 2 (Hebrew). The Chief Rabbis returned to Jerusalem on 1 July 1948.

a public assembly with those who entertained thoughts of surrender. Echoing this stance, Simcha Isarov emphatically declared, "We have no dealings with defeatists." As the assembly concluded, a committee was elected to act decisively on behalf of the participants. Rabbi Berlin was appointed chair, with Rabbi Zwebner serving as coordinator, alongside five representatives from various sectors, including Rabbi Yehuda Blau of Agudat Yisrael. This committee was charged with presenting the assembly's resolute demands to the government of Israel.[48]

Shmuel Hacohen Weingarten, who participated in the meeting at Rabbi Berlin's home, decided to call a meeting of Jerusalem's rabbis to express their opposition to the internationalization of the city. He convinced Rabbi Meir Stolovitz, Rabbi of the Zikhron Moshe neighborhood, who was the chairman of the Association of Rabbis and Halakhic Authorities in Jerusalem, to call a meeting of the rabbis and teachers in Jerusalem. This meeting was held on July 26 at the Central Committee Building for the Knesset Yisrael on Rabbi Kook Street, with many of the neighborhood rabbis and teachers in Jerusalem participating. Those who could not attend sent their opinions in writing. The meeting's chairman was Rabbi Yosef Gershon Horowitz, Rabbi of the Meah Shearim neighborhood. At the end of the discussion, these decisions were formulated:[49]

1. Profound joy at the establishment of the State of Israel and heartfelt gratitude to the Rock of Israel for this historic milestone.

2. Sincere blessings and unreserved admiration for the Israel Defense Forces (IDF) for their dedication and sacrifice.

---

48 Protocol of the Meeting, 28 June 1948, file 26/1, The Archive of Religious Zionism.

49 Shmuel HaKohen Weingarten, "The Opinions of Jerusalem's Rabbis During the War of Independence: 'Jerusalem Is the Heart of the Nation and the Capital of the State of Israel,'" *ha-Tsofeh* (21 September 1979) (Hebrew); "Jerusalem's Rabbis Demand Its Inclusion in the State of Israel," *Ha Yom* (7 July 1948): 1 (Hebrew).

3. A fervent aspiration that the eternal laws of the Torah will be firmly enshrined within the legislative framework of the state.

4. A solemn declaration: "It is a sacred and unwavering obligation, rooted in our holy Torah, to ensure that the holy city of Jerusalem—the heart of our nation and its eternal capital—be fully included within the sovereign borders of the State of Israel. We resolutely call upon the government to restore Jerusalem to its rightful glory and position as the capital of Israel and the seat of its sovereignty."

5. An unequivocal demand to grant the Chief Rabbis and Rabbi Frank, the Rabbi of Jerusalem, an active and pivotal role in all deliberations concerning the future of Jerusalem.

6. A heartfelt expression of esteem for the Minister of Religious Affairs for steadfastly upholding and advancing the values of Torah and Judaism within the governance of the state.

THE JEWISH QUARTER IN THE OLD CITY OF JERUSALEM

In the mid-1940s, Avraham Halperin, commander of the Jewish Quarter, sought to establish a central silik—a hidden weapons cache—in a room adjacent to one of the Sephardic synagogues. However, the synagogue caretakers he approached hesitated, expressing reluctance to grant their approval. Determined to resolve the issue, Halperin turned to Rabbi Ben-Zion Meir Hai Uziel, presenting the matter directly to him. Rabbi Uziel promptly summoned the gabbaim and firmly instructed them to comply with Halperin's directives without reservation. Within days, the silik was successfully constructed, and the weapons it concealed later proved instrumental in arming the defenders of the Quarter during the War of Independence.[50]

Rabbi Yitzchak Avigdor Orenstein, a native of Jerusalem and a student of its yeshivot, was a resident of the Jewish Quarter. He served

---

50 Avraham Halperin, "From Those Days (Events and Episodes)," *Alon la-Haverim* (Jerusalem: Havrei Hahaganah, 1971): 19 (Hebrew).

as the rabbi responsible for the Western Wall on behalf of the national institutions and the Chief Rabbinate, as well as the director of Kollel Chabad in the Land of Israel. At the start of the siege, he was outside the Quarter and was unable to return due to British opposition. His home in the Quarter housed a position for members of the Haganah until the British demolished it on January 25, 1948.[51] It was only on February 11, 1948, that the British authorities allowed him to return to the Quarter. In March 1948, Rabbi Orenstein was appointed to oversee the civilian affairs of the Quarter and was entrusted with managing all essential aspects of life for the residents under siege. All his sons were enlisted and fought on various fronts, one of them, Avraham, serving as a commander in one of the two sections of the Quarter. He was responsible for the burial of fallen fighters and residents of the besieged Quarter in a cemetery consecrated in the courtyard of the Batei Mahase. On May 23, Rabbi Yitzchak Avigdor Orenstein and his wife, Mushka-Liba, were killed by shrapnel from a shell. After his death, he was posthumously enlisted and officially recognized as a fallen member of the Israeli defense establishment.

The two rabbis of the Jewish Quarter, Rabbi Yisrael Ze'ev Mintzberg (age 76), who served as the Ashkenazi rabbi of the Quarter during the siege and fighting, and Rabbi Ben-Zion Hazzan (age 63), one of the rabbis of the Sephardic Porat Yosef Yeshiva, sent a telegram on May 22 to Rabbi Herzog and Yitzhak Ben-Zvi, describing the dire situation in the Quarter: "The settlement is on the verge of massacre. On behalf of the population, we issue a desperate plea. The synagogues have been destroyed, and all the Torah scrolls within them have been burned. [Details of the synagogues] 'Misgav LaDan' is under a barrage of gunfire and shelling. Shake the supreme institutions and the entire world to save us."[52] This telegram prompted discussions among Jerusalem's civic

---

51 Aharon Liron, *The Old City of Jerusalem Under Siege and in Battle* (Tel Aviv: Maarachot and Ministry of Defense, 1985), 59-62 (Hebrew).

52 David Ben-Gurion, *The War Diary*, vol. 2 (Tel Aviv: Ministry of Defense, 1983), 451 [3 May 1948] (Hebrew).

and rabbinic leadership about how to assist the Quarter. The contents of the telegram were conveyed that same day to David Ben-Gurion by Chaim Herzog. Ben-Gurion noted in his diary: "There are many peace-seekers—meaning advocates of surrender—pressuring Rabbi [Yitzhak Isaac Halevi] Herzog."[53]

On the morning of Friday, May 28, 1948, Rabbis Mintzberg and Hazan went out to the enemy lines under a white flag to initiate negotiations aimed at ending the fighting in the Jewish Quarter. This mission was undertaken on their own initiative. The forces of the Arab Legion and irregular fighters were very close to the cellars where the civilian population was hiding, and there was grave concern that continued fighting would result in a massacre. The rabbis attempted several times to approach the Arab lines, but the defenders of the Quarter prevented them. Ultimately, the commander of the Quarter approved their mission and instructed them on how to negotiate for a ceasefire, emphasizing that it was to be a negotiation for a truce, not for surrender.[54]

Abdullah al-Tal, the commander of the Arab forces with whom the rabbis sought to negotiate, refused to discuss a ceasefire and demanded surrender. He sent Rabbi Ben-Zion Hazan to inform the Quarter's command of his terms, while holding Rabbi Mintzberg as a hostage.[55] Years later, Rabbi Mintzberg recounted this mission, which he had undertaken voluntarily. According to his account, heavy fighting continued even after the burials of the Quarter's residents and fighters. On May 25, Rabbi Mintzberg approached the commander

---

53 Ibid. Chaim Herzog, the son of Rabbi Yitzhak Isaac Halevi Herzog, served as the head of the Security Department in the Jewish Agency and as a senior liaison officer with the British and other parties in Jerusalem.

54 Testimony of Moshe Rusnak, file 922/75, Israel State Archives, p. 291, item 1960, pp. 7–29.

55 Abdullah al-Tal, *Memoirs*, trans. Yehoshua Halamish (IDF: Maarachot, 1960), 103–104 (Hebrew); John Roy Carlson, *From Cairo to Damascus: With the Arab Armies Against Israel* (Jerusalem: Achiasaf, 1952), 229 (Hebrew).

of the Quarter and asked, "What will be the end of this?" He was told that reinforcements had been promised. When it became clear that no reinforcements would arrive, a meeting of the Quarter's elders—both Sephardic and Ashkenazi—was held on May 26 at Rabbi Mintzberg's home, with a representative of the Quarter's command also present. After the meeting, a shell exploded on the steps of his house, damaging Rabbi Mintzberg's hearing. The following day, they met with the commander of the Quarter, and it was decided to surrender. Rabbi Mintzberg persuaded Rabbi Ben-Zion Hazan to join him in going to the enemy lines under a white flag. Despite his family's pleas, Rabbi Mintzberg declared, "I am offering my life for the sake of all of Israel." The two went out several times, waving the white flag, but the gunfire did not cease, and Rabbi Hazan was lightly wounded. Only after Rabbi Hazan shouted in Arabic to the Arab fighters did the shooting stop, and they were led to the Arab forces' commander. The commander sent Rabbi Hazan back to the Quarter's command to summon the commander of the Quarter to surrender, while Rabbi Mintzberg remained a hostage until representatives of the Quarter arrived to negotiate the terms of the surrender.[56] Abdullah al-Tal, the commander of the Arab forces fighting in the Quarter, described in his memoirs how Rabbi Mintzberg, whom he referred to as the "Polish rabbi," immersed himself in deep Torah study while in their custody, until Rabbi Hazan returned from his mission to the Quarter's commander.[57] Approximately a month after the surrender of the Quarter, Rabbi Ben-Zion Hazan spoke about his considerations and feelings during those critical moments.[58]

> "I was entrusted with the sad duty of approaching the enemy lines and raising a flag of surrender. It was the

---

56 Aharon Sorasky, *Demuyot Hod* (Jerusalem, 1978), 227-228 (Hebrew).

57 Abdullah al-Tal, *Memoirs*, trans. Yehoshua Halamish (IDF: Maarachot, 1960), 103–104 (Hebrew).

58 Yonah Cohen, "The Last Fighters in the Old City," *ha-Tsofeh* (28 June 1948): 2 (Hebrew).

bitterest day of my life. Right before my eyes, on my way to fulfill my mission to save whatever could be saved from the fire, my beloved son was injured. It was not easy to make the bitter decision. For half a year, the Old City waged a David and Goliath war. Unfortunately, this time, the miracle did not happen.

We, the elders, could no longer stand idly by and see the best of the youth sacrificing their lives on the altar of the homeland. The wounded multiplied, and the fallen were not brought to Jewish burial. We cried out to the community, the Diaspora, and the whole world. We warned of the desecration of the sacred, the destruction of our holy places, the shelling of hospitals and residences, the abuse of the fallen and wounded. We struggled to bring the world to understand the enemy's savagery, but the world kept silent. The community comforted us and promised help and reinforcements. We knew that the heart of the entire community and the people beat with the heart of the defenders of the walls of Jerusalem, but we could no longer endure.

Four times I was on my way to the enemy lines with the white flag in my hand, and four times I returned. Our brave young men, who had not yet known their commander's order, stopped me, took the flag from my hand, and tore it to pieces. It took a special armed guard to escort us, me and the elderly Rabbi Mintzberg, my fate-sharing companion, otherwise, I am sure they would have torn us to shreds. The hours of negotiation were like a bitter exile to us. The seven circles of hell are nothing compared to these infernal tortures of exchanges with Abdullah's representatives, despite the courtesy and respect they showed us. My only consolation was that I succeeded in saving almost all the residents of the Old City.

The mission these two rabbis took upon themselves, to walk toward the enemy lines during combat, involved great personal risk and required courage and determination. The residents of the Quarter knew the fate of the residents of Kfar Etzion after their surrender about two weeks earlier. The two rabbis also had to stand before their families' pleas not to endanger themselves. An American journalist present at their arrival described it in a book he wrote several years later:[59]

> The flag was carried by a patriarchal figure of an old rabbi. Dressed in black, his long beard hair fluttered wildly as he walked upright, leaning on his cane. Next to Rabbi Ben-Zion Chazan, seventy-six years old, tall and holding his head high like a man who knows no fear, walked Rabbi Yisrael Ze'ev Mintzberg, thin, short, fearful. His sad eyes were set in pale, furrowed faces. Mintzberg walked in small, quick steps, occasionally turning his head backward. The two, surrounded by legionnaires, looked as if they had just emerged from a dark cellar. The Legion soldiers showed no signs of hostility or gloating. However, the representatives of the 'Muslim Brotherhood' from Egypt, Syria, and Palestine grumbled about the lenient treatment of the Jewish emissaries, 'The Jews deserve only this...' they said, making a gesture around their neck.

The Legion soldiers, under the command of Abdullah el-Tell, treated the two rabbis with respect and courtesy.[60] Eventually, officials from the Jewish Quarter's headquarters, along with Mordechai Hacohen Weingarten, the head of the Quarter, joined the negotiations. Moshe Rusnak, the Quarter commander, signed the surrender agreement.

59 John Roy Carlson, *From Cairo to Damascus*, trans. Shalom Rosenfeld (Jerusalem: Achiasaf, 1952), 228-229 (Hebrew).

60 Puah Steiner, *The Good Mountain: The Life and Work of Rabbi Shlomo Z. Min-Hahar* (Jerusalem: Tzvi Publishing Network, 2008), 199-200 (Hebrew).

Approximately 340 fighters and residents of the Quarter, including those with minor injuries, were taken as prisoners to the Kingdom of Jordan. The remaining residents of the Quarter were transported to New Jerusalem through Zion Gate and housed in the Katamon neighborhood, which had been vacated by its Arab residents about a month earlier.[61]

Rabbis' Attitude Towards Population Evacuation and Surrender

Many rabbis chose to remain within their communities, even in perilous situations, viewing it as a duty inherent to their role and a personal example expected of public leaders. Rabbi Aryeh Levine's home in the Mishkenot neighborhood suffered severe damage during a bombing. Yehoshua Israeli, a member of Lehi, approached Rabbi Levine and offered to relocate him and his family to safety. Rabbi Levine refused, fearing that his departure would leave the neighborhood's residents without encouragement and support during their long hours in bomb shelters. Israeli brought food to Rabbi Levine, but he distributed it to his neighbors, keeping none for himself.[62]

Rabbi Dushinsky was compelled to leave Jerusalem for several weeks and relocate to the Tel Aviv area for medical reasons. A few days before Rosh Hashanah 5709, he sent a letter of blessing to the residents of Jerusalem, writing: "This was from God. Following the doctors' advice to seek healing, and with God's will, I am compelled by a mitzvah matter to be far from the place most dear to me—my place of rest and the aspiration of my spirit—Jerusalem, the holy city, the city of beauty, during these holy days approaching us for good." Rabbi Dushinsky

---

61 For details regarding the surrender, see Moshe Ehrenwald, *Siege within Siege: The Jewish Quarter in the Old City of Jerusalem During the War of Independence* (Sede Boqer: Ben-Gurion Research Institute, 2004), 229-241 (Hebrew).

62 Simcha Raz, *Tzaddik Yesod Olam: The Life of Rabbi Aryeh Levine* (Jerusalem: Yerid HaSfarim, 1996), 298 (Hebrew).

returned to Jerusalem on October 10, 1948, just before Yom Kippur 5709,[63] and passed away a few days later, on the eve of Sukkot.

Rabbis, like other civilian and military leaders, also grappled with the question of whether to evacuate non-combatant civilians from areas of conflict. At times, they had to address the possibility of surrender as well. In the first months following the adoption of the Partition Plan, the leadership of the Jewish Yishuv adhered to a policy of non-evacuation of settlements, including those located outside the boundaries outlined in the Partition Plan. Yisrael Galili, the head of the *Haganah*'s National Command, clarified this policy during a commanders' meeting on January 20, 1948: "*The decision is to hold all settlements. We do not ignore the fact that this decision means dispersing forces, tying up personnel and weapons for defensive positions, and bearing a heavy burden in terms of supply and transportation [...]. However, this decision is based on thoroughly examined political and military considerations.*"[64] Particular emphasis was placed on avoiding the evacuation of areas in Jerusalem. In David Ben-Gurion's directives to David Shaltiel upon his appointment as Jerusalem District Commander on January 31, 1948, Ben-Gurion stated: "*Do not allow any Jewish neighborhood to be abandoned. Demand that residents remain. If anyone leaves, bring others in [to replace them].*" Regarding settlements on Jerusalem's periphery, Ben-Gurion noted: "*Every single point must be held and its security reinforced, but a plan should be prepared for evacuating children and women when necessary.*"[65] He reiterated this stance during a Security Committee meeting on February 3, stating: "*Theoretically, should the need arise to evacuate certain points, it is unthinkable to consider evacuating Jerusalem.*" In contrast, policies regarding other areas were

63 *HaYoman* (8–11 October 1948)(Hebrew).

64 Zerubavel Gilad and Matti Megged, eds., *The Palmach Book*, vol. 2 (Tel Aviv: Palmach Veterans Organization, Hakibbutz Hameuchad Publishing, 1956), xviii (Hebrew).

65 David Ben-Gurion, *The War Diary*, vol. 1 (Tel-Aviv: Ministry of Defense, 1984), 196-197, 208 (Hebrew); "The Line of Action in Jerusalem," file 186, Israel State Archives.

more flexible. For example, in a Security Committee meeting on February 24, Galili stated: *"We found it appropriate to decide on the transfer of children from five settlements on the northern border [...]. These are communities that could be targeted from across the border. The children will be relocated primarily to the Jezreel Valley."*[66]

The evacuation was not carried out in most locations until the invasion by Arab states following the end of the British Mandate. One of the areas from which children and most women were evacuated as early as June 7, 1948, was the besieged Gush Etzion. There was ongoing debate about the benefits of evacuation, as David Ben-Gurion noted in his remarks to the Provisional State Council on May 12, 1948: "There will be places where it will be necessary to evacuate women and children because there is no place safe enough for them."[67]

Despite the policy of the settlement leadership, proposals to evacuate the non-combatant population from Jerusalem occasionally arose. For example, senior members of the political department of the Jewish Agency in Jerusalem - Chaim Berman, Walter Eytan, Chaim Herzog, and Eliahu Sasson - proposed this in a telegram sent on March 30 to their department head, Moshe Sharett, who was in New York at the time. Eliahu Dobkin said at a Jewish Agency executive meeting on April 21: "There are activists who claim that it is essential to remove 10,000 children from Jerusalem and evacuate Talpiot, the university, Hadassah [on Mount Scopus], and Atarot." These proposals were not accepted by

---

[66] Protocols of the Security Committee Meetings, 3–24 February 1948, file S25/9346, Central Zionist Archives.

[67] Description of the evacuation from Gush Etzion under British military escort, David Ben-Gurion, *The War Diary*, vol. 1 (Tel-Aviv: Ministry of Defense, 1984), 121 (Hebrew); protocol of the discussion held on 12 May 1948, *Protocols of the Meetings of the People's Administration*, 18 April–13 May 1948, Israel State Archives.

the settlement leadership, and Sharett rejected the proposal of the four senior department members.[68]

The prolonged siege on Jerusalem caused shortages of the most essential goods, and the fighting throughout the city resulted in many casualties among the fighters (most of whom were city residents) and the civilian population. There were serious concerns about Jerusalem's ability to hold out for long. These feelings were shared by the military and civilian leadership in the city. Chaim Salomon, chairman of the Jerusalem Community Committee, expressed his pressures and anxieties about the situation at the start of the war. In a telegram sent to Ben-Gurion, it was said:

> "The severity of the situation in the city is indescribable. More than two thousand people have been trapped in the Old City since yesterday morning without bread. [...] If quick assistance is not provided to them, people, women, and children will perish from hunger. [...] More than twenty bodies of the murdered [...] lie in the hospital and cannot be buried. [...] From every corner of the city, residents want to leave their homes. More than one hundred and fifty families have yet to be housed. This is the situation in our capital city. Take counsel - hasten assistance."

When there was no response, he sent another letter the next day, stating: "If I do not receive a reply tonight to this letter and quick assistance, I will leave the community and announce it publicly. Like all of you, you have left Jerusalem. [...] The Old City has been closed

---

68 Telegram from Berman, Eitan, Herzog, and Sasson in Jerusalem to Sharett, 30 March 1948, file S25/2558, Central Zionist Archives; "Moshe Sharett, 1 April 1948, file S100/53, protocol of the Jewish Agency Executive discussion," in Gedalia Yogev, ed., *Political and Diplomatic Documents: December 1947 – May 1948* (Jerusalem: Israel State Archives and the Central Zionist Archives, 1980), 533 [document 339] (Hebrew); Moshe Sharett and Eliahu Sasson (4 April 1948)(Hebrew).

to us for three days. We cannot provide them with food, and they are literally starving to death. [...] At the Jewish Agency, there is no one to turn to. The Haganah does not want to break into the Old City, and the government promises but has not fulfilled its promises. Disaster is about to break out at any moment. [...] This is your last warning."[69]

At the end of March, David Shaltiel wrote to Ben-Gurion, Galili, Dori, and Yadin: "I must inform you that if we do not evacuate the isolated places and if you do not send us substantial reinforcements in commanders, people, weapons, armor, and supplies, and if the city remains without food and people capable of organizing the food distribution (not amateur activists), Jerusalem will not hold out even until May 15."[70] On April 3, the British expressed their willingness to mediate between the parties to achieve a ceasefire. Yitzhak Ben-Zvi, the President of the National Committee, who was in Jerusalem, demanded a response to the High Commissioner's call for a truce and wrote:[71]

---

69 Salomon requested that his letters be delivered immediately to Ben-Gurion and not be published. Letter from Chaim Salomon to Ben-Gurion, 31 December 1947 – 1 January 1948, file J2/3800, Jerusalem Municipal Archives.

70 The boundaries of the Jerusalem sector were as follows: the Dead Sea to the east, Atarot and Neve Yaakov to the north, Sha'ar HaGai and Hartuv to the west, and Gush Etzion to the south. Most of the settlements on the periphery of Jerusalem were isolated, and a significant portion of the limited forces in the Jerusalem District were stationed in these disconnected locations. Shaltiel proposed evacuating the isolated settlements and concentrating all forces and their weaponry on the defense of the city itself. However, his request was denied due to the prevailing policy of not evacuating settlements. See David (Shaltiel) to Amitei (Ben-Gurion), Dan, Hillel, and Yizin, correspondence dated March 8, 1948, file 80/50/25, IDF Archive.

71 Letter from Yitzhak Ben-Zvi to the Members of the Jewish Agency Executive, 5 April 1948, "On the Temporary Ceasefire in Light of the Situation in Jerusalem," in Gedalia Yogev, ed., *Political and Diplomatic Documents: December 1947 – May 1948* (Jerusalem: Israel State Archives

"[...] and hunger has already begun to manifest in Jerusalem, [...] all of Jerusalem is in the same state as the Old City. [...] Let us not forget that half of the city's residents belong to the Sephardic communities, among whom there has long been a nest of separatism, and even among the Ashkenazi settlement, half are dragged after the Agudah, etc. All these are elements among whom national discipline is lacking, and demoralization has already begun - let us not ignore it. There has been sharp incitement against the institutions, and there have already been threats to establish separate institutions and even attempts to go out with white flags and ask for mercy from the governor and the Arabs. [...] There is no certainty that we will hold out on this front as the distress grows. We need a truce, first and foremost for the salvation of Jerusalem. [...] Without additional people, supplies, and weapons, we cannot stand, and we are facing a fatal decision against us in Jerusalem, a decision that heralds destruction and ruin for the Jewish settlement in Jerusalem."

Eliahu Dobkin, a member of the Jewish Agency Executive, who had returned from Jerusalem to Tel Aviv at the start of the first truce, gave an overview of Jerusalem's situation during a meeting of the Mapai Secretariat and called for action to prevent the phenomenon of fleeing. In his remarks, he stated:[72] "Within the Jerusalemite Yishuv, not only among the circles of Agudath Israel and those lagging behind, such as the Sephardi communities, there were manifestations of terrible and horrifying defeatism [...]. On several occasions, people came to us [to him and Zalman Aran] and suggested surrender. I do not wish to name

and the Central Zionist Archives, 1980), 559-561 [document 344] (Hebrew).

72 Remarks by Eliahu Dobkin, protocol of the Mapai Secretariat meeting, 13 June 1948, p. 18, Labor Movement Archive.

who proposed surrender; you would be shocked to hear the names." He further added: "If you ask me what the Jews of Jerusalem want now [...], you must understand that every Jew in Jerusalem would tell you—they want to flee. Of course, there will be the impoverished by the Kotel who will not want to flee. I assume even Ben-Zvi does not want to flee. But if we are to speak about the dream of the Jew in Jerusalem, you must know—they dream of leaving."

The issue of evacuation arose among Jerusalem's rabbis as well, particularly after the intensification of fighting and the entry of Legion forces into the battle for the city on the morning of May 19. On May 12, Rabbi Uziel responded to a request from Rabbis Minzberg and Chazan, the rabbis of the Jewish Quarter, seeking his opinion on whether women and children should be evacuated from the Quarter:[73]

> "Your letter from the fourth day of the intermediate days of the festival [Chol HaMoed] was read with my full attention. I was unable to respond until now, and I ask for your forgiveness. Now, I am honored to inform you: My heart and soul are with you and with all those under siege within the walls of Jerusalem, the holy and revered city, praying fervently to God, who dwells in Zion and has chosen Jerusalem, for your swift redemption. My concern grew greatly during the days when transportation ceased until, by God's grace, the last convoy departed. Surely, you have received news of the negotiations for a ceasefire in Jerusalem. My confidence in the Rock of our Salvation is strong—that this will end well, and all barriers of the siege will be removed. At present, there is a ceasefire in Jerusalem, and therefore, there is no need to relocate the women and children outside of Jerusalem. Such an action would cause great

---

73 Shmuel Katz and Ezra Barnea, eds., *Sefer Mikhmanei Uziel*, vol. 5 (Jerusalem: The Committee for the Publication of the Writings of Rav Uziel, 2004), 561-562 (Hebrew), based on file P2/888/5, Central Zionist Archives.

sorrow to both the men and their wives and children, being uprooted from their homes. Instead, we should all lift our eyes and hearts to our Father in Heaven, who will once again have mercy upon us, ensuring that no destruction or calamity will be heard within our borders, and that light will shine upon all the people of Israel, bringing peace and comfort."

Rabbi Uziel wrote in his personal diary on June 15:

"I declined the invitation to the World Jewish Congress to be held in Zurich on July 22, as I could not find any justification to leave the Land of Israel during these times, when it is our collective duty to fulfill the verse, 'I am with him in distress' (Psalms 91:15)."[74]

Rabbi Herzog, who regularly assisted the besieged Jewish Quarter in the Old City, was very concerned about the fate of its residents following the heavy attacks on it from May 16. On the 17th, he wrote to Ben-Gurion:[75]

"Assuming that the chances of success in the Old City are slim, according to estimates (may this assumption have no basis)! I suggest that I contact the Christian religious leaders here to approach Amman, which is the main decider among the Arabs, to ask them, in the name of religion, since the Jewish residents of the Old City, who are all non-combatants, are a holy group maintaining the religious connection between the Holy City and the people of Israel, to grant them guaranteed

---

74   Shmuel Katz and Ezra Barnea, eds., *Sefer Mikhmanei Uziel*, vol. 6 (Jerusalem: The Committee for the Publication of the Writings of Rav Uziel, 2004), 687 [8 Sivan 5708] (Hebrew).

75   Letter from Rabbi Isaac Isaac Halevi Herzog to David Ben-Gurion, 17 May 1948, file S44/499, Central Zionist Archives.

free passage from the Old City to the Jewish area in the New City."

Rabbi Herzog was prepared to consider relinquishing the Jewish Quarter due to concerns for the lives of its residents if the fighting there were to continue. It can be assumed that Rabbi Herzog was aware of the content of the desperate telegrams sent from the Quarter's headquarters on the afternoon of May 16, which raised the possibility of surrender. At 2:20 PM, a telegram was sent to the Moriah Battalion: "We are under constant bombardment and attack. What is the approach—political or military?" The response they received was: "We are addressing this militarily. Hold your ground at all costs." By 4:20 PM, another message came from the Quarter: "They are blowing up house by house. We cannot hold on for even one more minute. At the very least, tell us how to surrender. This is the result of three years of neglect." The massive attack on the Quarter continued the following day, during which the Arab forces succeeded in capturing part of it.[76]

The situation of the Jewish Quarter and its residents also worried the rabbis of Agudath Israel. Menachem Porush, an activist of Agudath Israel, contacted Rabbi Berlin, the president of the Mizrachi, on May 20 and stated that he was speaking on behalf of Rabbis Dushinsky and Yitzchak Ze'ev Soloveitchik. Porush reported that a telegram was received from the rabbis of the Quarter, Rabbi Mintzberg and Rabbi Chazan, "crying out for help and demanding the evacuation of the Old City," and asked Rabbi Berlin to use his influence with the Jewish Agency's leadership to agree to it. Rabbi Berlin approached Minister Yitzhak Gruenbaum, a member of the Jewish Agency executive, who was in Jerusalem and relayed Porush's message to him. Gruenbaum replied that this matter had already been raised with King Abdullah, and in light of his response,

---

76 Telegrams from the Old City to the Moriah Battalion (responsible for the quarter), file 500/48–52, May 16–17, 1948, Israel State Archives; Aharon Liron, *The Old City of Jerusalem Under Siege and in Battle* (Tel Aviv: Maarachot and Ministry of Defense, 1985), 191-277 (Hebrew), providing a detailed account of the battles in the quarter from May 7–16.

there was no place for the demand to evacuate the Quarter. Gruenbaum added that Agudath Israel activists were causing panic, and this should not be done. On May 21, Agudath Israel members, including Menachem Porush, met at Rabbi Herzog's home with Dov Yosef to discuss the matter, but no conclusions were reached. A discussion was held on the morning of May 23, attended by the Chief Rabbis Herzog and Uziel, Rabbi Dushinsky, Dov Yosef, Yitzhak Ben-Zvi, Chaim Solomon, and Agudath Israel members—Dr. Buxbaum, Porush, Yehuda Blau, Mokotovsky, Raphel Katzenellenbogen, and others. They also waited for Rabbi Soloveitchik, but he did not attend (the reason for his absence is unknown). Rabbi Berlin suggested establishing a special committee that included the Chief Rabbis and Rabbi Dushinsky to manage the political affairs of Jerusalem. Dov Yosef opposed this, explaining that it was the government's role, and they would not relinquish it. It was decided to draft a telegram, signed by the Chief Rabbis, addressed to the five major powers, the UN, and the international press. The telegram would describe the dire situation in Jerusalem, the harm to its civilians and holy places, and the demand for an immediate ceasefire. It was agreed that the final version of the telegram would be drafted by the Chief Rabbis, Rabbi Dushinsky, Rabbi Berlin, and Dr. Buxbaum from Agudath Israel. Meanwhile, residents who had left the Jewish Quarter arrived and demanded its immediate evacuation. Following Rabbi Berlin's request, Shaltiel sent his adjutant to the meeting, who stated that the Haganah forces would not leave the Old City due to its strategic importance. He noted that they had decided to break into the Quarter and evacuate its residents. The rabbis, including Rabbi Dushinsky, agreed that they had no place to interfere in military considerations and hoped that the Haganah would succeed in implementing their plan.[77]

At a meeting held at Rabbi Berlin's home on June 28, attended by rabbis from various circles, party representatives, communities, and

---

77 Rabbi Meir Berlin, "On the Situation in Jerusalem and the Old City," file 26/2, The Archive of Religious Zionism. Although undated, the document was written by Rabbi Berlin close to the time of the events.

different organizations, Rabbi Tikochinsky, head of the Etz Chaim Yeshiva, suggested allowing anyone who wants to leave Jerusalem, especially women and children, who might be better off evacuating the city entirely.[78] With the opening of the "Burma Road" and improved access to leave Jerusalem during the first truce, Rabbi Yonah Merzbach, a leader of the Kol Torah Yeshiva and Agudath Israel activist, composed an opinion on leaving Jerusalem under the title "Descent":[79]

> "Every person is entitled to do what they can to save themselves, and they would give everything they have for their soul. Nevertheless, the law is not according to one who interprets scripture for himself. And the law sets a limit on saving oneself. What is this text about? About all those who make many calculations and leave Jerusalem. Indeed, your captors are not driven away because of the world's need, but the captive himself is allowed to escape and need not worry about others.

If someone's heart tells them they cannot withstand the bonds of war and must save their life—let them do what their heart desires, as the elders of the parties did at first, those who worried about themselves, and others followed. The future will show if they are right or not. But our great ones have already spoken on this question, and these are their words: if they can save with their body and money, Heaven forbid, let them not withhold themselves and withdraw from the public's distress and not see Zion's comfort. If, Heaven forbid, there is no result from them, then they said not to stand in a place of danger.

---

78 Protocol of the discussion, 8 June 1948, file 26/1, The Archive of Religious Zionism.

79 *HaYoman* (7 July 1948): 2 (Hebrew). Rabbi Merzbach served as a rabbi in Germany while also pursuing studies in mathematics, physics, and astronomy at the University of Marburg, where he earned his doctorate. His youngest son enlisted in the Haganah and served in Company A of Battalion 62 (the Beit-Hadaron Battalion).

People responsible for others, people whose personality, role, wealth, etc., can ease others' suffering—may God prevent this suffering—how can they leave Jerusalem? Moreover, if they already leave, they should remember the others, they should not close their doors when there are those who must find shelter, they should dedicate their money to those most distressed by the times and participate in the public's distress this way!

And thirdly, they should not weaken the people's heart with their actions. And they should not forget that there is merit in being distressed in Jerusalem, the holy city. And remember the verse, 'Trust in the Lord with all your heart and lean not on your understanding' (Proverbs 3:5). Not so much the calculations of intellect and understanding. Trust in Him at all times. And indeed, if around him—Jerusalem, the surroundings of the Divine presence—is very stormy, and the storm has already flared too much; then we bless especially the one who spreads the tabernacle of peace—not only on His people Israel—but also on Jerusalem. Descent from Jerusalem can be a moral decline. And such will not be in Israel. All go up to Jerusalem, and not all are taken out."

Conclusion:

After the opening of the "Burma Road" for traffic, Ben-Gurion traveled to Jerusalem on October 23, 1948. Upon his arrival, he was informed that approximately 20,000 people had left the city, a minority during the first truce and the majority during the second truce.[80] Indeed, the war brought about a significant decrease in Jerusalem's Jewish population. In 1947, the city was home to approximately 90,000 Jews, which had dropped to about 87,000 by the spring of 1948. By November 1948, the number had fallen to approximately 83,000 Jews who reported Jerusalem as their permanent address (of whom only about 8,000 were

---

80 David Ben-Gurion, *The War Diary*, vol. 3 (Tel-Aviv: Ministry of Defense, 1984), 769 [4 October 1948] (Hebrew).

physically present in the city or were enlisted in the military).[81] The residents of Jerusalem's peripheral neighborhoods, which included a significant concentration of religious and ultra-Orthodox Jews, were regarded by the Yishuv leadership as a problematic population unlikely to withstand the hardships of war. Yet, it was this observant community that demonstrated remarkable resilience and steadfastness during the time of trial, remaining in the city despite suffering significant losses in both lives and property. Their endurance was influenced by the leadership of their rabbis, who stood with them in their time of need.[82] The rabbis of Jerusalem made a point of remaining in the city during its most difficult hours, in contrast to other leaders who left when the opportunity arose. Rabbis who did leave the city for personal or communal reasons were careful to return promptly. Their presence in the city and their spiritual activities were crucial to the resilience of the civilian population, which suffered greatly under the siege and during the fighting. The rabbis' regular and wartime-specific activities played a vital role in maintaining communal life under the conditions of war. They took on full responsibility and demonstrated proactive involvement to support the political leadership and military command in the battle for Jerusalem.

[This chapter is an English translation of Moshe Ehrenwald, "The Involvement of Jerusalem's Rabbis in Security Matters During the War of Independence," *Aley Zayit Vacherev*, vol. 10 (2010): 251-279 (Hebrew).]

---

81 Uziel Schmelz, "The Development of the Jewish Population in Jerusalem Over the Last Century," (PhD Dissertation, Hebrew University of Jerusalem, 1959), 14 (Hebrew).

82 Moshe Ehrenwald, "Civilians in the Northern Border Neighborhoods of Jerusalem," in Mordechai Bar-On and Meir Chazan, eds., *Civilians in War: A Collection of Studies on Civil Society During the War of Independence* (Jerusalem: Yad Yitzhak Ben-Zvi, 2010), 155-170 (Hebrew).

Dr. Moshe Ehrenwald is a graduate of the Department of History of the Modern Middle East and the Department of International Relations, holding a master's degree in Contemporary Jewry from the Hebrew University of Jerusalem. His book on the Jewish Quarter of Jerusalem's Old City during the War of Independence, based on his doctoral dissertation in the Department of History at the Hebrew University, was awarded the Yitzhak Sadeh Prize for Military Literature. His book on Mount Scopus in the War of Independence received the Moldovan Prize for Military Literature at Ariel University. His 2017 book, *The Haredim During the Independence War*, was published by Modan Publishing House.

Made in United States
North Haven, CT
08 April 2025

67741441R00241